MW01227894

The Book of Enoch

Volume III

The Lions are Coming

Michael B. Rush

Chapter 1 – Fragments from the Book of Noah

The Book of Noah is an intriguing document. Extracts from this ancient book are included in the Book of Enoch and are also cited in the Book of Jubilees. Additionally, twenty-one fragments of the Book of Noah were discovered in Cave 1 at Qumran, with two potentially complete books found in Cave 4. The translation of the two large scrolls from Cave 4 has yet to be released. The withholding of these two scrolls has raised eyebrows among some, particularly given the allegations of Dr. John Strugnell that the Ultra-Orthodox Jews would censor the Dead Sea Scrolls if they could.

You will recall from Volume II of this series that Dr. Strugnell was fired from the Dead Sea Scroll project after an interview that many considered to be antisemitic. In that interview, he suggested that one of the reasons the scrolls were hidden in the first place was to keep them out of the hands of the orthodox. Historically, the orthodox—think Pharisees and Sadducees—have not had the best track record regarding information that counters their narrative. Dr. Strugnell's concern gained support when it became evident that the Book of Noah contained prophecies about the Jewish Messiah.

Because the whole text has not been made public, we lack the context for this fragment, but it provides a description of the physical appearance of the Messiah. This fragment has been dated to the second century BCE. Consider the following:

> On His hair a birthmark of reddish color. And the shape of a lentil will be on [his face?], and small birthmarks on his thigh. And after two years He will know how to distinguish one thing from another in his heart. In His youth, He will be like [*missing text*] a man who knows nothing until the time when he knows the three Books. And then He will acquire prudence and learn understanding [*missing text*] wise seers come to Him, to his knees.

> And with His father and His ancestors [*missing text*] of brothers will hurt Him. Counsel and prudence will be with Him, and He will know the secrets of man. His wisdom will reach all the peoples, and He will know the secrets of all the living. And all their designs against Him will come to

nothing, and His rule over the living will be great. His designs will succeed, for He is the Elect of God. His birth and the breath of His spirit [*missing text*] and His designs shall be for ever (Qumran fragment 4Q534)

This fragment from the Book of Noah is incredible and, if taken at face value, suggests that Noah knew important details of Christ's life thousands of years before His birth. Curiously, this Noah fragment aligns with another description of Jesus Christ written by Publius Lentulus to Tiberius Caesar. In that account, Christ was described as having hair the color of ripe chestnuts, which are a deep reddish-brown. Therefore, the only two physical descriptions we have of Christ refer to Him as having reddish hair. This is very curious because red hair is a recessive trait, meaning that in order for Christ to have red hair, both of His parents had to carry the gene.

It is not surprising that Mary, Christ's mother, carried the recessive gene for red hair. She was a direct descendant of David, who was described as being of ruddy countenance, which most Bible scholars interpret as the complexion of a redhead. What is more curious is the suggestion that God the Father also carries the gene for red hair. Joseph Smith described Jesus Christ as looking "exactly similar" to His Father. Therefore, if Christ had reddish or auburn hair, it suggests that God the Father does as well. This is fascinating to me.

Red hair is highly unusual. Anyone with red hair knows how difficult life can be as a result. My wife has red hair, as do three of my children. There have been many tears in my household over this fact and the relentless bullying that it brought on. Curiously, one of my family members was feeling particularly sad as a result of relentless bullying. They were praying for comfort when they were given a very strong impression that simply came across as, "You are in the very best of company." This prompting is much more meaningful in light of the physical description of Christ given above.

I do not want to belabor this point, but before moving past the topic of red hair and the House of Israel, I think it is worth pointing out some other interesting facts. In the book *Pharaohs and Kings*, written by Egyptologist David M. Rohl, a description was given of a very curious statue that was excavated from Tell ed-Daba (Avaris) in the eastern Nile delta in the location identified with the biblical lands of Goshen. Goshen is where the Hebrews lived while in Egypt. The statue was discovered by an Austrian/German archaeologist and Director of the Austrian Institute for Egyptology in Vienna. He believed that the statue was of Amenemhat III's great Asiatic vizier, who was second only to Pharaoh in authority. If so, the statue was none other than Joseph of

Egypt, the great patriarch of Ephraim and Manasseh. As such, consider the following description of that statue:

> The sculptor has captured him in the prime of life, his upright seated posture full of dignity and assuredness, as befits the chief minister of the Black Land. The vizier's face is painted in pale ochre – the standard pigment used by the Egyptian artists to indicate the skin color of a northerner heralding from the Levant. Although he is an Asiatic, Joseph does not carry the usual beard. He is clean shaven. One of the most unusual features of this remarkable statue is the coiffure or wig. Joseph's hair is flame red, fashioned into what can only be described as a mushroom-shape. It has been carefully trimmed and is neatly curled under at the back and sides.
>
> Across his right breast the vizier holds his insignia of office. Pharaoh holds the crook and flail, but Joseph holds his 'throw stick' – the Egyptian hieroglyphic symbol used to denote a foreigner. The imagery of the cult statue is telling us to recognize a man of foreign origins – but a man who has become completely integrated in the highest reaches of Egyptian culture. (Pharaohs and Kings – David M. Rohl)

In addition to this incredible statue, the remnants of an Egyptian palace were found, and behind the palace, twelve tombs, which some believe were built to house the twelve sons of Jacob. This is an extraordinary find, and it is particularly curious that Joseph is depicted as having red hair.

During the Spanish Inquisition, anyone with red hair was assumed to be a Jew by default and was rounded up by the Catholic Church and forced to convert to Catholicism. Having recently visited Jerusalem, I can confirm that red hair is not uncommon among the Jews to this day. There are beautiful redheads all over Israel.

Furthermore, Christ was described as having lentil-shaped birthmarks on His face and legs. Any child who grew up with red hair is no stranger to marks upon the skin, be they freckles or red dots. When you combine the Savior's red hair with these prominent facial markings, Isaiah's Suffering Servant prophecy begins to make more sense.

He hath no form nor comeliness; and when we shall see Him, *there is* no beauty that we should desire Him. He is despised and rejected of men; a man of sorrows, and acquainted with grief: and we hid as it were *our* faces from Him; He was despised, and we esteemed Him not. Surely He hath borne our griefs, and carried our sorrows: yet we did esteem Him stricken, smitten of God, and afflicted. But He *was* wounded for our transgressions, *He was* bruised for our iniquities: the chastisement of our peace *was* upon Him; and with His stripes we are healed. (Isaiah 53:2-5)

You will recall from the New Testament that it was this specific revelation of Isaiah's that was being studied by an Ethiopian eunuch, the emissary of Queen Candace of Ethiopia. This eunuch was struggling to make sense of the prophecy. The Spirit prompted Philip to ask the eunuch if he understood what he was reading. "How can I unless someone guides me?" was his response. Philip then preached the Lord Jesus Christ to the eunuch, who asked to be baptized in the Lord's name on the spot. Philip did so, and immediately after coming out of the water, Philip was miraculously transported by the Spirit of God.

This Ethiopian eunuch serves as our segue back to the fragmentary Book of Noah, for the Ethiopians were great custodians of Israel's ancient libraries. After all, it is thanks to the Ethiopians that we have access to the Book of Enoch today. This eunuch is not the only encounter between Israel and Ethiopia. Makeda, the Queen of Sheba (now Ethiopia), traveled to Israel to pay homage to King Solomon. She spent six months with Solomon, during which time she became pregnant and returned home to bear Solomon's son, the grandson of King David. We are also told in the scriptures that Moses married an Ethiopian woman. Ethiopia's ties to the House of Israel have always been a point of great pride to the Ethiopian Church. It is therefore no surprise that the Ethiopian Church has safeguarded so many of Israel's ancient scriptural texts.

Embedded within the Book of Enoch is an excerpt from the Book of Noah. It is this fragment that will now become the focus of our study. The Noah fragments included in the Book of Enoch were not arranged in chronological order; rather, they seem to have been inserted based on their relevance to the subject matter of the Book of Enoch.

For the purposes of my analysis, I will examine the Enochian fragments of the Book of Noah in what I perceive their chronological order to be. As such, we will begin by looking at two of the last chapters in the Book of Enoch, which provide a fascinating account of Noah's birth. This account was written from the perspective of Enoch and will make more sense at its end than at its beginning.

106.1 And after some days my son Methuselah took a wife for his son Lamech, and she became pregnant by him and bore a son.

106.2 And his body was white as snow and red as the blooming of a rose, and the hair of his head †and his long locks were white as wool, and his eyes beautiful†. And when he opened his eyes, he lighted up the whole house like the sun, and the whole house was very bright.

106.3 And thereupon he arose in the hands of the midwife, opened his mouth, and †conversed with† the Lord of righteousness.

106.4 And his father Lamech was afraid of him and fled, and came to his father Methuselah.

106.5 And he said unto him: 'I have begotten a strange son, diverse from and unlike man, and resembling the sons of the God of heaven [*meaning the Watchers*]; and his nature is different and he is not like us, and his eyes are as the rays of the sun, and his countenance is glorious.

106.6 And it seems to me that he is not sprung from me but from the angels [*Watchers*], and I fear that in his days a wonder may be wrought on the earth.

106.7 And now, my father, I am here to petition thee and implore thee that thou mayest go to Enoch, our father, and learn from him the truth, for his dwelling-place is amongst the angels. [*Enoch and his city had already be lifted up in to the cosmos*]

106.8 And when Methuselah heard the words of his son, he came to me to the ends of the earth; for he had heard that I was there, and he cried aloud, and I heard his voice and I came to him. And I said unto him: 'Behold, here am I, my son, wherefore hast thou come to me?'

106.9 And he answered and said: 'Because of a great cause of anxiety have I come to thee, and because of a disturbing vision have I approached.

From the translation of the account above, it is not clear if Lamech is describing Noah's actual birth or a vision regarding the same. I tend to believe that Lamech had a vision of his son before he was born, and the vision terrified him. Methuselah, who was a visionary man himself, quickly understood that the Lord was doing something new with Noah, and they needed to understand why. Therefore, they sought clarification from the greatest seer the world had known, his grandfather Enoch.

For context, Noah was born approximately 2,945 BC, or sixty-nine years after Enoch and his city were translated. In the context of this series, the concept of translation is synonymous with being called on a cosmic mission. Enoch and his people were working with the inhabitants of innumerable worlds (Moses 7:31). The understanding that Enoch was translated, or taken up into heaven while still alive, along with his entire city, is not common knowledge. However, this is what is referenced in **106.7** above.

Lamech, and all righteous people for that matter, understood that Enoch was no longer living on the earth. Methuselah was alive when Enoch and his people were translated but was asked to remain upon the earth so that Enoch's posterity might continue. By this, we should understand that Enoch had obtained the same covenant from the Lord that Abraham had sought. Indeed, Abraham sought this covenant because he knew that the great patriarchs before him had obtained it. Therefore, Enoch's posterity will always be found upon the earth, just like Abraham's.

Apparently, Lamech understood that Methuselah had some means of communicating with his father that we do not presently understand. How else would Methuselah know that his father Enoch had temporarily returned to the Earth, and precisely where to go to find him? Lamech's vision had disturbed him so much that he begged Methuselah to take advantage of Enoch's return to discuss the perplexing vision with him and get his take on the matter.

Lamech was clearly concerned that his wife had been impregnated by a Watcher, and that as a result, his future son had become unnatural. The vision had so rattled him that he did not believe his poor wife, who was surely at her wits' end. He needed third-party confirmation from someone he knew could tell him all things – his grandfather. Lamech could have no solace until he had it from Enoch that Noah was not the offspring of the Watchers. This is a reminder of how prevalent such things were in the prediluvian world. It is important to understand that Lamech, Enoch's grandson, lived with his grandfather for over a hundred and ten years before both he and his people were translated. Therefore, he knew his grandfather very well and trusted him implicitly. Enoch would have been the hero of every righteous man.

Seeing how distressed Lamech had become, Methuselah agreed to travel to where he knew his father Enoch would be. It is entirely possible that Enoch's visit to Earth may have corresponded with the account of the extraterrestrial whistleblowers discussed in Volume I of this series and in verses **12.3** to **12.6**. Whether for that reason or another, the fact remains that Enoch had returned after a sixty-nine-year absence, and his son Methuselah knew it. The narrative continues with Methuselah speaking to his father:

> **106.10** And now, my father, hear me: unto Lamech my son there hath been born a son, [*at least according to the vision there soon would be*] the like of whom there is none, and his nature is not like man's nature, and the color of his body is whiter than snow and redder than the bloom of a rose, and the hair of his head is whiter than white wool, and his eyes are like the rays of the sun, and he opened his eyes and thereupon lighted up the whole house.

> **106.11** And he arose in the hands of the midwife, and opened his mouth and blessed the Lord of heaven.

> **106.12** And his father Lamech became afraid and fled to me, and did not believe that he was sprung from him, but that he was in the likeness of the angels of heaven; and behold I have come to thee that thou mayest make known to me the truth.'

> **106.13** And I, Enoch, answered and said unto him: 'The Lord will do a new thing on the earth, and this I have already seen in a vision, and make known to thee that in the generation of my father Jared some of the angels of heaven [*Watchers*] transgressed the word of the Lord.

> **106.14** And behold they commit sin and transgress the law, and have united themselves with women and commit sin with them, and have married some of them, and have begot children by them.

Note that in the passages above, Enoch is speaking in the present tense, indicating that the Watchers were still uniting themselves with the women of Earth at that moment and had been doing so for over five hundred years since the days of his father Jared. Enoch claimed that he had seen a similar vision wherein he knew that the Lord was about to do something new upon the Earth. The birth of Noah marked the beginning of a new age in the Earth's temporal history.

Our days mirror the antediluvian world in many ways. It should not be lost upon the reader that the Lord said He would do another new thing upon the Earth in the last days (see Isaiah 43:19, Isaiah 28:21, D&C 94:4, D&C 101:95, and Joel 1:2 for examples). In the last days, the Lord describes what He is about to do as not only new but also strange. There is definitely a status quo that has existed upon the Earth throughout time. The Lord does not needlessly act in ways that disrupt that status quo. After all, we were sent to Earth not for the shock and awe of His power, but so that we could exercise our agency while under the influence of the veil. Therefore, when the Lord gets involved, it is usually to steady the ark Himself. As Satan's power grew in ancient times, so did the endowment of power that was poured out upon the righteous. When the world became too wicked, the righteous were literally lifted up into the heavens in the eyes of all people.

In the last days, the righteous civilizations of times past will be restored to the Earth, for it is their covenanted land of inheritance, just as it is ours. These restoration events will result in some of the strange and new acts that the Lord is referring to. After all, prior to these events, while cities and people have been lifted up into the heavens, they have never been restored. This will indeed be a new thing. Beyond this, however, the Lord will pour out His Spirit in greater abundance than He ever has before. The righteous will be armed with power and great glory. In that day, one of the new things the Lord says He will do is give a woman power to compass a man. The reasons for the outpouring of God's power both anciently and in modern times will be to preserve His people. In both instances, this preservation will involve protecting us from the Watchers.

Enoch continues speaking of the ramifications of the Watchers, which I must assume may be something that we will see again upon the Earth.

> **106.15** And they shall produce on the earth giants not according to the spirit, but according to the flesh, and there shall be a great punishment on the earth, and the earth shall be cleansed from all impurity.

In the passage above, Enoch makes a distinction that the giants on the Earth in his day were giants in the flesh only. Their spiritual capacity did not match their physical stature. Indeed, while their bodies were enormous, they were spiritually inept. These giants, which were clearly the result of some natural anomaly the Watchers intentionally exploited, lived their lives in pursuit of unbridled and insatiable carnal desire. As a result, the Earth was filled with violence and iniquity. The Earth cried out in anguish because of the never-ending cycle of wickedness that the Watchers had introduced and that humanity had embraced.

Due to this wickedness, many were killed and cried out for justice from the Spirit World. As we have seen earlier, the Lord takes the cries of the righteous very seriously.

He will not stay silent for long. Consequently, the Lord revealed His plans for the Earth to Enoch. Enoch explained what these plans entailed in the subsequent verses.

> **106.16** Yea, there shall come a great destruction over the whole earth, and there shall be a deluge and a great destruction for one year.

> **106.17** And this son who has been born unto you shall be left on the earth, and his three children shall be saved with him: when all mankind that are on the earth shall die [he and his sons shall be saved].

Enoch declared that all mankind upon the Earth would perish. This statement acknowledges that many were removed from the face of the Earth before the great flood of Noah. Nephi prophesied that in the last days, the righteous would be spared, even if it must be by fire. Similarly, the righteous in the antediluvian world were saved from water by miraculous means, being lifted up and taken into the heavens.

Lamech's son Noah was destined to inherit the Enochian covenant of his great-grandfather, thereby becoming a father of nations. It is crucial to note that Noah could not become a father of nations without also elevating his forefathers. If Noah was the Father of Mankind, so too were Enoch, Methuselah, and Lamech, along with their wives. Thus, we see that the righteousness of the children can profoundly impact the lives of their ancestors.

There were ten generations between Adam and Noah, and ten generations between Noah and Abraham. At the beginning, middle, and end of the first twenty generations of this Earth's temporal history, there have been men whose covenantal relationships with God had eternal consequences for the human family. This pattern can and should be mirrored by each covenant-keeping disciple of Christ who obtains a throne and a kingdom in the courts of the Most High God. As eternal parents, they become the fathers and mothers whose joint offspring populate the multiverse. In so doing, we bless, honor, and exalt those who came before us. Righteousness is the only true form of repayment we can offer our heavenly parents. In righteousness, we not only magnify ourselves but them as well.

Enoch now addresses Lamech's pressing question regarding whether Noah was his son or the illegitimate offspring of a Watcher:

> **106.18** And now make known to thy son Lamech that he who has been born is in truth his son, and call his name Noah; for he shall be left to you, and he and his sons shall be saved

from the destruction, which shall come upon the earth on account of all the sin and all the unrighteousness, which shall be consummated on the earth in his days.

106.19 And after that there shall be still more unrighteousness than that which was first consummated on the earth; for I know the mysteries of the holy ones; for He, the Lord, has showed me and informed me, and I have read (them) in the heavenly tablets.

107.1 And I saw written on them that generation upon generation shall transgress, till a generation of righteousness arises, and transgression is destroyed, and sin passes away from the earth, and all manner of good comes upon it.

107.2 And now, my son, go and make known to thy son Lamech that this son, which has been born, is in truth his son, and that this is no lie.'

107.3. And when Methuselah had heard the words of his father Enoch--for he had shown to him everything in secret--he returned and showed them to him and called the name of that son Noah; for he will comfort the earth after all the destruction.

Enoch is the quintessential seer. He understood the mysteries of God. He foresaw that in the last days, the Earth would become even more wicked than it was in the antediluvian world. This should give us pause. The wickedness that pervades our societies today would have shocked many in the ancient world. We must comprehend this fact. We have become accustomed to the ubiquitous nature of gross iniquity. However, this does not rationalize immoral behavior—the "everybody is doing it" mentality holds no sway in the courts of God. The moral standard for our society is the same standard that exists among the residents of the City of Enoch or the Lost Ten Tribes. We simply are not rising to the occasion.

Those who justify sinful practices simply because they are ubiquitous have chosen to be carnally minded rather than spiritually minded. The carnally minded segregate themselves from the Saints of God in their hearts, though they might still honor God with their lips. The Lord takes no delight in such hollow praise. True disciples of His Son know Him and follow Him. This means that the Saints of God can and do discern between truth and error, and seeing both, they cleave unto truth.

As Enoch noted, the events that will transpire upon the Earth in the last days are both known and written and have been from the beginning. On the other side of the veil, before we came into mortality, we knew exactly what we were signing up for. However, this knowledge is lost to us on this side of the veil. Through discernment and the miraculous gifts of transcendent seers such as Enoch, this knowledge can be restored. For those with eyes to see and hearts to feel, such knowledge is readily recognizable. For others, they must work diligently to accept such truths. On the other hand, for those not seeking to be instructed by the Lord, it would be easier for a camel to pass through the eye of a needle than for them to comprehend the mysteries of God.

Enoch's writings are among the first recorded, and through divine providence, they have been preserved to the point that five thousand years later, you are reading and comprehending their meaning. Before the end of this book, you will see that Enoch foresaw this. He saw that the Earth would be filled with wickedness and occult knowledge. However, he saw that his words would be brought forth in faithfulness and that other books would come forth that would enable his writings to be understood. He saw that the righteous would rejoice in them and retain their faith in the Father's Hidden Son as a result. Enoch also saw that in that day, the Father would send those of understanding into the world to help others make sense of what was happening to them, and in so doing, they would become Saviors on Mount Zion. Yet, such things will come to relatively few because of the hardness of their hearts and the blindness of their minds.

This brings us back to Noah and the peculiarities of his birth. It is clear that Noah was reserved to be born when he was so that he could help heal the Earth from the tremendous iniquity that had transpired upon its surface. From this vision, we understand that Noah's spiritual gifts were so powerful and unique that his father feared him. We are therefore left to ask ourselves, if Noah was such a powerful soul, why were only eight people saved on the ark? I believe our understanding of the true nature of ancient events has been obscured by the zealous editing of the Bible by the post-Babylonian Jews. We obtain more insight into what actually happened during this time period from the Pearl of Great Price.

You will recall that Noah was born sixty-nine years after Enoch's people were lifted up into the heavens. Therefore, the following passages discussing Noah's days are very instructive. Consider the following:

> And after that Zion was taken up into heaven, Enoch beheld, and lo, all the nations of the earth were before him; and there came generation upon generation; and Enoch was high and lifted up, even in the bosom of the Father, and of the Son of Man; and behold, the power of Satan was upon all the face of the earth.

And he saw angels descending out of heaven; and he heard a loud voice saying: Wo, wo be unto the inhabitants of the earth. And he beheld Satan; and he had a great chain in his hand, and it veiled the whole face of the earth with darkness; and he looked up and laughed, and his angels rejoiced.

And Enoch beheld angels descending out of heaven, bearing testimony of the Father and Son; and the Holy Ghost fell on many, and they were caught up by the powers of heaven into Zion. And it came to pass that the God of heaven looked upon the residue of the people, and He wept...
(Moses 7:23-28)

Angels are not distant, dispassionate servants of heaven; they are us. All angels sent to minister to the people of Earth have, or will, experience mortality here. This includes Michael, Gabriel, Phanuel, and Raphael. When the Lord says He sent angels to proclaim the gospel to the people of Earth, He could be referring to righteous individuals reserved for such times to enlighten others. Noah was one of these people. Joseph Smith even proclaimed that Noah and the archangel Gabriel were one and the same.

Despite Satan's chains encircling this planet, the Spirit of the Lord can still pierce the darkness and liberate the captives. Between the days of Enoch's city and the destruction in Noah's time, many were translated despite the Earth's corruption. When we read of only eight people being saved from the flood, it is because the other righteous individuals had been translated before the flood. Noah and his family remained to fulfill the covenants of the fathers on Earth.

The ancient happenings on Earth were well-known, not hidden. Enoch's city was the first to ascend into the heavens, but not the only one. Many others in Noah's days were lifted up. Melchizedek and his people sought and obtained the city of Enoch in Abraham's day. The Rechabites and the main body of the Lost Ten Tribes of Israel were also lifted up. The modern world has lost its bearings on reality, unlike the ancient world, which understood the cosmos far better than today's greatest scientific minds.

When the cosmic veil is pulled back and the heavens are rolled together as a scroll, the shock will be overwhelming. Even the most faithful will struggle under its weight. Many will cry out in anguish, feeling deceived, not because the Father and His prophets were silent, but because we were deaf, dumb, and blind. We were warned about taking lightly the things we received, yet we did not change our view. The Lord will try the faith of His people, and the trial will be severe, deceiving even the very elect.

Just as the Lord reserved angels to minister before the prediluvian destruction, He has done the same for our day. Many have been reserved to be a light unto others, helping them make sense of the darkening world. It is hard to imagine anyone coming to this knowledge by chance; the Lord has brought them forth for a wise purpose, and He will magnify that purpose in the hearts of those who receive them.

Returning to the narrative of this Enochian fragment from the Book of Noah, Enoch proclaimed that Lamech should call his son Noah because Noah would comfort the post-diluvian world. After our greatest tribulation, we too will have a comforter, the Prince of Peace, who will heal the nations. He will dry all tears and restore the Earth to a state of joy and wonder. Wickedness will be abolished, and righteousness will prevail for a thousand years.

This concludes my analysis of the first Enochian fragment of the Book of Noah. This will not be the only fragment we consider. How these fragments became part of the Book of Enoch is a mystery. It is possible that Noah, his son Seth, or even Abraham, who were custodians of the early records, added them. Regardless of how they were preserved, I thank Almighty God for them. It is a true miracle to read and be edified by such writings thousands of years later.

Chapter 2 – The Heavens Will Shake

In the previous chapter, we explored an extraordinary vision of Noah's birth received by his father, Lamech. This vision revealed that Noah was a profoundly righteous spirit in the premortal realms, chosen to rejuvenate humanity in the post-diluvian world. This portrayal starkly contrasts with the common image of a frail old man clumsily constructing an ark. Joseph Smith taught that Noah was the premortal Gabriel, a spiritual powerhouse and fervent servant of the Father.

Lamech was terrified by the vision of Noah's formidable spiritual nature. This reaction would likely be shared by many today if they were to glimpse their premortal status and achievements, especially when compared to their current state. The veil of forgetfulness diminishes the confidence of even the most steadfast premortal warriors. Before the world was, we valiantly opposed Lucifer alongside Michael, Gabriel, Raphael, and the Son of Man. Like them, we too stood with authority in the presence of God. Yet, with the veil, we have forgotten everything and now stumble like blind men in a minefield.

As we navigate life in our weakened state, we must remember to be merciful to ourselves and others. Enoch began his mortal journey as a stuttering young boy, dismissed by the world as insignificant. Yet, by the end, mountains moved at his command, and giants trembled at the mention of his name.

The Lord often uses the small and insignificant to accomplish His work. He humbled the King of England through an illiterate seventeen-year-old French farm maid and defeated Goliath with a young boy's sling. Therefore, let us take courage in knowing that we are in the midst of our own stories, not at their end. Though things may seem bleak and hope distant, every good story has such moments. If we endure well, with hope in Christ, we will not recognize ourselves by the end for what the Lord has made of us.

In this chapter, we begin our analysis of what many consider the first fragment of the Book of Noah transcribed into the Book of Enoch. This fragment, possibly added by Noah himself, includes some of Enoch's visions retold from Noah's perspective. This particular vision occurred 135 years after Enoch's translation, when Noah was sixty-six years old.

Consider the following fascinating account:

60.1. In the year five hundred, in the seventh month, on the fourteenth day of the month in the life of †Enoch†. In that Parable I saw how a mighty quaking made the heaven of heavens to quake, and the host of the Most High, and the angels, a thousand thousands and ten thousand times ten thousand, were disquieted with a great disquiet.

In the opening verse Noah confirms that Enoch did not die at the age of three-hundred and sixty-five, but was alive and well in the heavens at the age of five hundred. This is another miraculous confirmation of restored knowledge from an ancient text, as the Pearl of Great Price spoke of Enoch's translation before this book was available. In this passage, Noah describes the same innumerable host of gods before the Father's throne that Enoch described in Volume II of this series. In that volume, we learned how the gods diligently petitioned God the Father for the well-being of Earth's inhabitants. In the context of this vision, Noah is witnessing a similar meeting, if not the same event described in Volume II.

A story is never told the same way twice and varies depending on the audience. Nephi's account of Lehi's dream was very different from Lehi's retelling of the same event. Different things stand out to different people. In Noah's account, the focus is not on the innumerable gods before the Father's throne but on an event that causes the heavens themselves to quake and tremble. What could cause the heavens to shake?

If you recall Enoch's vision of the innumerable host of gods before the Father's throne, he witnessed a sense of urgency among the hosts of heaven. In Enoch's vision, the heavens were intently focused on the inhabitants of the Earth and were praying for their welfare, as if they knew something was about to happen that would try them beyond the breaking point. Noah's vision of the heavens shaking must be the realization of this long-awaited and distressing event that caused even the Throne of God, in the heaven of heavens, of the Celestial Kingdom, to shake terribly.

Some might think it impossible for such an event to occur. After all, why would God permit His own household to be shaken terribly in a manner that disquiets even gods? What could cause such an event? The initial presumption is to attribute this terrible shaking to opposing forces, for why would God shake His own household? Who would be able to attack heaven and the council of the gods in their stronghold? Such audacity and power indeed raise eyebrows in astonishment.

As we consider Noah's vision, we must do so in light of the greater gospel whole into which all truth must reconcile. Are there other prophecies that speak of the heavens shaking under such conditions as Noah witnessed? As it turns out, there are. Reviewing these additional accounts will be critical to understanding what Noah saw transpire in the heavens. Consider the following prophecy given by none other than the Son of Man, the keeper of all the mysteries of God.

> Then said [*Jesus*] unto [*His disciples*] Nation shall rise against nation, and kingdom against kingdom: and great earthquakes shall be in divers places, and famines, and pestilences; and fearful sights and great signs and great signs shall there be from heaven.
>
> And there shall be signs in the sun, and in the moon, and in the stars; and upon the earth distress of nations, with perplexity; the sea and the waves roaring; men's hearts failing them for fear, and for looking after those things which are coming on the earth: **for the powers of heaven shall be shaken**. And then shall they see the Son of man coming in a cloud with power and great glory. And when these things begin to come to pass, then look up, and lift up your heads; for your redemption draweth nigh. (Luke 21:10-11,25-28)

When Christ explained these things, He used the Enochian marker—Son of Man—which we discussed in depth in Volume II as marking something of particular significance best understood in the context of the writings of Enoch. Furthermore, Christ used additional Enochian imagery: "then shall they see the Son of Man coming in a cloud with power and glory." This is clearly reminiscent of Enoch's statement about the Son of Man coming in the clouds of heaven with ten thousand of His saints.

However, before this day happens, Christ stated that we would see fearful signs in the heavens, and the world would have great fear for the things they see coming to the Earth. Indeed, just the sight of these things would cause the hearts of many to fail them for fear! In layman's terms, this pending event will be so terrifying that merely witnessing it will cause many to have deadly heart attacks. This is incredible!

In addition, Christ explicitly stated that this event would cause the powers of heaven themselves to be shaken. Given that the heavens represent the epicenter of God's power, the shaking of the heavens in such a manner cannot be a common occurrence. As such, the event witnessed by Noah and described by Christ as happening in the last days before the Second Coming must be the same event. The primary difference between the accounts is one of perspective. Christ's explanation was from the perspective of the Earth's inhabitants gazing up into the heavens, while Noah's perspective was of Heaven's inhabitants looking down upon the Earth.

Therefore, when other prophecies speak of the heavens shaking, we can rightly presume that they are also speaking of this same event, for the shaking of the heavens is certainly a singular event that might happen once a cycle, and no more. Therefore, any additional passages that speak of this event become critically relevant to our present understanding of the topic. As such, we would do well to consider them. Here, then, is another prophecy regarding the shaking of the heavens for your consideration:

> Let the heathen be wakened, and come up to the valley of Jehoshaphat [*the valley in between the Mount of Olives and Jerusalem, aka the Kidron Valley*]: for there will I sit to judge all the heathen round about. Put ye in the sickle, for the harvest is ripe: come, get you down; for the press is full, the fats overflow; for their wickedness *is* great. Multitudes, multitudes in the valley of decision: for the day of the LORD *is* near in the valley of decision.
>
> The sun and the moon shall be darkened, and the stars shall withdraw their shining. The LORD also shall roar out of Zion, and utter His voice from Jerusalem; and **the heavens and the earth shall shake**: but the LORD *will be* the hope of His people, and the strength of the children of Israel. So shall ye know that I *am* the LORD your God dwelling in Zion, my holy mountain: then shall Jerusalem be holy, and there shall no strangers pass through her any more. (Joel 3:12-16)

The passages above clearly speak of when the Lord will come to save the Jews from destruction in the first of the bookend battles of Armageddon. He will divide the Mount of Olives, allowing the Jews to flee to safety, and then utterly destroy the enemies of Israel. This interpretation is validated by modern revelation as well. Consider the following passage from the Doctrine and Covenants, which speaks of this same event:

> Then shall the arm of the Lord fall upon the nations. And then shall the Lord set His foot upon this mount [*meaning the Mount of Olives*], and it shall cleave in twain, and **the earth shall tremble, and reel to and fro, and the heavens also shall shake**. And the Lord shall utter His voice, and all the ends of the earth shall hear it; and the nations of the earth shall mourn, and they that have laughed shall see their folly. And calamity shall cover the mocker, and the scorner shall be consumed; and they that have watched for iniquity shall be hewn down and cast into the fire.

And then shall the Jews look upon me and say: What are these wounds in thine hands and in thy feet? Then shall they know that I am the Lord; for I will say unto them: These wounds are the wounds with which I was wounded in the house of My friends. I am He who was lifted up. I am Jesus that was crucified. I am the Son of God. And then shall they weep because of their iniquities; then shall they lament because they persecuted their King. (D&C 45:47-53)

The passage above clearly associates the shaking of the heavens with the events of the Second Coming. If you study other passages in modern revelation that mention the heavens shaking for the benefit of the saints, you will find that they also refer to the day when the wicked will be swept from the Earth, and the Kingdom will be given to the meek and humble saints who remain. However, before the meek can inherit the Earth, the vineyard must be fully cleared; thus, all that is evil and bitter will be cut off and burned.

The following passage from the Book of Ether describes what the brother of Jared saw regarding the last days. Consider the following:

In that day that they shall exercise faith in Me, saith the Lord, even as the brother of Jared did, that they may become sanctified in me, then will I manifest unto them the things which the brother of Jared saw, even to the unfolding unto them all my revelations, saith Jesus Christ, the Son of God, the FATHER of the heavens and of the earth, and all things that in them are. And he that will contend against the word of the Lord, let him be accursed; and he that shall deny these things, let him be accursed; for unto them will I show no greater things, saith Jesus Christ; for I am He who speaketh. And at my command the heavens are opened and are shut; and at my word the earth shall shake; and at my command the inhabitants thereof shall pass away, even so as by fire. And he that believeth not My words believeth not My disciples; and if it so be that I do not speak, judge ye; for ye shall know that it is I that speaketh, at the last day. (Ether 4:7-10)

Christ's words of warning to the hard-hearted are sobering. It is clear from the passages above that many who come across these things beforehand will not believe them. To me, this likely refers to the saints, for who else would be reading the words of the brother of Jared? Specifically, Christ states that He is willing to make known to His children the things the brother of Jared saw, if they seek them. Curiously, Christ does not say that He will give the saints the writings of the brother of Jared; rather, He says that He will manifest the things the brother of Jared saw by unfolding His revelations.

In other words, Christ is saying that through the Spirit, we can come to understand the same things the brother of Jared saw, even if we never read his record. Jared received all that he saw through the Spirit of God, which is the same Spirit that teaches us. Therefore, the brother of Jared's visions are not mysterious to those who seek to be taught by the Spirit; they are already known to us. Yet, because of unbelief, most of the saints will not receive these things and, as a result, will be unprepared for what is about to take place upon the Earth.

The saints believe that the writings of the brother of Jared will be revealed to the entire world in the form of a written book, just like the Book of Mormon. The day will certainly come when that happens. However, Mahonri received his comprehension from the Lord, and so must we. After all, Mahonri is not the gatekeeper of the mysteries of heaven; the Son of Man is. Jesus Christ is no respecter of persons; He is just as willing to teach you through the Spirit as any other person who has ever lived. However, that teaching will happen through the spiritual gifts you have received and in accordance with your seeking. Therefore, while the manner in which you learn these things may be more mundane than Mahonri's experience, knowledge is knowledge.

In this way, those who have sought to be taught by the Lord will find that when the writings of Mahonri are read from the housetops, there is little they had not already come to understand through the Spirit of God. God has opened the eyes of many regarding the mysteries of the Kingdom of Heaven. The Lord has already revealed all that He will do to His servants, the prophets. It is up to us to study their words. These incredible seers have all lived upon the Earth at diverse times, and not all of their writings are found together. Yet, their writings have been preserved by miraculous means and are available to all who seek further light and knowledge.

The Lord has commanded His saints to seek knowledge from the best books, but this admonition is a little too general for most. Particularly when many of the saints have taken the exact opposite approach to the Jews regarding this subject. The Jews rejected living prophets for the words of the dead, while many of the saints are only interested in the words of living prophets. Yet, a prophet is a prophet. The word of God, once uttered, stands for all time. If we do not study all the words of the prophets, then it does not matter to us that the Lord has revealed to them all His secrets.

The mysteries of God are mysteries because, to learn of them, you must seek to be taught by God Himself. The words and writings of the prophets are simply tools to facilitate that process. This process takes place over time, line upon line, precept upon precept. As we begin to understand one concept, another one opens to us. By this process, God will both teach and prove the world. Those who mock and scorn those who engage in this process will eventually see the error of their ways. For the days will soon come when the world will realize with both shock and horror that they were willfully ignorant of the mysteries of God, having despised those who could have helped them.

We now return to the topic at hand, which is the terrible shaking of the heavens and Earth that will occur in the last days at the time of the great and coming purge. We have another insightful passage of scripture on this topic in the Pearl of Great Price. It should be no surprise that this particular passage is taken from a conversation between Enoch and the Lord regarding the last days. Consider the following:

> And the Lord said unto Enoch: As I live, even so will I come in the last days, in the days of wickedness and vengeance, to fulfil the oath which I have made unto you concerning the children of Noah; and the day shall come that the earth shall rest, but before that day the heavens shall be darkened, and a veil of darkness shall cover the earth; and the heavens shall shake, and also the earth; and great tribulations shall be among the children of men, but my people will I preserve (Moses 7:60-61)

We have read numerous examples of the shaking of the heavens from the Old Testament, the New Testament, the Book of Mormon, the Doctrine and Covenants, and now the Pearl of Great Price. The volume of witnesses attests that this is not an obscure or isolated teaching. It has always been there, yet only available to those with eyes to see it. The Lord will preserve the righteous, even if that salvation comes by supernatural means that we cannot understand. God desires all His children to understand these things, for His words can have a more profound impact upon the hearts of men than anything else. Yet, with God, agency is of paramount importance. If the inhabitants of this Earth are willing to call Him Father and be taught by Him, His arms are open to receive them.

> And every one that hearkeneth to the voice of the Spirit cometh unto God, even the Father. And the Father teacheth him of the covenant which He has renewed and confirmed upon you, which is confirmed upon you for your

sakes, and not for your sakes only, but for the sake of the whole world.

And the whole world lieth in sin, and groaneth under darkness and under the bondage of sin. And by this you may know they are under the bondage of sin, because they come not unto Me. For whoso cometh not unto me is under the bondage of sin.

And whoso receiveth not My voice is not acquainted with My voice, and is not of me. And by this you may know the righteous from the wicked, and that the whole world groaneth under sin and darkness even now.

And your minds in times past have been darkened because of unbelief, and because you have treated lightly the things you have received— Which vanity and unbelief have brought the whole church under condemnation. And this condemnation resteth upon the children of Zion, even all. (D&C 84:47-56)

The world rejects the light and knowledge of the restored gospel of Jesus Christ. They call it a cult and deride those who seek to be taught by the Father as fools. Yet, when the heavens and the earth begin to shake, those who have been taught by the Father will understand, while those without understanding will fall to the earth in fear. When the heavens shake, it will be for the good of the Lord's people and the destruction of the wicked. On that last and great day, when the earth reels to and fro like a drunken man, the Father will make a final end of wickedness upon the earth.

There is one more scriptural passage regarding this topic that I feel impressed to share before returning to Noah's vision. This example comes from Paul's teachings to the Hebrews. In this passage, Paul draws upon the House of Israel's experience at Mount Sinai, when God wanted to speak to His people directly, without a prophet as an intermediary. It was the Lord's objective to establish once and for all that Israel was His chosen people and that He was their God. In preparation for this event, He gave the people explicit instructions not to touch the mountain upon which He would descend. To the people, it seemed that the mountain itself was about to burst into flames under the tremendous weight of God's unparalleled power and glory. Indeed, the House of Israel greatly feared that they might be consumed by fire simply from hearing the Lord's voice.

Paul's retelling of this account is particularly interesting because his knowledge of the event must have been supplemented by information we do not have. I say this because he speaks of the fear that overcame not only Israel but Moses himself. Paul then uses Moses' own terror as a point of reference for the events of the last days. Consider the following:

> For ye are not come unto the mount that [ye] might be touched, and burned with fire, nor unto blackness, and darkness, and tempest, and the sound of a trumpet, and the voice of words; which voice they that heard entreated that the word should not be spoken to them any more... And so terrible was the sight, that Moses said, I exceedingly fear and quake.
>
> See that ye refuse not Him that speaketh. For if they escaped not who refused Him that spake on earth, much more shall not we escape, if we turn away from Him that speaketh from heaven: Whose voice then shook the earth: but now He hath promised, saying, Yet once more I shake not the earth only, but also heaven... For our God is a consuming fire. (Hebrews 12:18-19,21,26,29)

Just as both Moses and the House of Israel were frightened by the majesty and power of the Lord, so too will the events of the last days strike terror in the hearts of the righteous and wicked alike. Yet, as Nephi has stated, the righteous have no need to fear the coming day, for the very flames that consume the wicked around them will result in their salvation and the dawning of the greatest age the world has ever known.

As we consider these things, we must remember the purpose of the Book of Enoch, as stated in its opening verses:

> The words of the blessing of Enoch, wherewith he blessed the elect and righteous who will be living in the day of tribulation, when all the wicked and godless are to be removed... not for this generation, but for a remote one which is for to come. (BoE 1:1-2)

Enoch's words were meant to bless and prepare the elect and righteous for what is coming. In this chapter we have only covered the first verse of the sixtieth chapter of Enoch's writings, in the next chapter we will cover the next two verses. There is much to unpack.

Chapter 3 – The Ancient of Days

In the previous chapter, we reviewed the first verse of Noah's incredible vision of the last days. In that verse, Noah witnessed an event so powerful that it caused both the heavens and the Earth to shake. I shared numerous sources linking this event to the latter-day restoration of the House of Israel. There is much more to explore as we delve deeper into Noah's vision with the second verse. For context, we will examine this passage together with the second verse.

> **60.1**. In the year five hundred, in the seventh month, on the fourteenth day of the month in the life of †Enoch†. In that Parable I saw how a mighty quaking made the heaven of heavens to quake, and the host of the Most High, and the angels, a thousand thousands and ten thousand times ten thousand, were disquieted with a great disquiet.

> **60.2**. And the Head of Days [*also translated as Ancient of Days*] sat on the throne of his glory, and the angels and the righteous stood around Him.

In these two passages, Noah refers to both the Most High and the Head of Days in the context of the terrible shaking that will occur in both heaven and earth. Also noted are the hundreds of trillions of gods who pray over their children participating in this cycle of salvation, all of whom are disquieted by the terrible shaking. We have learned that this shaking corresponds with the cleansing of the Earth, which, of necessity, will result in the mortal destruction of billions of the offspring of this heavenly host.

In the second passage, we are introduced to a second godly figure, the Head of Days, who is described as sitting upon a throne of his own, surrounded by both angels and the righteous.

Who is the Head of Days, or Ancient of Days, as translated by Richard Laurence and others? Why is he described as sitting on his own throne apart from the Most High and His hosts? You will recall that this is not the first time we have been introduced to this title in the Book of Enoch. We learned of this same individual from Enoch's vision of this event. Noah and Enoch were not the only ones to have seen this vision. Daniel also saw this in a vision, and it is from Daniel's vision that this man's identity becomes clear.

The chapter heading of Daniel 7 states the following: "[Daniel] sees the Ancient of Days (Adam) to whom the Son of Man (Christ) will come." Note the Enochian marker—Son of Man. After reading Volume II of this series, you should understand that this singular title indicates that we are to understand Daniel's vision in the context of the Book of Enoch. This we will do. Consider Daniel's supplemental vision of these things for context:

> After this I saw in the night visions, and behold a fourth beast, dreadful and terrible, and strong exceedingly; and it had great iron teeth: it devoured and brake in pieces, and stamped the residue with the feet of it: and it was diverse from all the beasts that were before it; and it had ten horns.
>
> I considered the horns, and, behold, there came up among them another little horn, before whom there were three of the first horns plucked up by the roots: and, behold, in this horn were eyes like the eyes of man, and a mouth speaking great things.
>
> I beheld till the thrones were cast down, and the Ancient of days did sit, whose garment was white as snow, and the hair of his head like the pure wool: his throne was like the fiery flame, and his wheels as burning fire. A fiery stream issued and came forth from before him: thousand thousands ministered unto him, and ten thousand times ten thousand stood before him: the judgment was set, and the books were opened.
>
> I beheld then because of the voice of the great words which the horn spake: I beheld even till the beast was slain, and his body destroyed, and given to the burning flame. As concerning the rest of the beasts, they had their dominion taken away: yet their lives were prolonged for a season and time.
>
> I saw in the night visions, and, behold, one like the Son of man came with the clouds of heaven, and came to the Ancient of days, and they brought him near before Him. And there was given Him dominion, and glory, and a kingdom, that all people, nations, and languages, should serve Him: His dominion is an everlasting dominion, which shall not pass away, and His kingdom that which shall not be destroyed. (Daniel 7:7-14)

From the passage in Daniel, we understand that the great shaking of both heaven and Earth corresponds specifically to the destruction of the fourth kingdom. This fourth kingdom is the kingdom of Ezra's Eagle, as referred to in that vision. Therefore, this vision is highly relevant to us and our day. Daniel also saw the rise of the antichrist in the form of a horn with a blasphemous mouth and eyes like those of a man. Daniel saw that this horn would be joined by a beast, and that both the beast and the antichrist would be thrown into a burning fire. This same event is described in Revelation 19:20. Upon their destruction, the kingdom is given to the Son of Man, who in turn confers it upon His saints.

Embedded within Daniel's vision is the Ancient of Days, who sits upon a throne of flaming fire. The Ancient of Days is none other than Adam, also known as Michael—the Great Prince and leader of the noble and great ones. According to Daniel, what happens next is something of a whirlwind. Daniel saw flaming wheels, which are most certainly the ships of Chittim as described in Daniel 11:30 and in the first and tenth chapters of Ezekiel. Curiously, Daniel described these wheels as subservient to Michael. By this, we understand that just as Michael was the great general of the war in heaven, so he will be the great general of this last and great battle. John the Beloved and all the Host of Israel will report to him.

The war in heaven did not end; it simply changed venues. Apparently, Michael will return once more and drive Lucifer and his minions from the Americas. If my understanding of modern revelation is correct, Michael will coordinate most of this from his seat of power at Adam-Ondi-Ahman, which is also where he prophesied of all things that would befall his posterity. These events have been recorded in the Book of Enoch and analyzed in this series.

In the context of the Beast, as discussed in Volume II of this series, Daniel's statements regarding the beasts of the last days are all the more interesting.

> I beheld even till the beast was slain, and his body destroyed, and given to the burning flame. As concerning the rest of the beasts, they had their dominion taken away: yet their lives were prolonged for a season and time. (Daniel 7:11-12)

According to Joseph Smith, the Beast referred to as being consumed by fire is a literal beast that will reign in America alongside the antichrist, as detailed in the Book of Revelation. The Beast and the Antichrist are the last two little feathers mentioned in the vision of Ezra's Eagle. Therefore, let us review the relevant passages from the vision of Ezra's Eagle that speak of these things. We will begin our analysis with the first feather representing President Trump and continue through to the last two feathers with their corresponding interpretations.

I beheld, and lo, there was one set up, [*the result of the 2016 elections*] but shortly it appeared no more. And the second was sooner away than the first. And I beheld, and lo, the two that remained thought also in themselves to reign and when they so thought, behold, there awaked one of the heads that were at rest, namely, it that was in the midst [*the middle head*]; for that was greater than the other heads. And then I saw that the two other heads were joined with it. And, behold, the head was turned with them that were with it, and did eat up the two feathers under the wing that would have reigned. But this head put the whole Earth in fear, and bare rule in it over all those that dwelt upon the Earth with much oppression; and it had the governance of the world more than all the wings that had been.

After this I beheld and lo, the head that was in the midst [*middle*] suddenly appeared no more, like as the wings [*the previous feathers or presidents*]. But there remained the two heads, which also in like sort ruled upon the Earth, and over those that dwelt therein. And I beheld, and, lo, the head upon the right side devoured that which was upon the left side…

And whereas thou sawest three heads resting, this is the interpretation: in his last days shall the most High raise up three kingdoms [*presidential administrations*] and renew many things therein, [*meaning select knowledge of the ancient world will be restored*], and they shall have the dominion of the Earth, and of those that dwell therein with much oppression – above all those that were before them. Therefore, are they called the heads of the eagle. For these are they that shall accomplish his [*Satan's*] wickedness, and that shall finish his [*Satan*'s] last end [*meaning Satan final end game*].

And whereas thou sawest that the great head appeared no more, it signifies that one of them shall die upon his bed, and yet with pain. For the sword of the one shall devour the other: but at the last shall he fall through the sword himself. And whereas thou sawest two feathers [*the Beast and the Antichrist*] under the wings passing over the head that is on the right side; it signifies that these are they who the Highest hath kept unto their end: this is the small kingdom [*the short*

administration of the Antichrist and the Beast over America]
and full of trouble, as thou sawest.

The Lion, whom thou sawest rising up out of the wood, and
roaring, and speaking to the eagle, and rebuking her for her
unrighteousness with all the words which thou has heard [*the
Lion confronted the Eagle and accused it of being the forth
beast of Daniel's vision*]. This is the Anointed [*Christ*],
which the Highest hath kept for them and fore their
wickedness unto the end: He shall reprove them, and shall
upbraid them with their cruelty. For He shall set them before
Him alive in judgement, and shall rebuke them, and correct
them [*referring to Rev 19:20, when Christ casts the Beast
and antichrist into outer darkness – the burning pit of fire at
the end of all things*].   For the rest of my people shall He
deliver with mercy, those that have been pressed upon my
boarders, and He shall make them joyful until the coming
day of judgement, whereof I have spoken unto thee from the
beginning. (2 Esdras 11:26-35; 12:22-34)

I believe that the passages above are speaking of imminent events and that the world
will witness the rise of the three eagle heads by the end of January 2025. I hope that I
am wrong. How this will happen is not exactly clear, but the event will not only remove
Biden but also two other presidential hopefuls who think they are about to be set up but
are devoured before the process can occur. When this happens, the foremost of the three
eagle heads will seize power in the United States and oppress the citizens of the world
more than any before him.

However, these three eagle heads are not long for the land. Despite all their well-laid
plans and schemes, according to Daniel, they will be plucked up by their roots in short
order. This opens the way for the joint rule of the last two feathers of the kingdom.
These last two feathers are the antichrist and the Beast, which Daniel mentioned in the
context of Michael's burning wheels and streams of unquenchable fire.

Throughout my writings, the correlation between the restoration of the House of Israel
and the cleansing of America has been made clear. The role that Michael, the Great
Archangel and leader of the Noble and Great Ones, will play in these last events has
also been discussed in my prior writings. As the powers at play upon the Earth rise to
supernatural levels never before seen since the prediluvian world, Michael will step in
to intervene.

According to prophecy, these epic events will begin in the United States, first among the Lord's people who have professed to know the Father's Hidden Son but have not known Him. From the United States, these things will spread to the four corners of the globe. Keep this in mind as we continue with Noah's vision of the events of the last days. We now add a third verse to the two previously reviewed:

> **60.1**. In the year five hundred, in the seventh month, on the fourteenth day of the month in the life of †Enoch†. In that Parable I saw how a mighty quaking made the heaven of heavens to quake, and the host of the Most High, and the angels, a thousand thousands and ten thousand times ten thousand, were disquieted with a great disquiet.

> **60.2**. And the Head of Days [*also translated as Ancient of Days*] sat on the throne of his glory, and the angels and the righteous stood around him.

> **60.3**. And a great trembling seized me, and fear took hold of me, and my loins gave way, and dissolved were my reins, and I fell upon my face.

In the passage above, we learn that Noah was so frightened by the magnitude of the vision that he lost control of his bodily functions. Recall Lamech's description of Noah from the prior chapter of this book. Noah was a mighty man, an Archangel made flesh, yet, due to the veil and the magnitude of the events he saw would transpire upon the Earth in the last days, he lost all control of himself and fell to the ground in shock and shame.

Some have tried to soften this experience by suggesting that by "loins" we should understand "legs." Therefore, they say that Noah did not wet himself, but rather his legs simply gave out and he fell. However, throughout all scripture, I have never seen an instance in which loins and legs could be used interchangeably. The fruit of one's loins refers to one's posterity. What would the fruit of one's legs be, I wonder? Noah explained that his reins were dissolved. Reins are the tools that enable you to control something. If the reins of control are dissolved, you no longer have control. The dissolution of one's reins is not uncommon in both men and animals in the presence of intense primal fear. I am highlighting the significance of Noah's experience and the effect it had upon him because, while he saw these things in vision, you and I will see these things with our natural waking eyes. Of that great and terrible coming day, Christ stated that men's hearts will fail them for fear of the things they see coming upon the Earth (see Luke 21:26-28).

Therefore, we are left to contemplate the astounding magnitude of the events that lie at our door. If the coming events were not of such incredible magnitude, would Michael be called to intervene on our behalf? With this in mind, consider the interaction that Michael and Noah now have, while Noah is lying prostrate on the ground in a puddle of his own making.

> **60.4** And Michael sent another angel from among the holy ones and he raised me up, and when he had raised me up my spirit returned; for **I had not been able to endure the look of this host**, and **the commotion** and the **quaking of the heaven**.

In this passage, Noah describes three things that caused him to lose control of his loins. First, he stated that he could not endure the sight of the terrifying host arriving on Earth from the ends of heaven. We must presume that Christ was referring to this same host when He said that men's hearts would fail them for fear upon seeing "those things which are coming on the Earth."

Second, Noah collapsed because he could not endure the commotion, chaos, and destruction that occurred as a direct result of this incredible host's arrival. Although Noah did not explicitly state what this commotion was, numerous other passages suggest it is the wholesale destruction of the wicked in the Americas. This destruction will render the cities of the Gentiles desolate. This destruction and the coming host are the primary subjects of Christ's discourse to the Nephites, as recorded in 3 Nephi 15:10 through 3 Nephi 17:4, and again in 3 Nephi 20:10 through 3 Nephi 23:5.

Lastly, Noah could not endure the shaking of the heavens, which occurred as a direct result of these events. From prior passages, we know that this quaking impacts not only the heavens but also causes the Earth to wobble to and fro like a drunken man. This trembling of the Earth is caused by more than just the energy released from within; it will be driven by external forces. Consider the following numerous accounts of this teaching, in addition to those already provided elsewhere in this series:

> When the world was first made it was a tremendous big thing. The Lord concluded it was too big. We read in the scriptures that in the days of Peleg the earth was divided so the Lord divided the earth. When the ten tribes of the children of Israel went into the north country He divided it again, so the earth has been divided and subdivided. We also read in the scriptures that the earth shall reel to and fro like a drunken man. What shall cause this earth to reel to and fro like a drunken man? We read that the stars shall fall to the

earth like a fig falling from a fig tree. When these stars return to the place where they were taken from, it will cause the earth to reel to and fro. Not that the planets will come squarely against one another, in such case both planets would be broken to pieces. But in their rolling motion they will come together where they were taken from which will cause the earth to reel to and fro." (Joseph Smith, Winter 1840, Vincent Knight home, Samuel Holister Rogers Journal, p. 17.)

And

Coming in one day and seeing my geography on my lap, he [Jacob Hamblin] told [me] that the Prophet said to him that at the North Pole is [a] convex or cup shaped [depression] with the deepest sea resting there. The planet that belonged to that part of the world would in time return to its place, strike the earth at that part, complete the sphere. The result would be a 'reeling to and fro like a drunken man' by the Earth ... (Biographical Record of Martha Cragun Cox, p. 104.)

And

In the course of his [*Joseph's*] remarks he spoke of the earth being divided at various times. He said, "When Enoch and his City was taken away, a portion of the earth was taken and would again be restored. Also in the days of Peleg, the earth was divided, see Genesis 10th Chapter, 25th verse." He then referred to the 'Ten Tribes' saying, "You know a long time ago in the days of Shalmanezar King of Assyria when the Ten Tribes was taken away, and never heard of since." He said, "The Earth will be restored as at the beginning, and the last taken away will be the first to return; for the last shall be first, and the first will be last in all things." He illustrated the return by saying: "Some of you brethren have been coming up the river on a steamboat, and while seated at the table, the steamboat run against a snag which upset the table and scattered the dishes; so it will be when these portions of the earth return. It will make the earth reel to and fro like a drunken man," quoting 24th chapter [of] Isaiah, 20th verse. When speaking of the return of the Ten Tribes, he said, "The mountains of ice shall flow down at their presence, and a highway shall be cast up in the middle of the great deep." (Wandle Mace Journal, 1809-1890, p. 38-39.)

In the passages above, three separate saints recorded that Joseph taught them the incredible shaking of the Earth in the last days would result from the physical restoration of former fragments of the Earth. The last of these fragments to be removed was accompanied by the main body of the Lost Ten Tribes of Israel. This fragment will be the first to be restored, followed by others, and will conclude with the City of Enoch. As Joseph stated, "the first shall be last and the last shall be first" applies not only to Israel but also to the restoration of these fragments and people.

The combined spectacle of all three of these events—the host, the ensuing commotion, and the shaking of the heavens and Earth—overcame Noah, and it will likely overcome us as well. From the world's perspective, these things sound absolutely crazy, even cult-like. As such, many in the Church have simply chosen to ignore that they were ever taught in the first place. After all, such incredible events cannot be reconciled with Newtonian physics. These things fall squarely into the realm of the supernatural. Yet, God is first and foremost a supernatural being. Nothing in Christianity makes any sense outside of the supernatural. Either these things are true or they are false, but as Christ's life and mission attest, such things cannot simply be discounted because they sound crazy. After all, the events of the last days will prove beyond all doubt that the supernatural is the default state of reality, not Newtonian physics.

From this incredible revelation, we understand that the host coming to Earth in the latter days will be both great and terrible. This host will bring fire and destruction upon the wicked of Earth on a scale we have never heard of nor considered. Do you recall from Volume I of this series the Egyptians' reaction when fire disks filled their skies? That incredible event occurred when the Lord called the kings of heaven to battle against Sisera and his nine hundred iron chariots. Yet, from the perspective of the Egyptians, hundreds of miles away, the simple astounding presence of such things in their skies constituted the single greatest event in their history, even surpassing the Exodus. If hovering fire disks elicited such a reaction among the Egyptians, we can begin to understand why Noah was both astounded and terrified when he saw such an incredible host baptizing the Americas in flames.

As we pause to contemplate such incredible things, we would do well to consider that these are far from isolated events. We have already noted the final destruction of the Canaanites and their iron chariots at the hands of such a host. Yet, something very similar seems to have occurred at Christ's birth in both Judah and the Americas. Glowing heavenly orbs of light guided wise men from distant lands, going forth before them all the way to Bethlehem, where they rested upon the Savior's home. Samuel the

Lamanite prophesied that the Nephites would see signs and wonders of such an incredible magnitude that they would fall to the earth in shock and disbelief. I believe they were witnessing our brothers and sisters from other worlds coming to pay their respects to the Lord of Lords and King of Kings.

You will also recall Elisha's fearlessness in the face of an overwhelming host coming against the Northern Kingdom of Israel. When his servant feared and wondered at Elisha's confidence, Elisha prayed that the Lord would open his eyes. When the Lord did so, Elisha's servant witnessed that the skies were filled with flaming chariots ready to eliminate their enemies, as had been done in the days of Deborah (see 2 Kings 6).

Again, just before the destruction of the Kingdom of Judah by the Romans in 70 AD, Josephus claimed that the skies above Jerusalem were filled with signs and wonders of the most peculiar nature. According to his account, these signs lasted for over a year. Consider the following extracts from his descriptions of these incredible events.

> Now, there was then a great number of false prophets suborned by the tyrants to impose upon the people, who denounced this to them, that they should wait for deliverance from God: and this was in order to keep them from deserting, and that they might be buoyed up above fear and care by such hopes.

> Thus were the miserable people persuaded by these deceivers, and such as belied God himself; while they did not attend, nor give credit to the signs that were so evident and did so plainly foretell their future desolation; but, like men infatuated, without either eyes to see, or minds to consider, did not regard the denunciations that God made to them.

> Thus there was **a star resembling a sword, which stood over the city**, and a comet, that continued **a whole year**.

> Thus also, before the Jews' rebellion, and before those commotions which preceded the war, when the people were come in great crowds to the feast of unleavened bread, on the eighth day of the month Xanthicus [Nisan], and at the ninth hour of the night, so great a light shone round the altar and the holy house, that it appeared to be bright day time; which light lasted for half an hour. This light seemed to be a good sign to the unskillful, but was so interpreted by the

sacred scribes, as to portend those events that followed immediately upon it.

So these publicly declared that this signal foreshowed the desolation that was coming upon them. Besides these, a few days after that feast, on the twenty-first day of the month Artemisius [*Jyar*], a certain prodigious and incredible phenomenon appeared; I suppose the account of it would seem to be a fable, were it not related by those that saw it, and were not the events that followed it of so considerable a nature as to deserve such signals; for, before sunsetting, chariots and troops of soldiers in their armor were seen running about among the clouds, and surrounding of cities. Moreover at that feast which we call Pentecost, as the priests were going by night into the inner [court of the] temple, as their custom was, to perform their sacred ministrations, they said that, in the first place, they felt a quaking, and heard a great noise, and after that they heard a sound as of a great multitude, saying, "Let us remove hence." (Flavious Josephus – Jewish War pages 286 to 300)

Josephus was not the only Jewish historian to write about these events. Sepher Yosippon, another Jewish historian, also documented the fall of Jerusalem in a self-titled work dated to the 10th century. This document was translated and published by Steven B. Bowman. Consider the following extract from it:

Moreover, in those days were seen chariots of fire and horsemen, a great force flying across the sky near to the ground coming against Jerusalem and all the land of Judah, all of them horses of fire and riders of fire. When the holiday of Shavu'oth came in those days, during the night the priests heard within the Temple something like the sound of men going and the sound of men marching in a multitude going into the Temple, and a terrible and mighty voice was heard speaking: "Let's go and leave this House. (Sepher Yosippon – a Medieval History of Ancient Israel – Chapter 87 – Burning of the Temple)

Both of these accounts describe incredible hosts of inexplicable craft in the skies above Jerusalem, mirroring the descriptions of a similar host in the Book of Revelation. As astonishing as these events are, it wasn't just the Jews who witnessed them. A Roman historian also documented such phenomena from their perspective as they besieged the city, preparing to raze it to the ground. Consider the following example from the Roman historian Tacitus:

> Prodigies had occurred, which this nation, prone to superstition, but hating all religious rites, did not deem it lawful to expiate by offering and sacrifice. There had been seen hosts joining battle in the skies, the fiery gleam of arms, the temple illuminated by a sudden radiance from the clouds. The doors of the inner shrine were suddenly thrown open, and a voice of more than mortal tone was heard to cry that the Gods were departing. At the same instant there was a mighty stir of departure. Some few put a fearful meaning on these events, but in most there was a firm persuasion, that in the ancient records of their priests was contained a prediction of how at this very time the East was to grow powerful, and rulers, coming from Judaea, were to acquire universal empire. (Tacitus, Histories, Book 5)

The hidden history of the House of Israel and their encounters with the supernatural is right before our eyes, yet, because it is strange, we often fail to see it. How different would our approach to the events of the last days be as a Church if we could consider both these ancient occurrences and the exponential increase of trans-medium craft invading our skies, as noted by the United States Congress? Yet, such topics remain taboo, leaving us woefully unprepared for the coming day.

Israel's history, regardless of its fantastical nature, literally happened, no matter how cult-like its retelling sounds. Therefore, I believe it is wise, albeit irrational in the eyes of some, to conclude that Noah's vision is not a mysterious symbolic parable but rather a vision of literal events that will transpire in the near future. Unlike many, when I read prophecies of hosts coming to Earth from the ends of heaven to destroy the wicked with fire, I am compelled to consider the stark possibility that they are not speaking of figurative events. Therefore, I invite you to reconsider the following prophecy from Isaiah in light of Noah's vision of the incredible latter-day host that will come to Earth.

> They come from a far country, from the end of heaven, *even* the LORD, and the weapons of His indignation, to destroy the whole land. Howl ye; for the day of the LORD *is* at hand; it shall come as a destruction from the Almighty.
>
> Therefore shall all hands be faint, and every man's heart shall melt: and they shall be afraid: pangs and sorrows shall take hold of them; they shall be in pain as a woman that

travaileth: they shall be amazed one at another; their faces shall be as flames.

Behold, the day of the LORD cometh, cruel both with wrath and fierce anger, to lay the land desolate: and He shall destroy the sinners thereof out of it.

For the stars of heaven and the constellations thereof shall not give their light: the sun shall be darkened in his going forth, and the moon shall not cause her light to shine. And I will punish the world for their evil, and the wicked for their iniquity; and I will cause the arrogancy of the proud to cease, and will lay low the haughtiness of the terrible.

Therefore I will shake the heavens, and the earth shall remove out of her place, in the wrath of the LORD of hosts, and in the day of His fierce anger. And it [Earth] shall be as the chased roe, and as a sheep that no man taketh up: they shall every man turn to his own people, and flee every one into his own land.

Every one [*of the sinners*] that is found shall be thrust through; and every one that is joined *unto them* shall fall by the sword. Their children also shall be dashed to pieces before their eyes; their houses shall be spoiled, and their wives ravished. (Isaiah 13:5-16)

Isaiah's prophecy is a dual prophecy for both the destruction of Babylon and the purging of the Americas. To understand this, it is instructive to discuss the demise of Babylon as a type and shadow. Even today, the demise of Babylon remains something of a mystery. According to the Cyrus Cylinder, Cyrus the Great conquered Babylon without a fight. The Greeks claimed that Cyrus diverted the Euphrates River, enabling his armies to simply walk into Babylon under its walls via the now-dried riverbed. Thus, the conquering of Babylon was done secretly and strategically, not unlike the usurpation of America contemplated by Ezra's Eagle. Consequently, Babylon became Persia without a traditional fight.

Subsequently, King Darius III of Babylon was betrayed by three conspiring men: Bessus, Satribarzanes, and Barsaentes. These three had originally sought for King Darius to confer the kingdom to Bessus. When he refused, they stabbed him and left him in a wagon bed to die in pain. Alexander hunted down these three men and plucked them up by their roots, taking the Kingdom of Babylon for himself. The parallels between the demise of Babylon and the prophecy of Ezra's Eagle should not be lost on the reader.

Yet, all of this was done without a single battle being fought within the famous city of Babylon itself, which remained unspoiled and occupied by Alexander without the shedding of blood within its walls. However, after Alexander's untimely death, his kingdom was divided among his four generals. It was in this subsequent power vacuum that Babylon descended into chaos, not at the hands of enemies or armies, but through lawlessness and chaos. Sons revolted against their fathers, neighbors rose up against neighbors, city against city until nothing remained but ruins and rubble. So it has been prophesied for the last days.

Isaiah's prophecy stated that the men and children of Babylon would be killed, but that their women would be ravished. The word "ravished" means taken away by force or kidnapped. This is precisely what happened to Darius III's family. Alexander the Great kidnapped his wife and daughter. He married Darius's daughter and became a son to Darius's wife. The question then becomes, why did the Lord save many of the women but not their children or husbands? This is an important question to consider, particularly since the Babylonian destruction is a type and shadow of what will befall the world in the last days.

The Lord has declared that in the last days the wicked will be cut off both root and branch. By this, we understand that wicked men will be cut off and left without any living posterity. Yet, the Lord will have mercy upon the women. Many of these mothers and wives will be preserved and will live to see the world renewed in incredible and unprecedented ways. Indeed, they will live to become wives and mothers again, but to husbands worthy of their affections. Consider the following:

> **Thy men shall fall by the sword**, and thy mighty in the war. And her gates shall lament and mourn; and she being desolate shall sit upon the ground. And in that day seven women shall take hold of one man, saying, We will eat our own bread, and wear our own apparel: only let us be called by thy name, to take away our reproach.
>
> In that day shall the branch of the Lord be beautiful and glorious, and the fruit of the earth shall be excellent and comely for them that are escaped of Israel. And it shall come to pass, that he that is left in Zion, and he that remaineth in Jerusalem, shall be called holy, even every one that is written among the living in Jerusalem:

When the Lord shall have washed away the filth of the daughters of Zion, and shall have purged the blood of Jerusalem from the midst thereof by the spirit of judgment, and by the spirit of burning. And the Lord will create upon every dwelling place of mount Zion, and upon her assemblies, a cloud and smoke by day, and the shining of a flaming fire by night: for upon all the glory shall be for a defense. (Isaiah 3:24-26, 4:1-5)

The passages above confirm that many of the women of Zion will survive the great fiery purge of the last days. As such, they will vastly outnumber the men—seven to one. As I consider these things, I marvel at the mercy the Father shows towards His daughters and the firmness He shows His sons. Obviously, there are wicked women who will be destroyed as part of these events, but the fact that so many more women survive speaks to the Father's acknowledgment of the divine nature of women. Women are different from men; they willingly sacrifice everything they have for their children. This is godlike love, charity in its purest form. Mormon prophesied that it would be well with those who possessed charity in the last days. Because women exhibit charity in far greater numbers than their male counterparts, they will be saved in far greater numbers as well. Charitable women can be found in large quantities in every culture and faith across the world.

Still, such women will not come through these days unscathed. Their worldliness and vanity will be stripped away. Yet, after they have humbled themselves to the dust and repented in sackcloth and ashes, they will live to become mothers once again under the most favorable conditions the world has ever known. Their lifespans will be greatly expanded, returning to the ages of their prediluvian mothers. Therefore, even after experiencing the stinging loss of their first children, these women, unlike their wicked husbands, will not be cut off both root and branch. Thus, we see how important posterity is, regardless of how readily the world seems to disregard the traditional family. The world will mourn its woeful short-sightedness.

Returning to Noah's vision, Michael now has a conversation with Noah. Noah is clearly overwhelmed by the fiery destruction he witnessed would rain down upon the Earth from the heavens in the last days. Michael attempts to give Noah context for these great and terrible events.

60.5 And Michael said unto me: 'Why art thou disquieted with such a vision? Until this day lasted the day of His mercy; and He hath been merciful and long-suffering towards those who dwell on the Earth.

40

60.6. And when the day, and the power, and the punishment, and the judgement come, which the Lord of Spirits hath prepared for those who worship not the righteous law, and for those who deny the righteous judgement, and for those who take His name in vain--that day is prepared, for the elect a covenant, but for sinners an inquisition. When the punishment of the Lord of Spirits shall rest upon them, it shall rest in order that the punishment of the Lord of Spirits may not come, in vain, and it shall slay the children with their mothers and the children with their fathers. Afterwards the judgement shall take place according to His mercy and His patience.'

Michael confirms that women will not get a free pass. Not all mothers will be preserved; those who have embraced the wicked traditions of the world and imprinted them onto their children will perish with the world. Yet, according to Michael, the Father has been in no hurry to destroy the wicked. Indeed, it seems to many that the Lord is delaying His coming to the point that some are starting to say, "Get on with it already." Yet the Father is patient and longsuffering, and His arm is outstretched to any who will take it.

The Great and Terrible Day of the Lord is coming. When it does, it will be both terrifying and devastating. The wicked will be destroyed without mercy, but the righteous will live to see the dawning of a new day unlike anything they have ever imagined. Yet, as the Book of Enoch has made abundantly clear, the journey of the wicked does not end at death. For the wicked, death is another merciful opportunity for a great reset. This change of venue enables the wicked to consider their ways. In Spirit Prison, they will reflect on why they were destroyed and why those they oppressed were deemed worthy to inherit the Earth in their absence. Such reflection will hopefully be the beginning of great change. God is all about transformative change, and bringing about the conditions wherein the children of heaven will exercise their free agency to do so.

You will recall from the seventh chapter of Volume I of this series that God placed Michael in charge of the Watcher issue both anciently and when they return in the last days. As such, Michael, the Great Prince, will preside over the purging of America. This makes sense on many levels, beginning with the fact that America was Adam and Eve's first land of inheritance. The Garden of Eden was given to them. Their blessed inheritance will be at the center of the New Jerusalem, wherein the Tree of Life will be restored. From modern revelation, we know that this will be located near present-day Independence, MO.

In addition, at the end of Michael's mortal life, as the father of the human race, he stood in Adam-Ondi-Ahman and prophesied all things that would befall his posterity unto the last generation. According to the Lord, the things that Michael prophesied about would be recorded in the Book of Enoch. Michael also oversaw the banishment of Lucifer and his angels to this Earth. As such, it is no surprise to learn that in the last days, when Satan and his followers have amassed the greatest degree of power they have ever obtained, Michael will be there once more to oppose them.

We know that things will get very bad in the last days. However, I believe there is hope for the righteous in the following passage:

> And at that time shall Michael stand up, the great prince which standeth for the children of thy people: and there shall be a time of trouble, such as never was since there was a nation even to that same time: and at that time thy people shall be delivered, every one that shall be found written in the book. (Dan 12:1)

Michael's return will correspond with the arrival of the massive host of heaven that Noah saw. The first wave will be comprised of the ships of Chittim, or the fiery burning wheels of Daniel's vision previously discussed. These will come to render the wicked cities of the Gentiles desolate and to drive the Antichrist and the Beast from America. While this will be both great and terrible for the wicked, it will also mark the end of the tribulations in America, although the rest of the world will just be getting started. After the Beast and the Antichrist are ejected from America, they will pull out all the stops. With nothing to lose and the countdown to their elimination on, they will unleash everything they have. The terrible conditions the rest of the world will face will last for another three and a half years from the time they attack Israel. Lucifer, the Antichrist, and the Beast will be filled with fury at the covenant people of the Lord. If not for the miraculous gathering of the righteous to the lands of Zion by the 144,000, they would be utterly exterminated by the wicked, preventing them from entering the millennium in mortality.

With an eye towards extinction, this unholy trinity will seek to devour Israel with open mouth. If not for the two prophets who will come, they would accomplish their objective. Ultimately, they will overcome these two candlesticks and then be confronted by the Son of Man Himself. However, they will find that the Son of Man far outstrips their combined might, and they will effortlessly fall before Him. The Antichrist and the Beast will then be cast into outer darkness, and Lucifer and his minions will be bound in prison for a thousand years. Yet, as we will soon see, there is more to the terror that Noah witnessed in these events than has yet been discussed. You will understand what I mean as Noah's explanation of his vision continues in the next chapter.

Chapter 4 – The Terrifying Hosts of Heaven

In the prior chapter, we continued our analysis of Noah's terrifying vision in which he witnessed the latter-day shakings of the heavens and the Earth, and the coming of the Ancient of Days, together with a terrible host of heaven. This host, and the destruction that accompanied them, was so terrifying to Noah that he lost control of his loins and fell upon his face in terror. Given the first chapter of this book, the fact that such a one as Noah could have been overcome by fear at what he witnessed in vision speaks to the incredible nature of coming events. I expounded on more commonly understood reasons for why these things might have been so terrifying. However, in this chapter, Noah adds his own commentary on the things he saw, introducing a whole new dimension to the events of the last days, of which we have only just begun to scratch the surface at the end of volume II of this series. Therefore, grab your life jacket as we wade into the deeper end of the pool.

What comes next may likely be the strangest thing I have discussed in the Book of Enoch series so far. It is so strange, in fact, that many will most certainly consider the things Noah is about to discuss as being symbolic of the coming devastation and nothing more. Frankly, I hope this is right, because if what we are about to discuss has any semblance of truth, we will find it difficult to retain any vestiges of reality as we have been accustomed to accepting it.

In the last chapters of Volume II of this series, Joseph Smith taught a reality-shattering doctrine with respect to the diversity of cosmic creatures. In the context of what Noah is about to discuss, it would be a good idea to refresh ourselves regarding Joseph's teaching on the subject. Consider the following:

> The beasts which John saw and speaks of being in heaven, were actually living in heaven, and were actually to have power given to them over the inhabitants of the earth, precisely according to the plain reading of the revelations. I give this as a key to the elders of Israel. The independent beast is a beast that dwells in heaven, abstract from the human family…
>
> I suppose John saw beings [*in space*] of a thousand forms, that had been saved from ten thousand times ten thousand earths like this, --strange beasts of which we have no

conception: all might be seen in heaven. **The grand secret was to show John what there was in heaven**...

John saw beasts that had to do with things on the earth, but not in past ages. **The beasts which John saw had to devour the inhabitants of the earth in days to come**. (TPJS 287-294)

These doctrines are astounding and shocking, and most people have never heard of them. Why? Because they are as weird as all get out! In the Church, since the world already views us as peculiar, we tend to avoid discussing anything that might add fuel to that fire. Consequently, our core curriculum has largely been stripped of these earth-shattering doctrines, further stigmatizing them. Despite the amazing insights these doctrines could provide if taught in the proper context, they remain almost entirely unknown. As a result, the world generally, and the saints specifically, are woefully unprepared for what is about to be unleashed on the planet.

It's easy to understand why we don't speak of such things. The world already thinks "Mormons" are a cult, and such peculiar doctrines do little to dispel that notion. However, when it comes to truth, who cares what the world thinks! Yes, there are many in the great and spacious buildings of the world who would have a heyday with such doctrines, but fools have always mocked what they do not understand. If we give fools power over what we believe, we too will suppress the more supernatural aspects of the gospel because we are embarrassed by them. By disregarding truth in any of its forms, we stick our heads in the sand regarding the true nature of the world around us, and we have nobody to blame but ourselves and our own prejudice against knowledge. It is precisely for these reasons that the true nature of the Father and the Son has remained hidden from the world for millennia.

Therefore, I will not shy away from writing about such things. I will present my thoughts on the matter and let you decide for yourself what you believe, as I have done in every book I have written. Still, it is clear that Joseph did not speak of these things often. By his own admission, he had only spoken of them twice. If these things are true and important for us to understand, why were they not spoken of more broadly? It seems clear to me that Joseph was constrained by the Lord in what he shared with the saints in many aspects. That is to say, he clearly knew more than he taught. Why was he constrained? Because the Lord has plainly stated that He will try the faith of His people!

Consider that after Joseph Smith introduced the three degrees of glory as revealed in D&C 76, many in the new Church became incensed and left. If the body of the Church struggled with accepting various degrees of glory, how on earth could they be expected to accept the idea of strange beasts coming to the Earth and devouring its inhabitants in the last days? This is truly the stuff of nightmares. It sounds closer to a Godzilla movie than the Come Follow Me manuals we all study from. Yet, Joseph clearly taught that this understanding was a key of knowledge to the coming events.

Because of the rarity with which such things were spoken, it is easy for the "doctrinal Pharisees" to brush them aside as being spoken of in isolation. After all, for most, obscure passages from the Book of Revelation and a little-known discourse from Joseph Smith are not much to go on. As such, very few in the world have ever considered that such things are not symbolic, but literal. Obviously, considering everything symbolic is the easiest course of action. It makes it far easier to place otherwise important nuggets on the "who cares" shelf and move on. Yet, on the other hand, there is great danger in dismissing great truths as symbolism. After all, this is precisely what the Jews did regarding the Father's Hidden Son. They dismissed such references in the Old Testament as being symbolic, and as a result, made the biggest mistake of their lives. It is perhaps for this reason that Joseph Smith stated the following:

> I have never heard of a man being damned for believing too much; but they are damned for unbelief. (*History of the Church,* 6:477)

Still, the Lord has said that by the mouth of two or three witnesses shall all doctrines be established. John and Joseph are two strong witnesses to the reality of these strange things, but extraordinary claims require extraordinary evidence. As we are about to understand, the Book of Enoch is another witness that strange and terrifying creatures will come to the Earth in the last days. Whether such things are symbolic or real, you must decide for yourself. However, as the world has done an adequate job of demonstrating the symbolic nature of these things, in this book I will present these ideas from the possibility of their being indicative of actual events.

You will recall that in D&C 107:56-57, the Lord stated that Adam prophesied of all things that would befall his posterity unto the last generation. The Lord said that these things would be recorded in the Book of Enoch, and that the truthfulness of this book would be testified of in due time. You are now reading the last volume of my analysis of the Book of Enoch, and you must decide for yourself if the things you have read in it are truth or error. After all, I write these things while peeking through a darkened glass, and not with perfect knowledge. Therefore, the accuracy of my interpretations of the Book of Enoch is far from a foregone conclusion. Extraordinary doctrines require extraordinary validation, so, as with all my writings, let the Spirit be your guide. I do not write these things with the intent that you believe them, but rather to make you aware of their existence, that you might have a box to place such things in should the need arise. I guarantee you that most have no place for the things we are about to discuss.

Now, returning to Noah's vision. Noah has only just risen to his feet after collapsing in terror. Upon rising, Noah stated that his terror stemmed from the hosts he saw descending upon the Earth from the heavens. Apparently, the host he saw will be comprised of more than the House of Israel. Consider Noah's continued explanation of the terrifying things he witnessed on the great and terrible day of the Lord, when both the heavens and the Earth are shaken beyond belief:

> **60.7** And on that day were two monsters parted, a female monster named Leviathan, to dwell in the abysses of the ocean over the fountains of the waters.
>
> **60.8** But the male is named Behemoth, who occupied with his breast a waste wilderness named †Dûidâin†, on the east of the garden where the elect and righteous dwell, **where my grandfather was taken up,** the seventh from Adam, the first man whom the Lord of Spirits created.
>
> **60.9** And I besought the other angel that he should show me the might of those monsters, how they were parted on one day and cast, the one into the abysses of the sea, and the other unto the dry land of the wilderness.
>
> **60.10**. And he said to me: 'Thou son of man, herein thou dost seek to know what is hidden.'
>
> **60.11**. And the other angel who went with me and showed me what was hidden told me what is first and last in the heaven in the height, and beneath the earth in the depth, and at the ends of the heaven, and on the foundation of the heaven.
>
> **60.12**. And the chambers of the winds, and how the winds are divided, and how they are weighed, and (how) the **portals** of the winds are reckoned, each according to the power of the wind, and the power of the lights of the moon, and according to the power that is fitting: and the divisions of the stars according to their names, and how all the divisions are divided.

Noah was overwhelmed by the spectacular nature of these creatures and wanted to know where they came from and how they arrived on Earth. In response, he was instructed about the hidden things in the heavens and within the earth itself. This sounds very much like Joseph's grand key of knowledge discussed earlier. The multiverse is not a vast and empty vacuum; it is full of life and living creatures in all its parts. As strange and foreign as this concept might seem, it is true.

Why do you suppose the restoration began with the Pearl of Great Price, which is unique in all holy writ in that it gives three separate accounts from three separate men, stating that the multiverse is comprised of innumerable inhabited worlds? Because this knowledge is a grand key that we all need for what is coming. Furthermore, according to Joseph, not all intelligent life looks like us. There are intelligent beasts and monsters, and we may be about to find out from firsthand experience.

When Noah asked how these creatures arrived on Earth, his angelic guide began speaking about portals. You will recall from the first volume of the Book of Enoch that Enoch described solar/cosmic winds and how those winds created portals. In that volume, I shared NASA's acknowledgment that such portals do exist and are products of electromagnetic and gravitational fields. The fact that Noah is receiving this answer in conjunction with these incredible creatures is astonishing to me.

This should also remind you of the account in volume II of Dr. Steven Greer regarding the portal that was opened in a lab in Salt Lake City. He stated that when the portal was opened, the scientists filmed strange creatures coming out of it. In addition to this account, you may recall the bizarre reports of strange creatures emerging through a mysterious portal that allegedly appeared inside a Miami mall on New Year's Day 2024. If any of those accounts are true, then as crazy as it sounds, we must be talking about the same kinds of portals that will bring Leviathan and Behemoth to Earth in the last days. I realize this sounds crazy, but there was a reason Noah lost control of his bladder when he saw these things. There is also a very good reason that men's hearts will fail them for fear because of those things they see coming upon the Earth in the last days.

Curiously, the angel explained to Noah that Leviathan was female and would live in the sea, while Behemoth was male and would live on the land. Furthermore, the passage began with the monsters' respective sexes in the context of them being separated. The implication, therefore, is that these two creatures are companions. If this is true, while Noah observed that Leviathan would occupy the ocean, it would appear that either she was capable of living on land, or Behemoth was capable of living in the sea as well. Otherwise, how could they be companions?

While this sounds like fantasy, it is very important to understand that both of these epic creatures are found throughout the lore of the ancient world. Every culture of the world has depictions of dragons in some form or fashion. This is true from the Norse in the extreme North to the world's first advanced civilizations of the Fertile Crescent. In Norse mythology, Leviathan was referred to as Jormungandr, the World Serpent. This World Serpent was associated with Ragnarök, or the end of the world. Furthermore, according to their traditions, this titanic beast could only be overcome by Odin – the God of gods. The Norse typically depicted the World Serpent as a sea creature of such immense size that it encompassed the Earth. This creature was used by them as a symbol of eternity and the life cycle of the universe.

The Sumerians referred to Leviathan as Tiamat. Tiamat was so powerful she was considered to be the goddess of the primordial sea and the harbinger of chaos and destruction. Furthermore, as with the Norse tradition, only the God of gods was able to overcome Tiamat. These examples and many others like them mesh very well with Noah's vision of Leviathan.

Anciently, Behemoth was an epic land creature of incredible power. Similar to Leviathan, Behemoth was so powerful that he could only be controlled by God. I believe that the fact that Leviathan was described as being in the water and Behemoth on land is symbolic of the global chaos and destruction that will be present upon the Earth during the Great and Terrible Day of the Lord.

According to the passage above, Behemoth will be located near two ancient locations: the Garden of Eden and the location where Enoch, Noah's grandfather, was taken up into heaven. This is curious given both of these locations are associated with North America, with the Garden of Eden being associated with Missouri. Noah further clarified that eastward of this location was at one time associated with Dûidâin, the ancient desert prison where the Watchers were imprisoned for seventy generations. Therefore, there seems to be a link between the arrival of these two creatures and the return of the latter-day Watchers.

Furthermore, Noah identifies the location of Behemoth with the location where his grandfather was taken up into heaven. As has been discussed elsewhere in this series, the City of Enoch is believed to have occupied what is now the Gulf of Mexico. Therefore, according to Noah, Behemoth will be wandering around somewhere in the southeastern United States. To understand the significance of Behemoth in North America and Leviathan dominating the oceans around us, we need to turn to the oldest book in the Bible – the Book of Job.

You will recall that when the Book of Job was discovered among the Dead Sea Scrolls, similar to the Book of Enoch, it was written in ancient Aramaic. Aramaic was the precursor to Hebrew and therefore suggests that both these books predated Abraham. Indeed, given the lifespan of Job as discussed within that book's text, he had a prediluvian lifespan. As such, Job would have lived during the days of the Watchers. This makes his writings all the more relevant to the topic at hand.

I find it fascinating, therefore, that the Book of Job speaks extensively about Leviathan and also mentions Behemoth. Even more interesting is the fact that this information comes to us from a conversation between God and Job, wherein God is asking Job a series of questions, and in so doing sheds light upon the understanding that the ancient world had regarding the present topic. Consider this incredible conversation:

> Canst thou draw out leviathan with an hook? Or his tongue with a cord *which* thou lettest down? Canst thou put an hook into his nose? Or bore his jaw through with a thorn? Will he make many supplications unto thee? Will he speak soft *words* unto thee? Will he make a covenant with thee? Wilt thou take him for a servant forever? Wilt thou play with him as *with* a bird? Or wilt thou bind him for thy maidens? (Job 41:1-5)

God essentially asks Job a series of rhetorical questions regarding the Leviathan. These questions highlight the absurdity of Job being able to control or influence the Leviathan, which was considered indestructible by the ancient world. Furthermore, God asks Job if the Leviathan has ever pleaded with him or made covenants with him. The implication is that while Job could never exert such influence, the Leviathan had both pleaded and covenanted with the Lord. This suggests that Leviathan is not a mindless monster but an intelligent creature capable of making and keeping covenants with the Lord. This is an astounding concept and aligns with Joseph Smith's statement that all intelligent creatures are heirs to salvation if they so choose. According to the Lord's conversation with Job, we have an example of at least one Leviathan that did just that. This speaks volumes!

Of further interest is that in this instance, God is speaking of a male Leviathan. Noah saw that a female Leviathan would come to Earth in the last days via a portal. This suggests that the Leviathans are a race of creatures like any other. It further suggests that the bonding of Leviathan with the Behemoth, as noted by Noah, was voluntary. This is further evidence that these creatures are both intelligent and possess free will, and are capable of friendship. Indeed, God asked Job if he could play with Leviathan as with a bird. The inference here is that God can and does do so. This also speaks volumes about the nature of both God and the Leviathan, for who would have guessed that the most powerful being in the universe would take delight in playing with Leviathans as we play with cats and dogs?

The most interesting thing about these passages is that nothing in this interaction between Job and God suggests that Leviathan is anything other than a real living creature. Consider the absurdity if the Lord had asked Job if he had made a covenant with the Easter Bunny, for example, or if he had taken the tooth fairy as his servant forever. Yet, the Lord's questions imply that He has done both of these things with Leviathan. Such could not be the case if Leviathan were a mythical creature.

The continued conversation between the Lord and Job forces the reader to concede that either the story of Job is a fabrication, or Leviathan is real, for God's conversation implies Leviathan is as real as you and I.

Consider the following:

> Shall the companions make a banquet of him [*Leviathan*]? Shall they part him among the merchants? Canst thou fill his skin with barbed irons? or his head with fish spears? Lay thine hand upon him, remember the battle, do no more. Behold, the hope of him is in vain: shall not one be cast down even at the sight of him?
>
> None is so fierce that dare stir him up: who then is able to stand before Me? Who hath prevented Me, that I should repay him? Whatsoever is under the whole heaven is mine. I will not conceal his parts, nor his power, nor his comely proportion. (Job 41: 6-12)

In the passages above, the Lord is clearly playing off the fear and reverent respect that the pre-diluvian world held for this creature. From the Lord's questions to Job, we can deduce that at some point, a pre-diluvian civilization familiar to Job attempted to battle the Leviathan. Despite the presence and technology of the Watchers, the battle was a catastrophic failure. So much so that all the Lord had to say was, "Remember the battle, do no more."

According to the Lord, the pre-diluvian civilizations could not even pierce Leviathan's skin. The fact that the Lord is speaking of iron weapons before the flood is further evidence of the technology of the Watchers, as the Iron Age was not meant to begin for thousands of years. Given the apparent indestructibility of Leviathans and the resultant fear and respect they commanded, the Lord uses the Leviathan to highlight that the world should hold Him in greater regard, for He is far greater than any Leviathan. Implied in the Lord's conversation is the fact that God could easily kill and make a banquet of the Leviathan. Indeed, based on the conversation above, the Leviathan's covenant with the Lord seems to have been born from an act of self-preservation. If Leviathan was intelligent enough to save itself with a covenant with the Lord, how much more ought we to do so, having been created in God's own image?

It is also important to note from the passages above that God associated the Leviathan with the "whole heavens," meaning outer space. Furthermore, God's statement that He would not conceal Leviathans from the Earth's inhabitants makes it clear that the ancient world fully understood that the Leviathan had extraterrestrial origins. Therefore, the Leviathan likely arrived in ancient times in the same manner it will arrive in the future, via the types of portals that Noah witnessed. Also implied in the conversation is God's dominion over the entire multiverse and all things contained within it. We will keep this in mind as we continue God's conversation with Job regarding these peculiar things.

> Who can discover the face of his garment [*meaning use Leviathan's skin for a garment*]? *Or* who can come *to him* with his double bridle? Who can open the doors of his face [*jaws of his mouth*]? His teeth *are* terrible round about. *His* scales *are his* pride, shut up together *as with* a close seal. One is so near to another, that no air can come between them. They are joined one to another, they stick together, that they cannot be sundered. By his neesings [*sneezing*] a light doth shine, and his eyes *are* like the eyelids of the morning. Out of his mouth go burning lamps, *and* sparks of fire leap out. Out of his nostrils goeth smoke, as *out* of a seething pot or caldron. His breath kindleth coals, and a flame goeth out of his mouth. In his neck remaineth strength, and sorrow is turned into joy before him. The flakes of his flesh are joined together: they are firm in themselves; they cannot be moved. His heart is as firm as a stone; yea, as hard as a piece of the nether *millstone.* When he raiseth up himself, the mighty are afraid: by reason of breakings they purify themselves.

> The sword of him that layeth at him cannot hold: the spear, the dart, nor the habergeon. He esteemeth iron as straw, *and* brass as rotten wood. The arrow cannot make him flee: slingstones are turned with him into stubble. Darts are

counted as stubble: he laugheth at the shaking of a spear. Sharp stones *are* under him: he spreadeth sharp pointed things upon the mire. He maketh the deep to boil like a pot: he maketh the sea like a pot of ointment. He maketh a path to shine after him; *one* would think the deep *to be* hoary [icy]. **Upon earth there is not his like**, who is made without fear. (Job 41:13-33)

The Lord goes into great detail describing the anatomy of the Leviathan. If the Leviathan were a mythical creature, the Lord would not do this. The Lord describes the scales of the Leviathan as not only airtight but also impenetrable. The Lord literally describes the Leviathan as capable of breathing fire. Indeed, the Lord's manner of speech indicates that Leviathan is not only real but a creature of unparalleled power on Earth. Furthermore, the Lord's manner of speaking suggests that Job had firsthand knowledge of this creature's anatomy, power, and magnificence.

What are we to make of this? The Lord is clearly speaking of knowledge that has been lost to time. Truth has become legend, and modern society is no longer capable of distinguishing between the two. Yet, this is not the only passage in the Bible that speaks of such things. Consider the following additional reference to Leviathan from the ancient world:

> For God is my King of old, working salvation in the midst of the Earth. Thou didst divide the sea by Thy strength: Thou brakest the heads of the dragons in the waters. Thou brakest the heads of Leviathan in pieces, and gavest him to be meat to the people inhabiting the wilderness. (Psalm 74:12-14)

It would appear that this psalm is speaking of an ancient event very similar to that spoken of by the Lord to Job. Apparently, at some point in antiquity, the oceans were infested with Leviathans, and these creatures were wreaking havoc upon the Earth, and none but God could do anything about it. In those days, God slew these sea dragons and gave their flesh to the people as a banquet, just as was referenced in Job. Why would such specific things be spoken of in conjunction with this incredible creature if it was all a fabrication? Why do most of the ancient maps of the world's oceans include drawings of sea dragons? We presumed such drawings were the product of frenzied and foolish superstitious minds. Perhaps future events will prove that we are the fools.

Job and the Psalms are not the only references to Leviathan in scripture. The Lord told us that Isaiah spoke of all things pertaining to the House of Israel. Therefore, I find the following excerpt from one of his more incredible revelations to be particularly pertinent to the present analysis. Consider the following:

> Come, my people, enter thou into thy chambers, and shut thy doors about thee: hide thyself as it were for a little moment, until the indignation be overpast. For, behold, the Lord cometh out of His place to punish the inhabitants of the Earth for their iniquity: the Earth also shall disclose her blood, and shall no more cover her slain.
>
> In that day the Lord with His sore and great and strong sword shall punish Leviathan the piercing serpent, even Leviathan that crooked serpent; and He shall slay the dragon that is in the sea. (Isaiah 26:20-21; 27:1)

By the overall context of this revelation, it is clear that Isaiah is speaking of the events that will take place during the great and terrible day of the Lord. Curiously, Isaiah suggests that the Leviathan will be part of those events, mirroring Noah's vision. The revelation from which this passage was extracted is incredible and deserves an analysis of its own. As such, I will perform such an analysis in the subsequent chapter. For now, the point of this particular excerpt is that Isaiah prophesied that the Leviathan will be relevant to the events of the last days. Note that Isaiah says the Lord will kill this Leviathan. Many have suggested that this is speaking of Satan, but the Lord will not kill Satan. This passage deserves more consideration than we typically give it.

In addition to Leviathan, the Book of Enoch also spoke of Behemoth, a name which means the greatest of beasts. The Lord also spoke to Job regarding Behemoth. Consider the following:

> Behold now Behemoth, which I made with thee; he eateth grass as an ox. Lo now, his strength is in his loins, and his force is in the navel of his belly. He moveth his tail like a cedar: the sinews of his stones are wrapped together. His bones are as strong pieces of brass; his bones are like bars of iron. He is the chief of the ways of God: he that made him can make his sword to approach unto him. Surely the mountains bring him forth food, where all the beasts of the field play. He lieth under the shady trees, in the covert of the reed, and fens. The shady trees cover him with their shadow; the willows of the brook compass him about. Behold, he drinketh up a river, and hasteth not: he trusteth that he can

draw up Jordan into his mouth. He taketh it with his eyes:
his nose pierceth through snares. (Job 40:15-24)

Curiously, the Lord states that He made Behemoth at the same time He made Job, referring to the creation of this Earth. This implies that Behemoth originated here, whereas Leviathan is associated with the cosmos. The Lord told Job that the tail of the Behemoth was like a cedar tree and that its bones were nearly unbreakable. Behemoth was also created as a herbivore. Based on this description, Behemoth sounds like a dinosaur, the largest of which is the Amphicoelias. Amphicoelias is believed to have grown up to 230 feet in length and weighed approximately 140 tons. That is almost the length of a football field and the weight of over fifty Toyota Sequoias. But how could Behemoth be a dinosaur if dinosaurs have been extinct for millions of years?

This is a great question, and as it turns out, much more has come to light regarding dinosaurs than is being shared with the general public. You have probably never heard of Mary Schweitzer, and if you haven't, it is about time that you do. In 2005, Mary Schweitzer was working on her PhD when she observed what she believed to be red blood cells in a T-Rex fossil. Befuddled by her discovery, she placed her sample into an acid that would dissolve all mineral content from the fossil. What was left over

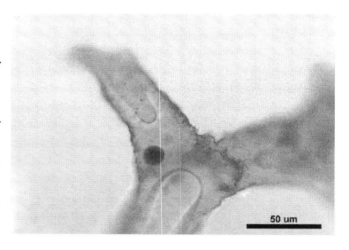

stunned the academic world. The fossil contained a shocking amount of soft organic material, including blood vessels, proteins, and cells. An image of one of Mary's samples has been included. These results have been replicated in labs to the disbelief of scientists around the world. Furthermore, the organic samples that have been recovered from these fossils include Carbon-14, which dates back thousands of years, not 65 million years ago.

Carbon-14 is only supposed to last approximately fifty thousand years or so. Therefore, its presence in large quantities within "fossilized" organic material is astounding. If dinosaur bones really were 65 million years old, there should be absolutely no organic materials remaining. The fact that we have discovered the widespread existence of soft organic material from dinosaurs should be one of the greatest discoveries of modern times. Why then have so few people heard about these things? Could it be that these findings are being suppressed because they challenge the evolutionary narrative? What might we learn if, instead of suppressing this information, it were widely shared so that further discoveries could be made?

With the things we have discussed thus far in this chapter in mind, there are some fascinating historical accounts of incredible beasts that readers of this book ought to be aware of. The first of these is taken from the writings of Claudius Aelianus in his book titled "On the Nature of Animals," written around 200 AD.

> When Alexander threw some parts of India into a commotion and took possession of others he encountered among many other animals a serpent which lived in a cavern and was regarded as sacred by the Indians who paid it great and superstitious reverence. Accordingly, Indians went to all lengths imploring Alexander to permit nobody to attack the Serpent; and he assented to their wish. Now as the army passed by the cavern and caused a noise, the Serpent was aware of it. (It has, you know, the sharpest hearing and the keenest sight of all animals.) And it hissed and snorted so violently that all were terrified and confounded. It was reported to measure 70 cubits although it was not visible in all its length, for it only put its head out. At any rate its eyes are said to have been the size of a large, round Macedonian shield. (Aelianus, Claudius, On Animals, Book #XV, Chapter 19-23, c.210-230.)

From Claudius's account, it is clear that he believed his audience was already familiar with dragons. What stands out is not just the existence of a dragon in India, but its immense size. Alexander's account is far from the only ancient record of this type. Another intriguing account comes from the travel logs of Marco Polo, who famously traveled the Silk Road between 1271 and 1295 AD. Consider the following account he recorded of an encounter with dragons during his journey.

> Leaving the city of Yachi, and traveling ten days in a westerly direction, you reach the province of Karazan, which is also the name of the chief city….Here are seen huge serpents, ten paces in length (about 30 feet), and ten spans (about 8 feet) girth of the body. At the fore part, near the head, they have two short legs, having three claws like those of a tiger, with eyes larger than a forepenny loaf (pane da quattro denari) and very glaring.
>
> The jaws are wide enough to swallow a man, the teeth are large and sharp, and their whole appearance is so formidable, that neither man, nor any kind of animal can approach them without terror. Others are met with of a smaller size, being

eight, six, or five paces long; and the following method is used for taking them. In the day-time, by reason of great heat, they lurk in caverns, from whence, at night, they issue to seek their food, and whatever beast they meet with and can lay hold of, whether tiger, wolf, or any other, they devour.

After which they drag themselves towards some lake, spring of water, or river, in order to drink. By their motion in this way along the shore, and their vast weight, they make a deep impression, as if a heavy beam had been drawn along the sands. Those whose employment is to hunt them observe the track by which they are most frequently accustomed to go, and fix into the ground several pieces of wood, armed with sharp iron spikes, which they cover with sand in such a manner as not to be perceptible.

The flesh also of the animal is sold at a dear rate, being thought to have a higher flavor than other kinds of meat, and by all persons it is esteemed a delicacy. (The Travels of Marco Polo, 1948, Book 2, Chapter XL, pg. 185-186)

Every student of history has been taught to some degree from the travel logs of Marco Polo. Why is it that accounts such as these have been omitted from his record? Was he considered a reliable resource in some areas of his accounts but a liar and a charlatan in others? There are incredible similarities between Marco Polo's account and the other ancient accounts we have reviewed above.

For example, God spoke of Leviathan's flesh to Job in the context of merchants and banquets, likely because of its renowned flavor. Alexander's army witnessed a large dragon lurking in a cave in the heat of the day, which is consistent with the dragons in Marco Polo's account. Both Claudius and Marco Polo also noted the size of dragons' eyes. One primary difference is that these latter dragons could be killed by iron spears, whereas Leviathan could not. Despite being terrible to behold, Marco Polo detailed an ingenious way in which these beasts could be hunted and killed at very low risk to the hunter. Given the delicacy of the beast's flesh, could it be that they were hunted to extinction in such a manner?

There are also numerous accounts of an entire Roman army battling a dragon as part of the Carthaginian war. This seems to be more than a passing rumor, as it is cited by numerous Roman historians, including three separate accounts of the same event written by three different Roman historians: Quintus Aelius Tubero, Valerius Maximus, and Orosius. Given their relevance to the present subject matter, I will share these fascinating accounts below:

Quintus Aelius Tubero

> The consul Atilius Regulus, when encamped at the Bagradas river in Africa, fought a stubborn and fierce battle with a single serpent of extraordinary size, which had its lair in that region; that in a mighty struggle with the entire army the reptile was attacked for a long time with hurling engines and catapults; and that when it was finally killed, its skin, a hundred and twenty feet long, was sent to Rome. (Tubero fragment - 1st Century AD)

Valerius Maximus

> The serpent of the Bagradas River in Africa was of such a size that it denied the army of Regulus access to the river. Many soldiers it seized in its enormous mouth and crushed to death not a few of them with its whirling tail. It could not be penetrated by the missiles thrown at it. Finally, they attacked it with many stones launched from ballistae from every side, it was brought down by the weighty blows. (Facta et Dicta Memorabilia)

Orosius

> Regulus, chosen by lot for the Carthaginian War, marched with his army to a point not far from the Bagrada River and there pitched his camp. In that place a reptile of astonishing size devoured many of the soldiers as they went down to the river to get water. Regulus set out with his army to attack the reptile. Neither the javelins they hurled nor the darts they rained upon its back had any effect. These glided off its horrible scaly fins as if from a slanting testudo of shields and were in some miraculous fashion turned away from its body so that the creature suffered no injury.

> Finally, when Regulus saw that it was killing a great number of his soldiers with its bites, was trampling them down by its charge, and driving them mad by its poisonous breath, he ordered *ballistae* brought up. A stone taken from a wall was

hurled by a *ballista;* this struck the spine of the serpent and caused its entire body to become numb. The formation of the reptile was such that, though it seemed to lack feet, yet it had ribs and scales graded evenly, extending from the top of its throat to the lowest part of its belly and so arranged that the creature rested upon its scales as if on claws and upon its ribs as if on legs.

But it did not move like the worm which has a flexible spine and moves by first stretching its contracted parts in the direction of its tiny body and then drawing together the stretched parts. This reptile made its way by a sinuous movement, extending its sides first right and then left, so that it might keep the line of ribs rigid along the exterior arch of the spine; nature fastened the claws of its scales to its ribs, which extend straight to their highest point; making these moves alternately and quickly, it not only glided over levels, but also mounted inclines, taking as many footsteps, so to speak, as it had ribs.

This is why the stone rendered the creature powerless. If struck by a blow in any part of the body from its bowels to its head, it is crippled and unable to move, because wherever the blow falls, it numbs the spine, which stimulates the feet of the ribs and the motion of the body. Hence this serpent, which had for a long time withstood so many javelins unharmed, moved about disabled from the blow of a single stone and, quickly overcome by spears, was easily destroyed. Its skin was brought to Rome—it is said to have been one hundred and twenty feet in length— and for some time was an object of wonder to all. (Historiarum Adversum Paganos Libri VII)

In all three of these accounts, the battle between the forces of Atilius Regulus and the dragon is spoken of as an actual event against a real creature, regardless of how fanciful it may sound. One or two accounts might be dismissed as lore, but there are many such accounts. Indeed, Europe is dotted with statues of St. George, who is said to have killed a fierce dragon that was terrorizing medieval villages. His story was deeply embedded within Christianity of that era.

As we contemplate these peculiar histories, we ought to do so in conjunction with another mysterious reference found within the Book of Mormon. Nephi, whose knowledge on the subject came from the Brass Plates, wrote about the mysterious serpents that plagued the House of Israel and prompted Moses to fashion a brass serpent upon a pole. According to Nephi, there was much more to that account than we have acknowledged. Consider his writings:

> He ruleth high in the heavens, for it is His throne, and this Earth is His footstool. And He loveth those who will have Him to be their God. Behold, He loved our fathers, and He covenanted with them, yea, even Abraham, Isaac, and Jacob; and He remembered the covenants which He had made; wherefore, He did bring them out of the land of Egypt.
>
> And He did straiten them in the wilderness with his rod; for they hardened their hearts, even as ye have; and the Lord straitened them because of their iniquity. He sent **fiery flying serpents** among them; and after they were bitten He prepared a way that they might be healed; and the labor which they had to perform was to look; and because of the simpleness of the way, or the easiness of it, there were many who perished. (1 Nephi 17:39-41)

What, pray tell, are fiery-flying serpents? The only fiery-flying serpents of which men have written are dragons. To make things even more interesting, Nephi stated that the Lord Himself sent these creatures. By this, we are to understand that these dragons came from somewhere else. Israel was wandering in the wilderness around the year 1440 BC, making this the earliest post-diluvian account of dragons of which I am aware. The Lord's introduction of these creatures into the post-diluvian world might have provided the source creatures from which the dragons of other accounts descended. It is curious that Nephi preceded his explanation by identifying God as the sovereign of the multiverse and that the Earth is merely His footstool. This suggests that God may have sent dragons to the Earth via a portal similar to that described by Noah and Enoch.

The Book of Mormon is the most correct book on Earth. It was translated by the power of God, with the Urim and Thummim, which provided the actual intended meaning of each word translated. As such, the phrase "fiery-flying serpents" should not be interpreted as a simple snake infestation. There are numerous passages about vipers in the scriptures. Fiery flying reptiles, on the other hand, are something altogether different. Indeed, this reminds me of another curious passage in the Book of Mormon, when the Lord again sent mysterious reptiles as a consequence of sin. Consider the following:

And THERE CAME FORTH poisonous serpents also upon the face of the land, and did poison many people. And it came to pass that their flocks began to flee before the poisonous serpents, towards the land southward, which was called by the Nephites Zarahemla. And it came to pass that there were many of them which did perish by the way; nevertheless, there were some which fled into the land southward.

And it came to pass that the Lord did cause the serpents that they should pursue them no more, but that they should hedge up the way that the people could not pass, that whoso should attempt to pass might fall by the poisonous serpents. (Ether 9:31-33)

The passage above is a highly abridged account of an event so traumatic that it relocated the most powerful nation on the planet (Ether 1:43). Again, the event involves mysterious reptiles sent by the Lord to bring about a specific end. From the context of the brief record we have, these creatures came forth upon the face of the land, presumably from somewhere else. Their origin was never provided, nor are they ever spoken of afterward. Their entire purpose was to drive and scatter the Jaredite nation and to keep them from retreating to the south.

Clearly, we are talking about something extraordinary here. After all, run-of-the-mill poisonous snakes are highly reclusive by nature and fear men as much as men fear them. Furthermore, recall that the Book of Mormon refers to the Jaredite nation as being highly advanced and powerful. When the Nephites found their breastplates, they were astounded by how massive the Jaredites were. How do snakes drive out an entire nation of armor-bearing giants? There is clearly more to this story than we know.

There is a third reference in the Book of Mormon regarding curious serpents that is even more relevant than those discussed so far. This comes by way of Nephi's transcription of a prophecy regarding the events of the latter days. In the passage, Isaiah warned the inhabitants of Palestine not to rejoice when the staff of the antichrist is broken. The reason they are not to rejoice is very curious. Consider the following passage:

Rejoice not thou, whole Palestina, because the rod of him that smote thee is broken; for out of the serpent's root shall come forth a cockatrice [*a two-legged dragon*], and his fruit shall be a fiery flying serpent [*a dragon*]. (2 Nephi 24:29)

According to the passage above, once the antichrist and his cohorts are driven from America, dragons will be reintroduced to the world. I have always assumed this reference was symbolic. After all, Lucifer is referred to as a dragon, but only symbolically. In light of Noah's prophetic vision and the historical accounts of strange creatures reviewed above, I am forced to wonder if there might be a more literal interpretation of these things than I initially thought.

I have mentioned Dr. Steven Greer's account of men who have weaponized the use of portals. He stated that when these men opened one of these portals, they encountered a variety of strange creatures, including a man who claimed to be the Savior of this Universe. If it is true that the Deep State has learned to weaponize portals, it should be expected that they will use them. What if, in response to the Remnant of Jacob ejecting these men from America, they open a portal as an act of revenge, unleashing Leviathan, Behemoth, Cockatrice, and fiery flying serpents upon us? As strange as these things sound, Joseph Smith prophesied that cosmic beasts of a cosmic nature would come to Earth in the last days and devour many of its inhabitants. This could be how that happens. If so, there may be far more to the coming days than any of us have dared imagine!

However bizarre this interpretation of Isaiah's words may sound, considering the subject matter of this chapter specifically, and this series in general, it does merit at least some degree of consideration. After all, according to the writings of Job, not even the Watchers were able to manage Leviathan in antiquity. Only the Lord could do so. We have also seen that while the Lord could easily kill the Leviathan, He could just as easily enter a covenant relationship with them. As such, if the Lord were to send Leviathan to Earth in the last days, why would He kill it for doing what He commanded it to do? The Lord is not in the habit of killing those who obey Him – He preserves such. Yet, regarding these creatures of the last days, Isaiah clearly states that the Lord will kill them. Therefore, it seems to me that these creatures are not brought here by the Lord as in times past, but by evil men. If so, we truly will experience a restoration of all things.

While it is fascinating to muse upon such things, it is important to acknowledge that we simply do not know their definitive meanings. Are these things purely symbolic, or do our forefathers' ancient tales of Ragnarök and world-ending serpents that are only killable by God Himself mean more than we have supposed? I cannot tell you the answers, but I can give you a box into which you can place such wild and crazy things until they may be needed in the future. Let this chapter be that box.

We now return to Noah's angelic guide, who continues answering Noah's question regarding how Leviathan and Behemoth arrive. You will recall that we left off in verse **60.12** above. In that verse the angel was talking about portals and cosmic winds in conjunction with Leviathan and Behemoth's arrival to Earth. The angel then begins a metaphorical conversation about the relationship between Leviathan and Behemoth, likening one to thunder and the other to lightning. Consider the following:

> **60.13**. And the thunders according to the places where they fall, and all the divisions that are made among the lightnings that it may lighten, and **their host** that they may at once obey.

> **60.14**. For the thunder has †places of rest† which are assigned to it while it is waiting for its peal; and the thunder and lightning are inseparable, and although not one and undivided, they both go together through the spirit and separate not.

> **60.15**. For when the lightning lightens, the thunder utters its voice, and the spirit enforces a pause during the peal, and divides equally between them; for the treasury of their peals is like the sand, and each one of them as it peals is held in with a bridle, and turned back by the power of the spirit, and pushed forward according to the many quarters of the earth.

> **60.16** And the spirit of the sea is masculine and strong, and according to the might of his strength he draws it back with a rein, and in like manner it is driven forward and disperses amid all the mountains of the earth.

Remember, everything we have discussed so far in this chapter has been in the context of the terrible host that Noah saw coming to Earth from the ends of heaven. From the description in **60.13**, it seems that Leviathan and Behemoth will not come to Earth alone but as part of a host of subservient creatures. This is consistent with Isaiah's reference to the coming Cockatrice and the host of fiery flying serpents. All these will have a role to play in the last days, whether metaphorically or literally, time alone will tell.

However, according to the angel's description, Leviathan and Behemoth are not just mindless beasts capable of nothing more than brute strength and force. They are highly intelligent entities who bide their time and use their power with skill and purpose. They unleash their power and then reign it back. Furthermore, it seems that the host that arrives with them will be subservient and obedient to them.

As the angel continues with his explanation, he likens the Spirit to the various known forms of water. Consider the following:

60.17. And the spirit of the hoar-frost is his own angel, and the spirit of the hail is a good angel.

60.18. And the spirit of the snow has forsaken his chambers on account of his strength--There is a special spirit therein, and that which ascends from it is like smoke, and its name is frost.

60.19. And the spirit of the mist is not united with them in their chambers, but it has a special chamber; for its course is †glorious† both in light and in darkness, and in winter and in summer, and in its chamber is an angel.

60.20. And the spirit of the dew has its dwelling at the ends of the heaven, and is connected with the chambers of the rain, and its course is in winter and summer: and its clouds and the clouds of the mist are connected, and the one gives to the other.

60.21. And when the spirit of the rain goes forth from its chamber, the angels come and open the chamber and lead it out, and when it is diffused over the whole earth it unites with the water on the earth. And whensoever it unites with the water on the earth . . .

60.22. For the waters are for those who dwell on the Earth; for they are nourishment for the Earth from the Most High who is in heaven: therefore there is a measure for the rain, and the angels take it in charge.

Water can take many forms: mist, humidity, rain, snow, frost, ice, dew, etc. Each of these unique forms has different properties and characteristics, yet ultimately, all are derived from the same substance. In like manner, the angel suggests that life throughout the multiverse, although incredibly diverse, is ultimately created from the same base material – intelligence/spirit. While humanity is created in the image of God, there are also other creatures of different forms that are capable of loving and serving the Lord.

Unlike the varied derivatives of water, intelligent life, regardless of its physical form, can exercise free will. Free will is what separates sentient beings from all other things throughout the cosmos. As we are free to choose good or evil, so are other lifeforms free to choose. The Spirit or Light of Christ, which enlightens the minds of men, also enlightens the minds of all sentient life. Thus, the gospel of Jesus Christ can and must be preached to every creature throughout the cosmos, and every creature must choose for themselves what they will do. This not only includes Leviathan and Behemoth but also the Watchers and the Beasts that will come, as well as their host of subservient followers. While it may be true that some of these creatures will be beyond our ability to destroy, the same spirit that can guide and redeem us can do the same for any creature. Therefore, as the word of God has had a more profound effect upon the hearts of men than anything else in the cosmos, we must believe that the same holds true for all creations derived from spiritual intelligence. As such, if peace cannot be found through strength of arms, perhaps it can be found through the gospel of Christ.

Noah now concludes his description of these events with a geographical identifier of where he saw them occur. Consider the following:

> **60.23**. And these things I saw towards the Garden of the Righteous.

> **60.24**. And the angel of peace who was with me said to me: 'These two monsters, prepared conformably to the greatness of God, shall feed . . .

According to Noah, he saw that these creatures made their first appearance near the Garden of Righteousness. By this, we understand that these creatures will first appear on the North American continent, which was home to the original Garden of Eden, the Earth's first temple. From there, they will go forth and feast upon the wicked inhabitants of the land and sea. Thus, we see that the cosmos will be rolled together as a scroll, and their inhabitants will perform many incredible things upon the Earth in the last days.

Therefore, if the things of this chapter are true, the world is about to witness some of the most incredible events that have ever transpired. Let us then remember Nephi's words of encouragement, for he looked forward to our days and promised that the righteous would have no need to fear the coming events. He saw that the saints would be preserved by the miraculous hand of God. Therefore, however strange the story becomes, let us sit back and marvel as the arm of God is laid bare before the eyes of all the nations!

Chapter 5 – Isaiah and the Leviathan

In the prior chapter, we reviewed Noah's terrifying vision wherein he saw a terrible host descend upon the Earth in the last days. This host included the Watchers, the Beast, the Remnant of Jacob, Leviathan and Behemoth, Cockatrice, and fiery flying serpents. Given the fantastical and mythical nature of some of these creatures, we examined several scriptural and historical accounts that suggest creatures of this nature did, in fact, exist. In this chapter, we will review a specific prophecy from Isaiah regarding the events of the last days that is particularly relevant to the present topic.

Jesus Christ stated that Isaiah prophesied of all things pertaining to the House of Israel, including key events among the Gentiles. If the things of the prior chapter are true, they are most certainly significant. As such, one would expect that Isaiah would have spoken regarding such things. In the prior chapter, we reviewed a passage from Isaiah that speaks of the Lord slaying Leviathan and the dragons of the sea as part of the events of the last days. In this chapter, we will review in detail the entire prophecy from which this passage was taken for context. I hope this chapter will lend credence to the Savior's admonition for us to study the words of Isaiah.

This is how Isaiah begins this prophecy:

> Behold, the Lord maketh the Earth empty, and maketh it waste, and turneth it upside down, and scattereth abroad the inhabitants thereof. And it shall be, as with the people, so with the priest; as with the servant, so with his master; as with the maid, so with her mistress; as with the buyer, so with the seller; as with the lender, so with the borrower; as with the taker of usury, so with the giver of usury to him.
>
> The land shall be utterly emptied, and utterly spoiled: for the Lord hath spoken this word. The Earth mourneth and fadeth away, the world languisheth and fadeth away, the haughty people of the Earth do languish. The Earth also is defiled under the inhabitants thereof; because they have transgressed the laws, changed the ordinance, broken the everlasting covenant. Therefore hath the curse devoured the Earth, and they that dwell therein are desolate: therefore the inhabitants of the Earth are burned, and FEW MEN LEFT. (Isaiah 24:1-6)

In the first six verses of this section, Isaiah mentions the Earth and her inhabitants six times. By doing so, Isaiah sets the stage for a catastrophic global extinction-level event for the wicked. We are to understand that the Great and Terrible Day of the Lord will be universal, impacting all of the world's inhabitants, rich and poor alike. This does not mean that the impact will be uniform across different geographies, as it will certainly vary. Isaiah delineates three specific reasons for this destruction. His reasons are as follows:

1. Earth's inhabitants have transgressed God's laws.
2. Earth's inhabitants have changed the ordinances.
3. Earth's inhabitants have broken the everlasting covenant.

Isaiah's first observation was that the Earth had transgressed the laws. What are we to understand by this? Jesus Christ once stated that all the laws and teachings of the prophets could be summarized by loving God and loving our fellow man as ourselves. Today, the world is divided and full of rage. Even good people turn into monsters online, attacking each other with vitriolic posts and slanderous language. Violence has increased in our cities, as dark forces have moved to import some of the world's most hardened criminals into otherwise peaceful cities around the world.

Enoch once witnessed God the Father weeping over this Earth. The image of the Almighty weeping over the children of heaven stunned Enoch. He therefore asked the Lord how it was that He could be so moved to tears by the events of this world when the multiverse is filled with innumerable inhabited worlds. The Father's response was very telling. He simply stated that He had commanded us to love one another, but instead, we hate our own flesh. Never has this been truer than today. No longer is hate limited to distant battlefields; it fills our civic discourse. We judge one another harshly, assuming the worst of others, without knowledge or wisdom.

Consider Paul's teachings on the matter:

> Though I speak with the tongues of men and of angels, and have not charity, I am become *as* sounding brass, or a tinkling cymbal. And though I have *the gift of* prophecy, and understand all mysteries, and all knowledge; and though I have all faith, so that I could remove mountains, and have not charity, I am nothing. (1 Cor 13:1-2)

According to Paul, if you have not filled your heart with the pure love of Christ, none of your other accomplishments matter. Specifically, Paul mentioned that it is more important to have charity than to understand the mysteries of God. This statement should impress upon the reader of this series the tremendous importance of the two great commandments. While pursuing knowledge is important, it pales in comparison to becoming Christlike. In the words of Christ, we should not do the one while leaving the other undone. Indeed, understanding the mysteries of God should motivate us to be filled with this love above all else, for it will not fail us in the days to come.

On one occasion, in a private moment, Brigham Young's secretary asked him why life was so hard and why God was not more active in shielding the saints from the troubles of this world. Brigham's response was powerful. Among other things, he said: "It is this way because we must learn to be righteous in the dark." (Brigham Young's Office Journal, January 28, 1857)

We are spending our second estate in the darkest recess of the mortal multiverse. No other mortal world has contemplated the degree of wickedness that has endured upon the face of Satan's prison planet since its creation. Therefore, there is no greater proving ground in the multiverse for us to learn how to be righteous in the dark than this Earth. How is our test going? According to Paul, the greatest indication of this fact is charity. If you can learn to love your fellow man here, in the multiverse's greatest bastion of hate and sin, then you have truly learned to be righteous in the dark. These things are easier said than done. It is impossible to do it on our own. We must petition the Father to send this transformative love to us. He has done so for all those who have sought it, from the beginning of days until now. But just as with seeking knowledge at His hand, we must seek this change at His hand as well. Consider the following passage that speaks to this:

> Charity is the pure love of Christ, and it endureth forever; and whoso is found possessed of it at the last day, it shall be well with him. Wherefore, my beloved brethren, pray unto the Father with all the energy of heart, that ye may be filled with this love, which He hath bestowed upon all who are true followers of His Son, Jesus Christ; that ye may become the sons of God; that when He shall appear we shall be like Him, for we shall see Him as He is; that we may have this hope; that we may be purified even as He is pure. Amen. (Moroni 7:47-48)

For students of Enoch's writings, the passage above should have special meaning. It speaks not of being the sons of God, but of **becoming** the Sons of God. It speaks of the Father bestowing charity upon all those who are true followers of His Son. To be a true follower of Jesus Christ, the Father must reveal Him to you. You must be seeking Him. Just as we must seek the Father's Hidden Son, so we must seek to be filled with charity by the Father. This does not happen passively. Just as we must pray to the Father that

He will teach us concerning His mysteries, so we must pray to the Father with all the energy of our hearts that He will fill our hearts with charity, which is the pure love of Christ. Becoming filled with the pure love of Christ is the magnum opus of any child of heaven. Without it, it matters little what else you accomplish. According to Isaiah, the fact that the world has broken these two great commandments and is now filled with anger and hate is the first of three reasons that the world has become ripe for destruction.

The second reason Isaiah gave for this pending extinction-level event was that God's people will have changed His ordinances. Christ taught that there was to be one Lord, one faith, and one baptism. Today, there are innumerable religions, and all of them seek different paths to God. In doing so, the world has created Ba'al of their own design and now worships them in place of the True and Living God. The world offers ordinances and sacraments without authority or priesthood power. Furthermore, the sacred sacraments are redefined, and if not, they are administered without the power or authority to do so.

Lastly, and perhaps most significantly, Isaiah foresaw that at the time of the end, the world would break the everlasting covenant. The everlasting covenant is the foundation upon which the Father's plan of salvation is based – the family. In "The Family: A Proclamation to the World," the prophets made numerous statements and warnings that in 1995 seemed simplistic. Today, they could not be more radical! Consider the following extracts taken from this singular document:

- Each human being is a beloved spirt son or daughter of heavenly parents.
- Gender is an essential characteristic of individual premortal, mortal, and eternal identity and purpose.
- The sacred powers of procreation are to be employed only between man and woman, lawfully wedded as husband and wife.
- Children are entitled to birth within the bonds of matrimony, and to be reared by a father and a mother.
- By divine design fathers are to preside over their families in love and righteousness and are responsible to provide the necessities of life and protection for their families.
- Mothers are primarily responsible for the nurture of their children.
- We warn that the disintegration of the family will bring upon individuals, communities, and nations the calamities foretold by ancient and modern prophets.

The world has indeed broken the everlasting covenant, and the family is disintegrating across the globe. Each of the topics mentioned above was inert when originally announced, but has since become a toxic live wire trigger for the woke generation.

Immorality is rampant. Gender fluidity is woven into grade school curriculums around the country. Traditional roles of men as providers and protectors have been recast as "toxic masculinity" – the oppressive artifacts of an unwanted patriarchy. Marriage has been redefined. Sexual restraint of any kind is seen as an oppressive Christian dogma. The new morality is "anything goes," with anyone, of any age. New York has become Sodom, and Los Angeles Gomorrah. From coast to coast, the family is collapsing. It is no better overseas; indeed, it may even be worse. Marriage rates in Europe have fallen 50%. The rising generation has traded the concept of traditional family for a life of whoredoms and lasciviousness, the likes of which we have not seen since Pompeii.

Isaiah prophesied that the breaking of the everlasting covenant would bring about the wholesale destruction of the Earth. Modern prophets have said the same. The world has ripened in iniquity. An extinction-level event now looms large on the horizon. The world had better awaken to the awfulness of its situation.

Isaiah's vision continues:

> The new wine mourneth, the vine languisheth, all the merryhearted do sigh. The mirth of tabrets ceaseth, the noise of them that rejoice endeth, the joy of the harp ceaseth. They shall not drink wine with a song; strong drink shall be bitter to them that drink it. The city of confusion is broken down: every house is shut up, that no man may come in. There is a crying for wine in the streets; all joy is darkened, the mirth of the land is gone.

> In the city is left desolation, and the gate is smitten with destruction. When thus it shall be in the midst of the land among the people, there shall be as the shaking of an olive tree, and as the gleaning grapes when the vintage is done.

> They shall lift up their voice, they shall sing for the majesty of the Lord, they shall cry aloud from the sea. Wherefore glorify ye the Lord in the fires, even the name of the Lord God of Israel in the isles of the sea.

> From the uttermost part of the earth have we heard songs, even glory to the righteous. But I said, my leanness, my leanness, woe unto me! the treacherous dealers have dealt treacherously; yea, the treacherous dealers have dealt very treacherously.

Fear, and the pit, and the snare, are upon thee, O inhabitant of the Earth. And it shall come to pass, that he who fleeth from the noise of the fear shall fall into the pit; and he that cometh up out of the midst of the pit shall be taken in the snare: for the windows from on high are open, and the foundations of the Earth do shake. The Earth is utterly broken down, the Earth is clean dissolved, the Earth is moved exceedingly. The Earth shall reel to and fro like a drunkard, and shall be removed like a cottage; and the transgression thereof shall be heavy upon it; and it shall fall, and not rise again. (Isaiah 24:7-20)

These passages open with the removal of joy from the cities of the world. By this, we understand that the days have come when the Lord will no longer permit the world to take joy in sin. This occurs once the righteous have been forced to abandon their homes in the cities, and only the wicked remain. In that day, vices will no longer bring pleasure to those who engage in them, but rather bitterness. Yet, songs of joy will still be heard at the ends of the Earth, among the righteous who, despite all that has happened, still know and trust in the Lord their God.

The righteous are those who were able to see through the lies and deception of the treacherous dealers. Those that deal in treachery are those who worked behind the scenes to deliberately flip the narrative and cause humanity to deviate from the Lord. They did not do this all at once, but by degrees. They infiltrated the entertainment industry, then corrupted the public school system. Colleges and universities became institutions of indoctrination. The twenty-four-hour mainstream news media was purchased in the dark and used as an echo chamber to reinforce their treachery.

This treachery will ultimately culminate in hatred and intolerance of such a degree that the righteous "bigots" will be driven out from among them "for the greater good." When the wicked have self-segregated, instead of finding joy and revelry in their victory over the righteous, they will find that peace and joy have fled with the righteous. In horror, they will soon realize that, as in the days of Sodom and Gomorrah, the only thing preserving them from destruction were the very people they had just cast out.

In that great and terrible day, when the wicked have isolated themselves, then shall the heavens and Earth tremble and stagger to and fro like a drunken man. In their own self-imposed quarantine, the isolated wicked, together with their cities, will then be consumed by the flames of those that come from the ends of heaven in fulfillment of the battles of the Lord.

The shaking of which Isaiah has spoken will be the same shaking event that we have learned of in the prior chapters of this volume. While the treacherous dealers may not have had a complete understanding of what their actions would unleash, Lucifer, who is the master choreographer of their treachery, most certainly does. He knows that their treacherous dealings will result in the destruction of humanity, and he rejoices in this fact. He knows that he is leading all who follow him to death and Hell. As he does so, he laughs at the degree to which his chains have encircled the Earth.

For further evidence that Satan will not be surprised by what is coming, consider the curious Marian apparition that occurred on October 13, 1973, to Sister Agnes Sasagawa of Akita, Japan. According to Sister Agnes, on this date, which oddly occurred precisely fifty years to the day from the global day of rage that the Lady recently predicted would occur, a three-foot wooden statue in the convent appeared to come alive and started speaking to Sister Sasagawa. In her own words, this is what the statue told her:

> My dear daughter, listen well to what I have to say to you. You will inform your superior. As I told you [*previously*], if men do not repent and better themselves, the Father will inflict a terrible punishment on all humanity. It will be a punishment greater than the deluge, such a one will never have seen before. Fire will fall from the sky and will wipe out a great part of humanity, the good as well as the bad, sparing neither priests nor faithful. The survivors will find themselves so desolate that they will envy the dead. The only arms which will remain for you will be the Rosary and the Sign left by My Son…
>
> Pray very much the prayers of the Rosary. I alone am able still to save you from the calamities which approach. Those who place their confidence in me will be saved.

If you are interested in learning more about what the Lady told Sister Sasagawa, you can easily find this information with a quick Google search. While it is clear that the Lady knows fire will rain down from the sky at some future point to cleanse the Earth from sin, she is mixing this truth with lies. Nephi clearly stated that the righteous have no need to fear and that the coming flames will save them, rather than destroying the righteous alongside the wicked. Furthermore, it is laughable to suggest that the Lady is the only one who can save the Earth from such things. The only thing that could spare the Earth was outlined by Jesus Christ in His sermon to the Nephites. We must repent and live the gospel to the best of our abilities.

We now return to Isaiah's revelation regarding the coming days:

And it shall come to pass in that day, that the Lord shall punish the host of the high ones that are on high, and the kings of the earth upon the earth. And they shall be gathered together, as prisoners are gathered in the pit, and shall be shut up in the prison, and after many days shall they be visited. (Isaiah 24:21-22)

Notice the difference between the two sets of rulers that Isaiah noted as being present upon the Earth during this period of great commotion. The difference lies in their origin. Isaiah spoke of "the high ones, that come from on high," and a separate group he calls "the kings of the Earth upon the Earth." You will recall from volume one of this series that after seventy generations, Enoch prophesied that the Watchers would return and walk among us openly as they had done in pre-diluvian days. The Watchers and their associates constitute the host of the high ones from on high who briefly join forces with the Whore of Babylon before they destroy her kingdom and usurp her governance of the nations.

Yet, despite all their well-laid plans and incredible technology and power, they too shall fall alongside the wicked and blind inhabitants of this world. When they do fall, their spirits will be resigned to that great and terrible prison which overlooks the open burning pit of outer darkness. There they will remain for a thousand years, in a process of refinement and purification, where they will atone for their own sins, having rejected the Savior of the multiverse.

After the thousand-year period is through, and they have completed the transformation process of their own atonements, the Savior of the multiverse will return to visit them. In that day, every one of them not destined for outer darkness will bend the knee, and every tongue will confess that Jesus is the Christ – the Son of the Most High God. When that occurs, they will be taken to a kingdom of Telestial glory, which will far outstrip anything we can presently contemplate. Yet, just as the stars are lights unto themselves, these too will be lights unto themselves, as one star differs from another star in glory. For these are quickened by their own suffering and atonements, and not by the redeeming power of Jesus Christ. As such, there are eternal limits placed upon them, and where God and Christ are, they cannot come, worlds without end.

Those who participated in the second estate who are not transformed through this process will be few and far between. However, they will exist. These will be cast into the pit with Lucifer and his terrible demonic host forevermore. This is where Isaiah's vision resumes.

How art thou fallen from heaven, O Lucifer, son of the morning! how art thou cut down to the ground, which didst weaken the nations! For thou hast said in thine heart, I will ascend into heaven, I will exalt my throne above the stars of God: I will sit also upon the mount of the congregation, in the sides of the north: I will ascend above the heights of the clouds; I will be like the most High.

Yet thou shalt be brought down to Hell, to the sides of the pit. They that see [*those in the burning mountain range overlooking outer-darkness*] thee shall narrowly look upon thee, and consider thee, saying, Is this the man that made the earth to tremble, that did shake kingdoms; That made the world as a wilderness, and destroyed the cities thereof; that opened not the house of his prisoners?

All the kings of the nations, even all of them, lie in glory, every one in his own house. But thou art cast out of thy grave like an abominable branch, and as the raiment of those that are slain, thrust through with a sword, that go down to the stones of the pit; as a carcass trodden under feet. Thou shalt not be joined with them in burial, because thou hast destroyed thy land, and slain thy people: the seed of evildoers shall never be renowned. (Isaiah 14:12-20)

The Son of the Morning will be sent into everlasting darkness, never to rise again, for his travel will be limited to kingdoms of equal or lesser glory to his own, and there is no place in the multiverse of lesser glory than outer darkness. Thus, we see that the mercy of God is staggering. He loves even those who turn on Him and seek to destroy the children of Heaven. For He knows that they do so because they have been deceived by Lucifer's masterful lies. As such, even these, after they have atoned for their own sins, will reject all that Lucifer had to offer them and cast him out from their hearts as an abominable branch.

Isaiah's vision continues by highlighting the Glory of the Lord and His role in the events of the great and terrible purging of the Earth.

Then the moon shall be confounded, and the sun ashamed, when the Lord of hosts shall reign in mount Zion, and in Jerusalem, and before His ancients gloriously. O Lord, thou art my God; I will exalt thee, I will praise thy name; for thou hast done wonderful things; thy counsels of old are faithfulness and truth.

For thou hast made of a city an heap; of a defenced city a ruin: a palace of strangers to be no city; it shall never be built. Therefore, shall the strong people glorify thee, the city of the terrible nations shall fear thee. For thou hast been a strength to the poor, a strength to the needy in his distress, a refuge from the storm, a shadow from the heat, when the blast of the terrible ones is as a storm against the wall.

Thou shalt bring down the noise of strangers, as the heat in a dry place; even the heat with the shadow of a cloud: the branch of the terrible ones shall be brought low. And in this mountain shall the Lord of hosts make unto all people a feast of fat things, a feast of wines on the lees, of fat things full of marrow, of wines on the lees well refined.

And He will destroy in this mountain the face of the covering cast over all people, and the veil that is spread over all nations. He will swallow up death in victory; and the Lord God will wipe away tears from off all faces; and the rebuke of His people shall He take away from off all the earth: for the Lord hath spoken it. (Isaiah 24:23; 25:1-8)

The verses above speak of the great and last day when the God of Israel shall make a full end of wickedness upon the Earth. The mountain that will be the epicenter of the Feast of Fat Things will be the Mount of Olives. At the time the Lord descends from the heavens to the Mount of Olives, the antichrist and the Beast will have at long last killed the two prophets protecting Jerusalem and will have overrun the city. As a result, the Jews will be in dire straits, having no recourse against their impending slaughter at the hands of their enemy. Yet now, suddenly, their Savior comes. When He does, the Mount of Olives will be split in two, and a miraculous highway of deliverance will be created for the desperate Jews to escape slaughter at the hands of their enemies.

Now their Savior will fight their battles for them. This marks the epic extinction-level event when the enemies of Israel fall and rise no more. The innumerable host will be consumed where they stand. Their eyes will dissolve in their sockets, and their tongues in their mouths. It will take many months for the Jews to bury the dead. The valley of Armageddon, which lies at the foot of Tel Megiddo, will become the world's largest graveyard. For seven years, the Jews will burn their armaments of war and pound the antichrist's swords into plowshares.

It is of this aftermath that Isaiah now speaks:

And it shall be said in that day, Lo, this is our God; we have waited for Him, and He will save us: this is the Lord; we have waited for Him, we will be glad and rejoice in His salvation. For in this mountain shall the hand of the Lord rest, and Moab shall be trodden down under Him, even as straw is trodden down for the dunghill.

And He shall spread forth His hands in the midst of them, as he that swimmeth spreadeth forth his hands to swim: and He shall bring down their pride together with the spoils of their hands. And the fortress of the high fort of thy walls shall He bring down, lay low, and bring to the ground, even to the dust. In that day shall this song be sung in the land of Judah; We have a strong city; salvation will God appoint for walls and bulwarks. Open ye the gates, that the righteous nation which keepeth the truth may enter in. (Isaiah 25:9-12; 26:1-2)

In that day, the Jews will finally recognize their Savior for who He is, and always has been – the Father's Hidden Son! This realization will be a shock for them. "What are these wounds in your hands?" they will exclaim in disbelief. "The wounds I received in the house of my friends," He will respond. In that day, the Jews will finally see eye to eye with their Savior. When that day occurs, the gates of Jerusalem shall be opened to the servants of Ephraim, who up until this point have been banned from bringing the Jews the restored gospel. None of their blind guides and foolish leaders will remain to hinder the spread of truth and light. At long last, the restored gospel will resound off the walls and stones of Jerusalem once more with joy and gladness!

Isaiah now breaks into prophetic verses of praise and song regarding the God of Israel. Consider the following:

Thou wilt keep him [*the righteous man*] in perfect peace, whose mind is stayed on Thee: because he trusteth in Thee. Trust ye in the Lord forever: for in the Lord Jehovah is everlasting strength: for He bringeth down them that dwell on high [*the Watchers*]; the lofty city [*the Whore of Babylon*], He layeth it low; He layeth it low, even to the ground; He bringeth it even to the dust.

The foot shall tread it down, even the feet of the poor, and the steps of the needy. The way of the just is uprightness: thou, most upright, dost weigh the path of the just. Yea, in the way of thy judgments, O Lord, have we waited for thee; the desire of our soul is to thy name, and to the remembrance of thee.

With my soul have I desired thee in the night; yea, with my spirit within me will I seek thee early: for when thy judgments are in the Earth, the inhabitants of the world will learn righteousness. Let favor be shewed to the wicked, yet will he not learn righteousness: in the land of uprightness will he deal unjustly, and will not behold the majesty of the Lord.

Lord, when thy hand is lifted up, they will not see: but they shall see, and be ashamed for their envy at the people; yea, the fire of thine enemies shall devour them. Lord, thou wilt ordain peace for us: for thou also hast wrought all our works in us. O Lord our God, other lords beside thee have had dominion over us: but by thee only will we make mention of thy name.

They are dead, they shall not live; they are deceased, they shall not rise: therefore hast thou visited and destroyed them, and made all their memory to perish. Thou hast increased the nation, O Lord, thou hast increased the nation: thou art glorified: thou hadst removed it far unto all the ends of the Earth.

Lord, in trouble have they visited thee, they poured out a prayer when thy chastening was upon them. Like as a woman with child, that draweth near the time of her delivery, is in pain, and crieth out in her pangs; so have we been in thy sight, O Lord. We have been with child, we have been in pain, we have as it were brought forth wind; we have not wrought any deliverance in the Earth; neither have the inhabitants of the world fallen [*meaning if the Jews had been righteous the inhabitants of the world would not have fallen*]. (Isaiah 26:3-18)

Isaiah prayed that the Lord would be merciful to the wicked and open the eyes of the righteous. As we saw earlier in this vision, the foremost among the wicked will be taken to the fiery mountain range at the end of all things, where they will atone for their own sins over the course of a thousand years. This they will do because they would not have the Lord be their Savior while in mortality. Yet, in the end, there will be mercy even for them. However, their own atonements will never be able to make of them what the master potter could have made of them if only they had entrusted themselves to the workmanship of His hands, instead of walking after the light of their own sparks.

Isaiah then likens Jerusalem to a woman in birth. Just as birthing pains do not let up until the child is born, so the pains of that day will not slacken in Jerusalem until Zion is restored. Yet Zion will not come forth from the Jews; it will come to the Jews. Because of their blindness and unbelief, all the birthing pains that the Jews endured only brought forth, as it were, a foul wind.

In like manner, Zion will not come forth from the Saints in America, but rather will descend to us from the heavens, as a bride adorned for her husband. The New Jerusalem, the City of Asenath's Refuge, will be beautiful and glorious beyond description. Had the Saints in America been capable of producing such a glorious city, the destruction that will shortly ravage our cities and render them desolate would never have happened. Still, under the stewardship of the Remnant of Jacob, we will be permitted to assist in the buildout of this incredible city.

Looking forward to the joyful restoration of all things that will occur once the Earth has been purged of wickedness, Isaiah now comes to the reason this particular revelation has been included in this volume. Consider the following:

> Thy dead men shall live, together with My dead body shall they arise. [*The righteous dead shall rise at Christ's return*] Awake and sing, ye that dwell in dust: for thy dew is as the dew of herbs, and the earth shall cast out the dead. Come, my people, enter thou into thy chambers, and shut thy doors about thee: hide thyself as it were for a little moment, until the indignation be overpast. For, behold, the Lord cometh out of His place to punish the inhabitants of the Earth for their iniquity: the Earth also shall disclose her blood, and shall no more cover her slain.
>
> In that day the Lord with His sore and great and strong sword shall punish Leviathan the piercing serpent, even Leviathan that crooked serpent; and He shall slay the dragon that is in the sea. (Isaiah 26:19-21; 27:1)

In this passage, Isaiah refers to the fact that Leviathan will be present in the sea at this time, and that it was even beyond the ability of the Remnant of Jacob to kill. As such, it will have been wreaking havoc throughout the oceans and among the islands of the sea. Yet, on that last and great day of the Lord's coming, even this terrible apocalypse beast shall be slain.

I confess that whenever I have read this passage before, I have always considered it to be symbolic. However, in light of the Book of Enoch and the Book of Job, I now believe there may be more to this passage than I had previously supposed. I had previously considered that this passage spoke of Lucifer's fall, but Isaiah has already spoken of that downfall and his banishment to outer darkness. Furthermore, Isaiah stated that the Lord will slay Leviathan; however, He will not slay Lucifer.

Lucifer is a spirit, and spirits are gnolaum, or eternal (see Abraham 3:18). The Leviathan, on the other hand, is mortal, albeit incredible and impossible for all but God to kill. Yet, at the Lord's return, the Leviathan will be killed. Lucifer, on the other hand, will be bound for a thousand years. Afterwards, he will be freed for a little season to wreak havoc throughout the multiverse once more.

As crazy as it sounds, the passage above therefore seems to speak of an actual event that will occur during the great and dreadful day of the Lord. That event will involve apocalypse beasts of great renown, for as the Book of Job teaches, nothing on the Earth is the equal of the fearless Leviathan (Job 41:33), for nothing on the Earth can harm it. Therefore, it seems to me that Lucifer is called the great dragon in honor of this beast's apocalyptic power, and not the other way around.

What makes Isaiah's prophecy all the more interesting is the additional context of global events that he associates with the Leviathan and its miraculous death at the hand of the Lord. Consider the following:

> In that day sing ye unto her, A vineyard of red wine. I the Lord do keep it; I will water it every moment: lest any hurt it, I will keep it night and day. Fury is not in me: who would set the briers and thorns against me in battle? I would go through them, I would burn them together.
>
> Or let him take hold of My strength, that he may make peace with Me; and he shall make peace with Me. He shall cause them that come of Jacob to take root: Israel shall blossom and bud, and fill the face of the world with fruit. Hath He smitten him, as He smote those that smote Him? or is he [*the Remnant of Jacob*] slain according to the slaughter of them that are slain by him? (Isaiah 27: 2-7)

In the passages above, the Lord refers to Himself as the master of a vineyard. This should call to the reader's mind the allegory of the Olive Tree, wherein the master of the vineyard performed three main graftings: the first, the second, and the last. You will remember that the first graftings were comprised of two cuttings, one in the worst place of the vineyard, and another somewhere worse than that. We are, of course, talking about the remnants of the Lost Ten Tribes of Israel that were led away out of the land by the hand of the Lord to the north countries. A portion of them stayed behind and became the Germanic tribes of northern Europe. However, the main body proceeded northward where, according to Joseph Smith, they were removed from the Earth altogether.

It is of this group the Lord spoke when He stated, "Let him take hold of My strength that he may make peace with Me, and he shall make peace with Me." This Remnant of Jacob made peace with the Lord in their Assyrian captivity, wherein they covenanted with the Lord to do His will. In return, He led them to a land where never before mankind had dwelt. Their return in the last days will rival the Exodus of Egypt for its wonder and might. It is pertaining to this group that the Lord asks the following two important questions:

1) Hath He smitten him, as He smote those that smote Him?
2) Is he slain according to the slaughter of them that are slain by him?

These two questions are meant to prompt the reader to consider Isaiah's prophetic words in the context of the identity and mission of the Remnant of Jacob. Let us examine this in light of the first question: Did the Lord smite the Remnant of Jacob as He smote the Jews who crucified their King? The answer is no. After the Jews smote the Lord, they became both a hiss and a byword. They were driven from their lands of inheritance and sold into slavery around the world. Even today, after being restored to their homeland, they continue to be demonized and persecuted. After all, the mantra "from the River to the Sea" is a call for the eradication of Israel and all Jews.

Therefore, Isaiah's question is meant to make us wonder what became of the Remnant of the Northern Kingdom of Israel. Specifically, we are to wonder if the Lord caused them to drink the dregs of the bitter cup, as He did with the Jews. The answer is, of course, no. While the Jews have been driven, scattered, and persecuted for centuries, we are told that the Remnant of Jacob was given the wings of a great eagle, allowing them to leave the Earth and prosper in the wilderness for a long season.

In the wilderness, they have become a mighty and holy people. As Isaiah stated, they sought peace with the Lord and obtained it. Consequently, the Lord has magnified them and made them more glorious than any other portion of the House of Israel known to us. They have become the Lord's covenant people and are truly worthy of the title.

This brings us to Isaiah's next question: Is the Remnant of Jacob slain according to the slaughter of those that are slain by him? The answer is a resounding no. We are told that no weapon formed by man will prosper against the Remnant of Jacob. Indeed, we are told that their enemies will become prey to them. Jeremiah stated that Israel will be the Lord's battle axe. Consider the following description of their future mission:

> The portion of Jacob [*Remnant of Jacob*] is not like them [*anyone else*]; for He [*God*] is the former of all things; and Israel is the rod of His inheritance; the Lord of hosts is His name. Thou [*speaking of the Remnant of Jacob*] art my battle axe and weapons of war; for with thee will I break in pieces the nations, and with thee will I destroy kingdoms. And with thee will I break in pieces the horse and his rider; and with thee will I break in pieces the chariot and his rider; With thee also will I break in pieces man and woman; and with thee will I break in pieces old and young; and with thee will I break in pieces the young man and the maid; I will also break in pieces with thee the shepherd and his flock; and with thee will I break in pieces the husbandman and his yoke of oxen; and with thee will I break in pieces captains and rulers. (Jeremiah 51:19-23)

Note that at the time Jeremiah wrote these things, both the Northern Kingdom of Israel and the Kingdom of Judah had been wiped out for worshiping the Queen of Heaven. Since that time, the Lord has never yet used the House of Israel as His battle axe to break in pieces the nations of the Earth. However, according to both Isaiah and Jeremiah, those days will come. Isaiah's question, "Is the Remnant of Jacob slain according to the slaughter of those that are slain by Him?" should be answered in this context. The answer is a resounding no. The prophet Micah also attests to this fact.

> And the remnant of Jacob shall be among the Gentiles in the midst of many people as a lion among the beasts of the forest, as a young lion among the flocks of sheep: who, if he go through, both treadeth down, and teareth in pieces, and none can deliver. Thine hand shall be lifted up upon thine adversaries, and all thine enemies shall be cut off. And I will execute vengeance in anger and fury upon the heathen, such as they have not heard. (Micah 5:8,9,15)

The Remnant of Jacob will destroy the wicked with a fury they have never before contemplated. Even the Antichrist and his beastly companion will be driven before them. Yes, the Antichrist will be able to take a few of them, cast them to the ground, and stomp upon them, but they will not be slain nearly to the degree of those that are slain by them. Indeed, the awesome destruction brought about by their hand is the inspiration for the cover art of this volume.

Isaiah's vision now speaks of the confusion and misunderstanding pertaining to the Remnant of Jacob's return.

> In measure, when it [*the Remnant of Jacob*] shooteth forth, thou wilt debate with it: he stayeth his rough wind in the day of the east wind. By this therefore shall the iniquity of Jacob be purged; and this is all the fruit to take away his sin; when he maketh all the stones of the altar as chalkstones that are beaten in sunder, the groves and images shall not stand up.
>
> Yet the defenced city shall be desolate, and the habitation forsaken, and left like a wilderness: there shall the calf feed, and there shall he lie down, and consume the branches thereof. When the boughs thereof are withered, they shall be broken off: the women come, and set them on fire: for it is a people of no understanding: therefore He that made them will not have mercy on them, and He that formed them will shew them no favor.
>
> And it shall come to pass in that day, that the Lord shall beat off from the channel of the river unto the stream of Egypt, and ye shall be gathered one by one, O ye children of Israel. And it shall come to pass in that day, that the great trumpet shall be blown, and they shall come which were ready to perish in the land of Assyria [*the Lost ten tribes*], and the outcasts in the land of Egypt [*the scattered remnants on Earth*], and shall worship the Lord in the holy mount at Jerusalem. (Isaiah 27:8-13)

According to Isaiah, although many have disputed and debated the identity and whereabouts of the Remnant of Jacob, when they are restored in the last days, all debates regarding them shall cease. In that day, all men will know that the sins of Jacob have been swallowed up by their liberation of the righteous. No longer will the Remnant of Jacob be remembered as those who were destroyed at the hands of Assyria's kings;

instead, they will be seen as the Lord's new threshing instrument with which He thrashes the nations.

From that day forward, the Remnant of Jacob will be remembered as the mighty host that delivered the children of Joseph from the hands of their mighty oppressors. When this incredible deliverance occurs, the righteous will look towards Jerusalem with joy and gladness, knowing that their salvation is not far distant. However, it should not be lost upon the reader that the House of Joseph would never have needed to be saved had it not strayed far from the covenant path.

Consider this in light of what Isaiah says next:

> Woe to the crown of pride, to the drunkards of Ephraim, whose glorious beauty is a fading flower, which are on the head of the fat valleys of them that are overcome with wine! Behold, the Lord hath a mighty and strong one [*the Remnant of Jacob*], which as a tempest of hail and a destroying storm, as a flood of mighty waters overflowing, shall cast down to the earth with the hand. The crown of pride, the drunkards of Ephraim, shall be trodden under feet: and the glorious beauty, which is on the head of the fat valley, shall be a fading flower, and as the hasty fruit before the summer; which when he that looketh upon it seeth, while it is yet in his hand he eateth it up. (Isaiah 28:1-5)

The United States of America is the nation of Joseph, set up to be a light on a hill. We are a nation comprised of the sons and daughters of Joseph and Asenath. Yet, as a nation, we have strayed from the faith of our fathers. We have broken the laws, changed the ordinances, and abandoned the everlasting covenant. As a nation, we have engaged in the same practices that led to the collapse of every major civilization before us. Whether knowingly or through demonic deception, many worship the gods of the ancient world. They do this through unbridled debauchery, abortions, human pollution, corruption of children, and with violence, hate, and prejudice.

When the Antichrist comes to these lands, many of the children of Joseph, in their drunken stupor, will hearken to his marvelous blasphemies and embrace him as their savior. In doing so, they turn from their inheritance like a dog to its vomit. When this happens, the grace that God shed upon these promised lands will fade like the beauty of a wilting flower. The sins of these lands will cause our cities to become abominable branches, good for nothing more than to be burned by those who come.

It will be in this drunken and wicked state that the drunkards of Ephraim will encounter the Lord's mighty and strong ones. There can be no doubt that these mighty and strong ones are the long-awaited Remnants of Jacob. They will come to the terror of the drunkards of Ephraim. In that day, it will be upon fear and blood that the drunkards of Ephraim will be inebriated, not with wine. In that great and terrible coming day, they will be swept off these lands of promise forevermore.

Yet, the same will not be true for the righteous who put their faith in God above all else. Isaiah speaks of these next.

> In that day shall the Lord of hosts be for a crown of glory, and for a diadem of beauty, unto the residue of His people, and for a spirit of judgment to him that sitteth in judgment, and for strength to them that turn the battle to the gate.
>
> But they also [*the Northern Kingdom of Israel who were scattered in Isaiah's day*] have erred through wine, and through strong drink are out of the way; the priest and the prophet have erred through strong drink, they are swallowed up of wine, they are out of the way through strong drink; they err in vision, they stumble in judgment. For all tables are full of vomit and filthiness, so that there is no place clean.
>
> Whom shall He teach knowledge? And whom shall He make to understand doctrine? Them that are weaned from the milk, and drawn from the breasts. For precept must be upon precept, precept upon precept; line upon line, line upon line; here a little, and there a little: for with stammering lips and another tongue will He speak to this people.
>
> To whom He said, This is the rest wherewith ye may cause the weary to rest; and this is the refreshing: yet they would not hear. But the word of the Lord was unto them precept upon precept, precept upon precept; line upon line, line upon line; here a little, and there a little; that they might go, and fall backward, and be broken, and snared, and taken. (Isaiah 28:6-13)

In these passages, the Lord is speaking of the Northern Kingdom of Israel before they were taken captive into Assyria in 720 BC. In that day, they were as blind as the drunkards of Ephraim will be in the last days. They would not hear the Lord. One does not simply hear the Lord and understand. The teachings of the Lord are intentionally layered. In this way, only those who truly seek to be instructed by the Lord will understand. This understanding does not come all at once but rather comes line upon line, precept upon precept, here a little, and there a little. As such, if a person is to understand the things of God, they must do so by intentionally seeking them. The mysteries of God can be learned in no other way. Yes, the milk of the gospel can be imparted to the young, as with a mother's milk, but the meat of the gospel is altogether different.

Those who have paid the price to understand know that a marvelous work is about to come forth among the children of men. In ancient days, the Lord led a remnant of the Northern Kingdom of Israel away out of the land, gave them wings of a great eagle, and planted the heavens with them. There they have flourished in the wilderness and have become mighty and strong, unlike any other portion of Jacob.

In this regard, the Lord planting the heavens with the lost tribes of Israel is no different than the Lord planting the Americas with the children of Ishmael, Lehi, and Mulek. Indeed, the only difference is that we have the written account of Joseph's ancient dealings in America, and only the promise of the records of the Lost Ten Tribes. Yet, as the sticks of Judah and Joseph can now be held in one hand, so too the day will come, and is not far distant, when those records will be supplemented with those of the Remnant of Jacob.

Yet, for those who have paid the price to be instructed by the Lord, such things are not nearly as mysterious as their milk-drinking brothers presume. For the Lord has done nothing upon this Earth, save He has revealed it to His servants the prophets. Yet, those revelations are of little value if they are not studied. When anyone embarks on a sincere journey of discovery, seeking to be taught by the Lord, this knowledge will come line upon line, precept upon precept, here a little, and there a little, until they too become astounded with just how much the Lord has revealed! The Father and His Hidden Son are just as active in the lives of their children today as they ever have been. Yet, those who take no initiative in these matters are just as blind as the drunkards of Ephraim.

As such, the vast majority of the children of heaven here upon the Earth know little of the mysteries of God, for they are unwilling to pay the price to learn of such things. They are content with milk and would that others might also be as content with milk as they. Yet, if milk is all they have, it will sour in their bellies when their worlds begin to collapse around them. In that great and terrible day, rather than being able to rise up as Saviors upon Mount Zion, these will either be deceived by the Antichrist's incredible blasphemies, or they will need to be taught by those who were willing to pay the price to be taught by the Lord.

Thus, the saints of God will find themselves in a very precarious position. If they are not capable of being led by the Holy Ghost, they will not survive. Theirs will be the unhappy task of reconciling the horrors overpowering the Earth in real time, without the spiritual infrastructure to do so.

Isaiah now leaves the children of Joseph and prophesies regarding the Jews and Jerusalem.

> Wherefore hear the word of the Lord, ye scornful men, that rule this people which is in Jerusalem. Because ye have said, We have made a covenant with death, and with hell are we at agreement; when the overflowing scourge shall pass through, it shall not come unto us: for we have made lies our refuge, and under falsehood have we hid ourselves.
>
> Therefore thus saith the Lord God, Behold, I lay in Zion for a foundation a stone, a tried stone, a precious corner stone, a sure foundation: he that believeth shall not make haste.
>
> Judgment also will I lay to the line, and righteousness to the plummet: and the hail shall sweep away the refuge of lies, and the waters shall overflow the hiding place. And your covenant with death shall be disannulled, and your agreement with hell shall not stand; when the overflowing scourge shall pass through, then ye shall be trodden down by it. From the time that it goeth forth it shall take you: for morning by morning shall it pass over, by day and by night: and it shall be a vexation only to understand the report.
>
> For the bed is shorter than that a man can stretch himself on it: and the covering narrower than that he can wrap himself in it. For the Lord shall rise up as in mount Perazim, He shall be wroth as in the valley of Gibeon, that He may do His work, His strange work; and bring to pass His act, His strange act. (Isaiah 28:14-21)

According to Isaiah, around the same time that Leviathan is wreaking havoc upon the world, a pestilence of epic proportions will sweep the planet. This pestilence will have been preceded by an earlier, less significant pestilence. Curiously, Isaiah calls out the leadership of Jerusalem for believing they would be delivered from the coming pestilence by making a covenant with death itself. What does this mean?

Isaiah's statement is cryptic, to say the least. However, it could very well refer to Israel's response to the recent global pandemic. According to an article published by Brookings titled "The secret sauce behind Israel's successful COVID-19 vaccination program" by Dany Bahar, shortly after the vaccines were made available, Israel's leadership entered into an agreement with pharmaceutical companies to act as the world's first test country. Given Israel's advanced healthcare system, after making the agreement, Israel became the most vaccinated country on the planet. The purpose of the agreement was to enable Israel to skip the pandemic altogether and keep their economy from shutting down.

Regrettably, that did not happen. Israel became just as sick and shut down as everywhere else in the world. Furthermore, while the country experienced 1.256 deaths per thousand people, it experienced 35 reported vaccine-related injuries per thousand people due to negative side effects from the vaccine. To make matters worse, a recent article by the Times of Israel titled "Ombudsman: Health Ministry didn't check 82% of reports on COVID vaccine side effects" by Toi Staff suggests that this number is dramatically underreported, and the negative side effects were intentionally not disclosed to the public. This implies that while one in a thousand died from COVID-19 in Israel, 233 out of every thousand of their population suffered negative side effects from the vaccine. Astoundingly, this is almost one out of every four people. This information was withheld from the general population by their government. I do not know if this is what Isaiah was referring to, but it is curious.

If this is what Isaiah was talking about, it would seem that something far worse than COVID-19 is coming down the pipeline. However, it seems that Israel will be worse off than other nations when the next pandemic hits, presumably as a result of the covenant with death their government made. Whether this is due to the negative repercussions of the vaccine on the immune systems of the people, we do not know, but Isaiah does seem to make a connection. However, Isaiah does say that the Lord will rise up on behalf of the people of Israel as He did at Mount Perazim and in the valley of Gibeon. Mount Perazim is where the Lord strengthened David's armies against the Philistines, resulting in the collapse of the Philistine nation. The valley of Gibeon is where the Lord caused the sun to stand still to give the Israelites more time to defeat the coalition of five Amorite nations in the land of Canaan. Presumably, the Lord's intervention on behalf of Israel at this time will result in another strange work just as perplexing as the halting of the sun.

Isaiah now concludes this epic revelation regarding the events of the last days:

> Now therefore be ye not mockers, lest your bands be made strong: for I have heard from the Lord God of hosts a consumption, even determined upon the whole earth. Give ye ear, and hear my voice; hearken, and hear my speech.

Doth the plowman plow all day to sow? Doth he open and break the clods of his ground? When he hath made plain the face thereof, doth he not cast abroad the fitches, and scatter the cummin, and cast in the principal wheat and the appointed barley and the rie in their place?

For his God doth instruct him to discretion, and doth teach him. For the fitches are not threshed with a threshing instrument, neither is a cart wheel turned about upon the cummin; but the fitches are beaten out with a staff, and the cummin with a rod. Bread corn is bruised; because he will not ever be threshing it, nor break it with the wheel of his cart, nor bruise it with his horsemen. This also cometh forth from the Lord of hosts, which is wonderful in counsel, and excellent in working. (Isaiah 28:22-29)

This seems a peculiar metaphor with which to conclude this incredible revelation. Yet the answer lies in the metaphor itself. Just as the farmer alters his actions to meet the specific circumstances and characteristics of the crop being harvested, so the world will require specific knowledge to navigate the last great reaping of the Earth. Just as the farmer obtained his knowledge regarding various reaping techniques from the Lord, so this knowledge must be received from the Lord via personal revelation.

Without personal revelation, the world will not survive these pending events. If we are to be prepared for the pending reaping of the Earth, we must put aside worldly wisdom and open our hearts and minds to the God of the Universe. After all, He is the keeper of these mysteries. As such, He is the only one who can truly prepare us for what is coming. We must humble ourselves before Him, pouring out all of our knowledge upon the ground, and giving our cups to the Lord so that He can fill them with His wisdom.

It has been said that it is impossible for a man to be saved in ignorance, and so it is. Yet why is the knowledge of God so hard to believe? An honest review of the history of humanity will demonstrate that there are few capable of hearing the Lord. God's truths have always been strange and rooted in the supernatural. We do ourselves no favors by filtering the supernatural from the gospel to make it more palatable for the masses. By doing so, we inevitably come to the same conclusions that the world has come to. Joseph Smith could not have seen God the Father and His Son, for they are unknowable. He could not have translated the Book of Mormon, because angels don't descend through cabin rooftops to bring tidings of gold plates buried in ancient hillsides. The Book of Mormon could not be real, because people of that era were incapable of traversing the oceans. Jesus Christ could not be the son of the virgin Mary, for such things are impossible. The Old Testament cannot be a historic account of the ancient world, for its pages are filled with giants and fairytale creatures. The reasoning of men precludes the world from true understanding.

Therefore, if we are to be taught of God, we must transcend the perceived boundaries and limitations of men. We must acknowledge that God is, at His very core, a supernatural being. As such, God is the rule, and the Newtonian world around us is what it is because of the good pleasure of God. He could alter it with a word if He so desired. Therefore, God is not bound by natural law; God is the Law Giver. When God states that He will perform His strange work in the last days, rest assured that Newtonian physics will have nothing to do with it.

Chapter 6 – The Holy Race - Above and Below

In the prior chapter, we reviewed one of Isaiah's epic visions regarding the last days. In that vision, Isaiah referred to a Leviathan and to the dragons of the sea that would be slain by the Lord. I reviewed that vision in conjunction with the terrifying things that Noah saw coming to the Earth in the last days. The things that Noah saw so terrified him that he lost control of his loins and fell upon his face in fear. Apparently, this heavenly host will be far more diverse and terrifying than a symbolic interpretation of the text would suggest.

While we can hope that such things are symbolic, thus far in Enoch's writings, when things are to be understood symbolically, there have been ample textual indications that such was the case. There were no such indications given with regards to the terrible hosts that Noah saw descending from the heavens in the last days. Indeed, if the Germans taught the world anything in WWII, it was that there was far more in the ancient world that was to be understood literally rather than figuratively. Unfortunately, few people understand much regarding these things today, for their discoveries became the property of the American Deep State after the war.

Yet, even without access to this information, the fact that Joseph Smith taught that there are intelligent creatures apart from the human family that will have roles to play in the last days should make us more alert. Indeed, if the Beast from the Book of Revelation will be an actual creature, as Joseph has said, why could there not be other beasts of an even more fantastical nature? Life in the cosmos is not limited to the imagination of man.

This current chapter will focus on life on Earth during the chaos of the last days, after our realities have been shattered by literal events of unimaginable consequence. Because of the world's hesitance to openly consider such things, most of the world's inhabitants will be forced to process them in real-time. As such, it is hard to imagine many surviving these days with their faith intact, much less their lives. After all, Jesus Christ Himself said this of coming events:

> And except those days should be shortened, there should none of their flesh be saved; but for the elect's sake, according to the covenant, those days shall be shortened. (JSM 1:20)

According to Jesus Christ, if the events of the last days were not cut short, no flesh would survive. This is a statement of fact regarding the physical dangers that will be present upon the planet in the last days, offered by the Savior Himself. However, for the sake of the elect, according to the covenant, those days shall be cut short. Clearly, the Lord is speaking of things that even the Remnant of Jacob are not equipped to handle. Perhaps this is one of the reasons that Michael, the Great Prince, John the Revelator, and many other translated beings will return in conjunction with the Remnant of Jacob in the last days. We will need all the priesthood power we can get just to survive until Christ comes and eliminates all threats with the word of His mouth.

To this end, Noah's vision of the last days now turns to the assistance that we will receive during these days of our greatest peril. Consider the following:

> **61.1**. And I saw in those days how long cords were given to those angels, and they took to themselves wings and flew, and they went towards the north.

> **61.2**. And I asked the angel, saying unto him: 'Why have those (angels) taken these cords and gone off?' And he said unto me: 'They have gone to measure.'

> **61.3**. And the angel who went with me said unto me: 'These shall bring the measures of the righteous, and the ropes of the righteous to the righteous, that they may stay themselves on the name of the Lord of Spirits for ever and ever.

It is important to remember that Noah is seeing the same things here that Enoch already saw in vision, but someone believed that Noah's perspective of these things would be important for us to have. As we learned with Nephi's take on his father's vision, different perspectives on the same events can be incredibly helpful.

The Christian world has often depicted angels as having wings. Noah's description of winged angels is insightful: "they took to themselves wings." We do not know exactly what this means, but it is clear that these angels took objects of power that enabled or enhanced them in ways that would not have otherwise occurred. We see this with other objects of power, such as the white stones spoken of in the Book of Revelation, and perhaps even the white robes given to the hosts of heaven. I believe that it is from this perspective that we are to understand these things. We will learn more about such enabling objects as this book continues.

Furthermore, Noah saw divine beings with cords measuring the righteous upon the Earth. By measuring, we are to understand that these angels can readily discern the wicked from the righteous. To the righteous, these ropes then serve as heavenly lifelines, with which they receive sustaining aid.

What Noah is seeing goes hand in hand with what both Daniel and Nephi saw. Nephi and Daniel saw that in the days of trial, the righteous would receive divine assistance and power from on high. This divine assistance will be like a rope thrown to a drowning man. If not for the rope, the drowning man would have perished. In other words, Noah's rope-bearing angels represent angels ministering to the children of men, helping them, strengthening them, and rebuffing both the satans and the cosmic creatures on their behalf. These angels will lighten the burdens from off our backs. For our own sakes, these burdens will not yet be removed from our shoulders, but through divine assistance, we will be able to survive the most challenging environment the world has ever seen.

Along the lines of divine assistance, Elder Bednar taught the following:

> I promise you will be protected against the intensifying influence of the adversary. As you participate in and love this holy work, you will be safeguarded in your youth and throughout your lives. (Elder Bednar – The Hearts of the Children Will Turn)

Elder Bednar specifically spoke about the divine protection received by those who perform temple work for the dead. Yet, the same principle applies to all those engaged in the Father's work. Those so engaged have been assured that they will not be taken before their time. If you are righteously engaged, the Father will not permit you to be taken before you have fulfilled your mission in life, though often, the Father's missions lie on the other side of the veil.

Regardless, we will not survive the coming days without divine assistance. By the end, we will need it desperately. Nobody will survive the supernatural nature of the coming events without divine intervention. Just as the hosts of Israel were dependent upon the Lord for their survival in the desolate Judean wilderness for forty years, so we too must rely upon the Lord for our deliverance in equal measure. He is just as capable of delivering us as He was our forefathers. Of this, there can be no doubt. Therefore, regardless of what the last days throw at us, even if it be the Leviathan itself, the righteous have no need to fear. For as our trials intensify, so will our divine aid.

> **61.4**. The elect shall begin to dwell with the elect, and those are the measures which shall be given to faith and which shall strengthen righteousness.

> **61.5**. And these measures shall reveal all the secrets of the depths of the earth…

These last verses are somewhat cryptic. There are clearly two events that will happen in the last days by divine design. Both of these measures, or divine aids, are meant to sustain the righteous through the days of trial. The first is described as the Elect returning to live with the Elect on Earth. The second divine aid will result in the secrets of the depths of the Earth being revealed. There is actually one more divine aid given in 61.5, but it is so incredible that I wanted to discuss it separately from the two above.

I believe that the verses above are best deciphered in the context of the Hopi prophecy reviewed in volume I of this series. In that series, we were told that two purifiers would come to America, one from the East and one from the West. The group from the East would be comprised of a remnant of the repentant Nazis who will have joined forces with a powerful group of righteous, highly advanced subterranean people. I believe that it was of this group that the Lord spoke in the context of the Second Coming in the following passages:

> I, the Lord God, have spoken it; but the hour and the day no man knoweth, neither the angels in heaven, nor shall they know until He comes. Wherefore, I will that all men shall repent, for all are under sin, except those which I have reserved unto myself, holy men that ye know not of. (D&C 49:7-8)

When this group starts to manifest itself to us, the secrets of the depths of the Earth will be made known to us. According to the Hopi prophecy, a second group will come from the West. The Doctrine and Covenants speaks of this mighty host first coming from the North and then traveling to the children of Ephraim in the West, who will be concentrated amongst the shadows of the everlasting hills. The Hopi prophecy stated that before the destruction of the Remnant of Jacob occurs, men will rain down like ants from the sky and cover the ground in untold multitudes. This incredible force will be the Lord's warriors from amongst the Lost Ten Tribes of Israel.

However, according to Noah, prior to the arrival of the main bodies of these two incredible hosts, righteous individuals from amongst their ranks will come to assist and preserve us. These righteous individuals will help us make sense of everything happening around us. At that time, we will finally understand the wise and glorious purpose for which the Lord planted the heavens and kept hidden from us many of the mysteries of the Earth. Neither of these two groups will be strangers to the cosmos, nor the dangers and challenges they possess. The illumination that these incredible men and women will share with us will be a literal godsend. Having lived in Zion-like societies, they will model for us what it truly means to have faith and to exercise priesthood power. The mixing of the Saints of God with these two groups will constitute the incredible event of which Nephi spoke, albeit cryptically. Nephi was constrained by the Holy Ghost at the time of his writing, but consider his words in this light:

> And it came to pass that I, Nephi, beheld the power of the Lamb of God, that it descended upon the saints of the church of the Lamb, and upon the covenant people of the Lord, who were scattered upon all the face of the earth; and they were armed with righteousness and with the power of God in great glory. (1 Nephi 14:14)

You will note that in the passage above, Nephi saw that scattered throughout the world, the saints of the Church of the Lamb would be joined by the covenant people of the Lord. This passage is confusing for some, as they consider the covenant people of the Lord and the Saints of the Church of the Lamb to be one and the same. Yet it is clear from the context of Nephi's writings, particularly the three subsequent verses that follow this, that the covenant people of the Lord are spoken of in conjunction with the restoration of the House of Israel. Apparently, this event will restore the seed of Joseph that has mingled with this subterranean group, as well as the Lost Tribes of Israel.

You will recall that in the chapters of this volume, Noah is seeing in vision what his great-grandfather Enoch saw. This is not dissimilar to Nephi seeing the vision of his father Lehi. Just as in that case, Nephi's vision brings a supplemental perspective that is very enriching. This is how Enoch described this portion of his vision of these events:

> **39.1.**[And it †shall come to pass in those days that elect and holy children †will descend from the high heaven, and their seed †will become one with the children of men.

Enoch is clearly talking about the same thing that Noah saw with regards to the angelic lifelines from on high. However, Noah used the very telling phrase, "the elect shall begin to dwell with the elect," and adds the insight that this process will also reveal the mysteries of the depths of the Earth. I consider this to be similar to Lehi's omission of detail regarding the filthiness of the river of water on account of his mind being caught up in other details. As such, the Lord provides two accounts of the same thing so that we might benefit from the additional perspective. Lehi's account was not untrue; it just was not complete. Few revelations are given in completeness. After all, regarding the three degrees of glory as recorded in Section 76 of the Doctrine and Covenants, Joseph Smith stated that he was able to reveal only the hundredth part.

I believe that the Lord will send advanced teams of people among the righteous early on in this process, likely shortly after they are driven from their homes. Furthermore, I believe that these reunions will happen among small isolated groups of saints throughout the world. As we will be cut off, without communication, the assistance that these will provide will be vital.

I envision kind and powerful strangers coming among us in our most dire hours of need. These will remain with us from this point forward. Apart from providing divine assistance to us, with their guidance, modeling, and the supplemental endowment of power which the Lord will pour out upon His saints at this time, we will quickly ascend in our faith and abilities. From these incredible people, we will learn how to truly live the gospel of Jesus Christ and what priesthood power truly means. Because of their assistance, the weak and humble of the Earth will be able to withstand the greatest trials the world has ever seen. To date, our instruction in these matters has been largely theoretical. However, of necessity, priesthood power will become the heavenly lifeline that will enable our survival.

As you consider these things, you might be somewhat frustrated that you have not been able to attain this kind of faith and priesthood power on your own. Know that any holder of the priesthood is keenly aware that this power is not our own but belongs to the Lord. Without the Lord, we have no power beyond that inherent in the flesh and will of all humanity. Obviously, desperate times call for desperate measures. Unless the Lord endows us with greater strength and power than we have previously known, we would not survive the coming day.

Even now, faith is increasing in the Earth. The scales of blindness are beginning to fall from the eyes of many, and the world around us is starting to be revealed for what it truly is. This ongoing restoration of truth will continue and even greatly accelerate. The acceleration of these revelations will not all come from predictable sources. Some restorations will be wielded like weapons by those in power. What do I mean by this? I am speaking of a specific cryptic portion of the prophecy of Ezra's Eagle.

This portion of that prophecy to which I am referring has to do with the rise of the three eagle heads to power in America. According to Ezra, something very interesting will occur during the consecutive administrations of the three heads of Ezra's Eagle. Consider the following passage:

> And whereas thou sawest three heads resting, this is the interpretation: In his last days shall the most High raise up three kingdoms [*three consecutive administrations of the three heads*], AND RENEW MANY THINGS THEREIN…
> (2 Esdras 12:22-23)

According to the prophecy, when the three heads of Ezra's Eagle rise to power, their consecutive administrations will renew many things. What things will they renew? As reviewed in the first volume of this series, the Nazis discovered many truths regarding the ancient world that inexplicably enabled them to leapfrog the rest of the world in technological advancement. Since the implementation of Project Paperclip, this esoteric knowledge has enabled, empowered, and emboldened the American Deep State. They have hoarded and coveted this ancient knowledge like Gollum with the Ring of Power. However, once the events of Ezra's Eagle have taken place, it seems they will begin to make this information known to the world. Given their objectives and track record, there can be no doubt that these long-awaited disclosures will be orchestrated and choreographed to support a meticulous predetermined agenda.

These revelations will be designed to legitimize their usurpation of power and will be used to unite the entire globe under their influence. In addition, such revelations will surely be used as a club with which they hope to bludgeon traditional Christian teachings into oblivion. In its place, they will offer and promote an alternative gospel that we see being taught with ever-increasing effectiveness among the rising generation. The restoration of these ancient truths will confound the Christian world, which up to this point has gone to great lengths to avoid considering such things in candid and open dialogue. As such, the preparations to counter such revelations must occur at the individual level. Without personal and immediate revelation, even the very elect according to the covenant will most certainly be deceived.

Obviously, both the Church specifically and the world generally are not prepared for supernatural events of this nature. This lack of preparedness on our part will stem directly from our taking lightly the incredible gifts and prophecies that we have received. Foremost among these are the Father's special message to the Gentiles in 3 Nephi, as well as the Isaiah chapters included within the Book of Mormon. For most of the saints, it is as if these resources were never given in the first place. It was for such complacency that the Lord proclaimed the entire Church to be under condemnation, which largely continues to this day.

Yet, despite our unbelief and stiff-neckedness, the Father will send us the aforementioned lifelines in our greatest hours of need. On account of our blindness, for many, if it were not for the Father sending elect emissaries from among these righteous covenant-keeping bodies, we would be destroyed along with the wicked. According to the evidence presented in this series so far, it appears that this process may have already started to a very limited degree. These interactions will soon increase, albeit gradually. After all, the Lord gave us the blueprint for the coming days in Zenos's allegory of the Olive Tree. According to that allegory, the Lord will not prune the vineyard all at once, but in accordance with the increased righteousness will the corrupt branches be cut off and burned. In this manner, the strength of the original root, which is in Christ, will not be too much for us to bear. But we, with the assistance of those who will come, will grow into the strength of the original tree until we are able to bear the full weight and glory of the author and finisher of our faith.

I acknowledge that Noah's prophecy of a holy and hidden race within the depths of the Earth sounds completely crazy. Nevertheless, some of academia's best and brightest are beginning to awaken to this as a real possibility. For example, in April 2024, Tim Lomas (Harvard), Brendan Case (Harvard), and Michael P. Masters (Montana Technological University) published a paper titled, "The Cryptoterrestrial Hypothesis: A Case for Scientific Openness to a Concealed Earthly Explanation for Unidentified Anomalous Phenomena."

The premise of the paper is that scientists need to be more open to the idea that a crypto or hidden civilization with advanced technology may already be present upon the Earth. The paper postulates that an advanced society may already be living within our oceans, deep within the Earth itself, or operating from the backside of the moon, or even all of the above.

As shocking as such an idea sounds, the paper argues that mounting evidence suggests that these wild scenarios are at least ten times more likely today than when the group first began evaluating the possibility. The paper links the dramatic increase of transmedium craft in our skies and oceans with a local presence of some kind. According to the paper's authors, if science were to examine the available evidence "in a spirit of epistemic humility and openness," we would need to rewrite our history books. The paper includes hundreds of references that create a compelling argument for their crypto-terrestrial hypothesis. Many of the references are firsthand accounts from government officials who have experience with these things.

Since David Grusch's bombshell testimony to Congress regarding the government's recovery of over one hundred transmedium crafts of incredible capabilities, more than eighty additional whistleblowers have come forward to corroborate his story. They have unbelievable stories of their own. All of these witnesses have come forward since September of 2023. This whistleblower movement is gaining momentum and exerting tremendous pressure upon the Deep State. Many feel the pressure building like the lead-up to a volcanic explosion. As such, this is a topic that every person in the world should be following as closely as they can. I believe that there are unseen connections between these events and those of Ezra's Eagle.

Furthermore, this Harvard study noted that the Senate attempted to pass the bipartisan Unidentified Anomalous Phenomena Disclosure Act (USC S2226, 2023) led by Senator Chuck Schumer, but it was undermined. This act would have empowered an oversight committee to penetrate the secrecy around all special access projects and declassify all information pertaining to UFOs. According to those familiar with the matter, special interest groups with close ties to the aerospace industry demanded that certain changes be implemented to safeguard the secrecy of the subject matter. The changes to the bill outraged Senator Schumer, who took to Twitter to vent his frustration. He tweeted the following:

> It is an outrage that the House didn't work with us on our UAP proposal for a review board. This means declassification of UAP records will be up to the same entities who have blocked and obfuscated their disclosure for decades. We will keep working to change the status quo.

It seems that many in Congress, who have become aware of this incredible phenomenon, are determined not to let this issue go. In May 2024, Robert Garcia filed an updated version of the UAP Disclosure Act as "A possible amendment to be considered on the floor of the House of Representatives during action on the Fiscal Year 2025 National Defense Authorization Act." The bill's official description is as follows:

> Enacts the remaining pieces of the Schumer-Rounds Unidentified Anomalous Phenomena Disclosure Act that passed the Senate [*in July 2023*], but were eliminated from the final FY24 NDAA. Creates an Unidentified Anomalous Phenomena Records Review Board, with exercise of eminent domain over UAP-related material controlled by private persons or entities, modeled on the President John F. Kennedy Assassination Records Act of 1992.

Former President Donald Trump has pledged to release all documents from government-affiliated programs if he retakes office. Since expressing his support for such transparency, there have been two assassination attempts on his life. These attempts, along with the act itself, draw intriguing connections to both the JFK assassination and the prophecy of Ezra's Eagle.

Conspiracy theories have long suggested that dark forces within the government were responsible for JFK's assassination. Supporters of these theories believe they have substantial reasons, and Trump has claimed that certain groups within the CIA urged him not to disclose all the investigation workpapers related to JFK's assassination. One key piece of evidence cited by conspiracy theorists is a speech JFK gave to the press on this subject. Below is a transcript of relevant portions of that address.

> My topic tonight is a more sober one of concern to publishers as well as editors. I want to talk about our common responsibilities in the face of a common danger. The events

of recent weeks [*referring to the Bay of Pigs*] may have helped to illuminate that challenge for some; but the dimensions of its threat have loomed large on the horizon for many years. Whatever our hopes may be for the future—for reducing this threat or living with it—there is no escaping either the gravity or the totality of its challenge to our survival and to our security—a challenge that confronts us in unaccustomed ways in every sphere of human activity.

This deadly challenge imposes upon our society two requirements of direct concern both to the press and to the President—two requirements that may seem almost contradictory in tone, but which must be reconciled and fulfilled if we are to meet this national peril. I refer, <u>first</u>, to the need for far greater public information; and, <u>second</u>, to the need for far greater official secrecy.

The very word "secrecy" is repugnant in a free and open society; and we are as a people inherently and historically are opposed to secret societies, to secret oaths and to secret proceedings. We decided long ago that the dangers of excessive and unwarranted concealment of pertinent facts far outweighed the dangers which are cited to justify it. Even today, there is little value in opposing the threat of a closed society by imitating its arbitrary restrictions. Even today, there is little value in insuring the survival of our nation if our traditions do not survive with it. And there is very grave danger that an announced need for increased security will be seized upon by those anxious to expand its meaning to the very limits of official censorship and concealment.

That I do not intend to permit to the extent that it's in my control. And no official of my Administration, whether his rank is high or low, civilian or military, should interpret my words here tonight as an excuse to censor the news, to stifle dissent, to cover up our mistakes or to withhold from the press and the public the facts they deserve to know.

But I do ask every publisher, every editor, and every newsman in the nation to re-examine his own standards, and to recognize the nature of our country's peril. In time of war, the government and the press have customarily joined in an effort, based largely on self-discipline, to prevent unauthorized disclosures to the enemy. In times of "clear and present danger," the courts have held that even the privileged rights of the First Amendment must yield to the public's need for national security.

Today no war has been declared—and however fierce the struggle may be, it may never be declared in the traditional fashion. Our way of life is under attack. Those who make themselves our enemy are advancing around the globe. The survival of our friends is in danger. And yet no war has been declared, no borders have been crossed by marching troops, no missiles have been fired.

If the press is awaiting a declaration of war before it imposes the self-discipline of combat conditions, then I can only say that no war ever posed a greater threat to our security. If you are awaiting a finding of "clear and present danger," then I can only say that the danger has never been more clear and its presence has never been more imminent.

It requires a change in outlook, a change in tactics, a change in missions—by the government, by the people, by every businessman or labor leader—and by every newspaper. For we are opposed around the world by a monolithic and ruthless conspiracy that relies primarily on covert means for expanding its sphere of influence—on infiltration instead of invasion, on subversion instead of elections, on intimidation instead of free choice, on guerrillas by night instead of armies by day. It is a system which has conscripted vast human and material resources into the building of a tightly-knit, highly efficient machine that combines military, diplomatic, intelligence, economic, scientific and political operations.

Its preparations are concealed, not published. Its mistakes are buried, not headlined. Its dissenters are silenced, not praised. No expenditure is questioned, no rumor is printed, no secret is revealed. It conducts the Cold War, in short, with a war-time discipline no democracy would ever hope or wish to match…

It is the unprecedented nature of this challenge that also gives rise to your second obligation—an obligation which I share. And that is our obligation to inform and alert the American people—to make certain that they possess all the facts that they need, and understand them as well—the perils, the prospects, the purposes of our program and the choices that we face.

No President should fear public scrutiny of his program. For from that scrutiny comes understanding; and from that understanding comes support or opposition. And both are necessary. I am not asking your newspapers to support an Administration, but I am asking your help in the tremendous task of informing and alerting the American people. For I have complete confidence in the response and dedication of our citizens whenever they are fully informed.

I not only could not stifle controversy among your readers— I welcome it. This Administration intends to be candid about its errors; for, as a wise man once said: "An error doesn't become a mistake until you refuse to correct it." We intend to accept full responsibility for our errors; and we expect you to point them out when we miss them.

Without debate, without criticism, no Administration and no country can succeed—and no republic can survive. That is why the Athenian law-maker Solon decreed it a crime for any citizen to shrink from controversy. And that is why our press was protected by the First Amendment—the only business in America specifically protected by the Constitution—not primarily to amuse and entertain, not to emphasize the trivial and the sentimental, not to simply "give the public what it wants"—but to inform, to arouse, to reflect, to state our dangers and our opportunities, to indicate our crises and our choices, to lead, mold, educate and sometimes even anger public opinion.

This means greater coverage and analysis of international news—for it is no longer far away and foreign but close at hand and local. It means greater attention to improved understanding of the news as well as improved transmission. And it means, finally, that government at all levels, must meet its obligation to provide you with the fullest possible information outside the narrowest limits of national security–and we intend to do it.

It was early in the Seventeenth Century that Francis Bacon remarked on three recent inventions already transforming the world: the compass, gunpowder and the printing press. Now the links between the nations first forged by the compass have made us all citizens of the world, the hopes and threats of one becoming the hopes and threats of us all. In that one world's effort to live together, the evolution of gunpowder to its ultimate limit has warned mankind of the terrible consequences of failure.

And so it is to the printing press—to the recorder of man's deeds, the keeper of his conscience, the courier of his news—that we look for strength and assistance, confident that with your help man will be what he was born to be: free and independent. (JFK – The President and the Press – April 27, 1961)

In his speech, JFK acknowledged the existence of a secret organization with a global reach and vast resources, working covertly to achieve its own objectives. He was not merely referring to the USSR but to what is now known as the American Deep State. This group operates transnationally, with influence, goals, and objectives that serve only its self-interests. It is seen as an enemy to both Russia and the American people. This organization has been likened to the Whore of Babylon, the secret combination that Moroni warned would threaten the freedom of all nations and people.

This topic serves as a compelling segue into an interview with Shawn Ryan and Steven Greer, which delves into these very issues. As of the date of this writing, the interview was available on YouTube under the title "JFK Assassination and the BIG UFO SECRET." Regardless of its current availability, a transcript of a portion of that interview is provided below:

Steven Greer - So some years ago I got from the vault from a National Security Agency guy, an envelope which had a big old Xerox of a document. The document was an order for a wiretap of Marilyn Monroe dated a couple of days before they found her dead. It was signed by the CIA guy James Jesus Angleton the third. He was a famous fanatical mole hunter and leak stopper at the agency back in the early 60s.

They wiretapped Marilyn Monroe's phone and learned that she was talking to Bobby Kennedy, and a friend of hers named Rothberg in New York. Rotherberg was an art dealer. She said that she was going to hold a press conference to tell the whole world what Kennedy had told her about the objects from outer space from the 40s found in New Mexico - a clear reference of Roswell and a couple of other events that happened out there.

That was not the only one, by the way. The first 1945 crash of an ET craft happened right after we detonated the first atomic bomb. That has just gotten documented by a good friend of mine, Paula Harris, she is a researcher. You know, it is a fascinating book. There are materials associated with that crash. So Marilyn, because I think the Kennedy brothers had distanced themselves from her because the affair she was having with Jack Kennedy was getting to be a little too well known. She was angry, and so she was threatening to spill the beans in a public news conference. The whole world would have been at that conference. So before she could do it, a wet-works killer made it look like she overdosed on drugs, but she didn't.

One of her friends way back in the day was this old cool guy named Burl Ives. He was an actor and singer back in the day. He was on my executive committee until he died. Interesting guy, 33rd degree Mason and all that. But he knew about the subject. So I go to his house in Washington and I show him this document. I didn't bring the original to him. It is this transcript of her telephone calls.

After he read it, he looks at me and he goes, "Now I know why they killed her!" I said, "Of course". And of course Kennedy was livid that they killed her. Because he had affection for her, even if he had to distance himself for political reasons. But he was working on an executive order at that time that would have dissolved the CIA agency and a lot of these [special access project] operations that were dealing with this. So before that could go through the executive review process, he was killed.

Now, interestingly, it wasn't just the UFO issue, it was a bunch of issues dealing with this whole constellation of problems, because remember he took office right after Eisenhower. Eisenhower's the one who coined the term "military industrial complex". Eisenhower was anti-fascist, which is the collusion and control of government by selfish corporate and money people. That's what Eisenhower was talking about. People have to get clarity on this because otherwise it gets politicized.

Now this is where Eisenhower was coming from. Now I have a witness, a guy named Stephen Lufkin, who is an attorney, at the time he was an Army core signal guy who was in the White House with Eisenhower. And he saw Eisenhower doodling pictures of UFO's and stuff and he talked to him. Eisenhower told him: "I've been cutoff, they're not telling me anything. I've lost control of these projects. This is all in my Disclosure book, it is an interesting read.

And so it it's a worrisome situation because I've been able to piece this together at the presidential level all the way to Roosevelt [*the second feather of Ezra's Eagle*]. By the way Foo Fighters, the rock band, they named their band Foo Fighters because that is what UFOs were called during World War II. We had these weird almost plasma light objects zipping around our aircraft. The Nazis thought it was a secret allied weapon, and the allies thought is was a weapon of the Nazis.

I was told by a pathologist in Denver whose uncle was General Jimmy Doolittle. He told me this story. So General Doolittle was sent over there [*to Europ*e] by Roosevelt to look into what the heck these Foo Fighters are. And General Doolittle comes back to the White House and tells Roosevelt, Sir, those are quote, "interplanetary vehicles". So that's how far back this knowledge is goes.

Lawrence Rockefeller, who was the brother of David Rockefeller, of Chase Manhattan, now JP Morgan Chase. wanted to help me with getting this problem fixed. So Lawrence hosted us at the Rockefeller Ranch in the Tetons. He was helping do things behind the scenes. He hosted the Clintons and I at his ranch under the cover of a summer vacation. While there I took the Clintons through all this material that we put together. However, Hillary said, "We don't want to hear too much more about this, it is too dangerous."

Lawrence and I got to know each other quite well. His heart was in the right place. He had people around him, we found out, who were actually deep cover intelligence operatives. I don't want to name them, but one of them, had been ambassador to France for Reagan, and served on the board of Morgan Stanley. He told me that he and William Buckley, a conservative journalist, were both recruited when they were at Yale to the CIA to be embedded in the corporate and political world. And so he and his wife sort of were a duo that ended up misdirecting Lawernce Rockefeller in the wrong directions to stop that initiative. People need to understand how counterintelligence operates, and how you have operatives who can go in and turn things sideways. Now that was in the nineties so we're talking ancient history here.

The big problem is people make these sweeping conspiracy theories. Most of the younger Rockefellers are actually supportive of this coming out. Lawrence was. Now Jay Rockefeller, who had been the chairman of Senate Intelligence Committee, and David, Lawrence's brother, were both members of this committee [*trying to keep disclosure from happening*]. And I went out on the deck late at night with Lawrence Rockefeller when we had this gathering at the at the ranch. This was before Clinton went there. And he turned to me and said, "My family is jumping up and down on my nuts because I'm even talking to you and doing this". I said, "Yeah, I'm sure because they have a very basic interest in maintaining the secrecy".

So you see, there are people who have been in the system who know but they will turn to their colleagues and lie to them and everybody. (Shawn Ryan Show clips: https://www.youtube.com/watch?v=gTUw-pEtpbc)

Dr. Stephen Greer's statements are indeed fascinating. He suggests that the Deep State has essentially become a breakaway civilization, viewing the universe in a completely different light than the average global citizen. Their perspective on reality is radically different from ours, and the knowledge they have acquired leads them to see the average American as both ignorant and insignificant. They have reasons for this belief, as the technology and intelligence they have amassed in secret far surpass what is available in the public domain. Despite this, we have funded their special access projects and enabled their incredible discoveries, which they hoard in the dark like Gollum with the ring of power.

As a result of their conspiring, they have created the antithesis of a holy race. With their unimaginable technology, which they have selfishly usurped, they consider themselves untouchable. Their confidence seems to be bolstered by intelligence from beings beyond our world. Thus, Satan will not be as blindsided by coming events as the world at large will be. He knows the ancient prophecies better than we do and is not constrained by the veil. He has been meticulously working behind the scenes to counter the Lord's plans. The Whore of Babylon has been a means for him to achieve these specific ends, but he will soon outgrow this phase of his plans.

The days are coming when the Whore of Babylon will openly usurp the people's power. Once this stage of Lucifer's plan is complete, Satan will use the Antichrist and the Beast to destroy the Whore of Babylon. This destruction will not be out of benevolence, but malevolence. Both the Beast and the Antichrist will be empowered not only by their advanced civilizations and technology but also by great supernatural powers of darkness. This, I believe, is the true meaning of Paul's words below:

> Put on the whole armor of God, that ye may be able to stand against the wiles of the devil. For we wrestle not against flesh and blood, but against principalities, against powers, against the rulers of the darkness of this world, against spiritual wickedness in high places.

> Wherefore take unto you the whole armor of God, that ye may be able to withstand in the evil day, and having done all, to stand. Stand therefore, having your loins girt about with truth, and having on the breastplate of righteousness; and your feet shod with the preparation of the gospel of

peace; above all, taking the shield of faith, wherewith ye shall be able to quench all the fiery darts of the wicked.

And take the helmet of salvation, and the sword of the Spirit, which is the word of God: praying always with all prayer and supplication in the Spirit, and watching thereunto with all perseverance and supplication for all saints; and for me, that utterance may be given unto me, that I may open my mouth boldly, to make known the mystery of the gospel (Eph 6:11-19)

Paul's oft-quoted rallying call to put on the full armor of Christ was a response to the forces of darkness, so that we might withstand the evil day. He urged us to prepare ourselves with the gospel, foreseeing that above all, we would need the shield of faith, as even the very elect according to the covenant could be deceived by the coming events. Paul concluded by pleading with the saints to pray for him specifically, so that he might boldly proclaim the mysteries of the gospel, which were meant to prepare them for the coming day.

It appears that Paul was constrained in what he could teach due to the desires of the people themselves. Thus, the Lord will not reveal these things to those who are not seeking to learn them. It seems that Paul's tongue was loosed in this regard. Consider the following teaching of his regarding the mysteries of the gospel, especially in light of what we have just reviewed:

Now we beseech you, brethren, by the coming of our Lord Jesus Christ, and by our gathering together unto Him, that ye be not soon shaken in mind, or be troubled, neither by spirit, nor by word, nor by letter as from us, as that the day of Christ is at hand. Let no man deceive you by any means: for that day shall not come, except there come a falling away first, and that man of sin be revealed, the son of perdition [*the antichrist*], who opposeth and exalteth himself above all that is called God, or that is worshipped; so that he as God sitteth in the temple of God, shewing himself that he is God.

Remember ye not, that, when I was yet with you, I told you these things? [*Paul taught the Saints things regarding the last days that are no longer common knowledge*] And now ye know what withholdeth that he might be revealed in his time. [*Paul is refering to the things that must occur before the antichrist rises to power in the last days. This is in reference to his previous statement. For a wise purpose in the Lord those teachings were not made public to us. I believe the reason is that the Lord will try the faith of His people.]*

For the mystery of iniquity doth already work: only He who now letteth will let, until he be taken out of the way. [*This knowledge is part of the mysteries of the gospel of which Paul asked the saints to pray that he might be able to teach them. Paul is saying that the secret workings of Satan are already under way in their days, yet the antichrist will not come forth until the Lord permits it to happen.*] And then shall that Wicked be revealed, whom the Lord shall consume with the spirit of his mouth, and shall destroy with the brightness of his coming: Even him, whose coming is after the working of Satan with all power and signs and lying wonders, and with all deceivableness of unrighteousness in them that perish; because they received not the love of the truth, that they might be saved.

And for this cause God shall send them strong delusion, that they should believe a lie: that they all might be damned who believed not the truth, but had pleasure in unrighteousness. But we are bound to give thanks always to God for you, brethren beloved of the Lord, because God hath from the beginning chosen you to salvation through sanctification of the Spirit and belief of the truth: whereunto He called you by our gospel, to the obtaining of the glory of our Lord Jesus Christ. (2 Th 2:1-14)

Paul clearly understood the mysteries of God and was permitted to teach the Saints about them, albeit under certain constraints. Only brief snippets of his teachings survive in the current canon. Those who seek to learn these things can be taught through the Spirit to the same degree that Paul taught others. God is no respecter of persons, but He will not force-feed us this information. He has given us tremendous resources, and we can learn everything today that was made known to the saints in antiquity. The responsibility to do so lies with us, not with anyone else. If we are ignorant of these matters, it is because we have not sought to be instructed through the Spirit.

Paul boldly stated that in the last days, we will not be battling against flesh and blood, but against powers in high places and supernatural forces of darkness. Until the arrival of the Antichrist, these forces will have been constrained to operate in the shadows.

However, the days are coming, and are not far distant, when the man of sin will be revealed to the world. When that day comes, Paul told us that his arrival will be magnified by the power and deception of Satan. This will occur so that all those who have distanced themselves from the Lord might be given over to believe this marvelous lie.

Paul taught that the gospel is meant to prepare us, serving as a shield against the power of the adversary. If we have not paid the price to put on the armor of God, we will be exposed to the lies and miracles of the Antichrist and the reality-shattering revelations that will be restored at that time. Without the shield of faith, even the very elect according to the covenant will fall.

Yet, the perils of that day will not all be spiritual in nature. Because the Whore of Babylon has amassed all her technology in the dark, when she falls, humanity's military forces will have no answer to check the power of the Antichrist and the Beast. Their global usurpation will be swift and absolute. However, Satan's ultimate objective is not to control the world of men, whatever the Antichrist and the Beast have been led to believe.

Lucifer's objective is to destroy the noble and great ones who banished him to the Earth. As John the Revelator said, these loved not their lives unto death. By this, we understand that the noble and great ones, who like Enoch, grew up in the Celestial Kingdom alongside the Father and the Son, left their heavenly homes to endure mortality upon Satan's prison planet. As a result, many of them will never return to the Celestial Kingdom again. It is perhaps the power of this incredible sacrifice that keeps the cancer of Satan's lies and deceptions quarantined to this prison planet. This is not an imagined sacrifice – it could not be more real. Satan's primary objective is to prevent as many of us from returning to the courts on high as possible. He knows that he cannot defeat God, but he also knows that he can and will defeat many of us.

Each of us is granted but a single chance at mortality, a fleeting moment in the grand tapestry of existence. Earth, a realm fraught with peril, challenges us at every turn. Yet, as the dangers loom large, so too do the rewards shine brighter. Therefore, let us heed Paul's call and don the full armor of Jesus Christ, fortifying ourselves with the profound mysteries of the gospel. Not the trivial mysteries that clutter our world, but the sacred truths that will guide us to salvation in the days of trial ahead, days unlike any the world has ever witnessed.

Chapter 7 – Additional Helpers

In the prior chapter, we reviewed the first four and a half verses of the sixty-first chapter of the Book of Enoch. In those verses, we learned about two groups of people that the Lord will send to live among the righteous in the coming days of trial. One group will reveal the mysteries of the Earth's depths, and the other will descend from the heavens. Their arrival will be a game changer for the righteous.

In this chapter, we focus on a third group that Noah saw would come to minister to the righteous in their hour of greatest need. However incredible you thought the first two groups were, to me, they pale in comparison to this third group. You will recall that up to this point, everything we have been discussing pertains to Noah's terrifying vision of the events of the last days and the terrible host that will come to the Earth. Therefore, this third group of helpers also comes in conjunction with this terrible host. Consider the remainder of verse 61.5:

> **61.5**. …and those who have been destroyed by the desert, and those who have been devoured by the Beasts, and those who have been devoured by the fish of the sea [*think Leviathans and sea*], that THEY MAY RETURN and stay themselves on the day of the Elect One [*think Great and Terrible Day of the Lord*]; for none shall be destroyed before the Lord of Spirits, and none can be destroyed.

According to Noah's vision, when the elect and holy races from both above and within the Earth begin to return to live among us, we will also be assisted by another group – our own righteous dead! Noah essentially tells us that even if the righteous are killed by the Beasts or by the monsters of the sea, they will be restored as resurrected beings. Taking this a step further, for these people to qualify to be resurrected at the forefront of the morning of the first resurrection, they must be Celestial beings. If Celestial Beings, then these departed family members will not return as we remember them, but as gods! As such, the greatest terrors this world has to offer will not even give them a second thought. Therefore, it seems to me that of the three coming groups, this one will spark the greatest reaction.

Imagine the joy and comfort such divine assistance will bring to both these newly minted gods and to the friends and family who will be assisted by them. Truly, the righteous have no need to fear death, for death may be precisely what is required to preserve their posterity. Thus, we see that certain individuals who are now well advanced in years and may lack the physical stamina to assist their posterity in mortality may have been reserved for this time for precisely this reason.

As you consider the fantastical nature of these ideas, remember that this is not the first time such things have happened. At the time of Christ's death in America, the righteous dead rose from their graves and ministered to their desperate posterity. Indeed, the context in which we learned of these events is extremely relevant to the circumstances of this chapter. Do you recall the context in which Christ spoke to the Nephites regarding these things? We learn of these events right after Christ finished expounding to the Nephites that the Remnant of Jacob would purge America. He then commanded both the Nephites and us to study these things. Right after that commandment, Christ did the following:

> And now it came to pass that when Jesus had said these words He said unto them again, after He had expounded all the scriptures unto them which they had received, He said unto them: Behold, other scriptures I would that ye should write, that ye have not. And it came to pass that He said unto Nephi: Bring forth the record which ye have kept.
>
> And when Nephi had brought forth the records, and laid them before Him, He cast His eyes upon them and said: Verily I say unto you, I commanded my servant Samuel, the Lamanite, that he should testify unto this people, that at the day that the Father should glorify His name in me that there were many saints who should arise from the dead, and should appear unto many, AND SHOULD MINISTER TO THEM. And He said unto them: Was it not so?
>
> And His disciples answered Him and said: Yea, Lord, Samuel did prophesy according to Thy words, and they were all fulfilled. And Jesus said unto them: How be it that ye have not written this thing, that many saints did arise and appear unto many and DID MINISTER UNTO THEM? And it came to pass that Nephi remembered that this thing had not been written. (3 Nephi 23:6-12)

It should be clear that this portion of the Book of Mormon was not included for the sake of the Nephites. They already knew this. Therefore, Christ wanted this knowledge to be included in their record for our sakes. Why? Because according to Noah, it will happen again! Consider the circumstances under which the dead originally rose to minister to their loved ones. The entire Nephite nation had just been destroyed. Many cities had been rendered completely desolate. Many were burned by fire. Others were buried in the Earth or in the depths of the sea.

This type of destruction had never before occurred. Destruction of this scale would have wiped out the Nephites' food supply and left them starving. Indeed, with dead and dying all around them, it would have been challenging to find clean water to drink. Had it not been for the resurrection of the righteous dead, who came to minister to them in their most desperate hour of need, they might not have survived what, for the wicked, was an extinction-level event. Today, the wicked await another extinction-level event which even now looms large on the horizon.

As we consider these things, it is important to contemplate who it was that rose from their graves to minister to them. Given the death and destruction that had occurred, do you suppose those who rose from the dead were long-deceased ancestors of whom they had little knowledge? No! These poor people had just lost their own loved ones – likely those most vulnerable to such events – the elderly. As such, these were loved ones with whom the Nephites were intimately familiar.

In this way, their resurrections were not just God-sent ministrations of temporal salvation; they were ministrations of healing and joy. The Lord did not eliminate the aftermath of the ancient American destruction. However, He did send divine aid to His surviving saints. His divine assistance at the hand of their loved ones enabled the survivors to overcome the last effectual struggle between them and what I refer to as the mini-millennium. So I believe it will be in our days!

It should be noted that this event does not appear to be linked to the universal resurrection of the righteous dead associated with the Second Coming of Jesus Christ. The morning of the first resurrection began with the resurrection of Jesus Christ, and He was the first person in this iteration of the Father's plan to rise from the dead with a glorified celestial body. At that time, many other saints rose from the dead, including those ancient American saints who ministered to their loved ones during their period of great need. Since the resurrection of Jesus Christ, many have been raised from the dead.

Peter and James appeared to Joseph Smith as resurrected beings and helped John the Beloved confer the Melchizedek priesthood upon Joseph Smith. Moroni, who was resurrected sometime between his death around 420 AD and his appearance to Joseph some 1,400 years later, is another example. This suggests that the Lord has already resurrected individuals at different times outside the primary window typically referred to as the morning of the first resurrection.

Indeed, it seems that those who have been resurrected thus far in the morning of the first resurrection have been relatively few. This should not be surprising, as the Lord has stated that comparatively few people will make it to the Celestial Kingdom, compared with the innumerable masses whose numbers are described as outstripping the sands of the sea. The resurrection of the dead is highly individualistic, correlating with an individual's final judgment. A person is raised from the dead with either a Celestial, Terrestrial, or Telestial body. These bodies correlate with kingdoms of glory, as described at length elsewhere. While there have been events where many people rose from the dead simultaneously, there have also been individual resurrections such as those described above.

It seems that the vision Noah saw, wherein the righteous dead rise up during times of trial to assist their families in their time of great need, will be highly targeted. Given that resurrection is correlated with a kingdom of glory, these individuals will have qualified themselves as Celestial Beings. That is to say, they remained valiant in their testimonies of Jesus Christ during mortality.

Additionally, I believe there will be a strong personal connection between those being ministered to and their resurrected ministers. In other words, the hearts of these fathers will be turned to their children, and the children to these fathers. Moroni proclaimed that if this were not the case, the entire Earth would be utterly wasted at Christ's coming. As such, we may find there is more to the revealing of priesthood by the hand of Elijah than we have supposed.

In addition to my hypothesis that these ministers will be known family members, there will also be a large force of resurrected beings ministering to the righteous across the world at this time. We refer to this group as the 144,000. According to the writings of John the Revelator, during the 6th seal, 12,000 righteous young men from every tribe of Israel were called and set apart for a particular mission. Consider the following passages which speak of these things:

> And I saw another angel ascending from the east, having the seal of the living God: and he cried with a loud voice to the four angels, to whom it was given to hurt the earth and the sea, Saying, Hurt not the earth, neither the sea, nor the trees, till we have sealed the servants of our God in their foreheads. And I heard the number of them which were sealed: and there were sealed an hundred and forty and four thousand of all the tribes of the children of Israel.

> And they sung as it were a new song before the throne, and before the four beasts, and the elders: and no man could learn that song but the hundred and forty and four thousand, which were redeemed from the earth. These are they which were

not defiled with women; for they are virgins. These are they which follow the Lamb whithersoever He goeth. These were redeemed from among men, being the firstfruits unto God and to the Lamb. And in their mouth was found no guile: for they are without fault before the throne of God. (Rev 7:2-4,14:3-5)

In these passages, the 144,000 young men were called and set apart by an angel who rose from the East. According to D&C 77:9&14, this angel is John the Revelator himself. John, who was translated by the Lord, is the great Elias overseeing the gathering of Israel and the restoration of all things. The 144,000 will coordinate their efforts with John.

These righteous men are described as standing before the throne of God, singing a song that no others could learn. This indicates that these young men, described as the first fruits unto God and the Lamb, are already Celestial beings, for they stand before the throne of God even now. Therefore, I believe that other righteous family members of the living will rise to minister alongside these 144,000 young men. However, their assignments will likely be very specific, while those given to the 144,000 will be broader.

As I consider the divine aid that the Father has promised to send to His saints in the last days, I am astounded by His foresight and mercy. I am overcome with gratitude for both the Father and His wonderful Son, and all they have done for the betterment of the human family. They have been the hope of ages past, and they are the only hope for our impending future. The powers of darkness are nothing before them. The only things that stand between us and Them are our own wickedness, unbelief, and the pride of the world that places a stigma upon Their truths.

I am amazed at the wonder of the Father's plan and the efficiency with which it segregates the sheep from the goats. The world has always placed a stigma around God's Eternal Truths. Those who would come unto God must bear the shame of the world to do so. The mocking scorn of the great and spacious buildings of Satan's kingdom is withering. Yet, it has always been so. The early saints were cast out of their synagogues and became social outcasts as a result of their belief in the Father's Hidden Son.

When the Romans usurped the "leadership" of the Church, those who disagreed with their apostate ideas were cast out of the churches, belittled, and derided. The Arian controversy is a perfect example of this. When the Church was restored in the latter days, the saints were once again persecuted and forced to bear the shame of the world. They were driven from place to place, enduring an endless stream of hardships. So it begins once more. In the comforting shadow of the Everlasting Hills, many of the Saints have forgotten the price their forefathers had to pay for the faith they now take for granted. Many among the Saints now heap derision and shame upon their fellow saints because they have sought to receive the greater light and knowledge the Father promised to send them. In their own spiritual blindness, these individuals bludgeon their fellows in the same ways Christ's true disciples have always been bludgeoned. It is for precisely this reason that the Lord has stated the following:

> Behold, vengeance cometh speedily upon the inhabitants of the earth, a day of wrath, a day of burning, a day of desolation, of weeping, of mourning, and of lamentation; and as a whirlwind it shall come upon all the face of the earth, saith the Lord. And upon My house shall it begin, and from My house shall it go forth, saith the Lord; first among those among you, saith the Lord, who have professed to know My name and have not known Me, and have blasphemed against Me in the midst of My house, saith the Lord. (D&C 112:24-26)

Jeremiah also spoke of this same cleansing event. The context in which he addressed it should be incredibly interesting to all students of the scriptures. Consider the profound words of Jeremiah:

> Therefore, behold, the days come, saith the Lord, that they shall no more say, The Lord liveth, which brought up the children of Israel out of the land of Egypt; but, The Lord liveth, which brought up and which led the seed of the house of Israel out of the north country, and from all countries whither I had driven them; and they shall dwell in their own land.
>
> Mine heart within Me is broken because of the prophets [*false teachers of Israel*]; all My bones shake; I am like a drunken man, and like a man whom wine hath overcome, because of the Lord, and because of the words of His holiness… For both prophet and priest are profane; yea, **in My house have I found their wickedness**, saith the Lord. Wherefore their way shall be unto them as slippery *ways* in the darkness: they shall be driven on, and fall therein: for I will bring evil upon them, *even* the year of their visitation, saith the Lord.

And I have seen folly in the prophets of Samaria; they prophesied in Baal, and caused my people Israel to err. I have seen also in the prophets of Jerusalem an horrible thing: they commit adultery, and walk in lies: they strengthen also the hands of evildoers, that none doth return from his wickedness: they are all of them unto me as Sodom, and the inhabitants thereof as Gomorrah.

Therefore thus saith the Lord of hosts concerning the prophets; Behold, I will feed them with wormwood, and make them drink the water of gall: for from the prophets of Jerusalem is profaneness gone forth into all the land. Thus saith the Lord of hosts, Hearken not unto the words of the prophets that prophesy unto you: they make you vain: they speak a vision of their own heart, *and* not out of the mouth of the Lord. They say still unto them that despise me, The Lord hath said, Ye shall have peace; and they say unto every one that walketh after the imagination of his own heart, No evil shall come upon you.

For who hath stood in the counsel of the Lord, and hath perceived and heard His word? who hath marked His word, and heard *it?* Behold, a whirlwind of the Lord is gone forth in fury, even a grievous whirlwind: it shall fall grievously upon the head of the wicked. The anger of the Lord shall not return, until he have executed, and till he have performed the thoughts of his heart: in the latter days ye shall consider it perfectly. (Jer 23:7-9,11-20)

Jeremiah began this incredible warning with a prophecy regarding the restoration of the House of Israel in the last days. According to Jeremiah, this restoration will rival the Exodus from Egypt, and once it happens, it will be the only thing anyone talks about. Yet, very few will see it coming, for the people will have chosen to heed the words of false teachers instead of the Lord Himself. Jeremiah proclaimed that this wickedness was occurring in the Lord's house, among His people – those who profess to know His name but do not know Him or His Hidden Son. Why do they not know them? Because they have relied on the teachings of men rather than the promptings of the Holy Spirit.

Jeremiah concludes his words by asking who has stood in the counsel of the Lord and hear His word. This sounds remarkably similar to President Nelson's admonition for us to learn to hear the Lord for ourselves. Jeremiah then states that a whirlwind is coming. Given the context of Jeremiah's warning and the modern revelation reviewed previously, this whirlwind will first start among the Lord's House. We are then left with the haunting prophetic statement that in the last days, we will consider these things perfectly. In other words, the saints of every age of this Earth's history have had the solemn responsibility of learning how to be taught by the Lord Himself, and not by men.

The Lord will send help to His Saints, but we are largely responsible for our own spiritual education and preparation for the events of the coming days. The world is almost entirely unprepared for what is coming. It is not that the Lord has not revealed these secrets to His servants the prophets, but that we do not seek them out. Instead, we wait for others to do all the heavy lifting for us and command us in all things. Yes, the Lord will help us, and yes, that help will come in miraculous ways, but there is a great amount of work left for us to perform. After all, if we are not willing to pay the price to prepare, why should anyone else?

Consider the example of Alma and his people when they were enslaved by the Lamanites in the land of Helam, or the people of Limhi who faced similar circumstances. The Lord sent divine aid to both of these groups, but He did not remove their burdens from their backs. They had to endure to the end. Yes, they were ultimately delivered, but not until their trials had run their course. As such, we must prepare ourselves for a period of spiritual trials the likes of which the world has never seen. To do so, we must engage with the Lord now!

The Lord requires effort! Consider the atonement of Jesus Christ, which is often described as being free. While salvation is a free gift, few people will take advantage of its full potential, as doing so requires the recipient of Christ's grace to fully engage in the process. Those who dip their toes in the pool will not have the same experience as those who immerse themselves in it. In like manner, the prophet cannot repent for us, nor can any other third party. If there are spiritual preparations to be made, we must be the ones to make them. As Elder Bednar stated, we must do what we must do, and we must learn what we must learn.

Furthermore, while the Lord will send divine aid to His saints, just as He did to the ancient American Saints, that aid will come after the full weight of the storm has passed. As such, do not suppose, as so many do, that the Lord will spare you from the trial of your faith through some rapture-like event. This is a false notion. You must be prepared to face the full fury of the coming storm. It is for this reason Paul implored us to prepare ourselves with the gospel and to forge for ourselves shields of faith, so that when the greatest storm the world has ever seen breaks down upon us, it will have no power over us because of our faith in the rock of our Redeemer – who is the Lord Jesus Christ.

As such, we had better start engaging more earnestly in this process; time is running out. The time will soon be upon us when the proverbial grocery store shelves will be barren. When that day comes, if you have not already obtained oil for your lamp, you will no longer be able to find it. After all, in the face of the unparalleled deceptions and marvelous blasphemies of the coming Antichrist, even the very elect according to the covenant will be swept away. When that day is upon us, hold fast, and know – HELP IS COMING!

Chapter 8– The Ascension of Christ and the Enuma Elish

In the prior chapter, we reviewed both Noah and Enoch's ancient prophecies regarding the divine helpers who will come in our hour of greatest need. We discussed the conditions of the world when they will arrive and, more importantly, the underlying cause for those conditions. The wickedness of the world will be augmented by the return of the Watchers and a non-human race of beast-like creatures that will align themselves with the Antichrist, Lucifer, the Lady, and each of their respective minions. Each of these different groups represents distinct classes of beings, all of which lie beyond our society's acknowledged reality.

Noah's version of this account was included in the Book of Enoch for a wise purpose. Keep in mind that everything Noah has discussed so far is related to the shaking of the heavens and the Earth and the fear-inducing descent of the terrifying hosts of heaven. In contrast to their descent, in this chapter, Noah discusses the ascension of the Son of Man to His Father's Throne. Consider the following verses:

> **61.6**. And all who dwell above in the heaven received a command and power and one voice and one light like unto fire.

> **61.7**. And that One [*the Son of Man*] with their first words they blessed, and extolled and lauded with wisdom, and they were wise in utterance and in the spirit of life.

> **61.8**. And the Lord of Spirits placed the Elect One on the Throne of Glory and He shall judge all the works of the holy above in the heaven, and in the balance shall their deeds be weighed.

In these opening passages, Noah's vision leaps forward to the culminating event of this iteration of the Father's grand plan of happiness. This occurs when the Elect One, Jesus Christ, completes all the work His Father gave Him to do and sits down upon the Throne of Glory, His Father's Throne. At this time, God the Father Himself ascends into the Mount of the Congregation to take His rightful place among His Father's thrones.

Noah foresaw that when this event takes place, the Son of Man will be surrounded by a host of newly resurrected gods. We know they are newly resurrected because their first words are to bless, extol, and laud the Son of Man, whom they refer to as "That One," meaning the One who made their ascensions possible. It seems their first act after rising from their graves in Celestial glory is to ascend to the Throne of God, where they present themselves to the Father and offer thanks, praise, and honor to the Son for elevating them. This behavior is reminiscent of Christ's resurrection, who was the first to rise from the dead in this iteration of the Father's plan.

You will recall from the New Testament that Mary Magdalene was the first to see the risen Lord. It is clear that Christ knew Mary was coming and waited for her to arrive. However, when she did, He prohibited her from touching Him before He had ascended to the Throne of His Father to present Himself. We see the same thing with the resurrected beings above. Their first act was to thank the Father and praise His First-Born Son.

There, surrounding the Father's Mercy Seat, this iteration of the Father's graduating class witnesses the ascension of He who conquered not only death and Hell but the Great Dragon himself. At this point, Lucifer has been cast into Outer Darkness, and the innumerable hosts of the unrepentant wicked have been relegated to the burning mountain range at the edge of all things. The culminating event of this cycle is now the coronation ceremony of Elohim's Beloved Son – our Champion and Savior, Jesus Christ.

We know that those who witnessed this incredible event had themselves been elevated to the status of gods for several reasons. First, they are standing in the presence of the Holiest Beings in the Multiverse in their full, unfiltered glory. Secondly, Noah perceived that all those present had received an endowment of great power, including the command of power, one voice, and a burning light. We understand that all these endowments are related to their ascension. By their receipt of command and power, they received the gift of Divine Utterance, the supreme gift of the gods, wherein they speak and the elements obey their commands. They receive one voice, meaning they are all of one mind in their honor and veneration of the Divine Godhead, acknowledging their supremacy in all things and recognizing that they were enabled by the Capital-G Gods in ways they could never have imagined or obtained for themselves. Lastly, they received a fiery burning light, an exceedingly great weight of glory at the Father's hand. As such, they have received all that the Father has to offer them.

As we consider these things, we do so in remembrance that these insights come from an ancient document preserved by the pre-diluvian Fathers. It is the closest source to the original belief system held by Adam. Recall that D&C 107:56-57 suggests that Adam's religious knowledge would be recorded and preserved within the Book of Enoch. Therefore, given that the Book of Enoch contains the original gospel as received by the ancient world, all other ancient religions would have become apostate derivatives of this original ancient religious tradition. By studying the ancient documents of the world, we should be able to find the fingerprints of this ancient religious tradition.

This concept becomes more intriguing when one considers the following words which the Lord gave to Nephi:

> Know ye not that there are more nations than one? Know ye not that I, the Lord your God, have created all men… and I bring forth my word unto the children of men, yea, even upon all the nations of the earth?... For I command all men, both in the east and in the west, and in the north, and in the south, and in the islands of the sea, that they shall write the words which I speak unto them; for out of the books which shall be written I will judge the world, every man according to their works, according to that which is written. (2 Nephi 29:7&11)

God explicitly told Nephi that He has spoken to all nations and commanded them to record the words He has spoken to their people. Furthermore, God stated that mankind will be judged out of the religious books that have been written. It is for this reason that I began my original search through surviving documents of the ancient world, looking for the ancient truths that the Lord said would whisper from the dust. Among these records, we find the Enuma Elish.

The Enuma Elish was first discovered in the ruins of an ancient library in Nineveh, the capital city of the Assyrian Empire, which carried away the Lost Ten Tribes. Today, most scholars agree that the oldest extant copies of the Enuma Elish were written around four thousand years ago. Yet, it seems to parallel older Sumerian texts and traditions that arose during the timeframe of the Book of Enoch, making them particularly relevant for us today. Furthermore, the ancient Canaanites recorded similar traditions in their own religious texts, one of the foremost being the Ba'al Cycle. While it is clear that all these ancient texts espouse apostate beliefs, it is equally evident that they point back in time to an original source. I believe this common source was the original religion of Adam, which he received directly from God and His messengers.

Assuming that the original religion of Adam is well represented by both the Book of Enoch, as D&C 107:57 attests, and the restored gospel of Jesus Christ, it should be quite easy to discern the original truths that became corrupted in antiquity by Satan and the philosophies of men. When the errors within these ancient texts are identified, isolated, and removed like a cancerous tumor, what remains is astounding truth!

However, before I begin my analysis, I must point out that not all the corruption of these ancient texts is of ancient origin. Many New Age ideas and philosophies have attached themselves to these ancient documents, which are every bit as false and dangerous as the original lies. As such, when studying ancient documents, it is paramount to consider the integrity of the source. It was for this reason that I based my commentary on R.H. Charles' translation of the Book of Enoch. He did a masterful job at translation, and his works withstand the rigor of academic scholarship.

Conversely, many of the dangerous New Age beliefs that have attached themselves to the ancient Sumerian texts like leeches and ticks wither away to dust under scholarship. As such, I will go to great lengths to use only commonly accepted translations and will demonstrate the tablet number and line of text where the reader can cite the account for their own study and benefit. The false New Age traditions offer no such opportunity, so I will ignore them in this analysis.

The Enuma Elish tells the story of the Godhead as recreated by the ancient Babylonians. You will recall that when Babylon conquered Jerusalem, they essentially kidnapped the promising youth and taught them in the ways of the Chaldeans (see Daniel 1:4). The Chaldeans were the foremost scholars of the ancient Sumerian culture. After the Sumerians were destroyed in the great flood, the Chaldeans made a name for themselves by hoarding and safeguarding the secrets of the ancient Sumerians. The Enuma Elish was likely the product of Chaldean scholarship attempting to recreate the original religious tradition espoused by the ancient world, particularly by the Sumerians themselves.

In light of the concepts and theories fleshed out within this series, I believe this chapter has the potential to be fascinating. Indeed, I would go further by stating that it could be one of the most meaningful I have ever written, if you have the eyes to see it. As such, I encourage you to take your time with this chapter. Do not rush through it. It is a long chapter and should take a long time to read. The value in this chapter does not come from the account of the Enuma Elish itself, but rather from the ancient doctrines hidden within it, like one of Christ's many parables. Surprisingly, the true hidden gems come less from the storyline and more from the titles ascribed to the story's main character and the respective meanings of those titles.

It should be understood that God has many names and is called differently by every people and tongue. Yet, whether we call the Son of Man Yeshua or Jesus Christ, light is light and is readily discernible as such for those with eyes to see. There is great meaning in a name. It is for this reason that President Nelson encouraged all the Saints to study all the names and titles given to the Lord. He said that even he was astounded by the knowledge and insight he gained by doing this. In this chapter, we will study the names and titles the ancients attributed to the Lord. This analysis, I believe, has the potential to be one of the most impactful subjects I have ever written about. However, before I can begin this analysis, I must first provide a summary of the main storyline of the Enuma Elish.

The Godhead described within the Enuma Elish is comprised of a patriarchal line of Firstborn Sons. The Patriarchs of the ancient Godhead each bore the title King of the gods, and each Father eventually gave their throne over to their Firstborn Son. The similarity to this concept and the opening verses of this chapter should not be lost upon the reader – indeed, it is the whole purpose of this analysis in the first place.

Similar concepts of the Godhead were the foundation of all the major religions of the ancient world. The Babylonian religious tradition named Marduk as the firstborn son of Ea – King of the Gods, while Ba'al was the firstborn son of El or Elohim, also described as the King of the gods. Out of reverence, Marduk was typically referred to simply as Bel, the Babylonian word for The Lord. A similar practice was adopted by both the Canaanites and the Hebrews. In order to preserve the sacredness of God's name, all these ancient people simply called Him the Lord in their respective tongues. Clearly, this practice stemmed from antiquity and was not jointly and severally developed by each culture spontaneously.

Let me specifically state here that the scriptures are very clear that both Bel and Ba'al should be considered apostate deviations of the God of Israel, and nothing more. Whereas the God of Israel created men in His own image, the nations of the world recrafted the concept of God's Firstborn Son into an image of their own design. By recrafting God in their own image, they permitted themselves to celebrate the natural man. As such, the worship of Ba'al and Asherah in Canaan, and Bel and Ishtar, their Babylonian counterparts, spread through the ancient world like wildfire. Yet, universal acceptance by man does not make something right. It was just as wrong for the apostate Babylonians to create their version of the Lord as it was for the Canaanites. Consider the following passage from Jeremiah:

> I will punish Bel in Babylon, and I will bring forth out
> of his mouth that which he hath swallowed up: and
> the nations shall not flow together any more unto him:
> yea, the wall of Babylon shall fall. (Jer 51:44)

As we consider the ancient records of the world, we must do so with our eyes wide open. With what I am about to discuss, I do not want anyone to take away the impression that I am venerating the apostate gods of antiquity. I am not. Rather, I am acknowledging that these apostate religious traditions did not spring forth from nothing but represent derivatives of an original truth. Think of this in terms of Catholicism. The religious traditions of Catholics today mingle the ancient ideas of venerating Heavenly Mother into Christianity. This is an apostate practice that can be traced back to the ancient religions of the world but has no bearing on the practices of the original or restored gospel. Still, it highlights aspects of truth, as each of us does have a Heavenly Mother. As such, let us not consider the religions of the ancient world on their own merits, but rather what they teach regarding the original truths from which they were derived.

Therefore, we return to the Babylonian godhead, seeking to forensically trace its origins to the original religious tradition as taught within the Book of Enoch. Marduk, or Bel, was the firstborn son of Ea – King of the Gods. In turn, Ea was the firstborn son of Anu – King of the Gods. Most scholars believe that the Babylonian Anu stemmed from the earlier Mesopotamian An, who was symbolized by a great bull before the flood. In turn, Anu was the firstborn son of Anshar – King of the Gods. Anshar was the firstborn son of Lahmu – King of the Gods. Before Lahmu, Tiamat, the great dragon, reigned in the primordial waters with her son Apsu. There is deep symbolism here which I shall now endeavor to unfold.

In the Enuma Elish, the Gods are born of the Queen of Heaven, and not the other way around. Thus, as with the ancient apostate mother goddess of the ancient world, Tiamat is attributed with being the mother of all life. Lucifer is famous for flipping the script, and this concept is evidence of his involvement in shaping religious thought from the very beginning. There is also great symbolism with Tiamat reigning over the multiverse as the Leviathan of the primordial sea.

As has been discussed elsewhere, the Leviathan has always been associated with cataclysmic extinction-level events. So it is within the Enuma Elish. In the context of the Enuma Elish, Apsu becomes enraged at the children of heaven and vows to exterminate them. More regarding this will be spoken of shortly. To this end, Apsu and Tiamat instigate a war in heaven. Thus, within the Enuma Elish, Tiamat and Apsu are the primary antagonists, with Apsu being the arch-rival of the children of heaven, specifically, and Tiamat being the general force of evil across the entire multiverse. It is therefore not difficult to find their gospel equivalents in the deceitful opposition and scheming of Lady Wisdom and Lucifer, as has been discussed throughout this series.

Thus far, we have been introduced to Tiamat, Apsu, and a royal lineage of Uppercase Gods representing the supreme sovereigns of the Universe. Among the Uppercase Gods, the kingdom is transferred from father to firstborn son. This is the same concept set forth in the opening verses of this chapter. This is also the pattern from which earthly kingship has been modeled from the beginning of time. It is therefore important to recognize that the Enuma Elish is modeling this concept as the order of heaven.

In addition to the two great antagonists and the royal line of Uppercase Gods, the Enuma Elish speaks of other heavenly beings. Two additional classes of heavenly entities are the Anunnaki, or the sons of Anu, and the Igigi – the children of heaven. The name Anunnaki actually has profound spiritual implications that should be considered regarding the ancient world's understanding of the true nature of the Godhead. These implications are perfectly aligned with the theories laid out in volume II of this series. Therefore, let us consider the Anunnaki in light of that theological framework.

In volume II, I speculated that each member of the Godhead progresses through the various roles of the Godhead with each successive iteration of the Cycle of Salvation. As such, in the prior iteration of the cycle, Christ's Grandfather would have served in the role of the sovereign power of the multiverse, while Elohim would have served as the cycle's Savior, with Christ serving in the capacity of the Faithful Witness or Holy Ghost. As such, through Elohim's atonement, the participants of the prior cycle would have become the begotten sons and daughters of Elohim's Father, in the same way we become Elohim's begotten children through Christ (see D&C 76:24).

John the Revelator spoke of this relationship in his writings. Consider the following verse:

> Jesus Christ who is the Faithful Witness…hath made us kings and priests unto God and His Father (Revelation 1:5-6)

Joseph Smith taught that this passage indeed speaks of Christ making us kings and priests to both His Father and His Grandfather (see *Teachings of the Prophet Joseph Smith*, page 373). We do not know the name of Christ's Grandfather, so for illustration purposes, let us presume that the Babylonians got it right and His name is Anu. Thus, the children of heaven redeemed by Elohim's atonement in the prior cycle would have become the begotten sons and daughters of Anu, or Anunnaki. I believe this is the precise meaning behind the term Anunnaki as used in the *Enuma Elish*. Therefore, the Anunnaki represent the hundreds of trillions of lowercase gods discussed numerous times in this series.

Now, let us discuss the Igigi. Most commentaries on the *Enuma Elish* suggest that the Igigi were the children of the Anunnaki. In the context of the restored gospel of Jesus Christ, the Igigi represent the premortal spirit children of the gods. This concept is further validated by the fact that the *Enuma Elish* attributes the war in heaven to the Igigi, or children of gods, making too much noise. The children of heaven so annoyed Apsu that in a fit of rage, he vowed to destroy them. Reading between the lines of the text, it is clear that Apsu's anger stems from his desire to become the undisputed sovereign of the multiverse, but the Uppercase Gods are intent on sharing the kingdom with the Igigi. Thus, Apsu planned to destroy them with the help of Tiamat, the Queen of Heaven.

Apsu and Tiamat's plan for destroying the Igigi and usurping control of the multiverse includes using powerful non-human creatures. The *Enuma Elish* refers to these creatures as monster-serpents. They are named as follows: Viper, Dragon, Monster Lahamu, The Great Lion, the Mad-Dog, the Scorpion-man, Mighty lion-demons, the Dragon-fly, and the Centaur. I find it very curious that Joseph Smith stated that the universe contains far more intelligent species than we can imagine, and that some of these Beasts will descend upon the Earth in the last days, as discussed throughout this series.

According to the account of the *Enuma Elish*, Ea – the King of the Gods – refuses to allow Apsu and Tiamat to destroy the children of heaven. Ea deals with Apsu himself but asks for a champion to confront the rebellious Queen of Heaven, Tiamat. In reality, the Book of Enoch shows that it was the exact opposite of this. God the Father cast out Lady Wisdom, or Tiamat, and Christ overcame Lucifer, the great dragon. Regardless, the symbolism and meaning within the *Enuma Elish* remain relevant.

According to the *Enuma Elish*, when Ea asks who shall be sent to overcome this great evil threatening the Igigi, His Firstborn son rises to the call by essentially stating, "Here am I, send me." He volunteers to overcome the Dragon in single combat. Ea calls a great council of the gods, in which His Son is put forward as the intended Savior. As part of that council, Ea's Firstborn demonstrates His mastery of the power of Divine Utterance. He does this by commanding a garment to disappear and reappear using only his command. The similarity between the Savior's mastery of power, which we refer to as the Light of Christ, should not go unrecognized.

In Apsu's war against the sons of heaven, we find the same profound irony within the history of Nazi Germany. Just as the Lady convinced the Nazis to destroy the Jews, Apsu sought to destroy his own. For Lucifer was the very thing he sought to destroy, a son of heaven, just as Hitler, undoubtedly descended from the House of Israel himself, was deceived into destroying his own. So it has always been that those who find themselves in Satan's service sooner or later come to understand that they have been engaged in the act of self-destruction, even as Satan was his own worst enemy.

After the conclusion of the council of the gods, Ea's Firstborn battles the cosmic Dragon and defeats it in single combat. According to the *Enuma Elish*, He then creates the Earth from the Dragon's body. This is consistent with the symbolism of Earth's uniqueness as the Dragon's prison. This symbolism further mirrors that of the twelfth chapter of the Book of Revelation.

The *Enuma Elish* ends with the heavens ringing with the Igigi's shouts of praise and joy for Ea's Firstborn Son, their Savior. This is reminiscent of the book of Job's description of the time "when the morning stars sang together, when all the sons of God shouted for joy." The Igigi's praise was given in the form of fifty prophetic names which they pronounced upon Ea's Beloved Son. The number fifty is meaningful as it represents Ea – King of the Gods. Therefore, to pronounce fifty names upon Ea's Firstborn suggests that the Son is destined to take upon Himself the role and responsibilities of His Father. Again, this is the true meaning behind the opening verses discussed at the beginning of this chapter.

As I list the Fifty Names below, know that I have deduced the implied meanings attributed to each from the context of the document itself, and not from a transliteration of the words themselves. As such, I encourage you to study these fifty names within the original context as found within the *Enuma Elish*'s tablets VI and VII. For your reference, I have included the tablet and line number where the name can be found. The version of the *Enuma Elish* that I have used is based upon that published by the Christian Resource Institute, and at the time of this writing, was available online at https://www.crivoice.org/enumaelish.html.

Their translation is primarily based on the work of E.A. Speiser, a renowned Assyriologist whose translations are highly regarded in academic circles. The Christian Resource Institute supplemented Speiser's work with that of L. W. King, another renowned Assyriologist. I have summarized the meaning of the names below but include this information so that you might be able to read the names in the original context at the previously cited website. Keep in mind that the *Enuma Elish* is not the original source document but was based upon far older Sumerian writings likely recreated by the Chaldeans. As such, the accounts herein predate the Bible. Indeed, George Smith first published these texts under the title *The Chaldean Genesis* in 1876. E.A. Speiser's translation was titled *Ancient Near Eastern Texts Relating to the Old Testament*. L. W. King's translation was called *The Seven Tablets of Creation*.

Many have been disturbed by the parallels between the Sumerian religious texts and those later recorded in the Bible. Indeed, many simply state that the Hebrews created their own versions of accounts that already existed in Mesopotamia or among the Canaanites. However, the real answer is that the Lord preserved the original records of the pre-diluvian fathers with Abraham.

As such, while the Mesopotamian and Canaanite texts have echoes of the truth, Abraham's records contained that truth in its pure form. The Bible as we have it today is not in the pure form that Abraham brought with him from the land of Ur. You can read excerpts from that account within the Book of Abraham. The Bible as we have it today is a product of the post-Babylonian Jews. Nephi prophesied that the Bible would pass through the hands of the Great and Abominable Church, which would strip many plain and precious things from it. By this, we understand that the Bible was edited by conspiring men with their own agendas. We know that this included zealous Jews who edited their own records, stripping out any references to a Godhead based on polytheism. As such, the Old Testament that we have today is not the same Old

Testament that was included within the Plates of Brass. This explains how the Nephites held such a clear understanding of the Godhead, while the Jews plunged themselves into a befuddlement of their own creation. Fascinating instructional examples of this will be shared in the next chapter.

With this understanding, here are the fifty ancient names that the ancients used to describe the Son of God. As I expound upon these names, I will refer to Ea's Firstborn Son either as such, or by the English version of Bel, His Babylonian common name – the Lord. Let the Spirit be your guide.

1. **Marduk: Son of the Sun, as named by His Father Anu from birth. Creation, destruction, deliverance, and grace shall all be at His command. They (the Igigi) shall look to Him! (TVI L124)** Honestly, Marduk is a name that I do not like very much. There is something about it that just does not sit well with me; however, it does help to shed light on some ancient practices that the Israelites struggled with throughout the Old Testament. I will get to those shortly. Before that, I want to focus on the fact that the *Enuma Elish* states that Marduk received this name from His Grandfather Anu. In the context of the Godhead as understood through the light of the restoration, this would be the equivalent of God the Father naming the Holy Ghost. This suggests that the ancients believed in a multi-generational Godhead. This is consistent with the theoretical framework I have laid out elsewhere in this series.

   Now, returning to the aspects of this name that caused the House of Israel so many problems. The name Marduk is literally translated as "Son of the Sun"; however, it can also be translated as "Bull Calf of the Sun." Marduk's Grandfather An/Anu was referred to as the Great Bull. The ancient apostate practice of worshiping golden bull calves likely had its origins in this concept.

   Among the ancients, references to bulls became a de facto way to reference the divine line of authority tracing back to the Great Bull of Heaven, An. This concept is likely why Ba'al, the Canaanite version of Elohim's Son, was also worshiped in the form of a calf, and why the apostate Queen of Heaven herself was associated with a bull or calf as well. Such symbolism was meant to link them to the divine right of kingship inherent within the Godhead.

   A further illustration of one's linkage to the ancient line of authority was to wear a hat or crown made from bull horns. We see this imagery throughout the carvings of the world's most ancient kingdoms. The concept being, anyone wearing such a hat could trace their line of authority back to the Godhead.

This symbolism, in some form or fashion, was perpetuated within the House of Israel. A reading of the eighth chapter of Leviticus is very illustrative in this regard. This chapter depicts the original temple ceremony. As part of that ceremony, a bull was sacrificed in order to consecrate Aaron and his sons for their work in the temple and cleanse them from their sins. They were then anointed with sacred oil that was to be held within the horn of an ox. The symbolism being that the authority to anoint and consecrate them could be traced directly back to God.

This symbolism is still used in the temples today. By it, we are meant to understand that the authority of the priest or priestess performing the anointing is of God. Furthermore, Ephraim's symbol as the Ox represented that he had become the birthright son of Israel. This is a direct linkage back to the original religion as revealed to Adam and was to be viewed as a symbol of divine kingship and a representation of the priesthood line of authority in which one had the authority to act in the name of the Capital Gods.

Whatever apostasy crept into the symbolism of this ancient truth over time, the true symbolic meaning was known to the original patriarchs from the earliest days of men's history on Earth. Furthermore, from the context of the text, it is clear that this name conveyed Ea's Firstborn Son's absolute authority to act in the name of His Father. Through power in the priesthood, the Son of God had the power to not only create or destroy but also to grant salvation through His atoning grace. It is also an indication that He followed the same tradition of salvation as His Fathers before Him.

2. **Mardukka: The Great Creator of all things, who brings joy to the gods and peace to their children. (TVI L134)** This name expounds upon the creative power of Ea's Son, who is described as the Great Creator of all things. This is in perfect harmony with John's description of Jesus Christ in John 1:1-3. This name further emphasizes that His creative abilities are used for the benefit of the Anunnaki, or gods, and their children – the Igigi.

We have seen elsewhere in the Book of Enoch that the gods are anxiously engaged with the Divine Throne regarding their earth-born children. You will recall that in one of those descriptions, Phanuel – the Face of God, who holds the keys of repentance and forgiveness, prohibited the satans from accusing the children of the gods before His Father's throne. He alone would be their advocate. Mardukka seems to emphasize this aspect of Ea's Firstborn.

3. **Marutukka: The Refuge of His People (TVI L136)** The third derived name of Marduk emphasizes that Ea's Son uses His divine power and authority to bless

and protect His people. Many passages within the scriptures describe the Lord as the refuge of His people. For examples, see Psalms 9:9; 46:1; 62:7-8; 91:2, and Nahum 1:7.

The first three names in this series are all derivatives of the name Marduk, as first pronounced upon Ea's Firstborn by His Grandfather Anu. These derivative names are meant to convey different aspects of His kingship, authority, and mission. The idea of taking one concept, such as the name Marduk, and subdividing and analyzing those subsets is an ancient philosophical method that the Greeks called collection and division. You will see this technique repeated throughout these fifty names. When you see it, you will know that the ancients are intentionally emphasizing particular aspects of the Lord that they considered critically important.

Right from the start, we are to understand that the Lord's role as heir to the Divine Throne, His priesthood line of authority, His ability to bring joy to His people, and to be their refuge in times of great need were of paramount importance for the reader to understand. Ea's Firstborn wields His unfathomable power not for His own benefit, but for the children of heaven!

We now continue with the fourth name.

4. **Barashakushu**: **The Empathetic Sovereign holds the reins of power (TVI L138)** The ancients wanted to communicate that Ea's almighty Son, although an Uppercase God, could still relate with the trials and hardships of His people. This same aspect is repeatedly emphasized in scripture regarding God's Beloved Son – see Alma 7:11-13; Hebrews 4:15, and Isaiah 53:5

5. **Lugaldimmerakia: Lord of the gods, as He was so called in the Council of gods before the world was (TVI L140)** Verse 9.4 of the Book of Enoch refers to a heavenly council in which Enoch hears the title "God of gods, Lord of lords, and King of kings." This gives us a second ancient text using this title in the same context as the Enuma Elish. There can be no doubt that this title is associated with Jesus Christ. After all, a similar title is written upon Christ's vesture and upon His thigh when He comes again in glory (see Revelation 19:16).

   Returning to the concept of a premortal council of gods, this idea is foreign to traditional Christianity. Yet, it is ubiquitous among all the ancient religions of the world. We have seen that Enoch spoke of such things, but they are also referenced in canonized texts. Examples can be found in Job 38:4-7, Abraham 3:22-28, D&C 29:36-38, Psalm 82:6, and John 10:34.

6. **Nari-Lugaldimmerankia: The Great Allocator of the exaltations of the gods (TVI L144)** This name is derived from the previous name – Lord of the gods.

By this, we understand that the supremacy of Ea's Firstborn Son was not simply a passing concept; it was a core tenet of the ancient tradition. Nari-Lugaldimmerankia is the maker of gods. This title communicates that the Igigi's exaltation was inextricably associated with Ea's Firstborn Son. Therefore, regardless of the apostasy that occurred in antiquity, at one point, the ancient world clearly understood that Ea's Firstborn was the gatekeeper of salvation. If the Igigi wanted to become like their heavenly parents, then Ea's Almighty Son was their only hope.

While mainstream Christianity does not fully appreciate this concept, they do acknowledge that no one comes to the Father except through Jesus Christ. John the Beloved, as a translated being, taught that God the Father has indeed placed our salvation into the hands of His Only Begotten Son (see John 3:35; 5:22, 27). If God has placed all things into Christ's hands, then He is indeed the great allocator of exaltation. This name reminds me of the following passage of scripture, particularly the last sentence.

> For behold, I, God, have suffered these things for all, that they might not suffer if they would repent; But if they would not repent they must suffer even as I; Which suffering caused myself, even God, the greatest of all, to tremble because of pain, and to bleed at every pore, and to suffer both body and spirit—and would that I might not drink the bitter cup, and shrink—Nevertheless, glory be to the Father, and I partook and finished My preparations unto the children of men. (D&C 19:16-19)

7. **Asaruludu: Light of the gods as named upon Him by His Grandfather Anu (TVI L152)** Here we have another curious reference to the three-generational aspect of the ancient Godhead. The first and seventh names given to Ea's Firstborn Son were bestowed by His Grandfather. The Babylonians followed a seven-day work week, likely stemming from the original creation story wherein the Earth was created in seven days. Therefore, having the Lord's first and seventh names given by His Grandfather is symbolic of the cycle of kingship in the Godhead and Anu's ability to foresee the end from the beginning, an attribute of all supreme deities.

While the first name in this list translates as Son of the Sun, a reference to light, Asaruludu means Light of the gods. As we progress through this list, we find that the next six names are based on the root word Asaru. From the context of these names, Asaru must mean light, as each subsequent name expounds upon attributes of light. Christ Himself stated that He was the Light of the world. This phrase means that Christ illuminates the Covenant Path that leads back to the presence of the Father. To return to the Father's presence as a resurrected being is to be a god. Thus, Jesus Christ is, in the truest sense, the Light of the gods, as this name proclaims Him to be.

8. **Asaruludu-Namtillaku: The Light which restores the lost gods and revives the dead ones (TVI L152)** We have already noted that the ancients wanted to emphasize the importance of light as it pertains to Ea's Firstborn Son, dedicating six names to explaining how the Light of the Lord is to be understood. In the previous name, we learned that Ea's Firstborn Son was the Light unto the gods, meaning those who would inherit His Father's kingdom. However, the ancients wanted us to understand that the Lord's Light fills the immensity of space, reaching even unto the lost gods and those who are spiritually dead.

Before this world was, we helped to cast out Lucifer and banish him to the Earth. In doing so, according to John, we loved not our lives unto the death. By this, we understand that many of us knew we would not return to the Celestial Kingdom. Additionally, we are taught in D&C 76 that of all the kingdoms of glory, only the Telestial Kingdom's inhabitants are described as innumerable. Indeed, Christ taught that the road to Hell is both broad and well-traveled, whereas the Covenant Path that leads back to the Father is both straight and narrow.

Those who inherit the Telestial Kingdom do so because they rejected Christ both in mortality and in the Spirit World. As such, they atone for their own sins in the burning mountain ranges at the end of all things. This separation from the presence of God is Spiritual Death. The ancients understood that God would not abandon these souls to the outer limits forever. The days will come when Jesus Christ will visit those who have been imprisoned at the edge of all things and will reclaim them through His power. This is what the ancients meant by Ea's Son being the Light unto the lost and dead gods. The Lord will eventually gather these souls and give them a kingdom of glory, the likes of which is beyond our ability to comprehend. When that happens, every knee will bow and every tongue confess that Jesus is the Christ, the Light of the Multiverse.

9. **Asaruludu-Namru: The Shinning God of which Anshar (His Great-Grandfather) and Lahmu (His Great-Great-Grandfather) prophesied (TVI L157)** In the context of the Book of Enoch, this name was prophetically given to the Lord by His Great Grandfathers before Christ even existed. This exemplifies how all things past, present, and future lay before the feet of the supreme deities. These two glorified beings are now enthroned in seats of honor upon the northern slopes of the Mount of the Congregation. Yet, long ago, they

prophesied the coming of the Shining God – the Great Jehovah – the Light of the Multiverse.

Why would the Gods prophesy of Jesus Christ if they had all fulfilled similar missions over prior cycles of salvation? This is a very good question. To me, it suggests that something would happen during the life and ministry of Jesus Christ that would deviate from prior iterations of the heavenly cycle – the War in Heaven.

The War in Heaven is the context from which the Enuma Elish was written. Ea's Firstborn Son was reserved to come forth when He did to overcome the dragon. As far as we know, nothing quite like this had ever happened before. At least, the Enuma Elish gives no indication that anything of the sort had occurred previously. It would seem that the supreme deities foresaw that one of the sons of heaven would rebel and cause one-third of the noble and great ones to rise up with him. These sought to usurp the Divine Kingship and obtain the Highest Heaven through alternate means. A great Shining God would be needed to overcome that threat. Jesus Christ, the Shining God, is so epic in nature that the very Light that shines forth from the Throne of God to fill the immensity of space bears His name – the Light of Christ!

10. **Asaru: Creator and sustainer of all vegetation (TVII L1)** Here we find the root word Asaru, which seems to mean full spectrum light, as it is used in conjunction with the creation and sustaining of vegetation. Christ was commissioned by His Father to create plant life upon the Earth, so we know that this title is literally true. But this name means more than that; not only did He create vegetation, He sustains it.

Vegetation is dependent upon full spectrum light for its survival. Plants actually synthesize light through a miraculous process called photosynthesis. Plants literally store light's energy to enable them to endure long periods of diminished light, and even outright darkness. It would seem that the ancients believed that, like plants, we too should synthesize the Light of Christ into our natures to enable us to withstand the darkness. Unfortunately, those who obtained their records either did not understand them or did not remain faithful to the doctrines they espoused.

11. **Asarualim: He who is honored in the council of the gods, and to whom they hope, He is the Fearless One. (TVII L3)** By the root of the word light in this name, the ancients desired to communicate the Lord's unique nature. We have seen with prior names of this root origin that His uniqueness was prophesied long before He stood before the council of gods. Because of the light that is so

indistinguishable from His nature as to bear His name, primordially He was fearless in the face of any challenge. Yet, the absence of fear is not what made Him great, but rather the absence of darkness within His soul. Even in His darkest hour in mortality, when He felt that both heaven and Earth had abandoned Him, He did not give in to darkness but overcame it, that we might have hope in Him. If this is the meaning of the title Asarualim, then no one is more deserving of it than Jesus Christ!

12. **Asarualimnunna: The Gracious Light of the Father. He directs the decrees of Anu, Enlil, Ea, and Ninigiku. He wears the horned cap and assigns the portions (TVII L5)** With this name, the ancients intended for us to understand that the Light associated with Ea's Firstborn Son came to Him from His Father. Four names are given as the object of His obedience. The first of these four names is Anu – His Grandfather. However, I believe that the next three names are all different cultural names for the same person. The first of these names is Enlil.

Enlil was the ancient Sumerian name for An's royal son and heir. As such, Enlil was the Sumerian equivalent to the Babylonian Ea. Ea is, of course, Marduk's Father. The last name used was Ninigiki, which is the Akkadian name for Marduk's Father, Ea. Therefore, the ancients wanted us to know that while the Lord was obedient to His Grandfather, in His new role, His obedience to His Father was absolute. To me, this suggests the turning of a cycle. The Lord served under His Grandfather, who named Him in the prior iteration of the cycle, but in the present iteration, where He now serves in the role of the Savior, His Father now sits as the supreme sovereign of the Multiverse.

Lastly, the Lord's horned cap, or priesthood right and authority, is mentioned in conjunction with His role of allocating the heavenly inheritances. This means that He holds in His hands the keys to the Igigi's godhood. If the Igigi are to obtain godhood, it will be by obeying His commands with the same diligence that He obeys the commands of His Father. The meaning inherent in these names is astounding and well worth our deliberate consideration!

The previous six names have all been related to the Light of Ea's Firstborn Son. The ancients believed that Light was an inextricable characteristic of the Lord. Note that in the way the ancients used these six titles, the Savior's light is never used for Himself, but always for others. He is the Light of the gods, the Shining God, the Light that restores the lost gods, the Light that gives life to the world, the Light of the Igigi's hope, and the Light of the Father. Each of these aspects mirrors the concept of Christ's Light that was restored through the prophet Joseph Smith. Consider the following passage in the context of the understanding of the ancients:

He that ascended up on high, as also He descended below all things, in that He comprehended all things, that He might be in all and through all things, the light of truth; which truth shineth. This is the light of Christ. As also He is in the sun, and the light of the sun, and the power thereof by which it was made. As also He is in the moon, and is the light of the moon, and the power thereof by which it was made; as also the light of the stars, and the power thereof by which they were made; and the earth also, and power of God who sitteth upon His throne, who is in the bosom of eternity, who is in the midst of all things. Now, verily I say unto you, that through the redemption which is made for you is brought to pass the resurrection from the dead. (D&C 88:6-14)

From modern revelation, we understand that Jesus Christ is the Light of the Multiverse and all things within it. He is the Light of the gods. He is the God who Shines. He is the Light of the world and of all creation. He is a Light to those who are lost and the means whereby they can be created anew. He is the Light of the Father. Therefore, this modern passage of scripture is not introducing new concepts to the world; rather, it is restoring ancient knowledge that had been lost. God the Father has not changed. He is the same today as He was thousands of years ago. Therefore, the knowledge He imparts to His children has not changed. If we seek, we will find, just as wise men through all generations of time have done before us. Let us seek the God who Shines, that His light might fill and renew our souls and cause us to be like Him.

We now move on to the next series of names.

13. **Tutu – The Unequaled Purifier that creates them anew (TVII L9)** The ancients understood that they were experiencing mortality on the most challenged planet in the multiverse, a planet symbolically forged from the flesh of the great dragon itself. This title demonstrates their awareness that, as a consequence of their fallen world, they too would fall. As a result, they had a choice to make: they could join the dead gods at the edge of all things, or they could rely on the merits of the Shining God and become purified and renewed in Him.

This understanding is consistent with the other titles given above. The ancients knew they could not be purified and born again through their own merits but were entirely dependent on Ea's Firstborn Son. It was His redeeming power that gave them hope. Ea's Firstborn was the hope of the gods, and none else. Only He could purify and create them anew. This concept is in perfect harmony with the restored knowledge of Christ's atonement. Yet, as these names clearly demonstrate, this understanding existed long before there was ever a prophet in Israel.

14. **Tutu-Ziukkinna: The Life of the host of the gods, the establisher of the Highest Heaven He will not be forgotten by the beclouded (TVII L15)** Again, we are shown the amazing level of comprehension that the ancient religion had regarding the life and mission of Ea's Firstborn. He gives life to the host of the gods. By this, we understand that while the Igigi were born into the Celestial Kingdom, they could not remain there as spirit children indefinitely. To obtain the highest heaven, one must die and be recreated with a Celestial body. Christ's resurrection is the power that gives life to the gods and establishes them in the highest heaven. This is the only way the Igigi could hope to rejoin the innumerable host of gods, their heavenly parents, who have successfully navigated prior iterations of the Cycle of Salvation.

I find the last phrase, "He shall not be forgotten by the beclouded," particularly interesting. Thus far, all of these titles pertain to the plan of salvation. Therefore, I believe that beclouding speaks of the introduction of the veil to the Igigi. While the veil will cause the children of heaven to forget everything they once knew, the Light of Truth will pierce the veil and enlighten the minds of those who seek Him. In this way, the Light of Truth will resonate in the hearts and minds of the wise, and they will not forget Ea's Firstborn Son. To these, the trinkets and baubles of this world will hold no sway. Instead, they will sell all that they have to obtain the Pearl of Great Price. Jesus Christ is that pearl!

15. **Tutu-Ziku: Bringer of purity and treasures (TVII L19)** The ancients associated Ea's Firstborn with heavenly treasures. The treasure they spoke of was exaltation and eternal life. Christ encouraged His disciples to lay up their treasures in heaven, where thieves could not break through and steal. The original keepers of these sacred truths understood that knowledge of the Father's Hidden Son was the greatest treasure the world could obtain. Without Him, nothing else matters. Compared to the Lord, all else is vanity and will pass away as if it were a dream – like the elusive treasures within a Minecraft chest.

16. **Tutu-Agaku: Reviver of the Dead, He who is merciful to the vanquished gods by removing the yoke from their neck (TVII L25)** From the context of the Book of Enoch and the titles that have come before, the meaning of this name is clear. It refers to the day when the Son of Man will visit those who rejected Him. These will be relegated to the burning mountain range overlooking Outer Darkness. There, because they would not be purified by Ea's Firstborn, they must atone for their own sins. Yet, if not for the Son of God, they would be forever imprisoned in that terrible landscape for all eternity. However, the Son of Man

will not forget them. After ten thousand years, He will come for them and break the yokes from off their necks. When that day comes, all those who rejected the Son of Man will bow the knee, and every tongue will confess that He is the Christ, the Son of the Living God!

17. **Tutu-Tuku: The Destroyer of all the Evil Ones (TVII L33)** This title refers to the destructive power of Jesus Christ. He destroyed the wicked of the pre-diluvian world and saved the righteous. At His second coming, He will do the same. Whereas the destruction of the ancient world came with the baptism of water, the coming destruction will be a baptism of fire. Therefore, this title refers to purity through the purging of the wicked by the heat of the great refiner's fire.

The previous five titles were all given by the ancients to illustrate different aspects of the Son of Man's power to purify. This purification can come through His ability to forgive sins and to recreate the children of heaven anew through the power of the resurrection. Yet, we have also learned that the ancients understood that Christ could purify with His power to destroy as well. In the coming days, Christ will purify the Earth by destroying the wicked through Divine Utterance. On the Great and Terrible Day of the Lord, the wicked will be consumed as they stand in rebellion against Him. In an instant, they will be relocated from mortality to the burning mountain ranges at the end of all things.

There, because they would not be purified by the Lord, they must atone for their own sins in a process that will last for ten thousand years. Yet, eventually, the day will come when the Lord will visit them in their distant prisons. On that day, He will break the heavy yokes of their bondage from off their necks and give them beauty for ashes. That beauty will come in the form of an inheritance beyond their wildest dreams. The Lord will do this because, as these names foretell, He is the generous allocator of heaven's treasures. These titles are an astounding display of the insight the ancients had into the true nature of the Father's Hidden Son! If only the Babylonians understood what it was that they possessed!

We now return to the next series of names:

18. **Shazu: He Who knows the heart of the Gods, sees what is inside, and segregates the wicked from the righteous, that the new assembly of the gods might be established (TVII L35)** It would appear that the title Shazu refers to the Lord's right and ability to execute judgment upon the wicked. This authority will manifest itself in all the derivative names that follow. From this name we understand that His judgment comes in the form of segregation or separation. Given that He knows the hearts of His Fathers and is of one mind with them, His judgments are their judgments. This means that nobody judged by the Son would have been judged differently by His Father. The judgment of the Lord is not rash but is based upon the sum of all the parts. He sees what is within us, the thoughts

and intents of our hearts. Not only this, but He takes into account the innumerable facets and nuances of our mortal bodies.

As we learn elsewhere, He knows our weaknesses because He gave them to us that we might be humble and submissive to His promptings and corrections. As such, the Lord does not punish the children of heaven for the weaknesses that He gave them but instead rewards them with power and appreciation when they overcome those weaknesses through His grace. Yet, there are many who do not sin out of weakness but out of rebellion and desire. These demonstrate that they are not capable of wielding power in their present state of being. Therefore, the Son of Man discerns who to "set up," meaning exalted into the congregation of gods, and who needs further refinement. He judges in perfect righteousness.

19. **Shazu-Zisi: He who banishes the insurrectionists from amongst the gods (TVII L41)**. With this derived title, the ancients wanted to communicate that the Lord was able to execute judgment on the wicked from the very beginning. He demonstrated this primordially when He caused the insurrectionists to be imprisoned upon this planet. In doing so, He isolated Lucifer and his minions from the vast majority of the children of heaven. Revelation twelve states that when this was done, the heavens rejoiced at the separation, for Lucifer and his minions accused them both night and day before the Throne of God.

The flipside of this is that He also judged the Noble and Great Ones and found many who were worthy and able to endure mortality upon Satan's prison planet. Only those whom He judged worthy would join the Firstborn in mortality upon the Dragon's prison planet. These would not overcome the Dragon on their own merits, but through their faith in the Father's Hidden Son.

20. **Shazu-Suhrim: He who roots out the enemies and frustrates their plans, and blots out their names – His ways the gods of the assembly exult (TVII L44)** In this title, the ancients related the Lord's discerning judgment to His ability to easily separate the wheat from the tares, the sheep from the goats, and the wolves from among the flock. To mortal men, the secret combinations and lying works of darkness make it hard to topple the hidden enemies around us. The ancients understood that the Lord had no such limitations. He sees through the lies and deceptions with ease and then blots their names out from the book of life.

Yet the Lord can do these things without malice, for He is slow to anger. Indeed, He does not root His enemies out straight away. Rather, He leaves the tares among the wheat for as long as possible in hopes that they might change and repent, for His arm is outstretched all the day long. However, when the night finally falls, the Lord will not hesitate. When He does, the entire assembly of the gods will acknowledge the wisdom and prudence of His actions, even when their own children are on the receiving end of His divine judgment.

This goes hand in hand with a prior vision of Enoch's wherein he witnessed the divine assembly of the gods before the Mercy Seat pleading on behalf of their posterity upon the Earth. The Lord acted in wisdom and mercy then, and He will do so when the day of the Gentiles comes to an end. You will recall that during Enoch's prior vision, he saw that the Son of Man prohibited the satans from accusing the children of heaven before the Throne of God. He permanently segregated them from the presence of God. Therefore, while the Firstborn will execute judgment upon the wicked, He will also advocate their cause before the Father, for He knows the horrors of Satan's prison planet.

21. **Shazu-Suhgurim: Ensurer of the judgement of the gods, which judgement was given to Him by His Fathers to cut off the progeny of the wicked (TVII L48)** As this title proclaims, the ancients understood that all judgment had been given into the hands of the Son. If the Igigi are to join their fathers among the council of the gods, it is by way of the Son and through no other means. The greatest gift that the multiverse holds is the ability to participate with the Father in the family business. There is no greater work or glory – no greater joy. Thus, the greatest judgment of heaven was to be cut off both root and branch from that potential. This is the point of this title.

The Father will only trust the next cycle's children to be raised by parents who were able to overcome the world through His Hidden Son. By divine design, this gives the next generation the best possible chance of replicating what their fathers before them did. Therefore, only those who found and trusted His Hidden Son, despite the lies and deceptions of Satan, will be entrusted to become heavenly parents and participate in the family business with Him.

22. **Shazu-Zahrim: Lord of the Living- eradicator of all wickedness, including amongst the fugitive gods who hold Him in their shrines (TVII L51)** The ancients wished to communicate that the Lord is able to create a clean and worthy people. Wickedness never was happiness. As man was created that he might have joy, wickedness must be eradicated for such joy to come. So it will be among all those who will be heirs of salvation, which will be all the children of heaven save those few sons of perdition who relish in darkness more than in light. Over the course of thousands of years, the wickedness will be consumed from the natures of the fugitive gods who were relegated to the burning mountains at the edge of all things. When at last they are free from sin, they will receive inheritances of great joy and glory, beyond their ability to comprehend. The inheritance they

will receive from the Lord will dwarf that which they had wrought for themselves.

The last aspect of this title speaks to the reason why the fugitive gods had to endure the long purification process of their own making. This was because they held Christ in their shrines, rather than in their hearts. The ancients understood shrines to be places where the false gods of this world were worshiped. As such, shrines represent the deception and subtle craft of the adversary. Through the adversary's stagecraft, he keeps the masses from accepting the Father's Hidden Son in their hearts. Instead, they house the world's Nehor-type concept of the Savior within the shrines of their own making. It is of this concept that the following passage from modern revelation speaks:

> And the glory of the telestial is one, even as the glory of the stars is one; for as one star differs from another star in glory, even so differs one from another in glory in the telestial world; for these are they who are of Paul, and of Apollos, and of Cephas. These are they who say they are some of one and some of another—some of Christ and some of John, and some of Moses, and some of Elias, and some of Esaias, and some of Isaiah, and some of Enoch; but received not the gospel, neither the testimony of Jesus, neither the prophets, neither the everlasting covenant.
>
> Last of all, these all are they who will not be gathered with the saints, to be caught up unto the church of the Firstborn, and received into the cloud. These are they who are liars, and sorcerers, and adulterers, and whoremongers, and whosoever loves and makes a lie. These are they who suffer the wrath of God on earth. These are they who suffer the vengeance of eternal fire. These are they who are cast down to Hell and suffer the wrath of Almighty God, until the fulness of times… (D&C 76:98-106)

In the passages above, the Lord described the inhabitants of the telestial world as those who rejected the truth for the diverse philosophies of men. Some followed one persuasion, and some followed another. Yet, while their philosophies may have contained varying degrees of light, as one star differs from another star in brightness, none of their man-made philosophies had the power to save them. As such, if Christ was found among their shrines, His true nature was not. Instead, they had fashioned their own versions of Ba'al, as so many before them had done, and worshiped its likeness in place of the True and Living God.

As a result, their beliefs could not save them, and they were left to pay the price for their own sins. According to the Son of Man, people with these kinds of ideas will be the largest contingent of people in the cosmos. You can hold fast to the philosophies of men, or you can hold fast to Jesus Christ, but you cannot serve both God and mammon. Therefore, choose your master wisely!

23. **Shazu-Zahgurim**: **Destroyer of all foes in battle (TVII L55)** The ancients have gone to great lengths to show their nuanced understanding of the Lord's discerning judgment. The last aspect of that judgment seems to refer to His role as Captain of the Lord's Hosts. In the end, it will be the Lord who purges the Earth of wickedness in the last great battle. This He will do with the words of His mouth. When He does so, the curse of the Lord will sweep the Earth like a relentless force, and not one wicked person will be counted among the living.

24. **Enbilulu: The Lord who makes them (the Igigi) flourish and gives them a new name. He instituted the original burnt offerings, and causes the dry places to bring forth water in abundance (TVII L57)** According to the ancients, Ea's Firstborn not only causes the Igigi to flourish but also revitalizes desolate and barren wastelands. Where there is death, He brings forth life. Where there are captives, He brings liberty. Where there is sin, He brings purity and revival. The ancients understood this.

They taught that it was Ea's Firstborn who instigated the first sacrifice. We understand that this sacrifice was to provide a covering for Adam and Eve. In ancient Hebrew, to cover is to atone. Thus, the Savior was both the author and finisher of their faith, first introducing the concept of sacrifice and then offering Himself as a ransom for sin. All this He did so that the Igigi might flourish because of Him.

25. **Enbilulu-Epadun: The Lord who caused things to grow (TVII L61)** With this name the ancients further expound upon the Lord's ability to make things grow. This title focuses upon things that grow from the Earth.

26. **Enbilulu-Ebilulugugal: Gardener of the plantations of the gods. (TVII L66)** The first title in this series demonstrated that the Igigi flourished under the Lord's care. The second title noted that the Lord caused the Earth itself to flourish. This title takes it one step further by stating that He is the caretaker of His Heavenly Father's many mansions. By this, we understand that He is the one who will be handing out the keys to our heavenly inheritances, for into His hands His Father has given all things.

27. **Enbilulu-Hegal: He who heaps up abundance for His people (TVII L68)** The ancients end this series of names with the concept that the Lord causes things to

flourish for the benefit of His people. He delights in blessing and prospering them. This series of titles causes me to ponder upon the following passage:

> I know the thoughts that I think toward you, saith the Lord,
> thoughts of peace, and not of evil, to give you an expected
> end. (Jer 29:11)

Most Bible translations replace "expected end" with the phrase "a future and a hope." This is consistent with the titles that the ancients attributed to the Lord above. He is for us, not against us. He wants us to flourish and to receive a fullness of joy. Nothing would make Him happier than to see all the children of heaven become even as He is. Yet, we must choose for ourselves.

28. **Sirsir: The Horn capped God who defeated the Dragon (TVII L70)** As we have noted from previously discussed titles, the ancients' reference to the horned cap signifies the Lord's divine authority. It is precisely because of His authority that His disciples are able to cast out demons in His name. All things in heaven and on Earth are subject to His authority. Yet, it is His will that we choose for ourselves what we will do. We have this agency because, as this title declares, He overcame the Dragon, who sought to usurp that freedom. Therefore, let us exercise our agency in wisdom, that we might obtain authority, or power, in the priesthood of our own.

29. **Sirsir-Malah: The Dragon Rider (TVII L76)**. This is one of my favorite titles of the ancients. It calls to mind the Lord's conversation with Job, wherein He asked Job if he could play with Leviathan as with a little bird. The implication was that God could and has done so. As such, we may find that Ea's Firstborn Son is a dragon rider in the most literal sense of the word. It doesn't get much cooler than that!

30. **Gil: The Storer of massive mounds of resources (TVII L78)** Again, the ancients are communicating their understanding of the Lord's role as the keeper of the Father's inheritances. Any inheritance that we receive will be at His hand. This concept is further elaborated upon in the next derivative name that follows.

31. **Gilma: The rock upon which heavenly things are built – the hoop which holds the barrel together (TVII L80)** By this title, we understand that Ea's Firstborn is the foundation upon which heavenly mansions must be built. To put it in the words of Helaman, "it is upon the rock of our Redeemer, who is Christ, the Son of God, that ye must build your foundation." It is possible that Helaman's comprehension of these things stemmed from far more ancient understandings contained within the Brass Plates. It is clear that the ancients understood that Ea's Firstborn was the iron band that held the whole plan together. Without Him, everything falls apart. The ancients' understanding of Ea's Firstborn and the vital

role He played is unrivaled in the ancient world. Who else could any of these titles be talking about? Outside of the Son of God, nothing else makes sense.

32. **Agilma: The Exalted One that rips the crowns from off the wrong heads (TVII L82)** This derivative title is the last one in the Gil series. The former titles seem to be related to Ea's Firstborn's ability to secure heavenly inheritances. This last title communicates the opposite: He has the ability to remove authority from those who exercise unrighteous dominion. Lucifer, the Son of the Morning, sought to usurp the Father's throne, to become a supreme deity, and to ascend into the northern slopes of the Mount of the Congregation himself. Yet Christ knew his heart, removed the crown from his head, and cast him down to the Earth. So it will be with all those who exercise unrighteous dominion over the children of heaven.

33. **Zulum: He who allots the heavenly inheritances (TVII L84)** Clearly, Ea's role as His Father's Firstborn and agent was something the ancients felt was important for us to understand. Paul understood this very well and spoke of these concepts in the language of the ancients themselves. Consider the following example:

> Blessed be the God and Father of our Lord Jesus Christ, who hath blessed us with all spiritual blessings in heavenly places [*the primordial assembly of the gods*] in Christ: according as [*God*] hath chosen us in [*Christ*] before the foundation of the world, that we should be holy and without blame before Him in love: having [*foreordained*] us unto the adoption of children by Jesus Christ to Himself, according to the good pleasure of His will, to the praise of the glory of [*Christ's*] grace, wherein [*God*] hath made us accepted in the Beloved. In whom we have redemption through His blood, the forgiveness of sins, according to the riches of [*Christ's*] grace…

> [*God*] Having made known unto us the mystery of His will, according to His good pleasure which [*God*] hath purposed in Himself: that in the dispensation of the fulness of times [*God*] might gather together in one all things in Christ, both which are in heaven, and which are on earth; *even* in [*Christ*]: In whom also we have obtained an inheritance, being [*foreordained*] according to the purpose of [*God*] who worketh all things after the counsel of His own will: that [*you might receive*] the spirit of wisdom and revelation in the knowledge of [*the true nature of the Godhead*]: The eyes of your understanding being [*thus*] enlightened; that ye may know what is the hope of [*Christ's*] calling, and what the riches of the glory of His inheritance [*is*

for] the saints, and what is the exceeding greatness of His power [*for us*] who believe, according to the working of His mighty power, Which [*God*] wrought [*through*] Christ, when [*God*] raised Him from the dead, and set Him at His own right hand in the heavenly *places [the assembly of the gods],* far above all principality, and power, and might, and dominion, and every name that is named, not only in this world, but also in that which is to come: and [*God*] hath put all *things* under [*Christ's*] feet, and gave Him to be the head over all things to the church [*meaning Christ will allocate the saints their respective inheritances Himself*] (Ephesians 1: 3-7,9-11,17-22)

In the passages above, Paul taught the early saints the same doctrines that the ancients embedded within the Enuma Elish. While these astounding doctrines are completely out of sync with the apostate traditions of the ancient world, they are perfectly harmonious with the restored gospel of Jesus Christ. For further evidence of this understanding in the early church, see John 3:35 and John 13:3.

34. **Mummu: Creator and sanctifier of Heaven and Earth who directs the gods (TVII L86)** We have already learned from the prior titles mentioned above that the ancients understood Ea's Firstborn to be both the creator of all things and the means by which they became pure. This title combines these two aspects and presents them alongside His divine right of Kingship over the gods. By this, we are to understand that any God who holds the illustrious title of King of the Gods has likewise been both a creator and a Savior to the previous iterations of the plans that came before.

35. **Zulummar: The God who no other among the gods can match in strength (TVII L87)** This title is meant to communicate the absolute, unquestioned supremacy of Ea's Firstborn among the assembly of the gods. There is no other who remotely matches Him in power. This passage further illustrates that there are gods, and there are Gods. Ea's Firstborn is a Capital God of the highest order, whose coming had been foretold since the days of His Great-Great-Grandfathers. There is nothing ordinary about the Son of God!

36. **Gishnumunab: Creator of all the noble and great ones that live upon the Dragon's prison planet (TVII L89)** From the context of the Enuma Elish, it is clear that Ea's Firstborn did not create the Igigi, but that they are the offspring of the Anunnaki. Therefore, this title is meant to convey the concept of the adoption of the Igigi into the royal line, which can only come through Ea's Firstborn. While the Igigi will always remain the offspring of their heavenly parents, their objective in coming to Satan's prison planet was to become like their heavenly parents. In other words, they hoped to become the begotten Sons

and Daughters of God (see D&C 76:24). Ea's Firstborn is their only hope in achieving this.

37. **Lugalabdubur: The Heavenly King that protects His people from the Dragon, providing safe ground both in front and behind them (TVII L91)** Many scriptures speak of Christ protecting His people from their enemies, both before and behind them. Examples of this concept, as understood by ancient Israel, can be found in Exodus 14:19, Deuteronomy 31:8, Psalm 125:2, and Isaiah 52:12. Jesus Christ confirmed this ancient understanding in modern scriptures as well, such as D&C 84:88 and D&C 49:27.

Thus, in these ancient names, we see relics of the ancient truths that were once known and taught among all the children of Adam but were lost due to the Watchers' corruption and Satan's cunning lies. Yet, for those with eyes to see, even now, the Father's Beloved goes before us and is our rearward. He is on our right hand and on our left. If Christ is with us, what have we to fear? Who can contend with Him?

38. **Pagalguenna: Foremost of all the lords, whose strength is outstanding, who is pre-eminent in the royal household - the most exalted of the gods (TVII L93)** Ea's Firstborn is the Lord of lords and the Father's chosen Heir. For many reasons discussed within these fifty names, no other child of heaven comes remotely close to Him. This makes Lucifer's premortal rebellion all the more audacious. Satan's strategy was cunning, which is why he did not challenge the Son of God outright. Instead, he sought to twist and mold the narrative, as he has so masterfully done here on Earth.

Before Lucifer's rebellion was over, he had successfully swayed one-third of the noble and great ones. He incredibly convinced them to back him rather than the Son of God. Yet, you and I could not be swayed. We knew the Father's Firstborn Son, and our testimonies in Him were unshakable. We knew Him to be the most glorious and righteous being of our generation. The heavenly scriptures, as dictated by the Gods themselves, foretold His coming many cycles before. We knew and believed these things, and we also believed in the words of our heavenly parents who testified to us of Him. As such, Satan's seeds of doubt found no fertile ground within our hearts. Alongside many other faithful, we cast the insurrectionist out through the power of our testimonies in God's Only Begotten Son. May we do the same here once more!

39. **Lagaldurmah: King of the Gods, Lord of the rulers (TVII L95)** Once again, the ancients reiterate the important doctrine of the existing celestial hierarchy

that governs the cosmos. This is consistent with the doctrine found within the ancient Book of Enoch, as we read early in the book's text.

> Lord of lords, God of gods, King of kings, and God of the ages, the throne of Thy glory standeth unto all the generation of the ages, and Thy name holy and glorious and blessed unto all the ages! (BOE 9.4)

We are reminded once again of the title Christ will wear across His chest and thigh upon His Return: "Lord of lords, and King of kings." This part of His title is well understood. However, with this title, the ancients wanted to communicate another important aspect of His divine heavenly authority—His being the Lord of the rulers. I believe we are to understand these things in the context of John's writings, which read as follows:

> [*Christ*] hath made us kings and priests unto God and His Father [*Elohim's Father meaning the line of Capital Gods*] to [Christ] be glory and dominon for ever and ever. Amen! (Rev 1:6)

And

> And [*Christ*] hast made us unto our God kings and priests: and we shall reign on the earth. (Rev 5:10)

In these two passages, John speaks of the future day when the Earth is transformed into the Celestial Kingdom and relocated into the Celestial Realm. In that day, those who have overcome the Dragon through the blood of the Lamb will serve under Christ as kings and queens, priests and priestesses. This is what the ancients meant when they taught that Ea's Firstborn was the Lord of rulers. They were not referring to earthly kingdoms but to eternal inheritances.

Ea's Firstborn will grant kingship through the authority of His own eternal and everlasting Kingship. We read of this transference of power throughout the scriptures. One of my favorite examples is found in the words of Isaiah:

> For unto us a Child is born, unto us a Son is given: and the government shall be upon His shoulder: and His name shall be called Wonderful, Counsellor, The Mighty God, The Everlasting Father, The Prince of Peace. Of the increase of *His* government and peace there shall be no end, **upon the throne of David, and upon His kingdom, to order it, and to establish it with judgment and with justice from henceforth even for ever**. The zeal of the Lord of hosts will perform this.

The Lord sent a word into Jacob, and it hath lighted upon Israel. And all the people shall know, *even* Ephraim and the inhabitant of Samaria (Isaiah 9:6-9)

Isaiah speaks of Christ's ascension to His Father's throne. When this happens, Jesus Christ—the Jewish Messiah—will appoint the House of Israel as the governing body of the multiverse. Through the House of Israel, Christ will order the Everlasting Kingdom. This means that from among the House of Israel, Christ will call and set up kings and queens, priests and priestesses, and allocate the kingdom into their hands. He is the allocator of the inheritances. Thus, we see that those kings and queens set up by Christ will rule and reign in and from the House of Israel forever.

This raises the question: why the House of Israel? From the names reviewed thus far, it is clear that the ancients understood Christ's preeminence was prophesied many generations before He was created spiritually. The Gods knew that a rebellion would occur in heaven and that this rebellion would also be fought on Earth. As the Enuma Elish attests, the ancients understood that Christ would overcome the Dragon both in heaven and on Earth. However, they also understood that Lucifer would not rebel in isolation but would turn a third of the hosts of heaven. Therefore, while Christ overcame the Dragon in both heaven and on Earth, the ancients understood that all of Earth's inhabitants would need to do the same.

Those who do so become the Lord's covenant people and are adopted into the Household of God, thus becoming part of the House of Israel. Therefore, as Christ's heavenly coming was long foretold, so too was the coming of the House of Israel. This is why Christ will organize His heavenly kingdom in and through the House of Israel.

It should be understood that Abraham did not seek this covenant of his own accord. By his own admission, he first read of these covenants in the records of the fathers, which the Lord God preserved in his hands for a wise purpose. When Abraham studied those records, they changed his life and set him on a lifelong mission to obtain the covenants of his fathers. Therefore, while Abraham and his posterity are specifically called out by name and honored for their role in this process, they were only following in the footsteps of their righteous fathers before them.

The frequency with which these incredible doctrines are woven throughout the narrative of the Enuma Elish speaks to the incredible degree of understanding that the ancients had obtained. These righteous followers of Jesus Christ were eventually taken from the Earth, where they continue to this day. In their absence, apostasy crept in, and great truths became hidden relics scattered throughout the ancient religions of the world. Yet, the light of the restored gospel of Jesus Christ illuminates and attests to the incredible knowledge once held by the ancient world. The days are coming, and are even now upon us, when the fullness of the gospel of Jesus Christ will be known in full, rather than in part. When that day comes, we will be surprised how much of this knowledge has been in front of us all along, but we simply did not have eyes to see it, nor the curiosity to seek it.

40. **Aranunna: Councilor of His Father (Ea), creator of the gods (TVII L97)** Wonderful, Counselor, Lord of lords, and King of kings—these titles were pronounced upon Ea's Firstborn Son thousands of years before the Bible was written. Thus, the Bible did not present the gospel to the House of Israel for the first time; it simply restored it once more.

41. **Dumuduku: The Decision Maker (TVII L100)** The meaning here is that the Father has given judgment into the hands of His Son, and His Son will have the final say regarding all aspects of salvation. We pray to the Father in the name of the Son, but there can be no doubt about the source of our salvation.

42. **Lugallanna: Strength of His Grandfather, whose supremacy was prophesied of by His Great Grand Father (TVII L101)** The recurring nature of this theme highlights the importance this doctrine held among the ancients. In light of the restoration, it would be like saying the Holy Ghost held the strength of God the Father and was prophesied of by Elohim's Father before the Holy Ghost came into being. However, these passages are not speaking of the Holy Ghost; they are speaking of Jesus Christ. This indicates that the ancients understood the Godhead itself progressed and advanced as the cycles of salvation progressed and advanced. This is an astounding insight into the ancient doctrine of the Godhead.

43. **Lugalugga: He whose broad wisdom and perception enables Him to liberate all of the captives (TVII L103)** This title seems to be the ancient equivalent to the following passage from Isaiah:

> Shall the prey be taken from the mighty, or the lawful captive delivered? But thus saith the LORD, Even the captives of the mighty shall be taken away, and the prey of the terrible shall be delivered: for I will contend with him that contendeth with thee, and I will save thy children. And I will feed them that oppress thee with their own flesh; and they shall be drunken with their own blood, as with sweet wine: and all flesh shall know that I the LORD *am* thy Savior and thy Redeemer, the Mighty One of Jacob. (Isaiah 49:24-26)

44. **Irkingu: Captor and binder of the Usurper, He that shows the way and determines Kingship (TVII L105)** Clearly, this title refers to the Firstborn's ability to bind Satan. The Firstborn first bound Lucifer to the Earth. Soon, He will bind him for a thousand years. After Lucifer's final rebellion, the Firstborn will bind him for all time and eternity in Outer Darkness. However, this title goes further than establishing the supremacy of Ea's Son over Lucifer. It also implies that He would guide us and show us the way back to the presence of the Father. It will be up to us to choose to follow Him. For those who do follow the Son, this title further attests that the Father has placed into the hands of His Son the sole power to convey Kingship. Thus, if we are to rule and reign in the House of Israel, it will be through Christ.

45. **Kinma: Director of the gods, whose name causes the gods themselves to tremble with fear (TVII L107)** This title continues the theme of the Firstborn's supremacy not just within the assembly of the gods, but throughout the cosmos. The latter part of this name may be confusing for some, who wonder why the gods would fear and tremble at the mention of the Firstborn's name. The first question we must ask is, "Is this true?" I believe that Mormon provides fantastic insight into this question from the perspective of the ancients themselves. Consider the following:

> O then despise not, and wonder not, but hearken unto the words of the Lord, and ask the Father in the name of Jesus for what things soever ye shall stand in need. Doubt not, but be believing, and begin AS IN TIMES OF OLD, and come unto the Lord with all your heart, and work out your own salvation with fear and trembling before Him. (Mormon 9:27)

According to Mormon, the ancients understood that they needed to work out their own salvation through God's Firstborn Son, and that they did so with both fear and trembling. This concept was also taught by Paul (see Philippians 2:12). Furthermore, Mormon admonished us to continue in the ancient tradition and do as they did, with fear and trembling. If God is love, as we are taught to believe, why must we work out our salvation with fear and trembling before Him? This is an excellent question, and its answer is of paramount importance.

The veil enables us to come boldly before the Throne of God because we have forgotten who He is. No one knows the Father's Hidden Son unless the Father Himself reveals Him. The Father does not reveal the true nature of His Hidden Son unless such an understanding is sought. Therefore, most stand behind the veil with only a rudimentary knowledge of the Son of God. Such individuals tend to equate themselves with Him. With this meager understanding, we refer to the Almighty Sovereign and Heir Apparent to the Father's Universal Throne as our brother. This creates a false sense of parity with the Son of God. However, as the Father slowly pulls back the curtain and begins to reveal the true nature of His Son, we become astounded by Him.

This newfound understanding opens the eyes of our understanding, and we no longer harbor any illusions of parity with the Father's Hidden Son. Instead, we become keenly aware of our comparative nothingness before Him. This was the experience that Moses had with the Son, after which he learned that man was nothing in comparison. If you diligently and prayerfully consider the profound doctrines regarding the true nature of the Father's Hidden Son, of which these fifty ancient names but hint, you can begin the process of having the Father reveal the true nature of His Hidden Son to you. Again, this process does not happen accidentally. If you are not seeking to be taught by the Father, you will not be. Conversely, if you want to know the true nature of the Father, He must be revealed to you by the Son. They bear witness of each other, and not of themselves.

Do you recall the admonition to the members of the Church from the incredible letter that was published on the front page of the Millennial Star on April 30, 1853? That letter spoke of the Son revealing the true nature of the Father, but the inverse is just as true. Consider this relevant extract from that letter:

> But it has been decided in the court of heaven [*the assemble of the gods*], that no man can know the Father but the Son, and he to whom the Son REVEALETH Him. Now, has Jesus Christ ever revealed God the Father to you, dear reader? Be honest with yourself, and do not err in your answer to this most important question. However much the Son may have revealed the Father to Prophets, Patriarchs, and Apostles of old, the question still remains in full force — has He revealed the Father to YOU? A revelation to another man is by no means a revelation to YOU!

We have a wonderful example of this in Christ's relationship with His beloved apostle John. No other apostle had the same relationship with the Lord as John. John knew the heart and mind of the Lord in ways the other apostles did not, and the Lord loved him for it, even entrusting His own mother to him as a result. I believe this is also why, among the original twelve apostles, John alone was translated, for he alone understood that feeding the Lord's sheep was of paramount importance to the Lord. John walked daily with the Lord as His friend. He even laid his head upon the Savior's chest during the Last Supper. Therefore, I find the following account very insightful in the context of the current subject matter:

> And after six days Jesus taketh Peter, James, and John his brother, and bringeth them up into an high mountain apart, and was transfigured before them: and His face did shine as the sun, and His raiment was white as the light. And, behold, there appeared unto them Moses and Elias talking with Him.
>
> Then answered Peter, and said unto Jesus, Lord, it is good for us to be here: if thou wilt, let us make here three tabernacles; one for Thee, and one for Moses, and one for Elias. While [Peter] yet spake, behold, a bright cloud overshadowed them: and behold a voice out of the cloud, which said, This is My Beloved Son, in whom I am well pleased; hear ye Him. And when the disciples heard it, they fell on their face, and were sore afraid. (Mathew 17:1-6)

Incredibly, in this account, it is not until the Father reveals His Son that the apostles fall to the ground with fear and trembling. The apostles were standing and talking in the presence of the Lord, Moses, and Elias, even after the Lord had been transfigured. Yet, when the Father opened their eyes to the identity of His Son, they could no longer stand nor even gaze upon their Friend and Savior. The disparity between themselves and the Father's Only Begotten Son was too much for them to bear. They could only rise to their feet after the Father had left, and their Savior and Friend came and touched them, telling them to arise and be not afraid. This is the meaning of this ancient name. The Son of God is Kinma!

46. **Esizkur: He who sits in the temple of prayer, four black-headed ones are among His creatures aside from Him, no god knows the answer as to their days (TVII L107)** This is perhaps the most mysterious title that the ancients bestowed upon Ea's Son. Who these black-headed creatures were and what their role was has never been discovered among extant Sumerian tablets. However, it cannot be a coincidence that the book of Revelation mirrors the Sumerian imagery associated with this title.

The book of Revelation speaks of God sitting within His heavenly temple upon His throne, with the prayers of the saints rising around Him in the form of incense. Before His mighty throne sit four mysterious creatures. John stated that these creatures were hybrid animals, representing component parts of lions, oxen, eagles, and men. Ezekiel also saw similar hybrid creatures created in a similar fashion.

There are no existing Sumerian tablets that describe the physical appearance of the four black-headed creatures that accompanied God's Son. However, based on archaeological digs, Sumerian temples were typically accompanied by impressive Lamassu statues. These statues were hybrid creatures comprised of the same four entities spoken of in the Book of Revelation—a lion, an ox, an eagle, and a man. I find these similarities astounding and impossible to ignore.

What, then, is the meaning of these strange hybrid creatures? Jewish tradition teaches that these creatures correspond with the ensigns borne by the four camps which encircled Israel's first temple. Therefore, these four creatures are symbolic representations of the Lord's people. Is the idea of these four creatures symbolizing God's people consistent with Sumerian religious beliefs? Indeed, it is!

The Sumerians referred to themselves as the black-headed people. I don't believe this had anything to do with the color of their heads. Rather, it had everything to do with proclaiming themselves to be the Lord's chosen people. This suggests that the idea of the Son of God having a covenant and chosen people was well known to the ancient religions of the world. However, from the context of the Enuma Elish, it is clear that nobody knew who or when the Lord's covenant people would appear. I believe this is the meaning of the phrase, "Aside from [the Son of God], no god knows the answer as to their days." Because no one knew when God's covenant people would rise, the Sumerians simply proclaimed themselves to be them.

The concept of these four creatures accompanying the Son of God in heaven, before the world was, suggests that the House of Israel was called and set apart primordially. Bruce R. McConkie taught that this was true. Consider the following extract from his seminal work, *Mormon Doctrine*:

> In the pre-mortal existence, faithful spirits were foreordained
> to be born into the House of Israel and to carry out the Lord's
> work in the latter days. This foreordination is a reflection of
> their faithfulness and valiance in the pre-mortal life.

If this is true, and I believe it is, this particular title suggests that Jesus Christ personally selected the House of Israel from amongst the Noble and Great Ones. According to His supreme intelligence and foresight, He determined when each of us would be born, that we might be able to fulfill our foreordained callings to the fullest measures of our respective creations. Furthermore, according to the Sumerians, not even the gods, or our heavenly parents, knew when we would be sent to mortality, it was Christ alone who decided.

Therefore, consider the lateness of the hour in which you have been called and set apart to come to the Earth and minister to its inhabitants. According to the ancient tradition, the Son of God Himself made this decision. He did so knowing that at this time, you would have the greatest opportunity to understand the fullness of His gospel. Yet, this fullness can only come if we have eyes to see and ears to hear His teachings. As His Father foreordained Him to the Savior of the Multiverse, so He as called us to be saviors on Mount Zion. As with all the titles in this series, the title Esizkur is incredible!

47. **Gibil: He who maintains the sharp point of His weapon, whose mind is so vast not even the gods, all of them, can comprehend (TVII L115)** As I consider this title, I cannot help but ponder a conversation that the Lord had with Abraham, which centered around Christ's intellect. Consider the following conversation in the context of this ancient title:

> And the Lord said unto me [*Abraham*]: These two facts do exist, that there are two spirits, one being more intelligent than the other; there shall be another more intelligent than they; I am the Lord thy God, I am more intelligent than they all. (Abr 3:19)

The Lord is certainly telling Abraham that He is more intelligent than any other child of heaven and may even be suggesting that His intellect exceeds their combined intelligence. Whatever the precise meaning, the Lord's conversation with Abraham certainly validates this ancient title.

48. **Addu: His name covers the sky, and may His roar forever hover over the Earth (TVII L119)** There are many times in scripture where God refers to His judgments as either the roaring of a lion or the roaring of the waves of the sea. This title seems to reference the ancients' understanding that the Lord's power was vast enough to fill the heavens and protect the entire Earth, much like a fearsome lion protects his own. I believe this title may suggest that the ancients understood the epic nature in which the Father's plan would come to its end.

After the millennium, when Satan is loosed from his prison, he will cause the entire cosmos to rebel against the Earth. When this cosmic revolt occurs, Lucifer will bring the heavens against the Earth to destroy it once and for all. However, when that day comes, all the hosts of heaven will hear the terrifying roar of the Lion of Judah. The hosts of heaven will literally dissolve before Him (see Isaiah 34:2-5 and Revelation 20:1-9). This epic, culminating exhibition of the Lord's unrivaled power will hang over the Earth and reverberate through the multiverse forevermore, and it seems the ancients understood that it would be so.

49. **Asharu: He who enables the gods to fulfill the measures of their creation (TVII L123)** The ancients understood that the Lord is not, nor ever will be, an ambivalent or dispassionate observer of humanity. He is involved in the details of our lives. If we seek Him and His wisdom and understanding, He will lead us to complete our missions in life and sustain us until they are complete. There has never been a righteous person who has diligently sought to be instructed and led by the Lord who died before their time or who did not fulfill their mission in life. The Lord prepares the way for His disciples to accomplish the things they are supposed to do, if, and only if, they put their trust in Him and not in man.

50. **Nibiru: He who is the Shepard of the gods, and who upholds the course of the stars (TVII L130)** In the New Testament, Christ is often referred to as the Good Shepherd. According to the ancients, the Lord's primary objective was to lead the children of heaven back to the presence of His Father. If they followed their Shepherd, they would be magnified, becoming like their heavenly parents. Thus, He was Nibiru, the Shepherd of the gods.

After the Igigi finished pronouncing these names upon the head of their Lord and Savior, Ea made one of the most profound statements in the entire Enuma Elish. Here is His profound statement:

> When all the names which the Igigi proclaimed, Ea [*God the Father*] had heard, His spirit rejoiced thus: "He whose names His Fathers have glorified, He is indeed even as I am; His name shall be Ea [*Father*]. All my combined rites He shall administer; all My instructions He shall carry out!" With the title "Fifty" the great Gods Proclaimed Him whose names are fifty and made His way supreme. (Enuma Elish tablet VII lines 137 – 144)

In this epic conclusion, the King of the Gods proclaimed, "He is indeed even as I AM." As such, the ancients would have understood Jehovah's assertion from the burning bush that He was "I AM" very differently from modern man. All those with knowledge of these ancient doctrines would have heard this as Jehovah's proclamation that He was the Son of God, with all the authority of His Father!

It now becomes clear that despite the apostasy present in the Enuma Elish, God spoke to the people of antiquity. They understood many of our doctrines better than we do. The fact that God spoke to the ancient people of Mesopotamia is also evident in the similarities between Hammurabi's code and the Ten Commandments. Hammurabi claimed to have received his code directly from the God of Heaven, just as Moses did!

Therefore, it is clear to me that God has not been a respecter of persons. He has not changed since antiquity—the world's perception of Him has. Yes, the ancient world fell into apostasy and committed innumerable atrocities which they ascribed to Him, but the folly was theirs, not God's. Above all the people of the Earth, the saints of the restored Gospel of Jesus Christ have the ability to understand these ancient truths and see them for what they are. This understanding is not new; we are just opening our eyes to the full measure of their meaning. That meaning is both ancient and incredible! Furthermore, given these names were allegedly proclaimed upon the premortal Savior by the children of heaven themselves, they are particularly relevant for us. After all, we are the sons of God who shouted for joy when the morning stars sang together in praise of the Son of God!

The ancient world clearly deviated from the pure worship of Ea's Firstborn as described by these prophetic names. Eventually, Marduk became little more than the Storm God, one of many in a vast pantheon. However, within the whispering of these fifty prophetic names, we understand that it was not always so, and this is the true wonder of the Enuma Elish. Therefore, I consider these fifty names to be evidence that God has indeed spoken to all nations, and they have written His words.

These fifty names clearly demonstrate that there was a time when these truths were not hidden but spoken of openly and understood broadly. Yet, because of apostasy and the post-Babylonian zeal of Israel's doctrinal police, all references to polytheism were removed from the Jews' scriptures, and much of the understanding of the ancient world fell by the wayside. Yet, the historic censoring of these concepts by the Jews does not make them any less true. It only makes them hidden. Truth is truth, and these things are as true today as they ever have been.

If these things are true, then that truth stems from the ancient truths held by the original church of the Firstborn, as it was known anciently. Those who believed and practiced this religion were eventually lifted up to join the people of Enoch. While most of their records likely went with them, some clearly remained behind, where they were clumsily rewoven into the religious narratives of the post-diluvian world. Yet, we live in the dispensation of the fullness of times, and we know that all truths will be restored in the last days. If you have eyes to see, it is clear that this continual restoration is happening right in front of our eyes. In the days of the three heads of Ezra's Eagle, many ancient truths will be restored. These truths will be revealed selectively and with an agenda that will seek to destroy faith in the Son of God.

However, while the secret combinations of this world have kept certain truths hidden from us, God has placed all truth into the hands of His Only Begotten Son. God the Father will reveal His Hidden Son to all those who seek Him. In turn, the Son will reveal the Father. In this, they are of one heart and one mind. I will close this chapter with a passage that Nephi wrote around the time that the Enuma Elish was at the height of its popularity among the Babylonians. Consider its implications for you:

> I, Nephi, was desirous also that I might see, and hear, and know of these things, by the power of the Holy Ghost, which is the gift of God unto all those who diligently seek Him, as well in times of old as in the time that He should manifest Himself unto the children of men. For He is the same yesterday, today, and forever; and the way is prepared for all men from the foundation of the world, if it so be that they repent and come unto Him.
>
> For he that diligently seeketh shall find; and the mysteries of God shall be unfolded unto them, by the power of the Holy Ghost, as well in these times as in times of old, and as well in times of old as in times to come; wherefore, the course of the Lord is one eternal round. (1 Nephi 10:17-19)

Chapter 9 – The Pride of Babylon

The previous chapter began with Noah witnessing the Son of Man ascending to the Throne of His Father. Following this, I reviewed the Babylonian creation epic, the *Enuma Elish*, which describes the ascension of Ea's Firstborn Son to His throne after He overcame the great Dragon that threatened to destroy the children of heaven. In their joy at their Savior's great victory, the children of heaven proclaimed fifty prophetic names, which I then analyzed in detail. The chapter concluded with Ea declaring that His Firstborn had now become as "I AM." Throughout the chapter, I referenced various ancient religions that shared common beliefs, suggesting their origin in an original source tradition—the pure religion of Adam.

In this chapter, I will further illustrate this concept by examining the fourth chapter of the Book of Daniel. This chapter provides a wonderful example of the interplay between the religious belief systems of Babylon and the pre-polytheistic purging of the Jewish scriptural canon post-Babylon. It offers insightful glimpses into the ancient underpinnings of Judaism.

Daniel rose to prominence in Babylon after receiving the same dream that King Nebuchadnezzar had previously experienced, and he then provided the interpretation of that dream. This is how Daniel prefaced his response to the King of Babylon in that instance:

> But there is a God in heaven that revealeth secrets, and maketh known to the king Nebuchadnezzar what shall be in the latter days. Thy dream, and the visions of thy head upon thy bed, are these: (Daniel 2:28)

After Daniel revealed the King's dream and its meaning, Nebuchadnezzar's reaction was particularly telling, especially in light of the previous chapter. Consider his response:

> The king Nebuchadnezzar fell upon his face, and worshipped Daniel, and commanded that they should offer an oblation and sweet odours unto him. The king answered unto Daniel, and said, Of a truth *it is,* that your God *is* a God of gods, and a Lord of kings, and a revealer of secrets, seeing thou couldest reveal this secret.

> Then the king made Daniel a great man, and gave him many great gifts, and made him ruler over the whole province of Babylon, and chief of the governors over all the wise *men* of Babylon. (Daniel 2:46-48)

The king responded by proclaiming Daniel's God—Lagaldurmah, the thirty-ninth holy name from the *Enuma Elish*—the King of gods and Lord of rulers. He then promoted Daniel to a position of great prominence in Babylon, where he oversaw all the wise men of the kingdom. In other words, Daniel was appointed as the supervisor of all the Chaldean and Sumerian scholars. With such a position of authority and the unquestioned backing of the king, it was clear that Daniel, along with Shadrach, Meshach, and Abed-nego, could correct many of the apostate traditions that had infiltrated the ancient religious practices of Babylon.

The king's vision profoundly impacted him. So much so that he ordered the creation of a great golden image, presumably a replica of the same image shown to him in his vision. Ancient literature refers to similar images as Bel statues, with Bel being the Babylonian name for the Lord—Ea's Firstborn Son. Given the king's recent declaration that Daniel's God was Bel, the King of gods and Lord of lords, this seems to be the most likely explanation for his actions. After all, each chapter in the Book of Daniel is iterative, building upon those that came before.

To honor Bel for granting him an answer to his dream, the king commanded all the citizens of Babylon to fall down and worship the image of Bel whenever they heard music playing. The worship of golden idols was expressly forbidden within the Ten Commandments, regardless of who the image was meant to depict. This is akin to falling down and worshiping an image of the Christus whenever a hymn played. The penalty for not worshiping the golden image was death by fire.

Predictably, the Jews, remaining faithful to the Ten Commandments, refused to bow down to the golden image. The Chaldeans attributed their obstinacy to Shadrach, Meshach, and Abed-nego. Consequently, all three men were cast alive into a burning furnace. This is what happened as a result:

> Then was Nebuchadnezzar full of fury, and the form of his visage was changed against Shadrach, Meshach, and Abed-nego: *therefore* he spake, and commanded that they should heat the furnace seven times more than it was wont to be heated.

And he commanded the most mighty men that *were* in his army to bind Shadrach, Meshach, and Abed-nego, *and* to cast *them* into the burning fiery furnace. Then these men were bound in their coats, their hosen, and their hats, and their *other* garments, and were cast into the midst of the burning fiery furnace. Therefore because the king's commandment was urgent, and the furnace exceeding hot, the flame of the fire slew those men that took up Shadrach, Meshach, and Abed-nego.

And these three men, Shadrach, Meshach, and Abed-nego, fell down bound into the midst of the burning fiery furnace. Then Nebuchadnezzar the king was astonied, and rose up in haste, *and* spake, and said unto his counsellors, Did not we cast three men bound into the midst of the fire? They answered and said unto the king, True, O king.

He answered and said, Lo, I see four men loose, walking in the midst of the fire, and they have no hurt; and the form of the fourth is like the Son of God [*meaning Ea's Firstborn Son – which is who Nebuchadnezzar would have understood the Son of God to be*].

Then Nebuchadnezzar came near to the mouth of the burning fiery furnace, *and* spake, and said, Shadrach, Meshach, and Abed-nego, ye servants of the Most High God [*Zulumar – name thirty-five – He who is above all gods*], come forth, and come *hither.* Then Shadrach, Meshach, and Abed-nego, came forth of the midst of the fire.

And the princes, governors, and captains, and the king's counsellors, being gathered together, saw these men, upon whose bodies the fire had no power, nor was an hair of their head singed, neither were their coats changed, nor the smell of fire had passed on them.

Then Nebuchadnezzar spake, and said, Blessed *be* the God of Shadrach, Meshach, and Abed-nego, who hath sent [*His Son*], and delivered His servants that trusted in Him, and have changed the king's word, and yielded their bodies, that they might not serve nor worship any god, except their own God.

Therefore I make a decree, That every people, nation, and language, which speak any thing amiss against the God of Shadrach, Meshach, and Abed-nego, shall be cut in pieces, and their houses shall be made a dunghill: because there is no other God that can deliver after this sort. Then the king promoted Shadrach, Meshach, and Abed-nego, in the province of Babylon. (Daniel 3:20-30)

After two supernatural experiences with the God of Israel, the king of Babylon clearly equated Him with the Most High God of his own religious tradition—the King of gods and Lord of lords. With these experiences in mind, we now turn to the incredible events of Daniel chapter four. This chapter was not written by Daniel; rather, it appears to be a transcription of a royal decree that King Nebuchadnezzar ordered to be circulated throughout all known kingdoms of the earth, not just his own. This, in itself, is fascinating!

What intrigues me most about the king's proclamation is the insight it provides into the ancient religious traditions of both Babylon and the Jews. After all, while Daniel did not write this proclamation, he included it in his record, indicating that he believed it to be true. You may find that this proclamation mirrors the *Book of Enoch* much more closely than the Bible does in its present altered state. This is the insight into the original ancient tradition that I wish to share. Consider the following:

Nebuchadnezzar the king, unto all people, nations, and languages, that dwell in all the earth; Peace be multiplied unto you. I thought it good to shew the signs and wonders that the High God hath wrought toward me. (Daniel 4:1-2)

From these opening words, we understand that this proclamation will contain Nebuchadnezzar's personal experiences with the High God. This is equivalent to him bearing his testimony to the nations. Note that Nebuchadnezzar does not refer to God as the God of Israel, but rather as the universal High God. This indicates that all the nations of the earth would have recognized to whom the king was referring with this title.

All the major religions practiced in the ancient world at the time of this proclamation were based on similar pantheons centered around a royal line of capital gods from whom the right of kingship was derived. Therefore, all the nations receiving this proclamation would have understood that the king of Babylon was referring to the King of Gods, the Most High, the All-Father—the center of their respective pantheons. One of the primary purposes of the previous chapter was to communicate the ancient world's understanding of that Godhead. Thus, consider everything discussed in this chapter within the context of the ancient writings previously mentioned, including both the *Enuma Elish* and the *Book of Enoch*.

> How great *are* His signs! How mighty *are* His wonders! His kingdom *is* an everlasting kingdom, and His dominion *is* from generation to generation. (Daniel 4:3)

It is clear from the passage above that Nebuchadnezzar is likening the Kingdom of God to the stone cut without hands that he saw fill the entire earth in the last days. Having conferred in council with Daniel for many years, the king would have also understood this from the following perspective:

> I saw in the night visions, and, behold, one like the Son of Man came with the clouds of heaven, and came to the Ancient of days, and they brought him near before Him. And there was given Him dominion, and glory, and a kingdom, that all people, nations, and languages, should serve Him: His dominion is an everlasting dominion, which shall not pass away, and his kingdom that which shall not be destroyed. (Daniel 7:13-14)

In the passage above, Daniel had a dream that reminded him of the *Book of Enoch*. This book prophesies that the Son of Man will descend to Earth in the last days with ten thousand of His saints. He will come from the clouds of heaven to inherit and establish an everlasting kingdom that will remain from that time forth and forever. This is the perspective from which the king was approaching the matter. Now, let us return to his recounting of his experience with the Most High God.

> I Nebuchadnezzar was at rest in mine house, and flourishing in my palace: (Daniel 4:4)

Those familiar with the ancient religions of the world would recognize Nebuchadnezzar's reference to flourishing in his palace as an acknowledgment of being prospered by the hand of Enbilulu—the Lord who makes them flourish—and Enbilulu-Enbilulugugal, the keeper of the heavenly mansions. In other words, the king believed that he and his kingdom were thriving due to the favor of Ea's Firstborn. This reflects the age-old problem of assuming that whatever we are doing is right, regardless of the reality around us. However, the king's reality is about to be altered in a significant way.

> I saw a dream which made me afraid, and the thoughts upon my bed and the visions of my head troubled me. Therefore made I a decree to bring in all the wise *men* of Babylon before me, that they might make known unto me the interpretation of the dream.
>
> Then came in the magicians, the astrologers, the Chaldeans, and the soothsayers: and I told the dream before them; but they did not make known unto me the interpretation thereof.
>
> But at the last Daniel came in before me, whose name *was* Belteshazzar, according to the name of my God, and in whom *is* the spirit of the holy gods: and before him I told the dream: (Daniel 4:5-8)

From the passages above, it is clear that although the king had multiple supernatural experiences with the Lord, he still did not fully understand. By his own admission, he had changed Daniel's name to Belteshazzar, which means "Bel, protect the king." As previously noted, "Bel" means "Lord" and was the typical name used by the Babylonians for Marduk, the Firstborn Son of Ea. Daniel would have also referred to Jehovah as "the Lord."

It is interesting that, despite his prior experiences, Daniel was the last person from whom the king sought counsel. This indicates that the king was living life on his own terms, believing that whatever he did was right. If we are honest, most people would acknowledge that this philosophy tends to be the default state of humanity. Unless God compels us to be humble, many tend to live according to their own wills.

However, when the Chaldeans could not answer the king, he began to realize that, for all their worldly wisdom, they could not replicate the power and authority that Daniel had received from the God of Israel. With this in mind, consider the precise language of the king's conversation with Daniel:

> O Belteshazzar, master of the magicians, because I know that the spirit of **the holy gods** *is* in thee, and no secret troubleth thee, tell me the visions of my dream that I have seen, and the interpretation thereof. (Daniel 4:9)

Notice that the king recognized that the Spirit of the holy gods was with Daniel. This suggests that Nebuchadnezzar was referring to a unified Godhead. From the Babylonian perspective, he understood this to mean Ea and His Firstborn Son. Daniel, on the other hand, would have interpreted this as Elohim and Jehovah, reflecting the understanding that Abraham passed down to his descendants. We know this because Abraham's writings frequently reference "the gods" rather than just Jehovah—whom, according to Abraham 1:16, he had personally met and spoken with. Consider how Abraham began his version of the creation account:

> And then the Lord said: Let us go down. And They went down at the beginning, and They, that is the Gods, organized and formed the heavens and the Earth. (Abraham 4:1)

As Abraham had met and talked with Jehovah numerous times throughout his life, his creation account is very instructive. He speaks of the Earth's creation in the context of the Father and His Son—the Gods. This knowledge was commonplace in the ancient world and was not at all mysterious. It only became so when misguided doctrinal policies edited polytheism out of the Bible after the Jews left Babylon.

The king now shares with Daniel his dream:

> Thus *were* the visions of mine head in my bed; I saw, and behold a tree in the midst of the earth, and the height thereof *was* great. The tree grew, and was strong, and the height thereof reached unto heaven, and the sight thereof to the end of all the earth: the leaves thereof *were* fair, and the fruit thereof much, and in it *was* meat for all: the beasts of the field had shadow under it, and the fowls of the heaven dwelt in the boughs thereof, and all flesh was fed of it.

> I saw in the visions of my head upon my bed, and, behold, a watcher and an holy one came down from heaven; he cried aloud, and said thus, Hew down the tree, and cut off his branches, shake off his leaves, and scatter his fruit: let the beasts get away from under it, and the fowls from his branches:

> Nevertheless leave the stump of his roots in the earth, even with a band of iron and brass, in the tender grass of the field; and let it be wet with the dew of heaven, and *let* his portion *be* with the beasts in the grass of the earth:

Let his heart be changed from man's, and let a beast's heart be given unto him; and let seven times pass over him. This matter *is* by the decree of the watchers, and the demand by the word of the holy ones: to the intent that the living may know that the most High ruleth in the kingdom of men, and giveth it to whomsoever He will, and setteth up over it the basest of men.

This dream I king Nebuchadnezzar have seen. Now thou, O Belteshazzar, declare the interpretation thereof, forasmuch as all the wise *men* of my kingdom are not able to make known unto me the interpretation: but thou *art* able; for the spirit of the holy gods *is* in thee. (Daniel 4:10-18)

It should be understood that the Lord speaks to people according to their own understanding. King Nebuchadnezzar viewed the world from the perspective of the Chaldeans, which is to say the Sumerians. Given that the king had appointed Daniel, Shadrach, Meshach, and Abed-nego to prominent positions in his kingdom, he also understood the world from the perspective of the Jews. Therefore, when the king stated that in his dream he saw a holy Watcher descend from the heavens, he was referencing this concept in the context of the *Book of Enoch*.

Within the *Book of Enoch*, there are both wicked and righteous Watchers. Indeed, after Enoch was translated, he mentioned that his dealings were with the Watchers (see verses 12.1 and 12.2). From Moses 7:30-31, we know that after their translation, Enoch and his people interacted with the mortal inhabitants of all the inhabited worlds of the cosmos. From this perspective, Enoch himself could be considered a holy Watcher, as he was a cosmic shepherd over a cosmic mortal flock. Therefore, when the king referred to a holy Watcher in his dream, I believe this is what he meant.

When the king approached Daniel, in whom the Spirit of the Holy Gods (Ea and His Firstborn Son) dwelt, he did so because he knew in his heart that only Daniel's understanding of these matters was correct. I am sure the Chaldeans provided him with explanations, but the king sensed they were wrong. Thus, Daniel's response to the king will offer critical insight into the original ancient tradition. Consider his words:

Then Daniel, whose name *was* Belteshazzar [*Bel save the king*], was astonied for one hour, and his thoughts troubled him. (Daniel 4:19)

It is important to note the reasoning behind Daniel's astonishment and subsequent troubled thoughts. Through his gift of discernment, he immediately understood the meaning of the king's dream. He was initially shocked because the Most High God was about to strike the king of Babylon with madness for a period of seven years. He then became troubled because he realized he would have to convey this grim message to the king. Given Nebuchadnezzar's tendency to make a spectacle of his enemies, this was not a matter to be taken lightly.

Daniel's response was critical. The king could see the wheels turning in Daniel's mind and understood the reason for his hesitance to share the interpretation. As such, the king offered the following prompt:

> The king spake, and said, Belteshazzar, let not the dream, or
> the interpretation thereof, trouble thee. (Daniel 4:19)

The king is reassuring Daniel not to worry about his reaction; he is more interested in hearing the truth than in political correctness. Emboldened by this encouragement, Daniel responds as follows:

> Belteshazzar answered and said, My lord, if only the dream
> applied to your enemies and its meaning to your adversaries!
> (Daniel 4:10 – New International Version)

> The tree that thou sawest, which grew, and was strong,
> whose height reached unto the heaven, and the sight thereof
> to all the earth; whose leaves *were* fair, and the fruit thereof
> much, and in it *was* meat for all; under which the beasts of
> the field dwelt, and upon whose branches the fowls of the
> heaven had their habitation:

> It *is* thou, O king, that art grown and become strong: for thy
> greatness is grown, and reacheth unto heaven, and
> thy dominion to the end of the earth.

> And whereas the king saw a watcher and an holy one coming
> down from heaven, and saying, Hew the tree down, and
> destroy it; yet leave the stump of the roots thereof in the
> earth, even with a band of iron and brass, in the tender grass
> of the field; and let it be wet with the dew of heaven, and *let*
> his portion *be* with the beasts of the field, till seven times
> pass over him; this *is* the interpretation, O king, and this *is*
> the decree of the most High, which is come upon my lord the

king: They [*the Gods*] shall drive thee from men, and thy dwelling shall be with the beasts of the field, and They [*the Gods*] shall make thee to eat grass as oxen, and They [*the Gods*] shall wet thee with the dew of heaven, and seven times shall pass over thee, till thou know that the Most High ruleth in the kingdom of men, and giveth it to whomsoever He will.

And whereas They [*the Gods*] commanded to leave the stump of the tree roots; thy kingdom shall be sure unto thee, after that thou shalt have known that the heavens do rule. Wherefore, O king, let my counsel be acceptable unto thee, and break off thy sins by righteousness, and thine iniquities by shewing mercy to the poor; if it may be a lengthening of thy tranquility. (Daniel 4:11-27)

Note that throughout Daniel's response to the king, he mirrored the king's understanding of a plurality of gods. It was never "God will do this to you," but rather "They will do this to you." Daniel then states that this judgment will remain upon the king until he knows that the Most High is in control. The title "Most High" itself implies a plurality of gods, over which there is One who presides—the Most High God, the King of the gods.

While the king understood these concepts, he did not live by this knowledge. He acted according to his own will and did not submit to the will of the Most High God. As a result, the Most High was about to teach him a lesson he would not soon forget. This serves as a striking example of Daniel's acknowledgment of polytheism in the Old Testament. The post-Babylonian Jews likely felt they could not edit this particular text because it was an official decree sent out to the entire known world, making it difficult to alter its wording.

The narrative now shifts to the words of a third party, acting as a narrator to describe what happened to the King of Babylon between Daniel's interpretation and its fulfillment. Consider the incredible nature of this narration:

All this came upon the king Nebuchadnezzar. At the end of twelve months he walked in the palace of the kingdom of Babylon. The king spake, and said, Is not this great Babylon, that I have built for the house of the kingdom by the might of my power, and for the honour of my majesty?

While the word *was* in the king's mouth, there fell a voice from heaven, *saying,* O king Nebuchadnezzar, to thee it is spoken; The kingdom is departed from thee.

And They [*the Gods*] shall drive thee from men, and thy dwelling *shall be* with the beasts of the field: They [*the Gods*] shall make thee to eat grass as oxen, and seven times shall pass over thee, until thou know that the most High ruleth in the kingdom of men, and giveth it to whomsoever He will.

The same hour was the thing fulfilled upon Nebuchadnezzar: and he was driven from men, and did eat grass as oxen, and his body was wet with the dew of heaven, till his hairs were grown like eagles' *feathers,* and his nails like birds' *claws.* (Daniel 4:28-33)

In the passage above, the narrator of this account confirms that Daniel's interpretation of the dream was true. Indeed, the narrator wrote that one year after Daniel's interpretation, these things came true. It happened in the very moment that the king was boasting in his own majesty and accomplishments. In an instant, God removed the king's sanity from him, and drove him into the field where he lived in the open for seven years, eating grass like a beast. All those that passed by marveled at this incredible spectacle for themselves. God put it in the hearts of all that this was His will, and as such, none dared to intercede on the king's behalf.

Now, King Nebuchadnezzar concludes with his own personal testimony of the Most High God, it is powerful.

And at the end of the days I Nebuchadnezzar lifted up mine eyes unto heaven, and mine understanding returned unto me, and I blessed the most High, and I praised and honoured Him that liveth for ever, whose dominion *is* an everlasting dominion, and His kingdom *is* from generation to generation: and all the inhabitants of the earth *are* reputed as nothing: and He doeth according to His will in the army of heaven, and *among* the inhabitants of the earth: and none can stay His hand, or say unto Him, What doest thou?

At the same time my reason returned unto me; and for the glory of my kingdom, mine honour and brightness returned unto me; and my counsellors and my lords sought unto me; and I was established in my kingdom, and excellent majesty was added unto me.

Now I Nebuchadnezzar praise and extol and honour the King of heaven, all whose works *are* truth, and His ways judgment: and those that walk in pride He is able to abase. (Daniel 4:34-37)

Was King Nebuchadnezzar prideful? Yes! Did he change? Absolutely. However, his transformation was not easy. Despite numerous experiences, he remained trapped in the pride and apostasy of his time. Yet, in the end, the Lord reached him. If God can change the heart of the King of Babylon, whose heart is beyond His reach?

It's important to note that it's not typical for the Lord to reveal Himself so forcefully in the lives of people. Nevertheless, this was a profound blessing for Nebuchadnezzar, as it transformed his life and turned him to God once and for all.

Chapter 10 - Daniel's Missing Chapter

Before returning to the narrative of the Book of Enoch, I would feel remiss if I did not introduce you to another ancient treasure. This gem comes from the Septuagint. The Septuagint is a Greek term meaning seventy, referring to the approximately seventy Jewish scholars who translated the Hebrew Scriptures into Greek around 300 BCE. The involvement of so many scholars is significant because the Septuagint includes some departures from the Old Testament as it reads today.

One of the anomalies within the Septuagint is an additional chapter in the book of Daniel, known today as Bel and the Dragon. From the prior two chapters, the reader should readily recognize the name Bel as the apostate Babylonian substitute for the Son of God. As such, it should come as no surprise that this chapter deals with another intersection that Daniel has with this apostate concept, this time with Nebuchadnezzar's successor, Cyrus.

I believe the primary reason this chapter was excluded from the modern Old Testament is that it refers to the Babylonians' ancient worship of an actual living dragon. Given that the modern world has taken the position that dragons were not real, it follows that any chapter suggesting otherwise must be apocryphal. As such, in the original King James Bible, this chapter was removed from Daniel and included within the Apocrypha.

With this in mind, I will share this curious chapter as it is found within the Apocrypha. Given the groundwork laid in the prior chapters, it will not be necessary for me to provide a verse-by-verse analysis. Instead, I will reserve my commentary until the end of the chapter. Here is the ancient missing chapter from the book of Daniel; you decide for yourself what you believe.

> 1 And king Astyages was gathered to his fathers, and Cyrus of Persia received his kingdom.
>
> 2 And Daniel conversed with the king, and was honoured above all his friends.
>
> 3 Now the Babylons had an idol, called Bel, and there were spent upon him every day twelve great measures of fine flour, and forty sheep, and six vessels of wine.
>
> 4 And the king worshipped it and went daily to adore it: but Daniel worshipped his own God. And the king said unto him, Why dost not thou worship Bel?

5 Who answered and said, Because I may not worship idols made with hands, but the living God, who hath created the heaven and the earth, and hath sovereignty over all flesh.

6 Then said the king unto him, Thinkest thou not that Bel is a living God? seest thou not how much he eateth and drinketh every day?

7 Then Daniel smiled, and said, O king, be not deceived: for this is but clay within, and brass without, and did never eat or drink any thing.

8 So the king was wroth, and called for his priests, and said unto them, If ye tell me not who this is that devoureth these expences, ye shall die.

9 But if ye can certify me that Bel devoureth them, then Daniel shall die: for he hath spoken blasphemy against Bel. And Daniel said unto the king, Let it be according to thy word.

10 Now the priests of Bel were threescore and ten, beside their wives and children. And the king went with Daniel into the temple of Bel.

11 So Bel's priests said, Lo, we go out: but thou, O king, set on the meat, and make ready the wine, and shut the door fast and seal it with thine own signet;

12 And tomorrow when thou comest in, if thou findest not that hath eaten up all, we will suffer death, or else Daniel, that speaketh falsely against us.

13 And they little regarded it: for under the table they had made a privy entrance, whereby they entered in continually, and consumed those things.

14 So when they were gone forth, the king set meats before Bel. Now Daniel had commanded his servants to bring ashes, and those they strewed throughout all the temple in the presence of the king alone: then went they out, and shut the door, and sealed it with the king's signet, and so departed.

15 Now in the night came the priests with their wives and children, as they were wont to do, and did eat and drink up all.

16 In the morning betime the king arose, and Daniel with him.

17 And the king said, Daniel, are the seals whole? And he said, Yea, O king, they be whole.

18 And as soon as he had opened the dour, the king looked upon the table, and cried with a loud voice, Great art thou, O Bel, and with thee is no deceit at all.

19 Then laughed Daniel, and held the king that he should not go in, and said, Behold now the pavement, and mark well whose footsteps are these.

20 And the king said, I see the footsteps of men, women, and children. And then the king was angry,

21 And took the priests with their wives and children, who shewed him the privy doors, where they came in, and consumed such things as were upon the table.

22 Therefore the king slew them, and delivered Bel into Daniel's power, who destroyed him and his temple.

23 And in that same place there was a great dragon, which they of Babylon worshipped.

24 And the king said unto Daniel, Wilt thou also say that this is of brass? lo, he liveth, he eateth and drinketh; thou canst not say that he is no living god: therefore worship him.

25 Then said Daniel unto the king, I will worship the Lord my God: for He is the living God.

26 But give me leave, O king, and I shall slay this dragon without sword or staff. The king said, I give thee leave.

27 Then Daniel took pitch, and fat, and hair, and did seethe them together, and made lumps thereof: this he put in the dragon's mouth, and so the dragon burst in sunder : and Daniel said, Lo, these are the gods ye worship.

28 When they of Babylon heard that, they took great indignation, and conspired against the king, saying, The king is become a Jew, and he hath destroyed Bel, he hath slain the dragon, and put the priests to death.

29 So they came to the king, and said, Deliver us Daniel, or else we will destroy thee and thine house.

30 Now when the king saw that they pressed him sore, being constrained, he delivered Daniel unto them:

31 Who cast him into the lions' den: where he was six days.

32 And in the den there were seven lions, and they had given them every day two carcases, and two sheep: which then were not given to them, to the intent they might devour Daniel.

33 Now there was in Jewry a prophet, called Habbacuc, who had made pottage, and had broken bread in a bowl, and was going into the field, for to bring it to the reapers.

34 But the angel of the Lord said unto Habbacuc, Go, carry the dinner that thou hast into Babylon unto Daniel, who is in the lions' den.

35 And Habbacuc said, Lord, I never saw Babylon; neither do I know where the den is.

36 Then the angel of the Lord took him by the crown, and bare him by the hair of his head, and through the vehemency of his spirit set him in Babylon over the den.

37 And Habbacuc cried, saying, O Daniel, Daniel, take the dinner which God hath sent thee.

38 And Daniel said, Thou hast remembered me, O God: neither hast thou forsaken them that seek thee and love thee.

39 So Daniel arose, and did eat: and the angel of the Lord set Habbacuc in his own place again immediately.

40 Upon the seventh day the king went to bewail Daniel: and when he came to the den, he looked in, and behold, Daniel was sitting.

41 Then cried the king with a loud voice, saying, Great art Lord God of Daniel, and there is none other beside thee.

42 And he drew him out, and cast those that were the cause of his destruction into the den: and they were devoured in a moment before his face.

There are many important aspects to this story that I would like to comment on, and I will do so sequentially. To begin, the above account highlights some fascinating aspects of human nature that are easy to observe in others but hard to see in ourselves. Consider that there were only three years between the reign of the great king Nebuchadnezzar and King Cyrus. Given Nebuchadnezzar's prominence and his proclamation, Cyrus would have most certainly known about the former king's personal experiences with the Most High God. Yet, it is clear that Cyrus still considered Bel to be the Most High God. How could this have been?

In the prior chapters, I reviewed several ancient records and testimonies that demonstrate just how much knowledge the ancient world once had regarding the nature of the Godhead. Yet, many Latter-day Saints are confused by the clarity that the people of the Book of Mormon had regarding the nature of the Godhead compared to the Old Testament. Honestly, the beliefs of the Book of Mormon prophets more closely aligned with the ancient religions of the world than with post-Babylonian Judaism for reasons that have been discussed. Keep in mind that the same Nebuchadnezzar we have been discussing was literally making preparations to wipe Jerusalem off the map at the time Lehi and his family fled. Nebuchadnezzar ardently worshiped Ea's Firstborn Son; he simply was doing so under the same false pretenses as Cyrus in the narrative above.

This is the second point that I am trying to make. The ancient world, including the Northern Kingdom of Israel and the Kingdom of Judah, had all deviated from the original religious tradition which had been restored through Abraham. However, it is important to understand that the ancient deviations espoused by each of these kingdoms are closely paralleled by a similar apostasy seen throughout modern Christianity today. These ancient sects each held about as much truth as the thousands of modern Christian sects hold today. While this may seem a shocking concept, it is nevertheless true. This is to say that the religious practices of Babylon, Assyria, Canaan, and Sumer were about as related to Abraham's originally revealed religion as Catholicism is to the Restored Gospel of Jesus Christ.

Catholics believe many things that are true, while at the same time they embrace many false doctrines which cause their creeds to be an abomination in the eyes of the Lord. The Lord told Joseph Smith as much in the Sacred Grove. So it was with the religions of the ancient world. Those religions were no more independently developed than were the myriad sects of Christianity. Indeed, one of the most trying aspects of the coming trial of faith will be how closely the coming deceptions will mirror the truth. If it were not so, it would not be possible to deceive even the very elect according to the covenant.

I give it as my opinion that in the coming days, the knowledge and religions of the ancient kingdoms of the Earth will play a very important role. These ancient traditions were close enough to the truth to constantly become a stumbling block for the House of Israel. The House of Israel did not believe that it was in the wrong when it was worshiping after the manner of the ancient traditions of their day because those ancient traditions so closely mirrored their own. Indeed, there are many archaeologists today that believe that Israel simply took the ancient records of Mesopotamia and gave them their own twist.

Hopefully, this explains why it was so easy for Cyrus to mistake the philosophies of men for truth, or why Israel fell so easily into the religious practices of the Canaanites. Each nation of the day believed that theirs was the one true original religion taught by the ancients. This is precisely what happened with Christianity. Regardless of what religious scholars think and say, Christianity did not begin with Christ; it was an extension and fulfillment of a much more ancient tradition that was restored with Abraham.

Yet, the same thing happened with Christianity that happened with the original religious tradition; through apostasy, it divested into many different religious practices, all believing that they are right. Therefore, the true and restored gospel of Jesus Christ should be just as easily reconcilable with the original ancient religious tradition as with the teachings of Christ in the meridian of time, for they are not two separate traditions, but one. However, only those with eyes to see can appreciate this fact. Once seen and understood, the religions of the ancient world fall into place. In my opinion, the Book of Enoch is the bridge.

This brings me to the third point I want to make about the narrative above. From the narrative above, we understand that there was a hidden power structure within Babylon. This power structure had usurped the religion of the people and operated behind the scenes, without even the king's knowledge. This group was a parasite that lived off of the people of Babylon. They were in it for themselves. This hidden aspect of society used stagecraft and its control over the narrative to exercise power over the populace. For those with eyes to see, it was obvious what was happening. However, to everyone else, including the king, it was a ridiculous conspiracy theory right up until the time it wasn't.

It is no mistake that Isaiah used Babylon as the prototype and backdrop for his prophecies regarding the last days. These same forces are at work in America and across the globe. For those with eyes to see, the workings of these secret combinations are as plain as day. For everyone else, it is nothing more than a crazy conspiracy theory. As such, we must learn from what happened in Babylon of old. The people were deceived because they were instructed and guided by the philosophies of men, and not by the true teachings of God.

Do not make the same mistake! Ours is the privilege to be instructed by the God of Heaven. But for this to happen, we must engage in the process. We must ask questions and seek answers. We must ponder in our hearts, acting upon the things we read in the scriptures, and not just going with the flow. Daniel engaged in this process, Nebuchadnezzar resisted it, and Cyrus was oblivious to it. Yet, in the end, these two great kings of Babylon had their eyes opened to the truth. Will the same be said for the Saints?

Next, we come to the dragon. In the prior chapters, I shared numerous accounts that speak of dragons not as mythical beasts, but as real-life creatures. This story is no different. For obvious reasons, it is easier to dismiss these things than to take them seriously. Therefore, let us consider for a moment that this chapter may be revealing a glimpse into ancient history as it really was, rather than as we perceive it to be.

Regardless of your personal opinion on the matter, in the narrative of the story, the Babylonians revered this dragon and even considered it to be a god. Furthermore, dragons played an important role in Babylon, not the least of which was Marduk's victory over the dragon. The mušḫuššu dragon adorned the great Ishtar Gate, which was spoken of in Volume I of this series, serving as the gateway into Babylon.

Somehow, Daniel understood that if the dragon ate a mixture of pitch, fat, and hair, it would burst. Why this was the case may be similar to documented accounts of certain animals bursting after eating calcium carbide. How Daniel came to understand such things may be traceable back to his Chaldean education. Regardless, this is another curious and noteworthy ancient account wherein dragons are discussed.

The last item of import is this version of the lion's den story. It is quite different from the regular account. Not only does this account attribute Daniel's being cast into the lion's den to killing the dragon, but it also speaks of the physical transduction of Habakkuk through the power of God from one location to another. This seems to be similar to Nephi being carried throughout the Americas by the Spirit to call its inhabitants to repentance.

All said, this is a very curious account, to say the least. It was provided by a quorum of seventy ancient Jewish Elders from Alexandria. Alexandria would become the world's greatest repository of ancient knowledge. The Septuagint would go on to become the de facto book of scripture for the early Christian church. The Masoretic Text would not provide an alternative narrative to this account for another thousand years, between 700 AD and 1000 AD. As such, this chapter should give the reader much food for thought. Regardless of your personal opinions on the matter, I have a feeling that the events of the ancient world are about to become very relevant once more! As such, ponder these things and come to your own conclusions. Doing so is a very healthy exercise.

Chapter 11 – The Classes of Heavenly Beings

In the previous chapters, I examined numerous examples of ancient texts. The purpose of this review was to illustrate how the Book of Enoch connects the original religious traditions of our forefathers with the restored gospel of Jesus Christ. The gospel did not begin with Abraham; rather, the ancient covenant and tradition were renewed through him. His understanding of the ancient world is evident in his creation account, where he consistently refers to the Gods.

I also shared these ancient accounts to highlight the similarities among the ancient apostate religions of the world. Just as many Christian denominations today claim to be rooted in the original apostolic tradition, I believe the ancient religions would assert their foundation in the original religious tradition of Adam. All of the world's ancient civilizations were built upon a similar tradition of an ascendant Son destined to inherit His Father's throne. This polytheistic tradition was widespread in Judaism but was largely purged after the Babylonian Exile by overly zealous doctrinal enforcers. The Book of Mormon reflects the polytheism of Israel before its apostasy and the subsequent overcorrection by its misguided leaders.

In this chapter, Noah will significantly expand upon the demographics of the cosmos. To fully appreciate Noah's teachings, let us revisit the last three verses that led us down the rabbit holes of the original ancient religious tradition.

> **61.6**. And all who dwell above in the heaven received a command and power and one voice and one light like unto fire.

> **61.7**. And that One [*the Son of Man*] with their first words they blessed, and extolled and lauded with wisdom, and they were wise in utterance and in the spirit of life.

> **61.8**. And the Lord of Spirits placed the Elect One on the Throne of Glory and He shall judge all the works of the holy above in the heaven, and in the balance shall their deeds be weighed.

These verses begin by referencing all who dwell above in "the heaven," as opposed to "all who dwell above in heaven." While this may seem like a minor distinction, it is significant. The Book of Enoch clearly illustrates that the multiverse is far more diverse and rich in its demographics than most realize. By mentioning those who dwell in "the heaven," Noah is referring to the realm where God and the Elect One reside. In the language of the restoration, this corresponds to the Celestial Kingdom. It appears that Noah is specifically addressing the new generation of gods and the new voices they have received.

Noah describes them as having received one voice, which suggests they possess the One Voice that commands all things and to which all must obey. This incredible power is known as Divine Utterance. We see this in the account of Ea's Firstborn Son, who used Utterance to bring forth a holy garment. With the power of Divine Utterance, the gods need only speak, and it is done, as evidenced in Abraham's creation account in the fourth chapter of his writings. The implication that these gods are newly resurrected is supported by Noah's statement that they praised His Son with their first words.

To recap, in this series we have explored Uppercase Gods, lowercase gods, and the children of heaven who chose to participate in mortality to become like their heavenly parents, as well as those who opted not to risk losing what they had obtained. We have also learned about the existence of other intelligent beings apart from humanity and the roles they will play.

It is essential to recognize that there is purpose in the tremendous diversity of the cosmos. One of these purposes is to provide opportunities and choices. Just as it can be challenging in mortality to maintain perspective amidst countless distractions, so it is in heaven. There have always been, and will always be, wonderful diversions throughout the multiverse. The cosmos is filled with wonder and awe. Even before the worlds were created, many, like the Lady, were captivated by such things. To illustrate this point, consider the following:

> And this is the manner after which they were ordained—being called and prepared from the foundation of the world according to the foreknowledge of God, on account of their exceeding faith and good works; in the first place being left to choose good or evil; therefore they having chosen good, and exercising exceedingly great faith [*in pre-mortality*], are called with a holy calling, yea, with that holy calling which was prepared with, and according to, a preparatory redemption for such.

And thus they have been called to this holy calling on account of their faith, while others would reject the Spirit of God [*such as Lucifer and the Lady*] on account of the hardness of their hearts and the blindness of their minds, while if it had not been for this they might have had as great privilege as their brethren.

Or in fine, in the first place they were on the same standing with their brethren [*that is to say all the children of heaven were on the same standing*]; thus this holy calling being prepared from the foundation of the world for such as would not harden their hearts, being in and through the atonement of the Only Begotten Son, who was prepared— And thus being called by this holy calling, and ordained unto the high priesthood of the holy order of God, to teach His commandments unto the children of men, that they also might enter into His rest—

This high priesthood being after the order of His Son, which order was from the foundation of the world; or in other words, being without beginning of days or end of years, being prepared from eternity to all eternity, according to His foreknowledge of all things (Alma 13:3-7)

I am continually amazed by the passages above; they convey these truths so clearly. As spirit children, we were all on equal footing, raised by loving heavenly parents who overcame the challenges of mortality through the grace and atonement of Uppercase Gods. When faced with the many cosmic distractions in heaven and on earth, some chose the better part, guided by the Holy Ghost. These individuals caught the vision of their parents, while others were sidetracked by the endless allurements of an infinite multiverse.

Just as I hope each person reading this book is doing so of their own free will, we chose to come to Satan's prison planet of our own volition. We began this journey with the end in mind, seeing in our parents the future we desired for ourselves. Thus, we were true and faithful above, hoping to replicate that faithfulness here below. Through our faith in God's Only Begotten Son, we distinguished ourselves from our peers through our obedience, rising to positions of leadership in the primordial Church of the Firstborn. The leaders of that ancient faith were known as the noble and great ones, and it was within their ranks that rebellion occurred, leading to the casting down of the anarchists.

Many in heaven watched from the sidelines, not participating. We would have surely tried our best to persuade the Lady and others like her to make better choices and be more valiant in their testimonies. Yet, the Great God of Heaven values agency and self-determination above all else. Our choices have shaped our current circumstances and those of others. We have arrived at this point because we have followed the Father's Hidden Son and strive to make and keep sacred covenants with Him. These covenants are the saving ordinances that can only be obtained and maintained through the constant guiding influence of the Holy Ghost.

This brings us to the next passage in the Book of Enoch, which discusses the great day of judgment. As we read these remarkable passages, I encourage you to take note of the various groups described by Noah, for not all those mentioned are created in the image of God. Consider the following:

> **61.9**. And when He shall lift up His countenance to judge their secret ways according to the word of the name of the Lord of Spirits, and their path according to the way of the righteous judgement of the Lord of Spirits, then shall they all with one voice speak and bless, and glorify and extol and sanctify the name of the Lord of Spirits.

The passage above describes the judgment of the Son as He takes His place upon the throne of His Father. When that day arrives, the heavens will resound with praise for the wonder and majesty of God the Father. Having completed His service to humanity, He is ready to assume His seat of honor on the Northern Face of the Mount of the Congregation. This will be a time of tremendous celebration, marking the great turning of the celestial wheel. As Noah continues his vivid account of this monumental changing of the guard ceremony, which will be the greatest in billions of years, pay attention to the three specific categories of beings invited to this joyous heavenly celebration.

> **61.10**. And He [*God the Father*] will summon all the host of the heavens, and all the holy ones above, and the host of God, the Cherubic, Seraphin and Ophanim, and all the angels of power, and all the angels of principalities, and the Elect One, and the other powers on the earth and over the water.

> **61.11**. On that day shall raise one voice, and bless and glorify and exalt in the spirit of faith, and in the spirit of wisdom, and in the spirit of patience, and in the spirit of mercy, and in the spirit of judgement and of peace, and in the spirit of goodness, and shall all say with one voice: "Blessed is He,

and may the name of the Lord of Spirits be blessed for ever
and ever."

God the Father will summon all the hosts of heaven to witness His Only Begotten Son's ascension to the Throne of Glory. In my opinion, this grand changing of the guard will not occur until all the work of this cycle has been completed. The final great work will be the redemption of the hosts of heaven, who will have atoned for their own sins in the fiery mountain range overlooking outer darkness at the end of all things. As we have learned, the days will come, after ten thousand years, when the Son will reclaim the spirits that rejected Him and His Father. They too will lend their voices in praise and honor, for every knee will bow, and every tongue will confess that He is the Christ, worthy of His Father's Throne.

Among the hosts of heaven, there are numerous classes of beings identified as separate from the sons and daughters of God. Noah describes some of these as the Holy Ones, while others are referred to as angels—servants of God. There are also angels of power and angels of principalities. Additionally, three other classes of beings are highlighted: the Cherubim, Seraphim, and Ophanim.

I will outline the differences among these categories of beings. You may recall that the Father and Son have promised to endow all that they have upon those who inherit the highest degree of glory in the Celestial Kingdom. What does this mean? The Father has much to bestow: kingdoms, thrones, powers, principalities, dominions, exaltations, and eternal lives. Those who receive such an extraordinary inheritance are magnified to such a degree that they are not merely angels, but gods. Yet, Noah speaks of both angels of power and angels of principalities, indicating that these angels serve the gods and are honored to do so.

It is possible that angels of principalities and angels of power represent different classes of servants assisting the gods, who have received far greater exaltation than they. After all, even the angels of the Telestial Kingdom are described as servants of God. Time will reveal their identities. The primary focus of this chapter will be on the other categories of beings identified by Noah: Cherubim, Seraphim, and Ophanim.

From the context of the scriptures, it is clear that Cherubim and Seraphim are glorified living creatures of tremendous power and light. However, Ophanim may be less familiar to many. The term Ophanim, also spelled Ofanim, or Ophannin comes from the Hebrew word meaning "wheels." It seems to refer to objects infused with spiritual intelligence to the point of sentience. For example, the crafts upon which the warriors from the Lost Ten Tribes will return are described as Ophanim in the original Hebrew text of Ezekiel chapter one.

All three of these creations are associated with stewardship, safeguarding, and protection. Cherubim and Seraphim are described as standing guard in the courts of God. Furthermore, a Cherubim and "a flaming sword that turned every way" were sent by Jehovah to guard the Tree of Life. We often overlook this detail, but the sword in this passage is a separate entity from the Cherubim, capable of protecting the Tree of Life on its own, turning "every way" by its own accord.

I believe the Flaming Sword falls into the category of Ophanim. Such creations seem to possess the ability to deter even powerful heavenly beings, which is significant. If you are familiar with the *Way of Kings* series, the Flaming Sword resembles Sword-Nimi, a sentient sword capable of consuming spiritual energy. Whatever Seraphim, Cherubim, and Ophanim are, they are neither human nor created in the image of God; they are something entirely different.

You may recall from volume II of this series that Joseph Smith taught that the multiverse is filled with sentient lifeforms beyond our comprehension. Consider the following to refresh your memory about Joseph's specific teachings in this regard:

> The beasts which John saw and speaks of being in heaven, were actually living in heaven, and were actually to have power given to them over the inhabitants of the earth, precisely according to the plain reading of the revelations. **I give this as a key to the elders of Israel. The independent beast is a beast that dwells in heaven, abstract from the human family...**
>
> I suppose John saw beings [*throughout the multiverse*] of a thousand forms, that had been saved from ten thousand times ten thousand earths like this, --strange beasts of which we have no conception: all might be seen in heaven. **The grand secret was to show John what there was in heaven**. John learned that God glorified Himself by saving all that His hands had made, whether beasts, fowls, fishes or men; and He will glorify Himself with them.
>
> Says one, "I cannot believe in the salvation of beasts." Any man who would tell you that this could not be, would tell you that the revelations are not true. (TPJS 287-294)

In the passage above, Joseph Smith expressed his understanding that there are thousands of forms of sentient beings from countless worlds throughout the cosmos that can be saved and exalted in the court of God. Just as Cherubim and Seraphim are exalted creatures outside the human family, we must assume there are many others as well. According to Joseph Smith, any sentient being can obtain exaltation through the atonement of Jesus Christ if they choose to do so.

I believe these classifications of sentient beings are broad enough to include members of the Leviathan family, with whom the Lord specifically stated He had covenanted. Therefore, salvation must necessarily be available even to the race of creatures from which the companion of the Antichrist will come—if they choose to seek it.

I would argue that salvation would not be withheld from the Lady's black servants with glowing red eyes, provided they repent and choose to follow Jesus Christ. After all, above all else, God honors and venerates the gift of self-determination through personal agency. All sentient beings are free to choose to follow God or reject Him. Our opinions and prejudices on such matters hold little weight. This seems to align perfectly with what the Lord intended when He gave the following commandment as part of the restoration:

> Go ye into all the world, preach the gospel of to every [*sentient*] creature that cometh under the sound of your voice. D&C 68:8

These passages should dispel the misguided notion that humans are the only intelligent species in the multiverse. While humans were created in the express image of God, this does not preclude the Great Creator from having fashioned other intelligent life forms, potentially of equal or even greater intelligence. If such beings fulfill the measure of their creation, why would God withhold His blessings from them? It is naive to believe that just because something is not human, it cannot serve and honor the Lord or have its own hopes and aspirations.

Some people foolishly presume that if they have not encountered something before, it cannot exist. Such is the folly of humanity. We often consider ourselves wise, yet we know no more about the cosmos than a babe in its mother's lap. Therefore, readers of this book should not be shocked or lose their faith if they encounter such creatures—whether for good or evil—within their lifetime. The universe is teeming with life in all its forms. We are far from cataloging all life on our own planet, let alone the vastness of space. Given the reality of countless worlds, it seems improbable to think of a creature that does not already exist in some form somewhere in the cosmos.

Just as Seraphim, Cherubim, and Ophanim are described as present in the courts of God, I suspect they are also scattered throughout the other kingdoms of glory. Indeed, it is entirely possible that, just as the Lady opted out of participating in the Father's plan, many other spiritual beings may have chosen to do the same. Such beings might be allowed to influence their mortal peers in the same way the Lady has influenced us. After all, there must be opposition in all things.

If we were to visit a zoo within the City of Enoch, we might encounter wonders that would astonish us. Diversity is the spice of life, and life throughout the multiverse is undoubtedly more varied than we currently acknowledge. Now, let us return to the intriguing class of beings known as the Ophanim.

For whatever reason, when William Tyndale and others translated the Bible into English, they chose to leave some words in Hebrew, such as Cherubim and Seraphim, while translating others, like Ophanim, into English. This practice has diminished our awareness of the Ophanim as a distinct category of sentient beings. As mentioned earlier, Ophanim is typically translated as "the Wheels." These remarkable Wheels have been discussed throughout these volumes, yet never as a category of sentient beings, as is now suggested within the context of the Book of Enoch.

Consider, therefore, that the Ophanim, as described in the first and tenth chapters of Enoch's writings, are said to have spirits. Reflect on the description of these living wheels in this new light.

> And when the living creatures went, the wheels [*Ophanim*] went by them: and when [*Israel's warriors*] were lifted up from the earth, the wheels were lifted up. Whithersoever the spirit was to go, they went, thither *was their [meaning the Ophanim's]* spirit to go; and the wheels were lifted up over against them: for the spirit of the living creature was in the wheels. When those went, *these* went; and when those stood, *these* stood; and when those were lifted up from the earth, the wheels were lifted up over against them: for the spirit of the living creature *was* in the wheels. (Ezekiel 1:19-21)

We must recognize that Ezekiel was not fabricating these visions; he truly saw them and received understanding through the Spirit of God. The Spirit revealed to Ezekiel that the Ophanim he witnessed were very special, possessing spiritual sentience that enabled them to interact with the House of Israel in extraordinary ways. Indeed, Ezekiel understood through the Spirit that the House of Israel was not merely driving the Ophanim, as one would drive a car. Instead, the Ophanim worked in harmony with the House of Israel, obeying the commands of the Almighty.

This leads me to believe that the Ophanim were created by God, not by man. Therefore, the manner in which God creates becomes paramount. Consider the following passage that describes God's creation process:

> But remember that all My judgments [*works*] are not given unto men; and as the words have gone forth out of My mouth even so shall they be fulfilled, that the first shall be last, and that the last shall be first in all things whatsoever I have created by the word of my power, which is the power of my Spirit. For by the power of My Spirit created I them; yea, all things both spiritual and temporal— First spiritual, secondly temporal (D&C 29:30-32)

And

> I the Lord God, created all things spiritually before they were naturally upon the face of the Earth. (Moses 3:5)

These two passages teach us, first, that we do not know everything the Lord has done, and we should not presume that we do. Secondly, when the Lord creates, He does so first spiritually and then physically. In contrast, human creations are typically physical only. However, as humanity begins to work with artificial intelligence, we are starting to embed it within our physical creations. The Lord has clearly taken things to a different level with the Ophanim. If He created the Ophanim, He first made them with a spiritual aspect, followed by a physical one.

The Liahona serves as a perfect example of this principle. The Book of Mormon teaches that the Liahona was made by God Himself, meaning He would have created it first spiritually and then physically. This explains the Liahona's spiritual sensitivity, as it functioned in accordance with the spiritual status of Lehi's family. When Nephi needed food, it pointed him in the direction to find it. When they needed to travel, it guided them, provided they were keeping the commandments of God.

As humanity continues to embed artificial intelligence into our creations, we draw closer to understanding the incredible capabilities of the Lord's workmanship. Alma, who possessed the Plates of Brass, the Sword of Laban, and the Liahona, described the Liahona to his son in this way:

> And now, my son, I have somewhat to say concerning the thing which our fathers call a ball, or director—or our fathers called it Liahona, which is, being interpreted, a compass; and the Lord prepared it. And behold, there cannot any man work

after the manner of so curious a workmanship. (Alma 37:38-39)

While the Liahona may not be classified as a "Wheel," I believe it can be seen as a sentient object of divine design, similar to the Ophanim and the Flaming Sword we discussed earlier. This idea might seem fanciful to some, but humanity's advancements in artificial intelligence are making it increasingly plausible. As you consider this topic, it's worth reflecting on the experiences of David Adair.

David Adair is a mathematical savant with a photographic memory. At just fifteen years old, his high school math teacher took some of his work to a local university, where it was recognized as remarkably similar to a complex problem Stephen Hawking was tackling at Cambridge. As a result, David was flown out to meet Hawking. When he entered the hall where Stephen was working, he saw numerous chalkboards filled with formulations similar to his own. Curious, he asked Stephen how he had obtained his private work. Stephen replied that no one had; the work on the boards was his own.

To Stephen's astonishment, David approached one of the chalkboards and began erasing parts of Hawking's computations. As a fifteen-year-old, he confidently told him, "You're doing it wrong," and proceeded to correct the formulations. Shocked, Stephen asked how David knew it was incorrect. David explained that he had been working on a rocket design based on those same formulations, claiming that the plans for his rocket engine had come to him in a series of consecutive dreams. To David's surprise, Stephen revealed that he too received his formulations through dreams, leading to a friendship between the two.

Thanks to his remarkable intellect, David applied for and received a government grant to build a rocket engine based on his designs. He claimed to have completed the first prototype by the age of 17. According to David, the engine he built was an electromagnetic fusion containment engine capable of accelerating from 0 to 8,654 miles per hour in just 4.1 seconds. The rocket was designed to be controlled by radio signals. A local newspaper published a story about David's rocket, which has been included below.

David Adair, 17, wins Air Force certificate for rocket project

Centerburg High School's rocket expert David Adair, 17, received a U.S. Air Force award at the 10th annual Central Ohio Regional Science Fair Friday and Saturday at Otterbein College.

Adair's entry was a 10-foot-tall rocket.

He improvised parts from automobiles and other equipment to construct the engine located inside the slim red, white and blue rocket.

The certificate given the high school junior says his exhibit "has been selected as the most outstanding in the field of engineering sciences."

Officials of the Center of Science and Industry in Columbus asked Adair to exhibit his rocket during the month of June.

Adair has named his rocket Pitholem, a Greek word which means center of energy.

Only 90 of the top student projects in Central Ohio had been selected for display and judging.

David claimed he could land his rocket anywhere for which he had coordinates. To test this ability, he was given the coordinates of a military testing ground in a remote area of Nevada, which he later learned was called Area 51. He successfully launched his rocket to the specified coordinates and was then escorted to the base to retrieve it.

Upon his arrival, David recounted that the government transported him in a golf cart to an underground facility. There, he entered a large room illuminated by arched lighting designed to eliminate shadows. In the center of the room stood a massive engine, larger than a school bus, resting on an elevated platform. The men present invited David to inspect this impressive engine. Here's how David Adair described his experience in his own words:

> It was an engine about the size of a school bus. This engine was a much larger version of the engine that I had built. It was also an electric magnetic fusion containment engine but was much more powerful than mine. My was like a Model A and this was a Ferrari. But they were both the same engine breed.
>
> This engine had been damaged right in the center of its core. In the type of configurations we built we have dual particle accelerators that caused the fusion reaction right in the center of these accelerators. I called that area the eye of the

186

hurricane, and it is like an infinity patter figure or a figure eight right in the center. This particular engine had a hole right there about four feet in diameter. That was the first thing that I noticed. The men that I was with asked me to look at it and describe to them how I thought that it functioned.

I asked them, "how come I'm telling you about your engine?" They said that the engine was from a project they were working with but that they were not sure how everything functioned. They said the personnel that were work on it in the past were not there anymore. They asked if I could help them out a little bit. Being seventeen years old at the time, they thought I didn't pick up on too many adult innuendos. But I was born old, and I knew exactly what they were doing.

So I said: "Fine, yeah, I'd be glad to help my county". So I played along. I asked if I could walk up to it. They said: "Sure, as a matter of fact you can climb on it if you want to". So I got up to the engine and then I noticed the alloys of the engine themselves had a sheen of color. It looked like an iridescent color, like when you hold a compact disk to the sun and you see the rainbows. Imagine those kinds of colors covering this entire engine. It was glowing in colors like that. It was really pretty. The color of the engine was unlike any metal or alloy that I was familiar with.

When I walked up to the engine my body made a shadow on the engine. Now the engine was in a room that was built to eliminate shadows. I saw my shadow on the engine, but not on the platform next to it. So I thought that the engine was picking up the heat radiation off of my body. So I backed away from it and the shadow dissipated. When I walked back up to it the shadow reappeared.

So then I put my hands on the engine to pull myself up on top of it, and that is where it got really interesting. The alloys were in some places so thin it was translucent. You could see through it like it was a sheet of amber. When I laid my hands on it, a really interesting swirl pattern came off from where my skin was touching the engine. The patterns swirled out through the metal and went out into the gallery around me. I did not know of any metal that could do that. So I thought, "How this could be so heat sensitive to pick up my body's heat waves and emulate them like that?"

Then I crawled up onto it and the patterns were really neat looking, like smooth waves flowing off of my hands. So I pulled myself up on the engine and started walking over it. It was huge and was radically different than my engine. The way they ran the fusion flows was the way you would run fuel in a fuel line. This thing was totally different. There was no wiring.

My engine was covered in four miles of wiring so I could get all the firing orders right for the particle accelerations. When I put my hands on it, it felt so different. It felt like a frog belly. It looked wet, but it wasn't wet. It was so slick looking but it wasn't slick. It was just amazing. It had such a texture and as soon as you touched it, it became your same temperature instantly, despite the cold temperature of the room. I didn't know of any alloy that could do this.

So I started going, "Oh, this is may not be from around here." So I am walking down the engine, and I go up to where the main core cells are, and the particle accelerators. This was where there was a hole blown out there. I stepped down into it just to get a better look. Now I am down in the hole in the engine and the walls are really smooth.

The temperatures in my electromagnetic fusion contained engine run at a hundred million degrees centigrade. They operate on plasma physics. So whatever caused the containment field to collapse in this engines caused its alloys to be exposed to those kinds of temperatures which vaporized them. However, the reaction must have been shut off within nanoseconds which limited the blast diameter to only four feet and stopped. But what was interesting was that where the engine's metal was torn, you could rub your hand over the jagged torn areas, but they would not cut your because it was more like flesh being torn, rather than metal.

Well, when I came up out of the hole and stood back on top of the engine I had enough of what I thought was going on that I turned around and said: "About this firing system here." And they said: "Yeah, where is the firing system?" I started to tell them, and then I said, "Why am I telling you about your own firing system? If all of this is yours. This isn't from here or anywhere in the area is?". Then I said: "I am assuming that this engine came out of a craft. A big one. By the size probably three hundred feet plus - the length of the football field. It must have had occupants. What have you done with them?"

Well that was the wrong thing to say. They jumped up on the engine and told me it was time to leave. Well, when I bent down to get off the engine, and placed my hands back on the engine something interesting happened. Instead of the nice smooth wave lines, the patterns now looked like small tornadoes coming off all of my finger tips and moving through the metal. I pulled my hands back from the engine and it started to calm down a bit.

Then I realized what this thing really was. They grabbed hold of me, the Air Force guys, and we got back into the golf cart and rode back up to the surface. As I sat there thinking I concluded that their engine was symbiotic. It was alive. It was an engine that was [*sentient*].

The reason I could not figure out the firing was that the tubing that was cascading all over the engine's body looked like the same pattern you would have from a neural synaptic firing order. So what was happening was when the pilots sat down in their seats their thought waves interfaced with the engine. When I first touched the engine, I was curious and awed by its wavelengths, how smooth they were off of my fingers. However, when I was getting down off of it I was totally angry. The engine was not picking up radiation heat waves. It was picking up mental thought energy [*spiritual energy*]. That engine was capable of a symbiotic relationship with the pilots. It was alive!

The transcription above is from an interview with David Adair, available on YouTube under the title "David Adair at Area 51 – Advanced Symbiotic Technology." David mentioned that he had a bad feeling about leaving his rocket with the men at the facility, so he applied graphite grease inside the door of his rocket, which caused it to explode. He said the men were furious with him, but since he was only 17, there was nothing they could do. However, when he turned 18, he was conscripted into service and forced to design projects for the U.S. military. He stated that he never built another engine like his original one because he felt the men he was working for could not be trusted.

David Adair is not the only government employee to claim he worked with living machines during his career. Bob Lazar also asserts that he worked at Area 51 with biologic machines, meaning sentient ones. There are many YouTube interviews featuring Mr. Lazar and David Adair that are worth watching for their insights on this unusual topic.

With this in mind, as I contemplate the remarkable ships of Chittim that will bring the vanguard of the Host of Israel to Earth from the far reaches of the heavens, I must consider that these ships themselves might be the servants of God. As such, what other technologies might exist that have been infused with sentience by the Master Artisan? The book of Revelation speaks of white stones which are given to the righteous, are these additional examples of spiritually infused technology? They are spoken of as being Urim and Thummim, which are additional examples of incredible technology. Truly, the cosmos contains more mysteries and wonders than we can possibly comprehend at this time. The coming restoration of all things will be amazing!

Noah continues with his narrative:

> **61.12**. All who sleep not above in heaven shall bless Him: all the holy ones who are in heaven shall bless Him, and all the elect who dwell in the garden of life: and every spirit of light who is able to bless, and glorify, and extol, and hallow Thy blessed name, and all flesh shall beyond measure glorify and bless Thy name for ever and ever.

Noah once again delineated the celestial inhabitants of the heavens. He began with those who do not slumber—the gods. These eternal beings have vigilantly petitioned for their posterity before the Throne of God from the beginning. From there, Noah broadened his vision to encompass all the holy ones dwelling in the celestial realms, a category that surely includes the non-human entities of which we have been discussing.

He then cast his gaze upon the Celestial people of this cycle who will inherit the Earth as their Celestial Kingdom. Afterall there a innumerable Celestialized worlds and realms throughout the multiverse. Finally, Noah expanded his proclamation to embrace all sentient beings throughout the vast multiverse, regardless of the kingdom of glory they inhabit, who are able to praise the Father and His Hidden Son will do so. Thus we see, every voice, every spirit, and every sentient creation will join in the heavenly chorus that will reverberate throughout the cosmos.

The vision continues:

> **61.13**. For great is the mercy of the Lord of Spirits, and He is long-suffering, and all His works and all that He has created He has revealed to the righteous and elect in the name of the Lord of Spirits.

God reigns supreme over all creation. Every sentient form of life will inevitably come to acknowledge and extol Him. This includes not only humanity but also the creatures of the earth, the lush vegetation, and even the very elements that compose our world. For God is the most loving being in the universe, the embodiment of kindness, the pinnacle of intelligence, and the essence of mercy. He stands as our unwavering ally, even as we often become our own worst adversaries, wrestling against our own nature and biting the hand that nourishes us.

Yet, we often find ourselves acting in ways born of the frailty inherent in the flesh—by divine design. Afterall, God gave us our weaknesses to enable us to grow and development in uniquely tailored ways. This divine intention is rooted in God's desire for our progression, though He will not compel us to change. If we lack vision and foresight, He stands ready to provide guidance, should we seek it. All things, both great and small, rest within His Almighty hand. We need only ask in faith and righteousness, with patience and belief that we will receive.

Therefore, we must approach our journey with the understanding that in all things, He works for our good. While He will not readily grant us the instruments of our own destruction, as Joseph Smith illustrated, we can, like the widow in the parable of the unrighteous judge, receive even that which may not serve our best interests. Thus, we are cautioned to exercise wisdom in our requests.

We should look forward with an eye of faith, trusting in the scriptures, for in them we believe we find Eternal Life. Yet, Eternal Life is not found in the words upon the page, but within the Father, His Son, and in the Holy Ghost. Therefore, our quest is not merely to read the scriptures, but to obtain and act upon the wisdom they are meant to convey. Afterall, the scriptures are not the destination; they are the beginning, guiding us toward the deeper knowledge that can only be revealed by the Gods. Such messages, imparted by the Spirit, are far more empowering than any written words could ever be. It is the Holy Ghost that imbues words with power; without this divine influence, they are simply ink on the page.

Chapter 12 – The True Nature of the Multiverse

In the previous chapter, we explored the various classes of beings that comprise the multiverse. We discovered that not only are there non-human entities throughout the cosmos, but some sentient life forms are not even made of flesh and bone. The Ophanim—known as the living wheels—are a prime example of such beings. We reviewed the experience of David Adair, who encountered a living engine, and I speculated that the Ships of Chittim might be examples of Ophanim. These life forms open doors to realms many never knew existed.

I also briefly touched upon the Cherubim and Seraphim, classes of non-human entities that typically serve as guardians and protectors. However, these wondrous creatures likely fulfill many other roles throughout the Kingdom of God, alongside countless others. Throughout this book, we have mentioned legendary creatures such as the Leviathan, Behemoth, and fiery flying serpents. The kingdoms of glory must be filled with exalted beings of all kinds, all of whom rejoice in their creation and their Creator. Through the power of the Atonement, and specifically the Resurrection, all these creatures call God their Father.

As we have seen with the Lady and her strange, black-skinned, red-eyed alien disciples, Lucifer is not the only opposition or deceptive force in the multiverse. According to General Jeremiah's account from Volume II, there are large reptilian beings who know more about scripture than anyone else he has encountered. These beings possess their own agency and must choose their paths.

Joseph Smith taught that all intelligent creatures who serve God can be saved. Therefore, if there are Greys that serve the Lady, it stands to reason that there are also Greys who serve the Lord and have thus obtained salvation. Indeed, Joseph Smith proclaimed this concept as the grand key of knowledge, meaning that the cosmos is filled with intelligent and diverse life forms—much more than any of us are currently prepared to accept. The Gods do not create any life forms unless they can be heirs of salvation if they so choose.

Such ideas are certainly incredible to contemplate, especially given the staggering diversity among the human family. If Earth is merely an example of that diversity, what other variations of humanity must exist throughout the infinite multiverse? The more we ponder these questions, the closer we come to understanding the true nature of reality. With such diversity filling the multiverse, what must the interactions between these varied classes of beings be like?

Joseph Smith explained that the social structure of the multiverse follows the same pattern as the social structure found on Earth.

> That same sociality which exists among us here will exist
> among us there, only it will be coupled with eternal glory,
> which glory we do not now enjoy. (D&C 130:2)

The root of the word "sociality" is "society." The complex macro social relationships of the human family stem from more intimate connections centered around the nuclear family. The human family is the fundamental unit upon which our plan of salvation is built. It is reasonable to extend this assumption to all other hyper-intelligent life forms, except perhaps the Ophanim, which, as far as we know, do not reproduce but are created. Nevertheless, many Ophanim have surely been adopted into family units, becoming cherished members for those fortunate enough to have them.

All the hosts of heaven have been created through a similar process as we have. Therefore, it stands to reason that salvation for them must resemble our own and be accomplished in similar ways—through the life and merits of our Lord and Savior, Jesus Christ. Before the worlds were created, we can assume that all hyper-intelligent species, like humans, were individually created as spiritual offspring of heavenly families that mirror our own. Their heavenly parents do not sleep, just as ours do not. Thus, their heavenly parents must be glorified and resurrected beings who fulfilled the full measure of their creations according to the Father's plan of salvation. Despite the incredible diversity that exists, all these beings look to the Great Creator as their Father, for He is the Father of their resurrected bodies, just as He is the Father of ours—regardless of species.

All hyper-intelligent life forms now participating in the Father's plan of salvation chose to do so before the worlds were created. However, as demonstrated by the Lady and her kind, participation in the Father's plan is not mandatory. Therefore, we must presume that the multiverse is home not only to spiritual beings like the Lady but also to countless spiritual creatures beyond our comprehension who opted out of the Father's plan.

Reason suggests that those who opted out did so out of fear of being worse off for having done so. If Earth is within the sphere of influence of the Lady, it may also be influenced by other non-human entities. However, like begets like, and the nature of these beings would naturally lead them to associate with their own kind. Thus, spiritual opposition likely pervades the multiverse, although it may not be organized in a unified front. This could change with the freeing of Lucifer from his prison after the millennium.

I presume that the fear of the agency inherent in the Father's plan arises from the veil of forgetfulness that accompanies all creation into mortality. Therefore, the sentient beings occupying the multiverse must operate under the same conditions as we do, requiring them to act by faith, just as we do. Furthermore, we must assume that their civilizations have received messengers—both genuine and fraudulent—for as long as the multiverse has existed. They must learn to discern truth for themselves, just as we must.

Thus, we can presume that the multiverse is filled with religions and belief systems as diverse as its inhabitants. It is not only possible but entirely probable that other intelligent life forms visiting Earth will possess belief systems entirely different from our own. These varied belief systems are likely the products of millennia of skillful deception and manipulation by negative forces and energies of those who chose not to participate in the Father's plan of redemption. This underscores the Father's admonition to preach the gospel of Jesus Christ to every creature within the sound of our voice. Therefore, it is crucial for readers to avoid equating technology with moral superiority. Truth is truth, and all truth must align with the restored gospel of Jesus Christ, which remains consistent throughout the cosmos.

Given the incredible diversity of the cosmos, I am confident that we interacted with countless species of intelligent life in the premortal realms, raised by their immortal parents. Many of these beings likely participated with us in the war in heaven to varying degrees. Just as Earth serves as the prison planet for Lucifer and his followers, there may be other prison planets for other rebellious entities. After all, Earth was specifically designated as the prison planet for Lucifer and his angels. However, there may have been other prominent entities that participated in that rebellion with their respective forces and were likewise cast out. Nevertheless, there can be no doubt that Lucifer was the great ringleader of that cosmic rebellion. The Enuma Elish suggests that many non-human creatures sought to destroy the Igigi in their pursuit of power. I mention this as speculation and nothing more.

As I contemplate these matters, one fact stands out: the human family was created in the very image of God. Why were some intelligences created as one thing while others were created as something else? Is there a specific reason behind the families into which spiritual entities were born? Certainly, creation is not left to random chance. Paul taught that not all flesh is the same; there is one kind of flesh for men, another for beasts, another for fishes, and another for birds (see 1 Corinthians 15:39). Paul was specifically addressing resurrection. Yet, if there is a difference in the end, might we not also presume that there was a difference to begin with? We know that spirit is intelligence, and intelligence is defined as truth and light. Not all light is the same; it exists on a spectrum. Therefore, I believe that the various forms of flesh created are based on the various forms of intelligence that exist.

Consider bacteria as an example. If all things were created spiritually before they were created physically, then bacteria must have a spiritual component. What about gnats, flies, mosquitoes, parasites, viruses, etc.? What happens to such beings when they die? Are they resurrected? Let's go even more basic: what about the elements themselves? We know that the Earth will join the Celestial Kingdom, which is the elemental equivalent of an entire planet becoming resurrected. Yet, will all planets be resurrected? This contemplation may not provide answers to all these questions, but it may offer a theoretical framework for them. Therefore, consider the following conversation between Moses and God regarding the creation of worlds:

> And now, behold, this one thing I show unto thee, Moses, my son, for thou art in the world, and now I show it unto thee. And it came to pass that Moses looked, and beheld the world upon which he was created; and Moses beheld the world and the ends thereof, and all the children of men which are, and which were created; of the same he greatly marveled and wondered.

> And it came to pass, as the voice was still speaking, Moses cast his eyes and beheld the earth, yea, even all of it; and there was not a particle of it which he did not behold, discerning it by the Spirit of God. And he beheld also the inhabitants thereof, and there was not a soul which he beheld not; and he discerned them by the Spirit of God; and their numbers were great, even numberless as the sand upon the sea shore.

> And he beheld many lands; and each land was called earth, and there were inhabitants on the face thereof. And it came to pass that Moses called upon God, saying: Tell me, I pray thee, why these things are so, and by what thou madest them? And behold, the glory of the Lord was upon Moses, so that Moses stood in the presence of God, and talked with Him face to face. And the Lord God said unto Moses: For mine own purpose have I made these things. Here is wisdom and it remaineth in me. And by the word of my power, have I created them, which is mine Only Begotten Son, who is full of grace and truth. And worlds without number have I created; and I also created them for mine own purpose; and by the Son I created them, which is mine Only Begotten.

And the Lord God spake unto Moses, saying: The heavens, they are many, and they cannot be numbered unto man; but they are numbered unto me, for they are mine. And as one earth shall pass away, and the heavens thereof even so shall another come; and there is no end to my works, neither to my words.(Moses 1:7-8,27-33,37-38)

In this profound conversation between God the Father and Moses, Moses learns that worlds have come and gone, only to be reformed again. Even the Earth we currently inhabit was reorganized from existing materials. At the quantum level, all matter possesses a spiritual component. Therefore, one cannot recycle the elemental components of matter without also recycling their corresponding spiritual counterparts. While matter cannot be created or destroyed, it can be recycled and transformed.

To illustrate this process, consider how suns function like massive cosmic vacuum cleaners, pulling in loose, disorganized matter into their orbits or into themselves. As they grow larger, the intensity of the fusion reactions within them increases, creating new elements. Within a sun's orbit, loose matter collides and consolidates. If this matter is rocky, it becomes spherical under the force of its own gravity once it reaches approximately 600 kilometers in diameter. The critical mass required for an object to become spherical varies by the state of matter: ice becomes spherical at lower thresholds, while gas requires higher ones. If a heavenly body grows to a critical mass—approximately eighty times larger than Jupiter—the force of its own gravity becomes strong enough to initiate nuclear fusion, leading to the birth of stars. The life cycle of a star can culminate in a supernova explosion, dispersing recycled matter throughout the cosmos, thus beginning the process anew.

At one level, the multiverse exists in a continual state of renewal, where old elements are transformed into new ones. It seems reasonable to suggest that lesser life forms, such as bacteria, viruses, and parasites, may also be recycled in a similar manner. However, just as we observe in the physical realms of the multiverse, I believe that once a critical mass of spiritual intelligence is attained, our cosmic trajectories are irrevocably altered. These changes occur not by cosmic chance but through the deliberate intervention of heavenly parents in an act of creation. There is nothing accidental about this process.

God does not create randomly. We are what we are because God willed us into being. However, what we become after our initial transformation is up to us. After all, the Household of God is not defined by pedigree but by agency. It matters little that we are gods in embryo if we choose to reject that legacy for the alluring mire of lesser pursuits. We are not cosmic debris; we choose our own orbits!

In this same vein, God did not send us to Satan's prison planet by mere chance. He knew we were capable of overcoming Satan through our faith in His Only Begotten Son, as we have done before. Given that this is the most challenging environment in the multiverse, one must suppose that the rewards for overcoming it through Christ are also the greatest. Indeed, Christ has promised that as He sits upon His Father's throne, those who overcome this world will likewise sit upon thrones of glory with Him (see Revelation 3:21).

That said, I believe that any creature in the multiverse can attain Celestial glory and qualify to participate in the Father's family business. Those who do become heavenly kings and queens, regardless of their class or creed. They will perpetuate the wonderful diversity that exists throughout the cosmos. I speak of these matters from a theoretical perspective, as our understanding is limited to the dealings upon this Earth.

However, our limited understanding does not imply that knowledge is confined to other worlds. After all, the inhabitants of all other worlds become the begotten sons and daughters of God through Jesus Christ's atonement. Joseph Smith taught that the covenants of salvation can be administered by the people of Earth to other worlds, but the reverse is prohibited.

One reason for this may be that other worlds in the cosmos are far older and have long histories of intertwined cosmic civilizations and colonization. They are likely more accustomed to the free flow of cosmic ideologies than we are today. Consequently, they may be more hesitant to accept something based solely on the novelty of a messenger with extraterrestrial origins.

Ancient history shows that our presence on Satan's prison planet makes us more susceptible to such influences. Indeed, the Book of Enoch recounts that when two hundred alien beings descended from the cosmos in the days of Enoch's father Jared, chaos ensued, necessitating a global reset. I believe that Earth is about to face similar tests, and soon. Those who have prepared in advance will fare far better than those who have buried their heads in the sand.

For those who have invested in acquiring such knowledge, the coming days will present an opportunity to testify to the truthfulness of the gospel to those who have never heard it in its pure form. When that day arrives, we will finally fulfill the Lord's commandment to preach the gospel to every creature within the sound of our voices. Some will heed this call, for Zion is destined to emerge from all of God's creations, including non-human entities.

The essence of Zion has never been based on physical appearance. Instead, the Household of God has always included the pure in heart who align themselves with His will, whether they are humans, Leviathans, Cherubim, Seraphim, or Ophanim. Diversity brings joy and excitement. In a realm associated with a fullness of joy, we must accept that diversity will exist in unfathomable abundance.

We must assume that the coming world will be radically different from our current understanding, yet it will be glorious and wonderful beyond description. A fullness of joy must inherently include wonder, awe, excitement, and splendor. After all, no matter how delicious a dessert may be, if you knew it was the only thing you would ever eat again, its appeal would quickly diminish. Thus, the Father rejoices in diversity!

Despite the differences that will exist, there are more similarities than disparities. All intelligent life throughout the cosmos must confront its own veil of unbelief and come to a realization of truth during mortality. Just as there are thousands of religious philosophies on Earth, we must prepare for countless religious ideas across the cosmos. Furthermore, as humanity has created gods in our own image, we can assume that other worlds and civilizations have done the same.

This situation may be compounded by the fact that various forms of creation likely have their own contingencies that opted not to participate in mortality, similar to the Lady, and for similar reasons. It is reasonable to expect that they may have encountered impressive, albeit deceptive, apparitions that have significantly influenced their belief systems over time. Such apparitions are no more from God than the many appearances of the Lady throughout history, asking the world to pray for her intercession. General Jeremiah's account in Volume II of this series indicates that a large reptilian creature believed their planet had been warned to prevent Earth from believing in Jesus Christ.

Regardless of cosmic geography, all truth must be encompassed within one great whole. Therefore, if the world is visited by a race of beings with vastly different religious beliefs, we should not be surprised. Yet, there is but one truth, and ultimately, all creation must come unto it, or they cannot be saved.

While evil certainly exists throughout the cosmos, nowhere has it taken such a hold on an intelligent species as it has on this planet. God Himself has proclaimed it the most wicked of all His creations. Here, we often harbor hatred for our own kind, a hatred stemming from the Father of Lies, who is bound to this Earth like a snake to the dust. Despite his chains, Satan is poised to gain unprecedented power, the ramifications of which will cause the heavens to tremble.

This is why Enoch spoke of the countless heavenly parents petitioning the Father on behalf of their children. The days are approaching when the entire multiverse will recognize that God the Father is the common denominator of all life. If we trust in Him and hold fast to His Hidden Son, all will be well with us. If not, we will be sent to the spirit world for another chance at repentance and change.

While the wicked on this world will be destroyed, wickedness will still exist elsewhere in the cosmos. Its influence will grow until Satan is released from his earthly prison and rallies the cosmos in rebellion against the great God of Heaven. This final battle, long in the making, will conclude in an instant, as God will dissolve the hosts of heaven in divine fire. The countless hosts of heaven will then be confined to the burning mountain range at the edge of outer darkness for ten thousand years, overlooking the fate of the sons and daughters of perdition.

There, at the edge of all things, they will pay the excruciating price for their sins, having rejected Jesus Christ. Yet, in the end, the scales will be removed from their eyes, and when that day comes, Christ will return to gather them in mercy once more. They will inherit the vast, expansive kingdoms of telestial glory, which are beyond comprehension in their goodness and majesty. This is by far the largest and most populated kingdom in the multiverse.

In the telestial realm, inhabitants will be limited in their interactions to kingdoms of equal or lesser glory. They will never be able to approach where God and His Christ dwell, worlds without end. However, both God and His Christ will be able to visit them, as will their loved ones who were worthy of a far greater reward. Thus, the same social dynamics that exist now will continue there, accompanied by eternal glory—a blessing we do not currently enjoy.

Chapter 13 – The Rise of the Hidden Son

In the previous chapter, we explored what I believe to be the true nature of the multiverse. As part of that discussion, I proposed a possibility for how intelligent life interacts both in heaven and in mortality. I speculated that just as it began, so it will end, with Zion, or the Kingdom of God, emerging from all the creations of the Father, encompassing life in all its forms.

While contemplating these matters is fascinating, it is far from the greatest mystery of the multiverse. The most profound mystery revolves around the singular covenant pathway back to the presence of God. There are over four thousand different religious traditions on Earth, with Christianity being the largest. However, it has splintered into more than forty-five thousand denominations. Only one of these is true, and even it is undergoing a continual process of restoration. Many plain and precious truths have yet to be fully restored. Due to spiritual blindness, most are not prepared for this personal restoration and must wait until global events remove the scales from their eyes, compelling them to believe.

Currently, only two out of every hundred thousand people have accepted the restored gospel at some point in their lives. Of those, less than half remain faithful to the covenants they once made. Thus, a faithful latter-day saint is one of the rarest beings in the multiverse—an astounding fact! Truly, narrow is the path to eternal life, and few there be that find it.

There are many reasons why the pathway to salvation and eternal life is so narrow and difficult to discern, not least of which is the reality that we live on Satan's prison planet. Too few seem capable of recognizing and acting upon the truth amidst Satan's lies and half-truths. Many perceive truth through the distorted lens of Satan's funhouse mirrors, rather than seeing it for what it truly is. Yet, against all odds, some manage to see through the lies. When they encounter the truth, they grasp it with both hands and refuse to let go, regardless of worldly temptations. It is to such individuals that the Father now speaks:

> **62.1**. And thus the Lord commanded the kings and the
> mighty and the exalted, and those who dwell on the earth,
> and said: 'Open your eyes and lift up your horns if ye are able
> to recognize the Elect One.'

From the context of the passage, it is evident that the identity of the Father's Elect One is not a foregone conclusion for the inhabitants of the multiverse. Since the dawn of time, He has remained hidden in the shadow of the Father's hand. However, the Father has consistently revealed Him to those who earnestly seek to know Him. For others, the true nature of the Hidden Son remains an enigmatic mystery of profound depth. This is true throughout the cosmos. Despite the lies and deceptions surrounding us, a day is approaching—one that is not far off—when the Father will call upon all inhabitants of the multiverse to raise their horns to the heavens if they have come to know His Hidden Son.

Historically, a horn has symbolized royal authority and heraldry. In ancient times, heralds blew their horns to alert the masses of significant events, summoned armies to battle, and proclaimed important messages from the King. Thus, horns became a sign of royal authority.

All divine authority originates from God, which is the core message of this passage. The right to heavenly kingship can only be bestowed by an uppercase God. Therefore, if you aspire to heavenly kingship, it is essential to know the Father's Hidden Son, for the Father has entrusted all authority to Him. In essence, if you do not know His Son, you possess no authority; your priesthood holds no power. Conversely, those who come to know the Father's Hidden Son through personal revelation become joint heirs with Him and receive all that the Father has to offer. In short, those with true horns of power are those of whom it has been said, "How beautiful upon the mountains are their feet, for they have published the Gospel of hope unto the nations."

The Father's call to raise your horn high if you have known His Hidden Son serves to distinguish those who hold His testimony from those who do not. This separation is inevitable and will be uncomfortable for many in the multiverse. Countless individuals profess to know and worship God, yet they do not truly know Him or His Hidden Son. The reason is simple: His identity cannot be revealed through words alone.

While heralds can proclaim the good news from the city walls, history shows that few are receptive to such declarations. Words alone cannot penetrate the hearts and minds of the people. Eternal salvation is not passively received; it is attained by acting upon the promptings of the Holy Ghost. This is why Christ told Peter he was blessed for recognizing Him as the Son of God, for such knowledge could not come from flesh and blood. This principle applies to all the mysteries of God.

Knowledge of God's Son is a privilege reserved for the humble and penitent who seek to know Him. Why is this knowledge so elusive? Because true understanding of Jesus Christ unlocks the gateway to the covenant path, leading to the greatest source of power and treasure the multiverse offers. Thus, such knowledge is reserved for those who earnestly seek it. Immortality and eternal life are not mere participation prizes;

resurrection is one such prize, but not this. This is done for a wise purpose in the Lord. If God wished to simplify matters, He certainly could.

Yet, God did not choose Caiaphas to announce His Son; He chose John the Baptist— the rugged wild man from the Judean wilderness. The fact that John was the Lord's mouthpiece, rather than Caiaphas, reveals much about the Father's ways. The Father tests the faith of His people, and such trials are inherently challenging. The Jews who accepted Jesus Christ as the Father's Hidden Son faced ostracism from friends and family, were cast out of synagogues, and were belittled by those they loved. They were labeled heretics, blasphemers, and apostates. Yet, those who truly know the Father's Hidden Son will endure all this and more, for they know Him, and He is with them. They are not alone in their suffering.

In the days to come, everyone who reads these words will come to understand their full significance. We will be compelled to make the same choices as our ancestors. Yet, we will endure, just as He bore the shame of our sins, and He will accompany us every step of the way.

Noah's vision continues:

> **62.2**. And the Lord of Spirits seated Him [*the Elect One*] on the throne of His glory, and the spirit of righteousness was poured out upon Him, and the word of His mouth slays all the sinners, and all the unrighteous are destroyed from before His face.

Once again, the Book of Enoch references the Son's ascension to the throne of His Father. This passage highlights how widely understood the concept of an ascending Son was in the ancient world. From the very beginning, it was foretold that the Father's Son would vanquish the wicked in the last days through divine proclamation. Recall the opening passage of the Book of Enoch. It clearly describes the latter-day event when the wicked will be removed from the Earth. Take a moment to reconsider those passages:

> **1.1.** The words of the blessing of Enoch, wherewith he blessed the elect[[and]]righteous, who will be living in the day of tribulation, when all the wicked[[and godless]]are to be removed.
> **1.2.** And he took up his parable and said--Enoch a righteous man, whose eyes were opened by God, saw the vision of the Holy One in the heavens, [which] the angels showed me, and from them I

heard everything, and from them I understood as I saw, but not for this generation, but for a remote one which is for to come.

The Lord has always known how things will end, and so have all who truly know Him. For millennia, He has prepared His people for what is to come. Yet, compared to the inhabitants of the Earth, which are as numerous as the sands of the sea, very few have sought to understand these truths. Consequently, only a small number have grasped them. Even when Israel's eyes were closed, wise men from the East came to honor the birth of the Son of God, having seen the signs. In contrast, the unwitting world remained largely unaware. So it will be in the last days. Given the Lord's foresight, it need not be this way, but human nature dictates otherwise.

As we discussed in the second chapter of this book, particularly regarding 60.1 of the Book of Enoch, everything that follows is framed within the context of that terrible event that will cause both the heavens and the Earth to tremble. On that great and terrible day, Jesus Christ will crush His enemies beneath His feet, and their blood will flow in the streets like new wine from the press, leaving cities desolate and uninhabited. New York will become like Assyria, Chicago like Babylon, Los Angeles like Sumer, and Seattle like Rome. This will occur in a single day. When it happens, the shame borne by the righteous children who have sought instruction from their Father's Hidden Son will be turned upon the heads of the wicked. On that day, the righteous and humble will ascend alongside the Son of Man.

Once again, we learn of the true nature of the Godhead. The Father will abdicate His throne to His Son, who will then assume the role of the Father, while the Father ascends to His seat of honor on the northern slope of the Mount of the Congregation, joining all the Uppercase Gods who have come before Him.

How confusing these passages must be for the Jews, who have historically expunged polytheism from their writings! The identity of this unknown Son, now seated upon the Father's throne, remains a mystery. Yet, to those with eyes to see, the identity of this Man is as clear as the sun in a blue sky. For them, this changing of the guard is no more perplexing than the setting of the sun. When Christ sits upon His Father's throne, the work of the Great Jehovah will be complete, and this iteration of the Father's great plan of happiness will reach its fulfillment.

The dead will rise from their graves and inherit the kingdoms of glory for which they are worthy, while those who reject the Son of Man will atone for their sins in the fiery mountains at the edge of the multiverse, where they will remain for ten thousand years. Meanwhile, the Earth will enter its glorified and celestial state, and the meek and righteous who endured the shame and scorn of the world will inherit it forever.

However, before the Son of Man ascends, the wicked will be removed from the face of the Earth, and the Earth will rest for a thousand years. Throughout this series, I have detailed how the events of the last days will unfold, including the kickoff events of Ezra's Eagle, the rise of the Antichrist, and the fall of the Whore of Babylon. I have also discussed the return of the Holy Race, the purging of America by the Remnant of Jacob, and the chaos and war that will engulf Europe and the rest of the world, culminating in the siege and capture of Jerusalem.

According to the writings of Daniel, there will be about a month and a half between the fall of Jerusalem and the appearance of the Son of God in the clouds above the city. John describes Him appearing on a white horse, clothed in red, with the armies of heaven at His back—this inspired the cover of Volume I of this series. Christ will then descend from the heavens to the horror of the wicked. At His command, the Mount of Olives will split in two, creating a great valley for the remaining Jews to escape Jerusalem. At that time, the Lord will save the Jews. The Son of Man, born a Jew, will return as the Jewish Savior.

By His word, the wicked will literally dissolve at their feet, not only in Jerusalem but across the globe. This will have occurred several years earlier in America, which will have begun the process of rebuilding. However, elsewhere, the great empires of the Earth will be destroyed and left desolate. The streets will be littered with corpses, reminiscent of the Nephite and Jaredite nations. This will serve as a terrible monument and testimony that the Lord God rules from heaven, and that the Earth is indeed His footstool.

On that great and terrible day, all that the wicked fought to control will be laid bare and unguarded. The meek and humble will now spoil the wicked. From the ashes of that day will rise a new and glorious civilization. The Earth will not remain desolate for long; the billions of wicked who were destroyed will be replaced by the hosts of Israel, of whom the world knows so little. They will return to inherit the desolate heritages of the Gentiles, as Christ has said.

In that day, there will be a new heaven and a new Earth. The heavens will be renewed as the portals open, allowing the righteous from all of God's creations to flow to Earth to pay homage to the Son of Man. The righteous will not be limited to those created in the image of God but will include all His varied creations who honor and uphold His ways. Thus, the diversity of Zion will be legendary, of a magnitude we are not yet prepared to accept. This will be what makes the heavens new to us.

The Earth will also be renewed, as the societies that rise from the ashes of the old will be unlike anything ever experienced. The greatest builders and designers from across the cosmos will come to create incredible things in the name of the Most High God.

Foremost among the Earth's new cities will be the New Jerusalem, which will descend from the heavens. Yet, the New Jerusalem will be just one of many interstellar cities, alongside those of Enoch, Melchizedek, and other righteous fragments of the Earth that have been removed throughout time.

Therefore, the cultures and societies that emerge from the ashes of the wicked will be far more glorious and exciting than we can currently imagine. These dramatic changes will renew both the heavens and the Earth, all brought about by the Son of Man. In that day, the hierarchy of the Church will no longer be vertical; all will know the Lord and have communion with Him, as He intended from the beginning. When this occurs, darkness and confusion will fade away, and our children will grow up in the light and presence of the Living God, with all things made known to them.

In that great and glorious day, our lives will be extended like those of Enoch's fathers. We will rejoice in mortality with the Lord upon the Earth, not for decades, but for centuries. When the time of death comes, we will be quickened in the blink of an eye, joining our heavenly parents as the sleepless heirs of salvation in the mansions of the Father. In that great day, full access to the multiverse will unfold before us and our spiritual posterity. We will know true freedom and joy unlike anything we have ever imagined. Truly, eye hath not seen, nor ear heard, nor hath entered into the hearts of man the things which the Lord hath done for those that love Him.

The vision now shifts to address the hosts of the wicked and powerful, who will have been cleansed from the Earth as they come to realize the gravity of their actions:

> **62.3**. And there shall stand up in that day all the kings and the mighty, and the exalted and those who hold the earth, and they shall see and recognize How He sits on the throne of His glory, and righteousness is judged before Him, and no lying word is spoken before Him.
>
> **62.4**. Then shall pain come upon them as on a woman in travail, [And she has pain in bringing forth] when her child enters the mouth of the womb, and she has pain in bringing forth.
>
> **62.5**. And one portion of them shall look on the other, and they shall be terrified, and they shall be downcast of countenance, and pain shall seize them, when they see that Son of Man Sitting on the throne of His glory.

62.6. And the kings and the mighty and all who possess the earth shall bless and glorify and extol Him who rules over all, who was hidden.

62.7. For from the beginning the Son of Man was hidden, and the Most High preserved Him in the presence of His might, and revealed Him to the elect.

This passage is one of the most remarkable in all of scripture to me. It speaks of the literal "come to Jesus" moment that the entire Earth will experience at the end of all things. Noah foresaw that the true nature of Christ has always been hidden. Only the elect know Him, and they know Him because the Father has revealed the true nature of His Hidden Son to them. This knowledge does not come passively; rather, it comes to those who actively seek it.

On the great day of judgment described above, the powerful of this world will realize that they never truly knew the Son of God. Indeed, many will come to realize that they venomously oppressed and persecuted His true disciples. Instead of truth, these embraced illusion. Now that illusion becomes a living nightmare for before the Father's throne of power Satan's lies fade to dust. All that was hidden behind half-truths and lies now lays bare in the open, the naked truth is seen by all.

When this happens, like the Israelites of old, many will realize that they fashioned for themselves Baalim, gods of their own creation, rather than worshiping the true and living God. Yet even now they see the differences between truth and error, but they cleave to error and reject the truth. With pride, they proclaim, "The 'Mormons' worship a different Jesus than us!" They are right, for we worship the Father's Hidden Son, and they worship Ba'al, a savior of their own making.

On that day, they will be utterly dumbfounded to find the resurrected Son standing at the right hand of His glorified Father, with the Holy Ghost at His left—three actual beings of power and glory beyond imagination, surrounded by an innumerable host of gods, of which their own heavenly parents will be numbered. Only then, in the blazing light of truth, will the true nature of the Godhead be revealed to the ignorant masses of this world.

Now they will comprehend that the Father's Son has been hidden by divine design so that only those who seek Him will find Him. This is both terrible and wonderful, as it places the responsibility for our relationship with the Godhead squarely on our own shoulders! This is the terrifying meaning behind the following passage:

> Many will say to me in that day, Lord, Lord... and then will I say, ye never knew me, depart from Me, ye that work iniquity. (JSM Matt 7:22-23)

We come unto Christ by doing the will of His Father, for such He proclaimed to be His gospel – 3 Nephi 27:13. Doing the will of the Father is much different than simply checking boxes on a list. Reading the scriptures, going to church, and attending the temple regularly are all good things. But you can do all of these things without fulfilling the Father's will in your life. If you want to know the will of the Father regarding your life, you must be actively seeking to understand His will. All of the good things previously mentioned should be seen as tools to come to know the will of the Father, rather than as the ends themselves.

The Pharisees and the Sadducees checked off many boxes and made many lists. Yet these were lists and checkboxes of their own design. In all their doings, they did nothing to actually come to know the Father's hidden Son. They knew not the God they claimed to serve. Can the same be said for us? In an attempt to do good things, many have built up churches unto Paul, some of Moses, and some of Christ. Yet the only thing that should matter for you is what the will of the Father is for your life. If you do many good things but leave His will in your life undone, you have missed the boat. On the flip side, if you fulfill the Father's will in your life but leave many other good things undone, who cares? If you do the will of the Father, you will make the choice of Mary rather than Martha, for there are many good things, but only one is needed.

The vision continues:

> **62.8**. And the congregation of the elect and holy shall be sown, and all the elect shall stand before Him on that day.

> **62.9**. And all the kings and the mighty and the exalted and those who rule the earth shall fall down before Him on their faces, and worship and set their hope upon that Son of Man, and petition Him and supplicate for mercy at His hands.

> **62.10**. Nevertheless, that Lord of Spirits will so press them that they shall hastily go forth from His presence, and their faces shall be filled with shame, and the darkness grow deeper on their faces.

62.11. And He will deliver them to the angels for punishment, to execute vengeance on them because they have oppressed His children and His elect

62.12. And they shall be a spectacle for the righteous and for His elect: they shall rejoice over them, because the wrath of the Lord of Spirits resteth upon them, and His sword is drunk with their blood.

The passages above are exceedingly harsh, and they explain the reason Christ asked us to pray for our enemies and for those who despitefully use and abuse us. At face value, these verses seem to take the perspective of vengeance and retribution, wherein the bad guys finally get what is coming to them. Indeed, the Lord has repeatedly said that vengeance is His and that He shall repay. These passages seem to indicate that this is precisely what will happen.

However, the Lord is not petty. He will not be vengeful for vengeance's sake. There is always purpose behind the Lord's actions. We must seek to understand what that purpose is. A good start for understanding the Lord's motivations for exacting vengeance can be found in the Book of Mormon. Consider the great destructions that took place upon the American continent before the Lord's first coming. It was catastrophic! This continent had never seen such things before, and the people were exceedingly amazed at the destruction that had taken place. In their amazement, the Son of God spoke to them and explained His actions. I believe that what He said has direct implications for the passages above. Consider the following:

> Wo, wo, wo unto this people; wo unto the inhabitants of the whole earth except they shall repent; for the devil laugheth, and his angels rejoice, because of the slain of the fair sons and daughters of my people; and it is because of their iniquity and abominations that they are fallen! Behold, that great city Zarahemla have I burned with fire, and the inhabitants thereof. And behold, that great city Moroni have I caused to be sunk in the depths of the sea, and the inhabitants thereof to be drowned. And behold, that great city Moronihah have I covered with earth, and the inhabitants thereof, to hide their iniquities and their abominations from before my face, **that the blood of the prophets and the saints shall not come any more unto me against them.**

Yea, and the city of Onihah and the inhabitants thereof, and the city of Mocum and the inhabitants thereof, and the city of Jerusalem and the inhabitants thereof; and waters have I caused to come up in the stead thereof, to hide their wickedness and abominations from before my face, **that the blood of the prophets and the saints shall not come up any more unto me against them.**

And behold, the city of Gadiandi, and the city of Gadiomnah, and the city of Jacob, and the city of Gimgimno, all these have I caused to be sunk, and made hills and valleys in the places thereof; and the inhabitants thereof have I buried up in the depths of the earth, to hide their wickedness and abominations from before my face, **that the blood of the prophets and the saints should not come up any more unto me against them**.

And behold, that great city Jacobugath, which was inhabited by the people of king Jacob, have I caused to be burned with fire because of their sins and their wickedness, which was above all the wickedness of the whole earth, because of their secret murders and combinations; for it was they that did destroy the peace of my people and the government of the land; therefore I did cause them to be burned, to destroy them from before my face, **that the blood of the prophets and the saints should not come up unto me any more against them.**

And behold, the city of Laman, and the city of Josh, and the city of Gad, and the city of Kishkumen, have I caused to be burned with fire, and the inhabitants thereof, because of their wickedness in casting out the prophets, and stoning those whom I did send to declare unto them concerning their wickedness and their abominations. And because they did cast them all out, that there were none righteous among them, I did send down fire and destroy them, that their wickedness and abominations might be hid from before my face, **that the blood of the prophets and the saints whom I sent among them might not cry unto me from the ground against them.** (3 Nephi 9:2-11)

In the passages above, the Lord states five times that He destroyed the wicked in order to stop the blood of the prophets and the saints from crying out in witness against them. The world is drenched in the blood of the innocent. How many lives have been lost because of special interest groups seeking their own best interests at all costs? The answer is hundreds of millions, if not billions. The blood of the innocent cries out to the Lord for justice. These lives had their mortal probations terminated by the conspiring few who, in their feckless pursuit of power and wealth, left unimaginable wakes of blood and carnage. For many of us, these are the stories of other people's lives in distant lands. Yet the days are coming when violence will rage upon the face of the entire Earth. As I contemplate these things, my mind goes to the following passage:

> For there shall be in every place and in the next cities a great insurrection upon those that fear the Lord. For they shall waste and take away their goods, and cast them out of their houses. Then shall they be known, who are my chosen: and they shall be tried as gold in the fire. Hear, O ye my beloved, saith the Lord; behold, the days of trouble are at hand, but I will deliver you from the same. Be not afraid neither doubt; for God is your guide. (2 Esdras 16:70-75)

The passage above is the embodiment of this concept. Ezra saw that in the last days, the righteous would be driven from their homes, as has happened to them throughout history so many times before. John validates this understanding by claiming that there will be many thousands of the righteous in the last days who will be beheaded and persecuted because they will not worship the Beast, nor take upon themselves the number of his name. These righteous individuals will starve, suffer, and see all of their earthly possessions stripped away from them. It is with regard to the perpetrators of these dark and terrible deeds that the Lord will rise up in vengeance and lay low.

When these are at last brought before the throne of God, to their shock and horror, they will find the Son of Man, whose followers they have so hatefully persecuted. At that moment, they will not be able to simply apologize before the throne of God, when kneeling before His majesty and might is the only option left. Such is not true repentance; it is desperation. As such, just as with the Watchers of old, the Almighty will not suffer their petitions to be heard. Instead, on that day, God will press upon them the full weight of their sins. This consciousness that they have ever abused the laws of God and persecuted His people will kindle a flame of unquenchable fire within them. When this occurs, they will realize that they will be far more comfortable in Hell than abiding in the presence of a just and perfect Being, knowing that they have ever abused both His laws and His people. As such, they will be cast out into that lake of fire and brimstone, where, for the first time in their probationary states, they will begin the process of true and lasting change.

When the justice of God is finally administered upon the wicked, the heavens will rejoice. This joy is not in the suffering of the wicked, but in the justice and mercy of the Father. He is the protector of His children. Vengeance is His, and He shall repay. You do not want to be on the receiving end of the Father's vengeance. His vengeance will be the legendary spectacle of the age. Those who witness it will be awed by it. Yet, such divine justice is the only hope they will have of transforming into something other than a dark and demonic resident of outer darkness. The choice will be entirely theirs. They can become further embittered by drinking the bitter cup of their own sins, or they can be radically transformed for the better in the stunning realization of what their sins have actually cost them.

However, for the weak and humble of the earth, who seek early for the mercy and grace of the Divine Throne, they shall find it. Rather than drinking the bitter cups of their own sins, the Son of Man will drink it for them, and their incredible transformations will come to pass through His suffering rather than their own. What the wicked took from them in life will be restored to them again a hundredfold. The tears of every eye shall be dried, and all will be made right.

Woe unto the mighty and powerful upon the earth who despised the humble disciples of Christ, for great will be the spectacle of their suffering if they do not humble themselves to the dust of the earth in sackcloth and ashes while it can yet be called day. For the night soon comes when they will be shut off from Christ's atonement, and then the awfulness of their state will be universally known. Therefore, truly we should pray for our enemies and those who persecute us, that their hearts may be softened, that they might turn unto the Lord before it is too late.

The vision continues:

> **62.13**. And the righteous and elect shall be saved on that day, and they shall never thenceforward see the face of the sinners and unrighteous.

> **62.14**. And the Lord of Spirits will abide over them, and with that Son of Man shall they eat and lie down and rise up for ever and ever.

> **62.15**. And the righteous and elect shall have risen from the earth, and ceased to be of downcast countenance. And they shall have been clothed with garments of glory,

62.16. And these shall be the garments of life from the Lord of Spirits: and your garments shall not grow old, nor your glory pass away before the Lord of Spirits.

The passages above hint at the blessings that await the righteous in the grand graduation ceremony of this iteration of the Father's plan of salvation. All of these will be heirs of either the Celestial or Terrestrial Kingdoms of glory. Upon these, the Lord will bestow His glory and blessings to the degree to which they were willing to receive it. The primary difference between these will be the timing of when they received and kept the testimony of the Lord.

Unto those that fulfilled the full measure of their creation, they will be welcomed into the Household of God. They will be magnified with honor and glory just as God Himself. Such will become joint heirs with the Son of Man, having done the will of the Father and navigated their mortal lives by the constant guidance of the Holy Ghost. These are they who could raise their horns in recognition of the Father's hidden Son.

The unfathomable joy that will radiate from all those who have received such an exceedingly great weight of glory will be incredible to behold. These are the only ones who will know what it means to receive an absolute fullness of joy. The sorrows, struggles, and weaknesses of mortality will forever lay behind them, while the work of bringing to pass the immortality and eternal life of man will lay before them, forevermore. The objective of these will be to enable others to accomplish what they have done. They will do this by raising up righteous posterity and pointing them in the way that they should go, and thus the great celestial wheel of the cosmos will keep on turning.

For those who did not qualify for Celestial glory, but rather Terrestrial glory, they will continue in their pathways of progression. Given that these are not damned, it is reasonable to believe that they may still obtain the Celestial Kingdom. Yet, I suppose that such progression will take far longer without the veil and with a resurrected body than it would have in mortality. How many future iterations of the Father's plan such progression might take, who can say but God alone, for He is the gatekeeper of exaltation and eternal lives. What is known is that it will take a minimum of ten thousand years for those in the fiery mountain range at the edge of all things to qualify themselves for the Telestial Kingdom. However, is this ten thousand years according to the timing of man or God? I rather believe it would be after the timing of God, for why would years be reckoned after the rotation of Earth at the burning mountain ranges at the edge of all things? If true, we are talking about a process of transition from the fires of Hell to a degree of Telestial glory that is equivalent to 3.7 billion years as we measure time.

Whatever the duration of time, the vision now speaks of that will happen with the wicked when their days in Hell are accomplished.

63.1. In those days shall the mighty and the kings who possess the Earth implore (Him) to grant them a little respite from His angels of punishment to whom they were delivered, that they might fall down and worship before the Lord of Spirits, and confess their sins before Him.

63.2. And they shall bless and glorify the Lord of Spirits, and say: 'Blessed is the Lord of Spirits and the Lord of kings, and the Lord of the mighty and the Lord of the rich, and the Lord of glory and the Lord of wisdom,

63.3. And splendid in every secret thing is Thy power from generation to generation, and Thy glory for ever and ever: Deep are all Thy secrets and innumerable, and Thy righteousness is beyond reckoning.

63.4. We have now learnt that we should glorify and bless the Lord of kings and Him who is King over all kings.'

63.5. And they shall say: 'Would that we had rest to glorify and give thanks and confess our faith before His glory!

63.6. And now we long for a little rest but find it not: We follow hard upon and obtain it not: And light has vanished from before us, and darkness is our dwelling-place for ever and ever:

63.7. For we have not believed before Him nor glorified the name of the Lord of Spirits, [nor glorified our Lord] But our hope was in the scepter of our kingdom, and in our glory.

63.8. And in the day of our suffering and tribulation He saves us not, and we find no respite for confession that our Lord is true in all His works, and in His judgements and His justice, and His judgements have no respect of persons.

63.9. And we pass away from before His face on account of our works, and all our sins are reckoned up in righteousness.'

63.10. Now they shall say unto themselves: 'Our souls are full of unrighteous gain, but it does not prevent us from descending from the midst thereof into the †burden† of Sheol.'

63.11. And after that their faces shall be filled with darkness and shame before that Son of Man, and they shall be driven from his presence, and the sword shall abide before His face in their midst.

63.12. Thus spake the Lord of Spirits: 'This is the ordinance and judgement with respect to the mighty and the kings and the exalted and those who possess the earth before the Lord of Spirits.'

Noah's vision is different from Enoch's in that Enoch saw to the end when the wicked were redeemed from Hell. Noah's vision of these things ends before redemption comes to those in Hell. For reference, here is what Enoch saw regarding this same group:

50.2. On the day of affliction on which evil shall have been treasured up against the sinners. And the righteous shall be victorious in the name of the Lord of Spirits: and He will cause the others to witness (this) that they may repent and forgo the works of their hands.

50.3. They shall have no honor through the name of the Lord of Spirits, yet through His name shall they be saved, and the Lord of Spirits will have compassion on them, for His compassion is great.

51.1. And in those days shall the earth also give back that which has been entrusted to it, and Sheol also shall give back that which it has received, and Hell shall give back that which it owes.

51.2. For in those days the Elect One shall arise, and He shall choose the righteous and holy from among them: for the day has drawn nigh that they should be saved.

From the combined visions of both Enoch and Noah, it is clear that all those who call upon the Father and His beloved Son for mercy will eventually receive it. Yet, not before their transformation is complete. Just as it takes a very long time for the blackness of coal to transform into a diamond, so the terrible spectacle of self-atonement takes a very long time. To be covered by the atoning blood of the Son of God, who was slain for the sins of the multiverse, is a tremendous honor. Yet, these will never know that honor, for they rejected Him and now suffer for their own sins, even as He suffered. Therefore, their redemption comes at a very heavy price and after a very long time. Yet, in the end, even the most vile of sinners, such as Stalin and Hitler, can, if they choose, be redeemed from Hell and become heirs of salvation. However, the spectacle of their suffering will be a thing of legend—a tremendous learning opportunity for the children of heaven, who will be redeemed in the next cycle.

It may be the witnessing of such terrible pain and suffering that caused so many to opt out of the Father's plan of salvation. I cannot say. However, ultimately, when the price has finally been paid to the last senine, these will rise from the flames of Hell, transformed. If even one such as Hitler were to pay such a price as this, nobody would ever associate the atrocities of his former sins with him ever again, for he will no longer be the same man. He, and all others like him, will have been transformed by their atonements. As such, in the end, even these can become the servants of God. Yet, the fact remains, where God and His Christ are, these cannot come, worlds without end. Thus, regardless of the price they have paid, their atonements could never make of themselves what God could have made of them, had they placed their trust in the Only Begotten Son.

The moral of this chapter is simply this: Know the Lord, and come before Him now, in fear and trembling, and work out your salvation before the Throne of God while it is yet day. Seek to do His will above your own, and it will be well with you. Otherwise, a long and terrible night is coming of indefinite duration, wherein only the labor of transformative suffering can be performed.

Jesus Christ and His infinite atonement are available now to all who will humble themselves before Him. But to the world, Christ's legendary power and might and righteousness and glory and wisdom and dominion are hidden. For the Son of the Great God of the multiverse is hidden. He is known only to the wise who seek Him. Therefore, be wise, and seek Him while it is still called today!

Chapter 14 – Noah's Vision of the Watchers

In the prior chapter, we learned once more that the identity of the Son is hidden from the world. No man knows the Son, save the Father reveals Him. Just as no man knows the Father, save by the Son. The Father and the Son are so similar to each other that to know one is to know the other. Yet, it takes effort to know them, but you can know the Ba'als of the world for free. Furthermore, Ba'al is pleasing to the carnally minded, for he enables the natural man to be unshackled. However, such unshackling comes with a terrible cost.

On the other hand, those that see will humble themselves before the True and Living God, learning to see things as they really are. As they do, they realize what a tremendous blessing mortality is, and what an astounding opportunity for growth. Such can use mortality to progress in a relatively short span of time in ways that could be possible in no other way. It would seem that the veil of forgetfulness is the vital component that enables this progress to happen through faith in the Son of God. Thus, Christ taught that those who accept things on faith alone are more blessed than those who believe because they have seen. As such, many prayers for great endowments of knowledge go unanswered. Not because God does not hear our prayers, but because He will act in our best interests.

The day will eventually come when every knee will bow, and every tongue confess that Jesus is the Christ. Today is the day for us to repent and change. If we wait to change until it is too late, our ability to transform is greatly diminished. It is not impossible—with God, nothing is. However, fundamental spiritual transformation takes a very long time on the other side of this veil of tears. Therefore, let us seize the gift of today and exercise our agency as befitting those of understanding.

In the present chapter, we continue our analysis of the Noah fragment that was included in the Book of Enoch. In this portion of the text, Noah sees the destruction of the Watchers in his day. You will note the strong parallels between the destruction described by Noah and the destruction of the latter-day Watchers that was described by Enoch earlier. This parallel is not coincidental. We will discuss these similarities as the narrative continues.

64.1. And other forms I saw hidden in that place.

64.2. I heard the voice of the angel saying: 'These are the angels who descended to the Earth, and revealed what was hidden to the children of men and seduced the children of men into committing sin.'

Noah is speaking of another group of beings which he saw suffering in the burning mountain range at the edge of all things. The mountains overlook the chaotic void of Outer Darkness. This other group of beings is the Watchers who descended to the Earth and corrupted the prediluvian world. You will recall from the first volume of this series that the Watchers were told that they would not have forgiveness for their sins. That is to say, the atonement of Christ would not "cover" them. As such, if an atonement was to be made, the Watchers themselves would need to make it.

The burning mountain ranges at the edge of all things overlook Outer Darkness to illustrate that it can always get worse. For those that look upon the horrible scenes of that darkness, there is a terrible choice to make: they must choose to join them or to atone and change. For all that dwell in the burning mountains know that their days there, while long, are nevertheless temporary. As such, these are locations of decision. Those that are making this decision are making it at the last possible hour, and right next to the red line from which, if crossed, there can be no return. Few would ever choose to cross that line, but some will, and some of the Watchers will be counted among their numbers. Who crosses the line and who doesn't is an individual choice, but one with everlasting consequences. Yet, for some, their hatred of the Father and His Hidden Son will be so great that they will cross the line and never return.

Noah's vision now turns from the fate of the Watchers to that of the prediluvian world.

65.1. And in those days Noah saw the earth that it had sunk down and its destruction was nigh.

65.2. And he arose from thence and went to the ends of the earth, and cried aloud to his grandfather Enoch: and Noah said three times with an embittered voice: Hear me, hear me, hear me.'

The ancients had a custom of calling out three times in order to be heard. It may be a pattern worthy of emulation. Enoch and his people had long since been removed from the Earth. Nevertheless, somehow Enoch responds to his grandson's petition. The following conversation ensues:

65.3. And Noah said unto Enoch: 'Tell me what it is that is falling out on the earth that the earth is in such evil plight and shaken, lest perchance I shall perish with it?'

65.4. And thereupon there was a great commotion, on the earth, and a voice was heard from heaven, and Noah fell on his face.

65.5. And Enoch, Noah's grandfather came and stood by him, and said unto him: 'Why hast thou cried unto me with a bitter cry and weeping?

You will recall that at the beginning of this book, Noah saw a vision of what would befall the Earth in the last days. That vision so terrified Noah that he lost control of his loins and fell upon his face. In the vision above, Noah witnesses the wickedness of the antediluvian world and its subsequent destruction. Once again, he falls upon his face, but nothing is said of his loins. As such, while Noah is terrified by the antediluvian destruction of the Earth and the wickedness upon its face, it does not rival the terror he experienced when he witnessed the Great and Terrible Day of the Lord.

Still, it was disturbing enough for Noah that he began to weep bitterly and called for his grandfather Enoch. Enoch, who comes to the aid of his grandson, does not seem to be as concerned with the antediluvian destruction of the Earth as Noah. Recall that Enoch wrote his book not for the antediluvian world, but for the generation in the last days that would live to see wickedness removed from the Earth. Enoch asks Noah why he is so terrified by the destruction of the wicked. Enoch knows that all the righteous have been spared, for they were lifted up from the Earth and have joined him in his city. Noah, on the other hand, is like Abraham with Sodom and Gomorrah. He has lived amongst the wicked. They are his neighbors and countrymen. He loves them and does not want to see them destroyed any more than Abraham wanted to see the Canaanites destroyed.

Enoch does not wait for Noah to explain himself; instead, he jumps right in to explaining the reasons that the antediluvian world must be reset.

65.6. A command has gone forth from the presence of the Lord concerning those who dwell on the earth that their ruin is accomplished because they have learnt all the secrets of the angels, and all the violence of the satans, and all their powers--the most secret ones--and all the power of those who practice sorcery, and the power of witchcraft, and the power of those who make molten images for the whole earth:

65.7. And how silver is produced from the dust of the earth, and how soft metal originates in the earth.

65.8. For lead and tin are not produced from the earth like the first: it is a fountain that produces them, and an angel stands therein, and that angel is Pre-Eminent.'

Enoch explains that the Father has decreed that the Earth will be destroyed. The reason for the destruction is the forbidden knowledge that the Watchers introduced to the sons and daughters of Adam and Eve. This knowledge involved demonic powers, sorcery, and witchcraft. Enoch stated that through these powers, silver was literally made from the dust of the earth. He also explained that tin and lead were not being mined from the earth but were also being made with devices that the Watchers had created.

Today, we understand that most elements in existence can be created throughout the life cycles of stars through nuclear fusion. Modern man has been able to replicate this to a limited degree in a process called nuclear transmutation. Furthermore, through nuclear detonations, new elements that did not exist before have been created. Supernova explosions create precious metals. Yet, like nuclear explosions, supernovae are incredibly destructive events and are therefore not an effective way of transforming elements. It would seem, however, that the Watchers did create a controllable process wherein this could be done. However, it would seem that there was something very ominous about the device they created.

Enoch described the device as a fountain/foundry wherein an angel/demon inhabited the device to facilitate the transformation. This sounds very much like the ancient practice of chrysopoeia, or alchemy, wherein base metals were transmuted into precious metals. The Lord was clearly not pleased with this technology. Enoch stated that the alchemy of the Watchers was enabled by a demon/fallen angel named Pre-eminent. It would appear that Pre-eminent is a separate entity from Lucifer. This should not surprise us, as the Earth is filled with such demons.

This mysterious process may explain how the Canaanites acquired iron chariots long before the introduction of the Iron Age. It may also explain why the Lord required the House of Israel to destroy all Canaanite artifacts. The Lord does not intend such practices to become commonplace, and entire civilizations have been eliminated to keep such things from happening. Zosimus, a Greek historian who lived around the fall of Rome, wrote that alchemy was a dark art of the ancient world and that it involved making sacrifices to demons in order to facilitate the transmutation of metals.

Apparently, the sacrifices involved were human. Allegedly, Native American witchdoctors utilized similar human sacrifices as part of their Skinwalker rituals. Such rituals, it is said, operate upon the same principle of elemental transmutation; however, rather than metals, the human body itself is transformed. There are many Native Americans today who believe such practices are very real and continue to take place around the country. Johnathan Dover is a Navajo Ranger who works for the US Government on paranormal cases, which seem to frequent Indian Reservations. The stories that he tells of transmutational demonic rituals will make your skin crawl. He unequivocally states that this process is real and that he has encountered it many times.

If such things happened in antiquity, is it surprising that the Lord caused a great flood to erase the sorceries, witchcrafts, and enchantments to hide these abominations from before the face of the Lord? Yet, it would seem that some of these ancient practices were preserved and safeguarded by the post-diluvian world as well. The satanic priests of Pharaoh, for instance, were able to replicate many of Moses' miracles through their secret arts and sorceries. No doubt this knowledge was of ancient date. It is clear that such knowledge was commonplace amongst the Nephites before their collapse as well. Consider the following:

> And it came to pass that there were sorceries, and witchcrafts, and magics; and the power of the evil one was wrought upon all the face of the land…(Mormon 1:19)

From Mormon's description above, there can be no doubt that the powers behind these sorceries were demonic. It seems to me that the horrible deeds that Mormon described in Moroni 9:9-10 may have actually been examples of these types of sorceries and abominations amongst the Nephites. Such unspeakable wickedness sounds more like a demonic ceremony than a random act of violence. Yet, the sorceries of the ancient world could not protect them from extinction. Therefore, all those who engage in the dark arts have given themselves over to the worthless mysteries of which Enoch spoke in the eleventh chapter of the first volume of this series. Isaiah prophesies that in the last days, the knowledge of these ancient practices would be restored and practiced. Consider his grave warning:

> But these two things shall come to thee in a moment in one day, the loss of children, and widowhood: they shall come upon thee in their perfection for the multitude of thy sorceries, and for the great abundance of thine enchantments. For thou hast trusted in thy wickedness: thou hast said, None seeth me. Thy wisdom and thy knowledge, it hath perverted thee; and thou hast said in thine heart, I am, and none else beside me.

Therefore shall evil come upon thee; thou shalt not know from whence it riseth: and mischief shall fall upon thee; thou shalt not be able to put it off: and desolation shall come upon thee suddenly, which thou shalt not know.

Stand now with thine enchantments, and with the multitude of thy sorceries, wherein thou hast labored from thy youth; if so be thou shalt be able to profit, if so be thou mayest prevail. Thou art wearied in the multitude of thy counsels. Let now the astrologers, the stargazers, the monthly prognosticators, stand up, and save thee from these things that shall come upon thee. Behold, they shall be as stubble; the fire shall burn them; they shall not deliver themselves from the power of the flame (Isaiah 47:9-14)

The power of Satan is evil, debasing, and corrosive, but it is real. The power of God is righteous, ennobling, and everlasting. In the last days, those who place their trust in the worthless mysteries will see everything they have trusted in overturned in a single day. The coming Remnant of Jacob will cut them off both root and branch in a mode and method they did not expect. All their work shall be undone. In that day, they will come to understand that their mysteries were truly worthless. Though the coming day will bring many incredible miracles wrought by the likes of Lucifer, Pre-eminent, the Lady, the Antichrist, and the Beast, none of these will be able to stand in the presence of the Savior. In that day, Satan's worthless mysteries will account for nothing.

Yet, the days will soon be upon us when we will be shocked to our core by the power and miracles of the modern-day Watchers. Their power will turn our world upside down. In that coming day, the ancient powers long since hidden will come to the fore. Not all of these powers will be evil, but they will all be used to deceive and defraud the faithful. It will be such a convincing display that even the very elect according to covenant will be deceived by such awesome displays of power. The Lord has warned and forewarned us that these things are coming. Let us therefore not give in to them when we see them, regardless of how impressive they appear.

We now return to Noah's vision. Noah fell to the earth on account of the calamities that he saw would fall upon the antediluvian world. Enoch now lifts his grandson up off the ground and shares with him a promise and covenant that he received from the Lord. It is clear that Enoch shared this covenant with Noah because he too had qualified himself for the same. Consider the following:

65.9. And after that my grandfather Enoch took hold of me by my hand and raised me up, and said unto me: 'Go, for I have asked the Lord of Spirits as touching this commotion on the earth.

65.10. And the Lord of Spirits said unto me [Enoch]: "Because of their unrighteousness their judgement has been determined upon and shall not be withheld by Me forever. Because of the sorceries which they have searched out and learnt, the earth and those who dwell upon it shall be destroyed."

65.11. And these [*the Watchers*]--they have no place of repentance forever, because they have shown them what was hidden, and they are the damned: but as for thee, my son, the Lord of Spirits knows that thou art pure, and guiltless of this reproach concerning the secrets.

65.12. And He has destined thy name to be among the holy, and will preserve thee amongst those who dwell on the earth, and has destined thy righteous seed both for kingship and for great honors, and from thy seed shall proceed a fountain of the righteous and holy without number for ever.

In the passages above, we learn that Enoch was rewarded by God for not being swayed or deceived by the mysteries of the Watchers. Enoch trusted in God more than the spectacle of the Watchers. He held fast to God in the face of such things. His grandson Noah seems to be cut from the same cloth as him, for Noah also refrained from such practices. It would seem that one of the reasons that the Lord considered Noah to be perfect in his generation was because he remained untainted by the Watchers' deceptions.

As such, Noah became the beneficiary of the covenant and blessing of his grandfather Enoch. What was this covenant? That divine kingship would descend from his loins, and that his posterity of kings and queens would eventually become innumerable, for they would have no end, for the Family Business of the Father has no end. This is the Abrahamic covenant! Abraham, by his own admission, sought for and obtained the covenant of the fathers, as is plainly attested to for those with eyes to see in Abraham 1:2-4. However, more will be spoken of regarding this in subsequent chapters. For now, the important consideration is that we are about to encounter the same circumstances that provided both Enoch and Noah an opportunity to distinguish themselves before the Lord.

According to Isaiah 10 (see the chapter heading), very few people will survive the trials of the coming day. This is true despite the promise that the righteous will be preserved by fire – see 1 Nephi 22:17. Therefore, we must suppose that the reason so few survive is because so many will be deceived by the miraculous powers and deceptions of the coming day. Never has there been a greater opportunity for us to demonstrate our faith than today. Let us resolve to stand firm, and if needs be, die in and for our faith in the Lord Jesus Christ, come what may. If we do, we will be worthy of the same covenants and promises of our fathers. This is my primary takeaway from this interaction between Enoch and Noah.

Enoch now shows Noah one final thing before he leaves him. Consider the following:

> **66.1**. And after that, Enoch showed me the angels of punishment who are prepared to come and let lose all the powers of the waters which are beneath in the earth in order to bring judgement and destruction on all who [abide and] dwell on the earth.

> **66.2**. And the Lord of Spirits gave commandment to the angels who were going forth, that they should not cause **the waters** to rise but should hold them in check; for those angels were over the powers of the waters.

> **66.3**. And I went away from the presence of Enoch.

Enoch showed Noah how the wickedness of his generation would be cleansed. That cleansing would come by way of a great flood. Noah observed that the Lord had placed a limit upon the flood itself and upon the angels that administered the destruction. The flood would rise to a certain limit, and then it would recede. The Lord has placed similar restrictions upon the angels of destruction in the last days. They are not to harm those who have the seal of God upon their foreheads. Ezekiel saw that this seal was associated with those who mourned for the sins of the world (Ezekiel 9:4). Therefore, let us come out from the world and be separate from their unclean things. If we must wash ourselves in the atoning blood of the Lamb from the blood and sins of this generation, let us do so quickly! For the days are soon coming when the wicked will be swept from off the face of these lands, and the meek will inherit not only the Earth, but the covenants of the ancient fathers!

Chapter 15 – The Third Wave

In the prior chapter, we learned more about the prediluvian destruction of the world. That destruction came in large part due to demon-fueled sorceries, witchcrafts, and enchantments that had spread throughout the whole earth. One of the ancient titles for the principal source of wickedness that will face the world in the last days is Belial, a name which means "worthless." By this title, the ancients meant to warn us that while his mysteries will be incredible and enticing, they will also be worthless with regard to our salvation.

Indeed, rather than storing up treasures in heaven, such worthless mysteries corrupt and eat away at our souls and will leave us empty and powerless before the Throne of God. Therefore, while there is secret knowledge that has been lauded and safeguarded by the secret combinations of the world for thousands of years, it is of no value and should not be sought. If Noah's days were a template for our own, life is about to get very interesting in the near future!

In this chapter, Noah received further instruction regarding the Watchers, the society in which he lived, and his own standing before God. I believe that these things will have great significance for us in the coming days.

> **67.1**. And in those days the word of God came unto me, and He said unto me: 'Noah, thy lot has come up before Me, a lot without blame, a lot of love and uprightness.

> **67.2**. And now the angels are making a wooden (building), and when they have completed that task I will place My hand upon it and preserve it, and there shall come forth from it the seed of life, and a change shall set in so that the earth will not remain without inhabitant.

> **67.3**. And I will make fast thy seed before me for ever and ever, and I will spread abroad those who dwell with thee: it shall not be unfruitful on the face of the earth, but it shall be blessed and multiply on the earth in the name of the Lord.'

The Lord states three very important things in the verses above. First, that Noah, despite living in a sinful and violent society, was a man of love and righteousness. Noah had charity. This gives us more insight into the following passage from one of the most curious chapters in the Bible:

Noah was a just man and perfect in his generations, and
Noah walked with God (Gen 6:9)

Taken together, we understand that Noah walked with God in precisely the same way as his grandfather Enoch walked with God (Gen 5:24). Both of these men walked with God because they walked after the manner of God. Their hearts and actions were aligned with those of the Father and His Hidden Son. If we would be justified and perfect in our generation, then we must also walk after the manner of God.

By this, I mean that we cannot be filled with hate and anger towards our fellow men, despite the wickedness and wrongdoing so prevalent in our days. Contention, rage, anger, and hatred are all attributes of darkness. If we exhibit these traits, it is a sign that we have darkness within us. In contrast, charity is the pure love of Christ. Charity is a defining attribute of those who walk with God. If you have charity, it will be well with you, just as it was well with Enoch and Noah.

Second, we learn from the passages above that the building of the Ark was a collaborative effort. Like Nephi, Noah did not build the ark by himself; rather, he did so with divine aid. This was not a foregone conclusion. The Brother of Jared knew that his barges had a major design flaw in that they were dark and dreary inside. They smelled awful, and living conditions were terrible. He knew all of these things, and yet, despite relaxing on the beach for several years with nothing but time on his hands, he did not collaborate with the Lord to improve the design. Indeed, he only went to the Lord once the barges were complete.

In this regard, the Brother of Jared lived well beneath his privileges, and his family felt the consequences of that fact when they were driven by the monster waves and shaken like beans in a maraca. Thus, one can be a righteous person and still live well beneath their divine privileges. We are in the driver's seat. By the collaborative ark-building process described above, we understand that Noah was exercising his privileges.

This brings us to the third and final observation. Because of Noah's collaborative effort with the Lord, he became heir to the covenant of his fathers. Today we know this covenant as the Abrahamic covenant, but it most certainly did not originate with Abraham. As we have seen throughout this series, this covenant was sought for and obtained by the original fathers. Indeed, the ark was the means whereby the records of the fathers were preserved so that Abraham could study and seek for them many years later (see Abraham 1:31).

If you have eyes to see, there is much to be seen in the passages above. Noah's encounter with God continues:

67.4. And He will imprison those angels, who have shown unrighteousness, in that burning valley which my grandfather Enoch had formerly shown to me in the west among the mountains of gold and silver and iron and soft metal and tin.

67.5. And I saw that valley in which there was a great convulsion and a convulsion of the waters.

67.6. And when all this took place, from that fiery molten metal and from the convulsion thereof in that place, there was produced a smell of sulphur, and it was connected with those waters, and that valley of the angels who had led astray (mankind) burned beneath that land.

67.7. And through its valleys proceed streams of fire, where these angels are punished who had led astray those who dwell upon the earth.

67.8. But those waters shall in those days serve for the kings and the mighty and the exalted, and those who dwell on the earth, for the healing of the body, but for the punishment of the spirit; now their spirit is full of lust, that they may be punished in their body, for they have denied the Lord of Spirits and see their punishment daily, and yet believe not in His name.

67.9. And in proportion as the burning of their bodies becomes severe, a corresponding change shall take place in their spirit for ever and ever; for before the Lord of Spirits none shall utter an idle word.

67.10. For the judgement shall come upon them, because they believe in the lust of their body and deny the Spirit of the Lord.

67.11. And those same waters will undergo a change in those days; for when those angels are punished in these waters, these water-springs shall change their temperature, and when the angels ascend, this water of the springs shall change and become cold.

67.12. And I heard Michael answering and saying: 'This judgement wherewith the angels are judged is a testimony for the kings and the mighty who possess the earth.'

67.13. Because these waters of judgement minister to the healing of the body of the kings and the lust of their body; therefore they will not see and will not believe that those waters will change and become a fire which burns for ever.

In the passages above, Noah speaks of the self-atonement that will be made by the Watchers because they would not accept the healing waters that might have otherwise changed them. The healing waters are symbolic of the Living Water, which is the Son of Man. Those who drink of the Living Water will never thirst again. Those who do not will never be satiated. As the Watchers rejected the Father's Hidden Son, they will atone for their own sins at the burning edge of all things. In that day, their own sufferings will be the catalyst for change. However, as has been previously discussed, that change will be very long in coming.

Let us purify ourselves in the Living Waters, that we might be able to overcome the lusts of the flesh, rather than being consumed by them, as the Watchers were. The theory of such things is simple. The practice of such things is hard. Yet, the sacrament prayers illustrate the transformative path. We must constantly remember the Son of God and seek to walk in His ways, as Enoch and Noah did. If we do not, we will walk the well-worn and heavily trodden ways of the world. The two paths are clear, and the choice as to which one we will take is ours alone.

68.1. And after that my grandfather Enoch gave me the teaching of all the secrets in the book in the Parables which had been given to him, and he put them together for me in the words of the book of the Parables.

68.2. And on that day Michael answered Raphael and said: 'The power of the spirit transports and makes me to tremble because of the severity of the judgement of the secrets, the judgement of the angels [*Watchers*]: Who can endure the severe judgement which has been executed, and before which they melt away?'

68.3. And Michael answered again, and said to Raphael: 'Who is he whose heart is not softened concerning it, and whose reins are not troubled by this word of judgement (that) has gone forth upon them because of those who have thus led them out?'

68.4. And it came to pass when he stood before the Lord of Spirits, Michael said thus to Raphael: 'I will not take their part under the eye of the Lord; for the Lord of Spirits has been angry with them because they do as if they were the Lord. Therefore all that is hidden shall come upon them [*the Watchers*] for ever and ever; for neither angel nor man shall have His portion, but alone they have received their judgement for ever and ever.'

69.1 And after this judgement they shall terrify and make them to tremble because they have shown this to those who dwell on the earth.

69.2 And behold the names of those angels [and these are their names: the first of them is Samjâzâ, the second Artâqîfâ, and the third Armên, the fourth Kôkabêl, the fifth †Tûrâêl†, the sixth Rûmjâl, the seventh Dânjâl, the eighth †Nêqâêl†, the ninth Barâqêl, the tenth Azâzêl, the eleventh Armârôs, the twelfth Batarjâl, the thirteenth †Busasêjal†, the fourteenth Hanânêl, the fifteenth †Tûrêl†, and the sixteenth Sîmâpêsîêl, the seventeenth Jetrêl, the eighteenth Tûmâêl, the nineteenth Tûrêl, the twentieth †Rumâêl†, the twenty-first †Azâzêl†.

69.3. And these are the chiefs of their angels and their names, and their chief ones over hundreds and over fifties and over tens].

According to the passages above, the punishment of the first two hundred prediluvian Watchers will be terrible. It caused Michael, the Great Prince, to tremble because of its severity. Michael observes that the Watchers and those who followed them will never be able to partake in God's portion but will receive their own portions forever and ever. This is the same teaching found within D&C 76 regarding those who atone for the price of their own sins. They can never come where God and Christ are, worlds without end.

Michael's observation about the severity of the Watchers' punishment is also reminiscent of Christ's warning regarding how heavy the price of personal atonement is. Consider His words in the context of the passages above:

> Therefore I command you to repent—repent, lest I smite you by the rod of my mouth, and by my wrath, and by my anger, and your sufferings be sore—how sore you know not, how exquisite you know not, yea, how hard to bear you know not.
>
> For behold, I, God, have suffered these things for all, that they might not suffer if they would repent; but if they would not repent they must suffer even as I; which suffering caused myself, even God, the greatest of all, to tremble because of pain, and to bleed at every pore, and to suffer both body and spirit—and would that I might not drink the bitter cup, and shrink (D&C 19:15-18)

Christ already suffered for the sins of the Watchers. They did not need to go through the terrible agonies of suffering that they will endure, but they rejected Jesus Christ and would not have Him as their Savior. As such, they will atone for their own sins, and their suffering will be exceedingly terrible and prolonged. How Christ was able to atone for the sins of all humanity within the Garden and upon the cross, I do not comprehend. However, just as with the brazen serpent upon the staff, I do not need to know how it works, only that it does. Therefore, let us look to the Son of Man with gratitude and humility that He has provided a better way for us, if we will but look to Him and live!

Another noteworthy observation from the above passages comes with a comparison of the Watchers' names to those found in Enoch 6:7 in volume I of this series. The names are very similar, but they are spelled differently. One might expect this to be the case if these two accounts were written by two separate people who lived hundreds of years apart, as Enoch and Noah did. Furthermore, in Enoch's writings, the names of the leaders of ten were provided, but Noah accounts for leaders of fifties and hundreds as well. This is a good reminder of the significance of multiple perspectives and descriptions, such as the added depth and clarity provided by Nephi in his retelling of Lehi's dream.

Now Noah's narrative introduces a new group of leaders, whose names are new to us. He does so without any contextual explanation, which in my opinion suggests that in his day these names were so well known as to not require explanation. Consider these additional characters:

> **69.4**. The name of the first Jeqôn: that is, the one who led astray [all] the sons of **God**, and brought them down to the earth, and led them astray through the daughters of men.

69.5. And the second was named Asbeêl: he imparted to the holy sons of God evil counsel, and led them astray so that they defiled their bodies with the daughters of men.

69.6. And the third was named Gâdreêl: he it is who showed the children of men all the blows of death, and he led astray [the daughters of Eve], and showed [the weapons of death to the sons of men] the shield and the coat of mail, and the sword for battle, and all the weapons of death to the children of men.

69.7. And from his hand they have proceeded against those who dwell on the earth from that day and for evermore.

69.8. And the fourth was named Pênêmûe: he taught the children of men the bitter and the sweet, and he taught them all the secrets of their wisdom.

69.9. And he instructed mankind in writing with ink and paper, and thereby many sinned from eternity to eternity and until this day.

69.10. For men were not created for such a purpose, to give confirmation to their good faith with pen and ink.

69.11. For men were created exactly like the angels, to the intent that they should continue pure and righteous, and death, which destroys everything, could not have taken hold of them, but through this their knowledge they are perishing, and **through this power it is consuming me†**.

I want to pause here a moment and discuss Noah's words above. Noah was particularly fearful of the teachings of Pênêmûe, who taught men how to write. It was not the act of writing that was the sin, but the ability to transfer forbidden knowledge from generation to generation that troubled Noah. You will recall that Giddianhi, the leader of the Gadianton robbers, boasted that their secret knowledge had been preserved in ancient writings and handed down to them (see 3 Nephi 3:9). Writing has enabled many dark arts to persist from one generation to another, when, if not for such writings, such practices would have died with the wicked.

It would appear that Noah was personally impacted by the philosophies of ancient writings. By saying that he was consumed by their power, he was saying that these ancient philosophies mingled with scripture, teased upon his mind, and tried his faith to the point that he wished writing had never been reintroduced. Yet, if Noah and Enoch had not learned and practiced the art of writing, we would not have their priceless words today. Thus, the power of the pen and letters is mighty indeed, both for good and for evil. Therefore, when it comes to ancient writings, it is of great importance to learn how to discern truth from error through the Spirit of God. The Nazis failed to do this and consumed many innocent lives as a result.

Given Noah's conversations with the Lord, while many of the ancient world's philosophies were apparently appealing to him, he clearly was able to discern between truth and error, bitter and sweet, light and darkness. Learning how to discern between the two is a painful process that results in much anguish of soul, as the psalm of Nephi recorded in 2 Nephi 4 clearly demonstrates. While the Earth is in its present state, good men and women still continuously struggle against the allure of sin and weakness. Such things are as common as gravity itself. Yet, if we endure such things well, the days will come when our weaknesses will be made strong and we will overcome all things through Christ, Jesus. Thus, the importance of enduring to the end!

Now, let us continue to ponder Noah's words above. We must remember that the world had been destroyed. The only survivors that remained were Noah's immediate family. As such, why would Noah be so concerned by the activities of these Watchers he is discussing, if their actions and records had been washed away by the prediluvian world? Herein is the mystery. I believe that Noah's greatest lament is that he is writing about a second wave of Watchers that had come to the Earth and corrupted the postdiluvian world. This second wave taught his posterity the written language of the prediluvian world, so that the ancient records and writings could be read by his posterity once more. Therefore, the ancient sins of the prediluvian world were able to live on. We will discuss this idea more as the narrative continues:

Noah's account continues:

> **69.12**. And the fifth was named Kâsdejâ: this is he who showed the children of men all the wicked smitings of spirits and demons, and the smitings of the embryo in the womb, that it may pass away, and [the smitings of the soul] the bites of the serpent, and the smitings which befall through the noontide heat, the son of the serpent named Tabââ'ĕt.

With the passage above, Noah concludes his description of five leaders of the Watchers, all of whom had major roles to play, and none of whom were included in Enoch's written record. These five leaders were Jeqon, Asbeel, Gadreel, Pênêmûe, and Kasdeja. I believe that these five leaders were not part of the original group of two hundred

Watchers that descended upon Mount Hermon in the days of Jared, Enoch's father, but rather the Watchers that returned to the postdiluvian world. If these Watchers were organized like their fathers, then these five men might represent fifty men. However, these five men could have been married to people of their own world and may have even had their wives with them. Either way, this group would have made a significant impact upon the population of the postdiluvian world.

More information regarding this second wave of Watchers is provided in the Book of Jubilees. Consider the following passage from this book:

> And in the third week of this jubilee the unclean demons [Watchers] began to lead astray †the children of† the sons of Noah; and to make to err and destroy them. And the sons of Noah came to Noah their father, and they told him concerning the demons which were, leading astray and blinding and slaying his sons' sons. And he prayed before the Lord his God, and said:
>
> God of the spirits of all flesh, who hast shown mercy unto me, and hast saved me and my sons from the waters of the flood, and hast not caused me to perish as Thou didst the sons of perdition; for Thy grace hath been great towards me, and great hath been Thy mercy to my soul; let Thy grace be lift up upon my sons, and let not wicked spirits rule over them lest they should destroy them from the earth. But do Thou bless me and my sons, that we may increase and multiply and replenish the earth. And Thou knowest how Thy Watchers, the fathers of these spirits, acted in my day: and as for these spirits which are living, imprison them and hold them fast in the place of condemnation, and let them not bring destruction on the sons of thy servant, my God; for these are malignant, and created in order to destroy. And let them not rule over the spirits of the living; for Thou alone canst exercise dominion over them. And let them not have power over the sons of the righteous from henceforth and for evermore."
>
> And the Lord our God bade [*Raphel*] to bind all. And the chief of the spirits, Mastêmâ [*Satan*], came and said: "Lord, Creator, let some of them remain before me, and let them hearken to my voice, and do all that I shall say unto them; for if some of them are not left to me, I shall not be able to

execute the power of my will on the sons of men; for these are for corruption and leading astray before my judgment, for great is the wickedness of the sons of men."

And He said: "Let the tenth part of them remain before him [*Satan*], and let nine parts descend into the place of condemnation." And one of [*the archangels*] He commanded that [*they*] should teach Noah all their medicines; for He knew that they would not walk in uprightness, nor strive in righteousness.

And [*the archangels*] did according to all His words: all the malignant evil ones [*were*] bound in the place of condemnation, and a tenth part of them [were] left that they might be subject before Satan on the earth. And [*the archangels*] explained to Noah all the medicines of their diseases, together with their seductions, how he might heal them with herbs of the earth. And Noah wrote down all things in a book as we instructed him concerning every kind of medicine. Thus the evil spirits [*Watchers*] were precluded from (hurting) the sons of Noah. (Book of Jubilees 10:1-13)

According to the passages above, this group of Watchers, whatever their number, had to have been much larger than five, or a tenth could not have remained, for you cannot have half of a person. Regardless of their population, Noah described them as being the sons of the original Watchers. By this, we are to understand their sons from their home world, for they are not described as being giants. However, because of them, giants were reintroduced into the lands of Canaan.

Furthermore, according to the narrative, it seems that the Watchers were poisoning the posterity of Noah. It would seem that the Watchers wanted to occupy the lands where these people were living and thought poisoning the inhabitants was the best way to obtain their desires. Given the history of the world, the lands they were seeking to obtain had to have been the lands of Canaan, for that was the home of the giants.

Curiously, Mastema, a name which means hate, hostility, or persecution, petitions the Lord that a tenth of the Watchers' population might be spared to facilitate his testing of mankind. The Lord consents, and the land of Canaan secured a place in history for the next seven hundred and fifty years or so, until the Lord commands the Children of Israel to destroy them. From this interaction, it is clear that the Lord is not concerned about making mortality easy. Indeed, without question, this action made life on Satan's prison planet that much more challenging.

Given the technological advancements of the Watchers, the grandsons of Noah had no recourse against them. They were dependent upon angels to teach them how to make antidotes to the poisons that were killing them. I find it fascinating today that Robert Kennedy Jr. has joined forces with Trump with the sole objective of eliminating poisons from our own food supplies. There can be no doubt that Americans are fed things that the rest of the world has prohibited from being added to their food supplies. The result has been a pandemic of obesity and sickness that is not seen elsewhere. This seems to be a curious parallel to the ancient world.

Because Pênêmûe taught Noah's posterity how to read the ancient scripts of the prediluvian world, the worthless mysteries were once again accessible. With the influx of ancient wisdom and the reduced power and influence of the Watchers by the Lord's intervention, the balance of power shifted back to the posterity of Noah, and they began to prosper exceedingly. Within one hundred and fifty years from the flood, the descendants of Noah began a massive construction project. Nothing like this project had ever been attempted before—the Tower of Babel.

Consider the following description of this project from the Bible.

> And they said, Go to, let us build us a city and a tower, whose top *may reach* unto heaven; and let us make us a name, lest we be scattered abroad upon the face of the whole earth. And the LORD came down to see the city and the tower, which the children of men built [*meaning that they had completed it*].
>
> And the LORD said, Behold, the people *is* one, and they have all one language; and this they begin to do: and now nothing will be restrained from them, which they have imagined to do. Go to, let us go down, and there confound their language, that they may not understand one another's speech. So the LORD scattered them abroad from thence upon the face of all the earth: and they left off to build the city.
>
> Therefore is the name of it called Babel; because the LORD did there confound the language of all the earth: and from thence did the LORD scatter them abroad upon the face of all the earth. (Gen 11:4-9)

The purpose of the Tower of Babel was for the people to make a name for themselves in the heavens. They wanted to build something that would astound even the Watchers. According to the Book of Jubilees, the descendants of Noah spent forty-three years building the Tower of Babel. When finished, according to that ancient text, the tower

234

was 5,433 cubits in height, with a base of thirteen by thirty stades. If my translation of these ancient units of measure is correct, the base of the Tower of Babel would have been an incredible 8,125 feet by 18,750 feet, or 5.5 square miles. It would have stood an astounding 8,150 feet high. If true, this structure would have easily dwarfed any man-made structure ever built. Given the tremendous size of its base, the tower would have most likely been built in the shape of a ziggurat, or stepped pyramid. It would have quite literally been the size of a mountain, even taller than Mount Hermon, the famous mountain peak of the original Watchers' first descent.

This project demonstrated that nothing was impossible for this determined people. As such, the Lord intervened by confounding the language of the people and literally dividing the Earth into multiple continents. Of this period of time, the famous Jewish historian Josephus wrote the following:

> After this they were dispersed abroad on account of their languages, and went out by colonies everywhere, and each colony took possession of that land which they light upon, and to which God led them… there were some also who passed over the sea in ships. (Josephus – book 1 chapter 5)

Josephus' account corresponds with that of the Jaredites, who crossed the sea in barges shortly after the events of the Tower of Babel. God then cast down the Tower of Babel, perhaps in the same event that divided Pangea, and things which should not have been forgotten were lost. The confounding of the languages seems to have also applied to the surviving Watchers, whose influence was now quarantined to the land of Canaan. The fall of the last Canaanite stronghold corresponded with the destruction of Sisera and his nine hundred mysterious chariots of iron at the hands of the kings of heaven, as discussed in Chapter 18 – Interstellar, in volume one of this work.

After this period, the Chaldeans seemed to be the only remaining group in the ancient world with the ability to read the prediluvian texts. Thankfully, they hoarded this information for their own benefit and advancement, rather than disseminating it throughout the ancient world once more. Thus, the knowledge of the ancients was muted, but not forgotten.

The knowledge of the Watchers among the Canaanites can be understood by the high strangeness of certain Biblical narratives, such as the presence of giants in the lands of Canaan and fiery flying serpents. We have briefly touched upon these fascinating creatures previously, but given the context of the present chapter, let's go into a little more detail about what is known of these creatures now. The footnotes in the LDS Bible are quick to rename fiery serpents as venomous serpents. However, if we believe that the Book of Mormon is the most correct book on Earth, these footnotes are not correct.

For the Book of Mormon does not call them venomous serpents, but rather "fiery flying serpents."

The Hebrew phrase for fiery serpents is "seraphim nachashim." As we have noted in a previous chapter, Seraphim are magnificent winged creatures with supernatural power. The original authors of the Bible associated these "fiery flying serpents" with Seraphim. Furthermore, the Hebrew word "nachashim" means snakes, sorceries, or witchcrafts. We learn about these events in Numbers 21. The context of this chapter is Israel destroying Canaanite settlements, and in the very next chapter, Balak, a Canaanite king, is offering money to anyone who can curse the Israelites. Is it possible that the fiery flying serpents were the result of just such a curse? The Egyptian priests were able to make snakes from staffs, after all.

This becomes particularly interesting in light of the specific knowledge attributed to one of these Watchers noted above. Consider the fiery flying serpents as being a potential Canaanite curse in light of the following verse:

> **69.12.** And the fifth was named Kâsdejâ: this is he who showed the children of men all the wicked smitings [*think curses*] of spirits and demons, and the smitings of the embryo in the womb, that it may pass away, and [*the smitings of the soul*] the bites of the serpent, and the smitings which befall through the noontide heat, the son of the serpent named Tabââ'ĕt.

Kasdeja is spoken of as having forbidden knowledge regarding smiting the souls of men through the power of spirits and demons. These curses are particularly linked to snakes, meaning sorceries and witchcraft. Specifically, Kasdeja is called the son of the serpent because of his forbidden abilities. This is a strange theory to consider, but the coming days will be filled with many strange things. I am concerned that the supernatural will soon become the default status of the Earth, and that we will have experiences with monsters of our own.

Thus, we must concede that the history of this world is more complicated and bizarre than most are prepared to accept. For a long time, it has been easy to dismiss these things. However, the blessed window of ignorance is closing. The prophecy of Ezra's Eagle states that much of the knowledge of the ancient world will be restored during the days of the three eagle heads (see 2 Esdras 12:23). To some, the restoration of this knowledge will have catastrophic consequences for their faith. This restoration will pave the way for the return of the demon-fueled gods of the ancient world.

Daniel prophesied that when the antichrist returns, he will pluck up three of the world's foremost rulers by their roots and supplant them. When he does:

> He shall speak great words against the most High, and shall wear out the saints of the most High, and think to change times and laws: and they shall be given into his hand until a time and times and the dividing of time. (Daniel 7:25)

That is to say, the antichrist will rewrite our history books and challenge our understanding of antiquity. With this power, he will overcome the saints of God, for the saints of God have no framework for such things. Yet, the antichrist's grip upon the saints will be broken when the Remnant of Jacob returns. At that time, America will be liberated, and a new era of peace and prosperity will be ushered in upon her hallowed shores, and the saints will have their eyes wide open to the true nature of the multiverse.

These things are both strange and uncomfortable for many. Yet, if such things are true, then they are critical to understand. Why? Because the first and second waves of the Watchers have now come and gone, but the third wave is at our doors. If you open your eyes and seek to reconcile the strange events that are happening on this planet with increasing regularity, rather than burying your head in the sand and ignoring them, you will be better prepared for the coming day.

I believe that this is the meaning behind the following prophecy found within the words of Isaiah:

> Bring forth the blind people that have eyes, and the deaf that have ears. Let all the nations be gathered together, and let the people be assembled: Who among them can declare this, and shew us former things? Let them bring forth their witnesses, that they may be justified: or let them hear, and say, It is truth. Ye are my witnesses, saith the LORD, and my servant whom I have chosen: that ye may know and believe Me, and understand that I am He: before Me there was no god formed, neither shall there be after me. I, even I, am the LORD; and beside me there is no savior. [*meaning the false Christ that will come in the last days may profess himself to be the savior of the Universe, but he is not.*]
>
> I have declared, and have saved, and I have shewed, when there was no strange god among you: therefore ye are My witnesses, saith the LORD, that I am God. Yea, before the day was I am He; and there is none that can deliver out of

My hand: I will work, and who shall [*turn it back*]? (Isaiah 43:8-13)

The prophecy above is incredible. The Lord began by stating that there would be those among His people who would have ears to hear and eyes to see, even when the majority would be both deaf and blind. The Lord proclaimed that these few who understood His words would be His witnesses before the nations. Such will testify that God spoke of these things long before the strange gods of the last days ever came among us, professing to be our saviors.

God alone is our Savior, and He is mighty to save us. What He has declared from before the foundations of the world will be fulfilled, every jot and every tittle. Those who ignore the Lord's warnings and do not follow His admonition to search the words of Isaiah will be blindsided by the coming events. In the coming day, unless the saints have the constant guiding influence of the Holy Ghost, even the very elect among us according to the covenant will be deceived. Yet, there is none that will be able to destroy those who rely upon the Lord in that day. He will perform His work, and no unhallowed hand will be able to stop it. Bring on the third wave!

Chapter 16 – The Oath and the Covenant

In the previous chapter, we learned about the second wave of Watchers that corrupted the Earth during the days of Noah's grandchildren. This led to the destruction of ninety percent of the Watchers and their descendants, the confounding of languages, and the division of Pangea. The Earth's corruption once again came through hidden knowledge. As we have learned throughout this book, the Lord has His own mysteries. However, His mysteries ennoble the soul, whereas those of the Watchers debase and defile.

In this chapter, we will delve into one of the most important mysteries of God. Consider the following passage from the writings of Noah:

> **69.13**. And this is the task of Kâsbeêl, the Chief of the Oath which He showed to the holy ones when He dwelt high above in glory, and its name is Beqa.

Kasbeel is a title that means the Fuller of God. A Fuller is someone who removes stains and impurities, making all that is impure or unclean become clean and acceptable before God (see Malachi 3:2-3). Such a title greatly limits the possibilities of whom it could apply to, especially given that the Lord specifically stated that besides Him there is no Savior.

Additionally, we learn that the Lord's Fuller is also the Chief of the Oath, meaning He is the One who judges whether an oath has been fulfilled or not. Furthermore, it is clear that this man was considered to be such before the world was, when the holy ones, or the Noble and Great Ones, still resided in heaven. Based on these descriptions, according to the knowledge of the ancient world, there can be only one man to whom these conditions apply – the Son of Man.

Jesus Christ is the Chief of the Oath and Covenant. For this reason, in ancient times, the priesthood, which is the oath and covenant, was called the Priesthood after the Order of the Son of God. Later, to avoid the constant repetition of the Lord's name, the ancients changed its name to the Priesthood after the Order of Enoch. This is because Enoch entered into this covenant with Christ and magnified it exceedingly well. After Enoch, the next man to magnify this covenant to an extraordinary degree was Melchizedek. It is for this reason that the oath and covenant of the priesthood bear his name today.

According to Noah, it was Christ who first taught the oath and covenant of the priesthood to the Noble and Great Ones before the world was. The power by which this oath operates also bears Christ's name. This power proceeds forth from the presence of God to fill the immensity of space. It is the power by which all things are governed – the Light of Christ.

According to Noah, this covenant was known by the ancients as Beqa. This is a very curious title, for in Hebrew, Beqa means half. In other words, this covenant was comprised of two parts. Thanks to the restoration of the gospel of Jesus Christ upon the Earth in the last days, we know that the oath and covenant of the priesthood is comprised of two parts: the Aaronic or lesser priesthood, and the Melchizedek priesthood. From this term, it is clear that the ancients held this same understanding.

We now return to Noah's writings as he further elaborates upon this sacred covenant.

> **69.14**. [Kasbeel] requested Michael to show him the hidden name, that he might enunciate it in the oath, so that those might quake before that name and oath who revealed all that was in secret to the children of men.

> **69.15**. And this is the power of this oath, for it is powerful and strong, and he placed this oath Akâe in the hand of Michael.

In the above passages, Noah appears to be referring to a sacred ceremony related to the Oath and Covenant of the Priesthood. Noah mentioned two specific aspects of this covenant, which we might assume pertain to the two halves of the covenant. Accordingly, the first half of this covenant was associated with a hidden name that only Michael knew. Michael enunciated this name as part of the priesthood oath. That this aspect of the ceremony was sacred is beyond question, for Noah stated that those who revealed what was secret to the children of men had great cause to fear.

The second aspect of this sacred oath and covenant of the Priesthood is associated with tremendous priesthood power. Apparently, God placed some token or sign into Michael's hand, which was called the Akâe. To this day, nobody knows what this sign or token was, or even what the name Akâe means. This may be precisely the point. Just as the Lord obtained the hidden name of the first sign or token of the priesthood from Michael, Michael was to obtain the meaning of the second sign or token of the priesthood from God Himself.

Noah goes on to further explain the incredible power and importance that these two components of the Oath and Covenant of the Priesthood had in antiquity. Consider the following:

> **69.16** And these are the secrets of this oath... and they [*referring to those that make and keep this covenant*] are strong through His oath: and the heaven was suspended before the world was created, and for ever.

By this last passage, we understand that those who made and kept this sacred oath and covenant became exceedingly strong. This means they obtained the same powers that formed the cosmos and all that is within it. The three dots (...) indicated in the passage above were present in all the twenty-plus copies of the Book of Enoch that R.H. Charles used to create this translation. As such, these are not an indication of missing text but rather a scribal indication that there was more to be said regarding these covenants, but it was not lawful to be written down by man. Therefore, if men are to learn of these things, they must be taught by God and God alone. May the Lord have mercy upon those who divulge what they ought not.

It is interesting that Noah provided this summarized account of the Oath and Covenant of the Priesthood shortly after describing the worthless mysteries of the Watchers. For all the power of the Watchers, there was nothing they could do when confronted with the true power of God. Therefore, Noah urges us to seek to be taught these things by the Lord rather than by men.

Nothing can stand before the power of God. Even Satan himself becomes as a wilted celery stalk before the Throne of God. Woe to the man or woman who trades the things of God for the trinkets and baubles of Watchers and demons. Such are destined to become the ashes beneath the beautiful feet of the Lord's humble followers—those who spent their days diligently seeking Him and His ways (see D&C 84:47-48).

> And he that receiveth my Father receiveth My Father's Kingdom, therefore all that My Father hath shall be given unto him. (D&C 84:38)

This is what it means to receive an exceedingly great weight of glory. Such promises and blessing are available to all, however, few will seek them, for it is the common practice of the Saints to live well beneath their privileges in this regard. Noah continues explaining the power that has been exercised through this oath and covenant in times past.

69.17. And through it the earth was founded upon the water, and from the secret recesses of the mountains come beautiful waters, from the creation of the world and unto eternity.

69.18. And through that oath the sea was created, and †as its foundation† He set for it the sand against the time of [His] anger, and it dare not pass beyond it from the creation of the world unto eternity.

69.19. And through that oath are the depths made fast, and abide and stir not from their place from eternity to eternity.

69.20. And through that oath the sun and moon complete their course, and deviate not from their ordinance from eternity to eternity.

69.21. And through that oath the stars complete their course, and He calls them by their names, and they answer Him from eternity to eternity.

69.22. [And in like manner the spirits of the water, and of the winds, and of all zephyrs [*gentle breezes*], and (their) paths from all the quarters of the winds.]

69.23. [And there are preserved the voices of the thunder and the light of the lightnings: and there are preserved the chambers of the hail and the chambers of the hoarfrost, and the chambers of the mist, and the chambers of the rain and the dew.]

69.24. [And all these believe and give thanks before the Lord of Spirits, and glorify (Him) with all their power, and their food is in every act of thanksgiving: they thank and glorify and extol the name of the Lord of Spirits for ever and ever.]

69.25. And this oath is mighty over them and through it [they are preserved and] their paths are preserved, and their course is not destroyed.

69.26. And there was great joy amongst them, and they blessed and glorified and extolled because the name of that Son of Man had been revealed unto them.

69.27. And He sat on the throne of His glory, and the sum of judgement was given unto the Son of Man, and He caused the sinners to pass away and be destroyed from off the face of the Earth, and those who have led the world astray.

69.28. With chains shall they be bound, and in their assemblage-place of destruction shall they be imprisoned, and all their works vanish from the face of the Earth.

69.29. And from henceforth there shall be nothing corruptible; for that Son of Man has appeared, and has seated Himself on the Throne of His glory, and all evil shall pass away before His face, and the word of that Son of Man shall go forth and be strong before the Lord of Spirits.

Here, at the end of chapter sixty-nine, the Son of Man is clearly identified as the master of this covenant, Kasbeel – the Fuller of God. Jesus Christ is the all-powerful Son of God. There is nothing that the Father has not placed into His hands. It is through Jesus Christ, and our covenant with the Father, that we obtain the full measure of our creation, wherein we become joint heirs with Him in the Kingdom of God. Without Jesus Christ, none of this is possible. Without the guiding influence of the Holy Ghost, none of these things can be known. This oath and covenant of the priesthood represents the highest and greatest mystery of God.

I am astounded that these things were recorded by Noah in the Book of Enoch, thousands of years prior to the restoration of the gospel of Jesus Christ. These revelations from the ancient world are a testament to Joseph's prophetic mantle. He was who he claimed to be, for how could he have possibly known such things if not from God?

It is for this reason that I have said, and will continue to say, that the Book of Enoch can only truly be understood by those who have embraced the restored gospel of Jesus Christ as held and preached by the Church of Jesus Christ of Latter-day Saints, and no one else. As such, if you have left the Church, repent and return. If you have dismissed the Church because of the deceptions of men, empty out your glass of the learning of men, and pray that God will fill it for you afresh. There can be nothing of more value to you than this. However, you are at the helm of your own ship, and you steer it whithersoever you will.

Now, speaking to those chosen few who see things as they really are, it is of the utmost importance that you understand that while certain covenants can be inherited by birthright, power in those covenants cannot be inherited. This is where the Jews have so often missed the boat, believing that because Abraham had obtained these blessings, they had obtained them too. Abraham sought these blessings with his whole soul. As a result, he ultimately obtained them, and there was nothing he valued more. Have you done the works of Abraham? If not, are you really an heir to these promises?

God is no respecter of persons. A man or woman is not saved because of his or her parents. They are saved because of their own choices and covenants. For surely salvation does not come to man through the words of his lips, but through the oath and covenant of the priesthood of God. It is for this reason we speak of the covenant path. There are many paths in the world, but there is only one covenant path.

Baptism by immersion, after having exercised faith and repentance in and through the Son of God, places one upon the covenant path. However, this path is long and narrow. The objective is not simply entering the gate. Yet this is as far as many will go. They see and acknowledge the covenant path, but they do not utilize it. Consider the following:

> And now, behold, my beloved brethren, I suppose that ye ponder somewhat in your hearts concerning that which ye should do after ye have entered in by the way. But, behold, why do ye ponder these things in your hearts? Do ye not remember that I said unto you that after ye had received the Holy Ghost ye could speak with the tongue of angels? And now, how could ye speak with the tongue of angels save it were by the Holy Ghost?

> Angels speak by the power of the Holy Ghost; wherefore, they speak the words of Christ. Wherefore, I said unto you, feast upon the words of Christ; for behold, the words of Christ will tell you all things what ye should do. Wherefore, now after I have spoken these words, if ye cannot understand them it will be because ye ask not, neither do ye knock; wherefore, ye are not brought into the light, but must perish in the dark.

> For behold, again I say unto you that if ye will enter in by the way, and receive the Holy Ghost, it will show unto you all things what ye should do. Behold, this is the doctrine of Christ, and there will be no more doctrine given until after He shall manifest Himself unto you in the flesh. And when He shall manifest Himself unto you in the flesh, the things which He shall say unto you shall ye observe to do.

And now I, Nephi, cannot say more; the Spirit stoppeth mine utterance, and I am left to mourn because of the unbelief, and the wickedness, and the ignorance, and the stiffneckedness of men; for they will not search knowledge, nor understand great knowledge, when it is given unto them in plainness, even as plain as word can be.

And now, my beloved brethren, I perceive that ye ponder still in your hearts; and it grieveth me that I must speak concerning this thing. For if ye would hearken unto the Spirit which teacheth a man to pray, ye would know that ye must pray; for the evil spirit teacheth not a man to pray, but teacheth him that he must not pray. But behold, I say unto you that ye must pray always, and not faint; that ye must not perform any thing unto the Lord save in the first place ye shall pray unto the Father in the name of Christ, that He will consecrate thy performance unto thee, that thy performance may be for the welfare of thy soul. (2 Nephi 32)

In the passages above, Nephi explained that once we have entered the covenant path, we must engage with the Lord. The means by which this is done is through the inspiration of the Holy Ghost. In other words, there is personal knowledge that you can obtain in no other way than by personally deciding to journey down this path. What good is a gift that is not received? You receive the gift of the Lord by acting upon it and coming to the Throne of God with fear and trembling to work out your own salvation with Him. If you do not do this, who do you have to blame?

Noah's vision now progresses, and he is shown what will transpire upon the Earth after his death, in the last days.

70.1. And it came to pass after this that his name during his lifetime [*Noah's hidden name associated with the oath and covenant*] was raised aloft to that Son of Man and to the Lord of Spirits from amongst those who dwell on the earth.

This is an exceedingly curious passage. It suggests that Noah obtained his hidden name while he was alive. The fact that this distinction was made suggests that Noah understood that others would receive their hidden names after they were dead. The book of Revelation speaks of the righteous dead who have overcome the world receiving new names which no man knew. According to the passage above, this name enabled Noah to enter into the presence of the Son of Man and the Lord of Spirits. Again, this is fantastic knowledge to be contained within an ancient record known to be in wide circulation hundreds of years before the birth of Christ. This is a testament to the truthfulness of the restoration and the veracity of the Book of Enoch itself!

> **70.2**. And he [Noah] was raised aloft on the chariots of the spirit and his name vanished among them.

> **70.3**. And from that day I was no longer numbered amongst them: and He set me between the two winds, between the North and the West, where the angels took the cords to measure for me the place for the elect and righteous.

> **70.4**. And there I saw the first fathers and the righteous who from the beginning dwell in that place.

This is another extremely interesting passage. Genesis 9:29 states that Noah died when he was 950 years old. The passage above states that Noah was raised aloft on the chariots of the spirit, and from that day forward no longer dwelt among the living. However, Noah is writing these things in the first person. How can this be? Is it possible that Noah did not die after all? Could he have been translated like his grandfather Enoch? If such was the case, it would explain how he could have written these things. That being said, God can do anything that He wants to do. I look forward to more clarity on this passage in a coming day.

Regardless of whether Noah was translated or not, a record of his subsequent journey was preserved and is noteworthy. After the flood, Noah ended up in the fertile crescent, in the lands of Mesopotamia. These are the lands of the first and second wave of the Watchers. However, he was taken by the chariot of the Spirit into lands that lay to the northwest of the fertile crescent. He provides two other references to the location of this place. First, he states that it was the land where the first dwelt. Through modern revelation, we understand that the location where the first fathers dwelt was North America. Specifically, Adam-Ondi-Ahman means the place where Adam walked with God.

Secondly, Noah stated that this was the location where he saw the angels with their life lines helping the latter-day inhabitants of those lands survive the challenging conditions that will exist in the last days. As such, what Noah described as happening next will occur on the North American continent in the last days. Consider the following:

> **71.1**. And it came to pass after this that my spirit was translated and it ascended into the heavens: and I saw the **holy sons of God**. They were stepping on flames of fire:

their garments were white [and their raiment], and their faces shone like snow.

71.2. And I saw two streams of fire, and the light of that fire shone like hyacinth, and I fell on my face before the Lord of Spirits.

71.3. And the angel Michael seized me by my right hand, and lifted me up and led me forth into all the secrets, and he showed me all the secrets of righteousness.

71.4. And he showed me all the secrets of the ends of the heaven, and all the chambers of all the stars, and all the luminaries, whence they proceed before the face of the holy ones.

71.5. And he translated my spirit into the heaven of heavens, and I saw there as it were a structure built of crystals, and between those crystals tongues of living fire.

71.6. And my spirit saw the girdle which girt that house of fire, and on its four sides were streams full of living fire, and they girt that house.

71.7. And round about were Seraphin, Cherubic, and Ophanim: and these are they who sleep not and guard the throne of His glory.

71.8. And I saw angels who could not be counted, a thousand thousands, and ten thousand times ten thousand, encircling that house. And Michael, and Raphael, and Gabriel, and Phanuel, and the holy angels who are above the heavens, go in and out of that house.

71.9. And they came forth from that house, and Michael and Gabriel, Raphael and Phanuel, and many holy angels without number.

71.10. And with them the Head of Days, His head white and pure as wool, and His raiment indescribable.

71.11. And I fell on my face, and my whole body became relaxed, and my spirit was transfigured; and I cried with a loud voice,... with the spirit of power, and blessed and glorified and extolled.

71.12. And these blessings which went forth out of my mouth were well pleasing before that Head of Days.

71.13. And that Head of Days came with Michael and Gabriel, Raphael and Phanuel, thousands and ten thousands of angels without number.

71.14. And He came to me and greeted me with His voice, and said unto me: 'This is the Son of Man who is born unto righteousness; and righteousness abides over him, and the righteousness of the Head of Days forsakes Him not.'

71.15. And He said unto me: 'He [*the Son of Man*] proclaims unto thee peace in the name of the world to come; for from hence has proceeded peace since the creation of the world, and so shall it be unto thee for ever and for ever and ever.

71.16. And all shall walk in His ways since righteousness never forsaketh Him: with Him will be their dwelling-places, and with Him their heritage, and they shall not be separated from Him for ever and ever and ever.

71.17. And so there shall be length of days with that Son of Man, and the righteous shall have peace and an upright way in the name of the Lord of Spirits for ever and ever.'

In the passages above, Noah was first taken to where Adam dwelt in mortality, and from that place, he was translated into the heavens. In the heavens, he briefly describes in passing some of the same landmarks that Enoch described in the prior chapters and volumes of this book. However, that was not the focus of his vision. His vision was centered around two majestic beings, the Head of Days and the Son of Man. Curiously, in verse 71.13, the Son of Man is not described as being present by title; however, Phanuel is. As mentioned in previous volumes, Phanuel means Face of God. Phanuel also held the keys to repentance and exaltation. Phanuel is the Son of Man.

God the Father, described above as the Head of Days, focuses Noah upon His Only Begotten Son. He then is taught about the world to come, which will center around the

Son of Man. It would seem that we are to conclude that this future world will be centered upon the Earth in the place where Noah's first fathers dwelt – Adam-Ondi-Ahman. This is an incredible prophecy, and one that could not be fabricated. It reconciles perfectly with the restored gospel of Jesus Christ and once again testifies of Joseph's prophetic mantle. So far as I can tell, apart from the Lord referring to the pending verification of the veracity of the Book of Enoch, no other LDS leader or scholar has ever elaborated upon it until Hugh Nibley did so in the 1970s. As far as I am aware, at the time of this writing, this series is the first and only comprehensive doctrinal review of the Book of Enoch since its coming forth from Bodleian obscurity.

The Book of Enoch clearly demonstrates that God made His mysteries known from before the foundations of the world. Joseph Smith simply could not have known these things. As such, the only reason the Book of Enoch reconciles so wonderfully with the gospel is because the gospel that Joseph restored is true! Second to the Book of Mormon itself, the Book of Enoch is one of the most powerful testaments to the truthfulness of the restored gospel on Earth today. This incredible book ought to be as familiar to the Latter-day Saints as any of our standard works.

Consider the following which was given to Joseph Smith specifically regarding these things:

> Noah was ten years old when he was ordained under the hand of Methuselah. Three years previous to the death of Adam, he called Seth, Enos, Cainan, Mahalaleel, Jared, Enoch, and Methuselah, who were all high priests, with the residue of his posterity who were righteous, into the valley of Adam-ondi-Ahman, and there bestowed upon them his last blessing.

> And the Lord appeared unto them, and they rose up and blessed Adam, and called him Michael, the prince, the archangel. And the Lord administered comfort unto Adam, and said unto him: I have set thee to be at the head; a multitude of nations shall come of thee, and thou art a prince over them forever.

> And Adam stood up in the midst of the congregation; and, notwithstanding he was bowed down with age, being full of the Holy Ghost, predicted whatsoever should befall his posterity unto the latest generation. These things were all written in the Book of Enoch, and are to be testified of in due time. (D&C 107:52-57)

I count it as one of the greatest privileges of my life to testify to you of the truthfulness of the Book of Enoch in fulfillment of the Lord's promise above. May we treasure this book and seek to prepare ourselves for the coming days based on its teachings!

Chapter 17 – The Book of the Luminaries

The Book of the Luminaries comprises chapters **71** to **82** of the Book of Enoch. These chapters detail a 364-day calendar system that was in effect during Enoch's time. Today, our calendars are based on 365.25 days. Interestingly, Enoch stated that while his calendar was precisely accurate in his days, he knew that due to the wickedness of men, the length of a day would be shortened, causing his calendar to become defunct.

Rather than spending time studying a defunct calendar system, I will focus on analyzing certain meaningful aspects of Enoch's writings from this book. The entire Book of Luminaries will be included in the appendix of this volume. With this in mind, consider the following extract from Enoch's Book of Luminaries:

> **80.1.** And in those days the angel Uriel answered and said to me: 'Behold, I have shown thee everything, Enoch, and I have revealed everything to thee that thou shouldst see this sun and this moon, and the leaders of the stars of the heaven and all those who turn them, their tasks and times and departures.

> **80.2.** And in the days of the sinners the years shall be shortened, And their seed shall be tardy on their lands and fields, and all things on the earth shall alter, And shall not appear in their time…

The passage above comes nine chapters into the Book of Luminaries. Uriel tells Enoch, "I have shown you the orbits pertaining to your world and how those orbits impact your calendar. However, because of unrighteousness, none of these things will be relevant to the people upon the Earth in the last days, as the timing of the Earth shall alter. Enoch's years will no longer be long enough to adequately account for the orbits of the Earth, nor its spinning upon its axis." The pivotal period wherein the days were shortened was linked to the days of the sinners – the Great Flood.

The explanation for how the flood occurred is found in Genesis. Consider the following passage:

> In the six hundredth year of Noah's life, in the second month, the seventeenth day of the month, the same day were all the fountains of the great deep broken up, and the windows of heaven were opened. (Gen 7:11)

If we were to liken Enoch's calendar to our own, the flood occurred on February 17th. According to the passage, the fountains of the great deep were broken, and it also started to rain. Of these two water sources, there can be no doubt that the former was the most devastating. There simply is not enough water upon the surface and firmament to flood the entire Earth to the degree that the Bible decrees. It is estimated that at any one point, there are approximately 3,100 cubic miles of water in the firmament above us. This amounts to approximately 12 trillion tons, enough to cover the entire Earth in between an inch and an inch and a half of water.

For the Earth to have been literally baptized in water, there must have been much more water than we see today. Note that the mountains of the Earth are formed by the tectonic movement of the continents. Prior to the flood, the Earth existed as one supercontinent—Pangea. As such, we might presume that many of the mountains as we know them did not exist. Therefore, to baptize the world, the water did not need to cover Mount Everest, as Everest was not yet there. Scientists have determined that the tallest mountain range during the days of Pangea included Mount Mitchell, located nineteen miles northeast of Asheville, North Carolina. This mountain is 6,684 feet above sea level. Anyone who has been in the Appalachian range understands that these mountains are very old and have been smoothed through erosion over long periods of time.

Mount Mitchell could not have been baptized by rainwater. It would have taken far more than this. It would have taken the fountains of the deep. What are the fountains of the deep? Scientists have recently discovered that vast quantities of water exist within the Earth itself in a mineral layer called ringwoodite. They estimate that this layer of the Earth's mantle contains 333 million cubic miles of water. If the fountains of the deep were released to the surface, the Earth would be covered in as much as 15,000 feet of water by this calculation. This would have easily submerged Mount Mitchell, despite the erosion that has taken place.

The Bible tells us that within approximately one year, the Lord caused the floodwaters to recede. Therefore, by Divine Utterance, the waters were reabsorbed by this ringwoodite layer, approximately four hundred miles beneath the Earth's surface. Such an event would have altered the Earth's center of gravity. The laws governing conservation of angular momentum state that when a spinning object's center of gravity becomes more concentrated, its rotational spin will increase. This is precisely what Uriel told Enoch would happen. Since the days of the sinners, of the Great Flood, the Earth's rotation has increased by approximately one third of one percent.

As such, after the waters of the flood receded, the increased rotational speed of the Earth shortened each day by approximately six minutes. Over the course of the year, this resulted in the need to add an additional 1.25 days to our year to keep time, whereas

Enoch needed only 364 days. As such, Enoch's prediluvian calendar became obsolete, just as he said it would.

As such, I do not consider it to be a valuable use of time to analyze a defunct calendar system for the purposes of these volumes. However, Enoch knew his calendar would be different than our own, and yet he still included it in his writings. What might his motivations have been? The way that the Book of Luminaries has been written makes it clear that it is more than an ancient calendar. Enoch's calendar writings describe the complex interactions between the Earth, Moon, and Sun.

These interactions are not the product of magic, but of gravity. While gravity may not be magic, it is still an incredibly curious force of nature that we are still in our infancy of understanding. What is known is that gravity is inextricably interconnected with space-time—meaning gravitational forces themselves not only govern the flow of physical time, but gravity can actually alter space-time itself. This phenomenon is known as gravitational time dilation.

Albert Einstein theorized that gravity could be used to generate portals through both space and time to remote locations too far to travel to in any other way. These theoretical portals are called Einstein-Rosen bridges, or more commonly—wormholes. In theory, wormholes can breach the immensity of space or even the dimensionality of the multiverse itself. This is where the Book of the Luminaries gets interesting.

Enoch discusses twelve portals, along with many other windows, that open to the four quarters of the heavens at different times of the year. The destinations to which these portals went also changed based upon the gravitational interactions between the Earth, Moon, and Sun, which changes were tracked by his calendar. This is the reason that Enoch wrote these things in his book; he wanted us to understand that this phenomenon is real, and that the days would come when they would be relevant to us.

Enoch demonstrated that these portals operated in accordance with divine law, and not some type of magic. As such, their operation could be readily predicted based upon the consistent gravitational interactions by anyone who understood such workings. Again, it appears to me that the Book of the Luminaries was less about establishing an ancient calendar system than it was about the mapping of Earth's portals. These portals were very sensitive. It seems plausible to me that one of the reasons that the Lord may have flooded the Earth was to increase the Earth's rotation so that these portals could no longer be used by the Watchers. Consider the following passages from the Book of Luminaries that point to these gravitational portals as means of transportation.

75.8. And **I saw chariots in the heaven**, running in the world, above those portals in which revolve the stars that never set.

75.9. And one is larger than all the rest, and it is that that makes its course through the entire world.

In the passages above, Enoch saw heavenly chariots coming to Earth through these celestial portals. What Enoch refers to as the stars that never set, the ancient Egyptians called the undying or imperishable stars. These are the circumpolar stars associated with the north and south poles. According to Enoch, there are portals to other solar systems accessible in these areas. Enoch discussed these portals in the sixteenth chapter of Volume I of this series.

You will recall from Volume II that the Lady had a chance encounter with a group she did not seek. This group was traversing the stars, presumably in one of the chariots Enoch described. Prior to this encounter, the Lady had visited Earth, where she found no place among the children of Adam. I postulated in that volume that she showed the crew of this star-chariot how to get to Earth. As a direct result, the two-hundred-member crew of this craft made the journey to Earth, forever altering the course of its history.

Yet, as Enoch mentioned chariots, there must have been more than one civilization that interacted with Earth's inhabitants. Indeed, we learned within this series that in the days of Sisera's nine-hundred mysterious iron chariots, the Lord rallied the kings of the stars to fight on Israel's behalf. I shared an account from the ancient records of Egypt that described Egypt's skies filled with fire disks from the eastern horizon to the western horizon, and from the north to the south. The Egyptians stated that this was the most spectacular event to ever transpire in their long storied history.

Based on the details of the Book of Luminaries, I speculate that the exact gravitational forces between bodies of a solar system are as unique to that system as fingerprints to an individual. Furthermore, if one were to understand these precise measurements, they act just like a cosmic address. Anyone with access to these variables and a portal could arrive at the location like a letter in a cosmic mailbox. The Lady imparted this critical information to the Watchers. However, by altering the spin of the Earth, the Lord essentially encrypted Earth's portals and changed our cosmic address. Therefore, the Watchers were locked out, at least for a time. It would seem that they decrypted the portal once more in the days of Noah's grandchildren.

Accordingly, the Lord wiped out ninety percent of those post-diluvian Watchers, which left the Canaanites with 900 iron chariots they may or may not have known how to use. Regardless, given the exponential increase in transmedium craft visiting Earth on a daily basis, it is clear that Earth's location is in the public domain once more. I believe that this was Enoch's primary motive for including these things in his writings. He did not want us to be blindsided by them in the last days. After all, if I am correct, anyone with our cosmic address can arrive on Earth in less time than it takes us to commute to work in the morning. This seems to be exactly what the next passages suggest:

> **76.1** And at the ends of the earth [*the poles*] I saw twelve portals open to ALL the quarters of heaven…

Enoch saw twelve portals that were open to all the quarters of heaven. "All" is a very large percentage, suggesting that from these twelve portals, you could travel anywhere in the cosmos, and anyone from the cosmos could travel here. Portals completely negate physical distances. You enter the portal from one cosmic address and exit at another. Enoch further explains the twelve portals with some very interesting supplemental details.

> **76.14.** And the twelve portals of the four quarters of the heaven are therewith completed, and all their laws and all their plagues and all their benefactions have I shown to thee, my son Methuselah.

According to Enoch, these portals have been the means whereby certain plagues have fallen upon the Earth in times past. What plagues might have been associated with cosmic portals? Fiery flying serpents come to mind. These fiery flying serpents appeared out of nowhere and then disappeared just as quickly.

Apart from plagues, Enoch stated that blessings have also come through these portals. Perhaps the greatest of these blessings is spoken of next. Consider the following:

> **77.1.** And the first quarter is called the east, because it is the first: and the second, the south, **because the Most High will descend there**, yea, there in quite a special sense He who is blessed forever will descend.

According to Enoch, the Most High would descend through the Southern portal. I associate the Most High with God the Father. Enoch did not give us a time frame for this, other than the fact that the Eastern portal would be used before the Most High Himself came through the Southern portal in what will most certainly be a spectacular way. I think this order is unique, but what might these things mean, and how did Enoch know about them?

I think the answers to these questions are fascinating. Jesus Christ clearly used the Eastern portal when He ascended into heaven in the eyes of over five hundred of His disciples. That was a spectacular event. Christ also descended from the heavens through a Western portal, which is described in fascinating detail in 3 Nephi 11. However, what is the event that Enoch knew about regarding the coming not of the Son, but of the Father through a Southern portal? Consider the following passage, which I believe speaks of this event:

> And the Lord said unto Enoch: Then shalt thou and all thy city meet them there, and we will receive them into our bosom, and they shall see us; and we will fall upon their necks, and they shall fall upon our necks, and we will kiss each other; and there shall be mine abode, and it shall be Zion, which shall come forth out of all the creations which I have made; and for the space of a thousand years the earth shall rest. (Moses 7:63-64)

Joseph Smith taught that the City of Enoch would descend into the Gulf of Mexico, just south of the United States. Such an event truly would be very special to witness. It will also involve Enoch. Given that the Most High told Enoch that these things would happen, it is probably to this event that he is referring. Note that it was in conjunction with this event that the Most High told Enoch that all the creations He had made would flow unto Zion, presumably through the kinds of portals that Enoch has been discussing.

Consider this additional extract from the Book of Luminaries:

> **77.2.** And the west quarter is named the diminished, because there all the luminaries of the heaven wane and go down.

This is a curious statement. Due to the rotation of the Earth, the Sun, Moon, and stars all set in the West. This may be why this portal was named "diminished," but I believe there was another reason for this. The New Jerusalem will be established in the West and will be the central hub of the cosmos for the space of a thousand years. All the righteous from the four quarters of heaven will come to the New Jerusalem through these portals. During this period of the Earth's history, Satan will be bound. Yet, we are told in Revelation chapter twenty that the time will come when he will be loosed from his prison for a little season. When that time comes, Satan will rally the hosts of heaven, and they will come and besiege the New Jerusalem. When that occurs, the Most High will destroy all the hosts of heaven with fire. Consider the following passages which speak of this:

And when the thousand years are expired, Satan shall be loosed out of his prison, and shall go out to deceive the nations which are in the four quarters of the earth, Gog and Magog, to gather them together to battle: the number of whom *is* as the sand of the sea. And they went up on the breadth of the earth, and compassed the camp of the saints about, and the beloved city: and fire came down from God out of heaven, and devoured them.

And the devil that deceived them was cast into the lake of fire and brimstone, where the beast and the false prophet *are,* and shall be tormented day and night for ever and ever. And I saw a great white throne, and him that sat on it, from whose face the earth and the heaven fled away; and there was found no place for them. (Rev 20:7-11)

And

But the day of the Lord will come as a thief in the night; in the which the heavens shall pass away with a great noise, and the elements shall melt with fervent heat, the earth also and the works that are therein shall be burned up. Seeing then that all these things shall be dissolved, what manner of persons ought ye to be in all holy conversation and godliness, Looking for and hasting unto the coming of the day of God, wherein the heavens being on fire shall be dissolved, and the elements shall melt with fervent heat? (2 Peter 3:10-12)

And

Their slain also shall be cast out, and their stink shall come up out of their carcases, and the mountains shall be melted with their blood. And **ALL the host of heaven shall be dissolved**, and the heavens shall be rolled together as a scroll: and all their host shall fall down, as the leaf falleth off from the vine, and as a falling fig from the fig tree. For my sword shall be bathed in heaven: behold, it shall come down upon Idumea, and upon the people of my curse, to judgment. (Isaiah 34:3-5)

I believe that each of the passages above speaks of the days when the inhabitants of the luminaries of heaven will rebel against God and the House of Israel. In that day, they will join forces with Satan and his minions one last time to attack the New Jerusalem in the West. When they do, they will be dissolved with fire from on high—meaning they will be diminished. These fallen foes will then be relegated to the fiery burning mountain ranges at the end of all things, where they will atone for their own sins in a process that will last ten thousand years.

Enoch now addresses the fourth quarter, which is to say the northern quarter of the twelve portals, three separate portals having been associated with each of the cardinal directions, as will be the case with the twelve gates of the New Jerusalem. Consider the following:

> **77.3.** And the fourth quarter, named the north, is divided into three parts: the first of them is for the dwelling of men: and the second contains seas of water, and the abysses and forests and rivers, and darkness and clouds; and the third part contains the garden of righteousness.

> **77.4.** I saw seven high mountains, higher than all the mountains which are on the earth: and thence comes forth hoar-frost, and days, seasons, and years pass away.

Through the northern portals, Enoch saw some curious things. I suspect that Enoch's observations are of great significance for us in the last days. For example, Enoch saw through the northern portal the dwelling place of men. I believe it is safe to assume that Enoch is seeing those from the northern countries who will come to Earth in the last days to free the saints and to sanctify North America. Consider the following passage that speaks of these things:

> And they who are in the north countries shall come in remembrance before the Lord; and their prophets shall hear his voice, and shall no longer stay themselves; and they shall smite the rocks, and the ice shall flow down at their presence. (D&C 133:26)

This leads us to the next thing that Enoch observed: the vast northern lands with mountains higher than any found on Earth. I believe that Enoch is witnessing the fragment of the world upon which the people of the northern countries presently reside, a place of rugged beauty. It seems to me that Enoch spoke of these things because, just as the City of Enoch will descend through the Southern portal to return to the Gulf of Mexico from whence it was taken in antiquity, so the lost tribes of Israel will be restored through the northern portal. When that restoration occurs, the northern ice caps will flow down at their presence, and the world will watch in both terror and amazement as it beholds one of the greatest miracles ever to occur.

Lastly, Enoch saw through one of the northern portals the garden of righteousness. There are many passages of scripture that suggest the Garden of Eden will be restored upon the North American continent. Indeed, the trees from the garden of righteousness will line the streets of the New Jerusalem, and their fruits and leaves will feed and heal the nations. These things can be studied in the twenty-first and twenty-second chapters of the book of Revelation.

According to the writings of Enoch, the people of his day were familiar with these ancient portals, as were the extraterrestrial civilizations that used them. While in his days these portals resulted in the corruption of the Earth, in the last days these portals will result in our salvation. I believe that the purpose of the Book of Luminaries was to bring these hidden mysteries to our attention. Incredible things will soon come upon the Earth, and Enoch thought you ought to be aware of them, for the wicked will use these portals before the righteous.

Chapter 18 - The Enochian Covenant

In the previous chapter, I reviewed excerpts from the Book of Luminaries, which is included in its entirety as Appendix One. I proposed that this ancient work is more about gravitational phenomena known as portals, than it is a defunct calendar system. Notably, Enoch taught that there are twelve portals through which all of the Father's creations are accessible. I suggested that these twelve portals correspond to the twelve gates of the New Jerusalem, which we are told will come forth from all the workmanship of the Lord's hands.

In this chapter, we will begin our analysis of the section of the Book of Enoch commonly referred to as the Book of Dreams. In this section, Enoch teaches his son Methuselah about numerous prophetic dreams he had throughout his life, the first of which occurred when Enoch was a young boy. Given that Enoch expressly stated that his writings were meant to bless the lives of the righteous during times of trial, we should understand that these dreams have been included in this book for our benefit. Therefore, as you study the writings in this chapter, you must ask yourself, "Why did Enoch think this dream was important enough to be preserved for thousands of years so that I could read it today?" If you seek this answer, you will find it, and it will bless your life. After all, Nephi taught long ago that we should liken all scriptures unto ourselves for our profit and learning.

This section of the book begins as follows:

> **83.1**. And now, my son Methuselah, I will show thee all my visions which I have seen, recounting them before thee.

> **83.2**. Two visions I saw before I took a wife, and the one was quite unlike the other: the first when I was learning to write: the second before I took thy mother, (when) I saw a terrible vision. And regarding them I prayed to the Lord.

> **83.3**. I had laid me down in the house of my grandfather Mahalalel, I saw in a vision how the heaven collapsed and was borne off and fell to the earth.

> **83.4**. And when it fell to the earth I saw how the earth was swallowed up in a great abyss, and mountains were suspended on mountains, and hills sank down on hills, and

> high trees were rent from their stems, and hurled down and
> sunk in the abyss.
>
> **83.5**. And thereupon a word fell into my mouth, and I lifted
> up my voice to cry aloud, and said: 'The Earth is destroyed!'

Enoch saw this vision while having a sleepover at his grandfather's house. In this dream, Enoch said that he saw five notable things that terrified him. The first of these was the collapsing of the heavens. The term "collapse" can have multiple meanings, one of which refers to the sudden and complete failure of the status quo. What could cause the order of heaven to collapse? Was Enoch witnessing something that had been, or something that would be? Think on this as we move to the next thing Enoch witnessed.

The second thing that Enoch saw in his dream was that after the order of heaven collapsed, the heavens themselves were "borne off." The phrase "borne off" means to carry or transport something from one location to another. In this instance, the heavens were borne to the Earth. This brings us to the third thing Enoch saw. Once the heavens were borne to the Earth, they fell upon it. This leads us to the last thing Enoch saw—the catastrophic supernatural destruction of the Earth. The scene that Enoch witnessed seemed to be one of reality inverting upon itself. Mountains were suspended and then dropped upon other mountains. Hills were lifted up and dropped upon other hills. Mighty trees were snapped at their bases and hurled into a terrible abyss. Enoch awoke from this dream with the shout, "The Earth is destroyed!"

Just what was it that Enoch saw? We will get to that, but first lets talk about Enoch. Enoch was called into the Lord's service when he was "but a lad" (see Moses 6:31). As such, it is possible that Enoch had already been called by the Lord at the time he had this vision. If such was the case, his grandfather surely knew about Enoch's calling. If this was true, Mahalalel knew that Enoch was special. Therefore, consider his reaction to his grandson's experience:

> **83.6.** And my grandfather Mahalalel waked me as I lay near
> him, and said unto me: 'Why dost thou cry so, my son, and
> why dost thou make such lamentation?'
>
> **83.7.** And I recounted to him the whole vision which I had
> seen, and he said unto me: 'A terrible thing hast thou seen,
> my son, and of grave moment is thy dream-vision as to the
> secrets of all the sin of the earth: it must sink into the abyss
> and be destroyed with a great destruction.

Enoch's grandfather recognized this dream as a prophetic warning regarding the state of the world. Therefore, we can begin to deduce the meaning of Enoch's dream. Specifically, in the days of Mahalalel's son Jared, the Watchers arrived on Earth and corrupted it. This must have been the meaning of the first thing that Enoch saw—the collapsing of the order of heaven. By this, we understand that what the Watchers did was an act of rebellion. They knew they were not supposed to do what they did, yet they did it anyway, and destruction followed after they fell upon the Earth. I believe that the reality-altering destruction Enoch witnessed in his dream was symbolic of how the pre-diluvian world's reality became inverted and subsequently collapsed beneath the inverted lie.

Enoch's grandfather may not have had it all figured out, but his response to Enoch shows that he clearly grasped the essence of the dream. Listen to his counsel to his grandson Enoch:

> **83.8.** And now, my son, arise and make petition to the Lord of glory, since thou art a believer, that a remnant may remain on the earth, and that He may not destroy the whole earth.

> **83.9.** My son, from heaven all this will come upon the earth, and upon the earth there will be great destruction.

Oh, that every child on Earth had a grandfather like Enoch's. Mahalalel recognized the implications of the dream right away. This clearly speaks to the type of man Mahalalel was—close to the spirit. The Lord knew how Mahalalel would respond. Therefore, there can be little doubt that Enoch had this vision at his grandfather's house for a reason. Mahalalel's counsel was profound, and I believe it profoundly shaped the destiny of his grandson. What was Mahalalel's counsel?

When Mahalalel understood that the Earth was about to be destroyed, his counsel to his grandson was to petition the Lord that a remnant of his seed might be preserved in the land. In other words, Mahalalel advised his grandson to enter into a covenantal relationship with God. This is most certainly the covenant that Abraham sought to emulate himself. In Abraham's own words, he described the inspiration for his actions:

> I sought for the blessings of the fathers, and the right whereunto I should be ordained to administer the same… desiring also to be one who possessed great knowledge… and to be a father of many nations, a prince of peace… (Abraham 1:2)

Abraham sought the blessing of the fathers. Specifically, he sought the blessings that Enoch had obtained many years prior. Because Abraham sought this blessing, he obtained it, but it was not easy. Indeed, Abraham never saw it fulfilled in his lifetime, but he died firm in the knowledge that God is the God of both the living and the dead, and His word never fails.

Specifically, Abraham received the promise that his posterity would never be completely destroyed and that through them, he would become a father of nations. Furthermore, he received a blessing that all future generations of the Earth would be blessed by way of his posterity, and that both he and his posterity would always have an inheritance before the Lord upon this Earth. Yet it was Mahalalel who put this idea into his grandson Enoch's head in the first place. It should be noted that Enoch could not be blessed in this way without his grandfather also being blessed in the same way. If Enoch would become a father of nations, so would Mahalalel.

Enoch took his grandfather's words to heart. In his own words, this is what happened next:

> **83.10.** After that I arose and <u>prayed</u> and <u>implored</u> and <u>besought</u>, and <u>wrote down my prayer</u> for the generations of the world, and I will show everything to thee, my son Methuselah.

Take note of the action verbs Enoch used to describe what he did to obtain this promise. Abraham used very similar language when he described how he obtained his blessings from the Lord. Nothing was more important to Abraham than obtaining these blessings. He left everything he knew and journeyed into the wilderness to parts unknown in pursuit of these blessings. Interestingly enough, just as Mahalalel instilled this desire in his grandson Enoch, Abraham instilled this desire in his grandson Jacob.

A study of Jacob's life demonstrates that there was nothing Jacob wanted more than to obtain the promised blessings of his grandfather. Jacob went to great lengths to obtain them. First, he attempted to purchase the birthright from his brother. Second, he sought to trick Isaac into giving him the birthright by disguising himself. Yet despite these strategies, many years later, when Jacob was old, it was clear that he was still seeking confirmation that his grandfather's blessings were his own.

When an angel of the Lord appeared to Jacob, he literally grabbed hold of Him and would not let Him leave until He promised him the blessings of his grandfather. It was only then that Jacob received the confirmation that he had finally obtained what he had been pursuing his whole life. Then and there, his name was changed to Israel.

Given Enoch's writings above, it seems clear that he engaged with the Lord. He prayed, he implored, he beseeched Him, and he wrote his promises down so that others might learn from his experiences. Melchizedek, Abraham, and Jacob all followed Enoch's example. Have you?

It is interesting how few people learn from the actions of their forefathers. Christ tried to teach this very message to His disciples, but they didn't get it—at least not at first. Consider the following:

> And in that day ye shall ask me nothing. Verily, verily, I say unto you, Whatsoever ye shall ask the Father in My name, He will give *it* you. Hitherto have ye asked nothing in My name: ask, and ye shall receive, that your joy may be full. These things have I spoken unto you in proverbs: but the time cometh, when I shall no more speak unto you in proverbs, but I shall shew you plainly of the Father. At that day ye shall ask in My name: and I SAY NOT UNTO YOU, that I will pray the Father for you. (John 16:23-26)

This is a very curious passage. Christ is essentially telling His apostles that they will not be able to ask Him for anything in His name after they are dead. He then tells them that they have not previously asked the Father for anything in His name because they did not know Him until now. By this, we understand that the apostles had not asked the Father for anything like Enoch, Melchizedek, Abraham, or Jacob did. Christ went on to say that if they did not ask for these things for themselves, He would not ask for them on their behalf. There is a very important lesson to be learned here.

The reason that Christ spoke in parables was so that only those who were truly seeking would understand. Christ then followed up this statement by saying that in the day when He no longer spoke in parables regarding these things, they did not have His assurances that the things they asked for would be granted to them. In other words, we need to work out our own salvation before the Throne of God while it is still today, and the veil is still drawn.

I feel constrained not to speak much more regarding these things. I have said enough. Indeed, I only feel comfortable writing what I have because I am doing what our fathers before us did. It is up to you to read and ponder these things for yourself. Millions have read of Abraham's struggle, yet very few have chosen to emulate it. Has Abraham done all the heavy lifting for you? No! Consider the following:

Then said Jesus to those Jews which believed on Him, If ye continue in my word, *then* are ye My disciples indeed; and ye shall know the truth, and the truth shall make you free. They answered Him, We be Abraham's seed…

[*And Jesus said unto them*] I know that ye are Abraham's seed; but ye seek to kill me, because My word hath no place in you. I speak that which I have seen with My Father: and ye do that which ye have seen with your father.

They answered and said unto Him, Abraham is our father. Jesus saith unto them, If ye were Abraham's children, ye would do the works of Abraham. (John 8:31-33;37-39)

According to Christ, the children of Abraham are his children because of their works, not their pedigrees. Abraham obtained his blessing because he saw that his fathers before him had obtained it, and he wanted what they had. Therefore, Abraham engaged the Lord as they had done. He who has ears to hear, let him hear.

Enoch now returns to his experience:

83.11. And when I had gone forth below and seen the heaven, and the sun rising in the east, and the moon setting in the west, and a few stars, and the whole earth, and everything as †He had known† it in the beginning, then I blessed the Lord of judgement and extolled Him because He had made the sun to go forth from the windows of the east, †and He ascended and rose on the face of the heaven, and set out and kept traversing the path shown unto him.

84.1. And I lifted up my hands in righteousness and blessed the Holy and Great One, and spake with the breath of my mouth, and with the tongue of flesh, which God has made for the children of the flesh of men, that they should speak therewith, and He gave them breath and a tongue and a mouth that they should speak therewith:

84.2. 'Blessed be Thou, O Lord, King, Great and mighty in Thy greatness, Lord of the whole creation of the heaven, King of kings and God of the whole world. And Thy power and kingship and greatness abide for ever and ever, and throughout all generations Thy dominion; and all the heavens are Thy throne forever, and the whole earth Thy footstool for ever and ever.

84.3. For Thou hast made and Thou rulest all things, and nothing is too hard for Thee, wisdom departs not from the place of Thy throne, nor turns away from Thy presence. And Thou knowest and seest and hearest everything, and there is nothing hidden from Thee [for Thou seest everything].

It should be noted that Enoch is praising the Lord in the context of the covenants he had just made with God. Elsewhere in Enoch's writings, he stated that the Father had promised him that he would return to His presence to go no more out, not because of any goodness in Enoch, but because of the goodness within the Father (see Moses 7:59). So it is with all those who obtain the highest degree of glory. Yet none obtain it who were not first seeking to obtain it.

Now Enoch's message turns to the root cause of the destruction that would wipe out all the ungodly in the day of sinners.

84.4. And now the angels of Thy heavens [*the Watchers*] are guilty of trespass, and upon the flesh of men abideth Thy wrath until the great day of judgement.

84.5. And now, O God and Lord and Great King, I implore and beseech Thee to fulfil my prayer, TO LEAVE ME a posterity on Earth, and not destroy all the flesh of man, and make the earth without inhabitant, so that there should be an eternal destruction.

Noah was Enoch's great-grandson. Noah sought for and obtained the blessings of his great-grandfather Enoch (see Genesis 6:18 footnote a JST). Therefore, Noah represented the Lord's fulfillment of Enoch's covenant upon the Earth. This means that every living person on the planet today has the blood of Enoch in their veins to the same degree that they have the blood of Adam in their veins. Why? Because his grandfather put the idea into his head, and he acted upon it. Enoch's covenant with the Lord was not only about himself but about you as well. Consider the following:

84.6. And now, My Lord, destroy from the Earth the flesh which has aroused Thy wrath, but the flesh of righteousness and uprightness establish as a plant of the eternal seed, and hide not Thy face from the prayer of Thy servant, O Lord.'

This is the concluding passage from Enoch's first vision. Part of Enoch's covenant with the Lord was that the Lord would preserve Enoch's righteous posterity and cause them to be part of the plant and the eternal seed. When we read this language, our minds should go to the branches of the original olive tree—those that will bring forth good fruit in the last days, when all the wild branches are cast into the fire and burned. The Lord will never hide His face from His servants. Therefore, we ought to be up and doing the works of our forefathers while there is still time…

Chapter 19 – Epic Vision – Part I – Prediluvian

In the previous chapter, we explored Enoch's first prophetic vision, which he experienced as a young boy during a sleepover at his grandfather's house. His wise grandfather encouraged Enoch to act upon the dream by working with the Lord to prepare a remnant of his seed to survive the impending destruction. This serves as a wonderful example of working out one's own salvation with the Lord.

In this chapter, Enoch shares another dream he had before getting married. According to D&C 107:56-57, the Book of Enoch contains a prophecy detailing everything that would happen to Adam's posterity from the beginning of time to the last generation. This chapter includes that prophecy, reaffirming the prophetic mantle of Joseph Smith.

The prophecy is presented as a parable, using animals to represent people. It spans the entire history of mankind, covering eight thousand years. Given the vastness of this timeframe, the prophecy highlights specific events for a reason. It is up to us to connect the dots. Considering Enoch's stated purpose for his book was to bless the generation that would endure the latter-day cleansing of the Earth, we must assume that the highlighted events are particularly relevant to us.

With this in mind, we begin our analysis of one of the most comprehensive visions ever given to mankind, yet known to but a few.

> **85.1**. And after this I saw another dream, and I will show the whole dream to thee, my son.

> **85.2**. And Enoch lifted up his voice and spake to his son Methuselah: 'To thee, my son, will I speak: hear my words--incline thine ear to the dream-vision of thy father.

> **85.3**. Before I took thy mother Edna…

Here we learn that Enoch's wife's name is Edna, which means "delightful." As a man and a woman are considered one before the Lord, the covenant that Enoch made with the Lord is now Edna's covenant as well. Similarly, Abraham's covenant became his wife Sarah's covenant, and Joseph's birthright became Asenath's birthright. This highlights the eternal importance of marriage, as the salvation of couples is deeply intertwined. Where in the cosmos is there a heavenly king and father without a heavenly queen and mother at his side? Thus, the responsibility of men is not only to provide for the physical welfare of their spouses but also for their spiritual welfare.

As we have seen in prior chapters, the Lord will not easily be separated from His daughters. While all human beings have their weaknesses and shortcomings, the divine nature of a woman is based on the Christlike attributes of love, nurture, and self-sacrifice. A woman places a tremendous amount of trust in the man she marries. Regardless of the caliber of the man she chooses to marry, a woman will typically pour her whole soul into the rearing of her children and the raising of her family. It is a wondrous thing to behold. In my opinion, a man who honors his priesthood must do everything he can to ensure the salvation and exaltation of his family, and that salvation is surely centered on the covenants he makes and keeps with God, as laid out in the previous chapter. Where in heaven is there a father of nations without a mother of nations at his side?

We now return to the vision:

> **85**.3… I saw in a vision on my bed, and behold a bull came forth from the earth, and that bull was white; and after it came forth a heifer, and along with this (latter) came forth two bulls, one of them black and the other red.

We learned from chapter eight of this volume that the ancient world associated the symbol of a bull with the Most High God. We see this same symbolism in the passages above. In addition to the bull itself, the color of the animals in this vison is telling. The white bull represents Adam, white being symbolic of his faithfulness to the light and knowledge he received from God, and his priesthood authority. The heifer obviously represents Eve. Note that a heifer is a young female bovine that has yet to give birth—the bovine equivalent to a virgin. That fact that she came after Adam is indicative of the creation narrative, in the which Eve is created from Adam's rib.

After Eve comes two young bulls which depict Cain and Abel. Again, we understand that the color of these oxen is significant. Cain is depicted as black or the opposite of white. This represents that rather than forming a covenantal relationship with God, as the White Bull had done, Cain entered into a covenant with Lucifer. The Pearl of Great Prices speaks of this in the following passage:

> And it came to pass that Cain took one of his brothers' daughters to wife, and they loved Satan more than God. And Satan said unto Cain: Swear unto me by thy throat, and if thou tell it thou shalt die; and swear thy brethren by their heads, and by the living God, that they tell it not; for if they tell it, they shall surely die; and this that thy father may not know it; and this day I will deliver thy brother Abel into thine hands.

And Satan sware unto Cain that he would do according to his commands. And all these things were done in secret. And Cain said: Truly I am Mahan, the master of this great secret, that I may murder and get gain. Wherefore Cain was called Master Mahan, and he gloried in his wickedness. (Moses 5:28-31)

Based on the passages above, it is clear why Cain was depicted as a black bull. Abel, on the other hand, was represented as a red bull because he was the first human being to have his blood shed through secret works of darkness. With these things in mind, the parable is not difficult to follow. This symbolism sets the stage for the rest of the prophetic allegory.

85.4. And that black bull gored the red one and pursued him over the earth, and thereupon I could no longer see that red bull.

85.5. But that black bull grew and that heifer went with him, and I saw that many oxen proceeded from him which resembled and followed him.

These passages refer to Cain's brethren and their numerous posterity which rejoiced in secret works of darkness with him, and therefore were described as resembling their father.

85.6. And that cow, that first one [*Eve*], went from the presence of that first bull [*Adam*] in order to seek that red one, but found him not, and lamented with a great lamentation over him and sought him.

85.7. And I looked till that first bull came to her and quieted her, and from that time onward she cried no more.

Notice above that since having children, Eve is now called the first cow, which means the first mother, as a cow differs from a heifer in that a cow has given birth. Eve was distraught that Abel was missing. She knew nothing of death and therefore spent her time scouring the countryside looking for him, assuming he was simply lost. This continued in the allegory until Adam came to her and comforted her. We do not know how Adam comforted Eve, but given the context of the vision, we may presume it had to do with the Oath and Covenant he had received from the Lord. This is the same covenant spoken of in the prior chapter. As such, Adam would have explained to Eve that through the power of that covenant, Abel was sealed to her for all time and eternity.

Though he was lost for the present, if they were true and faithful to the covenants they had made, they would be reunited. It was Eve's faith in the covenant that brought her comfort, not Adam's words. For without faith, words are just words.

The vision continues:

> **85.8.** And after that she [*Eve*] bore another white bull, and after him she bore many bulls and black cows.

After Abel was killed by Cain, Eve bore another son who was described as being a white bull like his father. In addition to this one bull, Eve bore other children who were not described as being white. Indeed, some are described as being black cows, meaning they were daughters of Eve who followed the ways of the world, and not the covenant path of their parents. However, according to this prophetic allegory, one male child did follow the covenant path of his parents. Who would this have been? Incredibly, the same section of the Doctrine and Covenants that prophesied that the Book of Enoch would be testified of in due time, and would contain this very revelation, also provides the answer to this question. Consider the following passage from that revelation:

> The order of this priesthood was confirmed to be handed down from father to son, and rightly belongs to the literal descendants of the chosen seed, to whom the promises were made. This order was instituted in the days of Adam, and came down by lineage in the following manner: From Adam to Seth, who was ordained by Adam at the age of sixty-nine years, and was blessed by him three years previous to his (Adam's) death, and received the promise of God by his father, that his posterity should be the chosen of the Lord, and that they should be preserved unto the end of the earth; because he (Seth) was a perfect man, and his likeness was the express likeness of his father, insomuch that he seemed to be like unto his father in all things, and could be distinguished from him only by his age. (D&C 107:40-43)

Remember, the Book of Enoch was not available to the Saints at the time this revelation was received in 1835. As such, it is another testament to the prophetic mantle of Joseph Smith and the veracity of the latter-day restoration. According to this revelation, Seth was not only born in the express image of his father Adam but also was the chosen line upon whom the Oath and Covenant of the Priesthood was passed down. This is why Seth was represented by a white bull like his father.

272

The ancient world honored and venerated Seth as a man of profound righteousness. This belief was particularly prevalent among the Sethians, a subset of the Gnostics. According to the Sethian Gnostics, Seth was the father of the Divine Lineage, who held sacred knowledge known only to the righteous. Furthermore, they revered Seth as the archetype of Christ, who would lead Seth's people. To the Sethians, it was not the posterity of Abraham that was chosen, but the posterity of Seth. Nevertheless, according to Abraham's genealogy, he too was a descendant of Seth.

The idea of Seth being the covenant son through whom the promised blessings of the Oath and Covenant of the Priesthood would flow, as put forth in the D&C, is remarkably consistent with the narrative of the Book of Enoch. Consider this as you read the following passage:

> **85.9.** And I saw in my sleep that white bull [*Seth*] likewise grow and become a great white bull, and from Him proceeded many white bulls, and they resembled him. And they began to beget many white bulls, which resembled them, one following the other, (even) many.

From Seth came a righteous posterity, which began to multiply exceedingly on the Earth. Mahalalel was Seth's great-grandson. Therefore, Mahalalel would have certainly known about Seth's covenant and would have sought it for himself. This is likely the reason that Mahalalel interpreted Enoch's dream from the prior chapter the way he did, and why he encouraged Enoch to enter into the same covenantal relationship with the Lord that Seth had.

There can be no doubt that the Lord highlighted this particular aspect of the vision for a reason. After all, He did so not only with the Book of Enoch but also with the modern revelation that speaks of such things. He wanted us to understand that from the very beginning, the righteous have sought to enter into customized covenantal relationships with Him. These covenants were a source of power to the mortals who made them, giving them both vision and purpose.

You will recall from Volume II of this work that when Lady Wisdom first visited the Earth, she found no place among the children of men. This must have had reference to the posterity of Seth, for Cain and Eve's black cow daughters delighted in Satan. However, things changed in the days of Enoch's father Jared, which seems to be what Enoch sees happen next.

> **86.1.** And again I saw with mine eyes as I slept, and I saw the heaven above, and behold a star fell from heaven, and it arose and eat and pastured amongst those oxen.

86.2. And after that I saw the large and the black oxen, and behold they all changed their stalls and pastures and their cattle, and began to live with each other.

In the account above, Enoch witnessed a pivotal event in human history. He saw one solitary star falling from the heavens to the Earth. This event is clearly reminiscent of Lucifer's fall from heaven as described in Isaiah 14:12. However, Lucifer's fall occurred before Adam and Eve were ever placed upon the Earth, as is clearly described in Revelation 12. This star, however, fell from heaven after Adam and Eve had begun to have children. Therefore, this star is not Lucifer, but Lady Wisdom, who came to visit Lucifer's prison planet after the fall of man. Enoch described Lady Wisdom's first visit to the Earth as follows:

42.1. Wisdom found no place where she might dwell; then a dwelling-place was assigned her in the heavens.

42.2 Wisdom went forth to make her dwelling among the children of men, and found no dwelling-place: Wisdom returned to her place, and took her seat among the angels.

According to Enoch's vision, Lady Wisdom visited Earth but chose not to stay. After her visit, she returned to the place created for her kind by the Father. Up to this point in the chapter, Cain and his descendants had already devoted themselves to worshiping Satan, while Seth's descendants wanted nothing to do with her or Satan. Consequently, she did not linger. According to verses **86.1** and **86.2**, the only outcome of her visit was that Satan's followers found new stalls and pastures for themselves. This is to say that they separated themselves from Seth's descendants and lived apart from that time forward. It sounds like the Book of Mormon, expect the with the Lamanites leaving the Nephites.

However, Lady Wisdom was not finished with Earth. Recall the following passage describing a chance encounter she had after returning to her dwelling place:

42.3 And unrighteousness went forth from her chambers: whom she sought not she found, and dwelt with them, as rain in a desert and dew on a thirsty land.

The passage above discussed a chance encounter that Lady Wisdom had with another group of men she was not seeking. Unlike Earth's inhabitants, this group embraced her wholeheartedly. In Volume II of this series, I speculated that these men were the two hundred Watchers who came to Earth in the days of Jared. This interpretation aligns with what Enoch's allegorical vision suggests happened next. Consider the following in this context:

> **86.3.** And again I saw in the vision, and looked towards the heaven, and behold I saw many stars descend and cast themselves down from heaven to that first star, and they became bulls amongst those cattle and pastured with them [amongst them].

> **86.4.** And I looked at them and saw, and behold they all let out their privy members, like horses, and began to cover the cows of the oxen, and they all became pregnant and bare elephants, camels, and asses.

We now have two separate arrivals of extraterrestrial beings on Earth since the fall of man. The first was Lady Wisdom, and the second was the two hundred Watchers who arrived in the days of Enoch's father, Jared. According to Enoch's vision, as soon as the Watchers arrived on Earth, they began having children with the black cow daughters of Eve. Enoch describes the offspring of the Watchers as entirely new races of people, depicted as elephants, camels, and mules. Given that an elephant is over three times the size of an ox, it clearly represents the giants who roamed the Earth in those days.

However, one group of Watchers with elephant offspring cannot account for the introduction of camels and mules. Therefore, Enoch's description of many stars coming to Earth from the heavens is intriguing. The Book of Job, a prediluvian text, refers to Earth being influenced by inhabitants from both the Pleiades and Orion star systems (see Job 38:31). While we do not know where the Watchers came from, there are claims today of inhabitants from many worlds coming to this one. If this is happening today, why couldn't it have happened in Enoch's day? Thus, as strange as it sounds, I believe the camels and mules represent additional hybrid races stemming from other off-world beings.

This concept may seem bizarre, but before dismissing it, consider this: if all people descend directly from Adam and Eve, why are humans so diverse? The Book of Enoch explicitly states that this diversity has extraterrestrial origins. Is such a theory reconcilable with the gospel? I think so. Our scriptures tell us that Adam and Eve themselves were extraterrestrials (see Moses 3:5). Our mortal DNA exists independently from our spirits, which were always destined for this Earth, regardless of our DNA's origins.

As expected, the introduction of new genetic material into the human gene pool resulted in increased fear, prejudice, and violence. Consider the following:

86.5. And all the oxen feared them [*the hybrids*] and were affrighted at them, and began to bite with their teeth and to devour, and to gore with their horns.

86.6. And they began, moreover, to devour those oxen; and behold all the children of the earth began to tremble and quake before them and to flee from them.

87.1. And again I saw how they began to gore each other and to devour each other, and the earth began to cry aloud.

According to the passages above, after the arrival of the Watchers, the Earth began to be filled with violence. Yet, Enoch's allegorical dream does not paint the complete picture of what was happening. Things were not all bad—yet. Consider the following passage that describes this period from the Book of Moses:

> And so great was the faith of Enoch that he led the people of God, and their enemies came to battle against them; and he spake the word of the Lord, and the earth trembled, and the mountains fled, even according to his command; and the rivers of water were turned out of their course; and the roar of the lions was heard out of the wilderness; and all nations feared greatly, so powerful was the word of Enoch, and so great was the power of the language which God had given him.

> There also came up a land out of the depth of the sea, and so great was the fear of the enemies of the people of God, that they fled and stood afar off and went upon the land which came up out of the depth of the sea. And the giants of the land, also, stood afar off; and there went forth a curse upon all people that fought against God; and from that time forth there were wars and bloodshed among them; but the Lord came and dwelt with His people, and they dwelt in righteousness.

> The fear of the Lord was upon all nations, so great was the glory of the Lord, which was upon His people. And the Lord blessed the land, and they were blessed upon the mountains, and upon the high places, and did flourish. And the Lord called His people Zion, because they were of one heart and one mind, and dwelt in righteousness; and there was no poor among them. And Enoch continued his preaching in

righteousness unto the people of God. And it came to pass in his days, that he built a city that was called the City of Holiness, even Zion. (Moses 7:13-19)

According to the passages above, despite the hatred, violence, and prejudice corrupting the rest of the world, Enoch and his people were safe, and the Lord was with them. Such will be the case in the last days as well. Every man who refuses to lift his sword against his neighbor must flee to Zion, which will be the only nation not at war. This is clearly why the Lord highlighted this point. However, eventually things became so bad that when Enoch was 365 years old, both he and his city were lifted up into the heavens, with the promise that they would return in the last days. When they do return, the following scripture will be fulfilled:

> Thy watchmen shall lift up the voice; with the voice together shall they sing, for they shall see eye to eye when the Lord shall bring again Zion. Break forth into joy, sing together, ye waste places of Jerusalem; for the Lord hath comforted His people, He hath redeemed Jerusalem. The Lord hath made bare His holy arm in the eyes of all the nations; and all the ends of the earth shall see the salvation of God. (3 Nephi 16:17-20)

We now return to Enoch's dream:

> **87.2.** And I raised mine eyes again to heaven, and I saw in the vision, and behold there came forth from heaven beings who were like white men: and **four** went forth from that place and three with them.

> **87.3.** And those three that had last come forth grasped me by my hand and took me up, away from the generations of the earth, and raised me up to a lofty place, and showed me a tower raised high above the earth, and all the hills were lower.

> **87.4.** And one said unto me: 'Remain here till thou seest everything that befalls those elephants, camels, and asses, and the stars and the oxen, and all of them.'

In the above passages, Enoch saw four men descend from heaven. The wording of the passage is a little awkward, which might lead to the idea there were seven men instead of four. However, from the context of the rest of the dream, it is clear there were only four. Enoch was trying to communicate that one of the four men came to Earth before the other three. Consistent with other aspects of this vision, the whiteness of these four men symbolizes their personal uprightness and priesthood power. Who were these four men?

You will recall that in Volume I of this series, many souls began to cry from Spirit Prison, asking God to intervene on behalf of their posterity who were being destroyed by the Watchers. As a result of their petition, four archangels approached the Lord of Spirits and asked Him what He intended to do. God responded by authorizing them to destroy the giants and bind the Watchers for seventy generations. This appears to be the context of these four men descending from the heavens. As such, these are the four archangels: Michael, Raphael, Uriel, and Gabriel. Of these four, Michael was the first man to come to Earth, and is the reason for the awkward phrasing previously mentioned. Thus, the following verse is speaking of the first thing that Michael did when he returned to Earth. Consider the following:

> **88.1**. And I saw one of those four who had come forth first [*Michael*], and he seized that first star which had fallen from the heaven, and bound it hand and foot and cast it into an abyss: now that abyss was narrow and deep, and horrible and dark.

If my interpretation is correct, the Lady did not go unpunished for her role in the prediluvian fiasco involving the Watchers. Michael bound her hand and foot and cast her into a narrow abyss that was deep, horrible, and dark. Notably absent from this passage is any indication of how long she would be bound. This is interesting because the Lady seems to have been active for most of Earth's history. As such, Lady Wisdom was either one of many engaged in such activities, or she was not imprisoned for long. Regardless, her punishment and confinement were separate from that of the Watchers and their offspring.

I believe Lady Wisdom was released from her confinement after a few hundred years. This opinion is based on the fact that the sons of the Watchers returned to Earth in the days of Noah's grandchildren. They returned despite the re-encryption of Earth's gravitational portals discussed in Chapter 17 of this volume. Such encryption is so complex that the children of the Watchers would have needed assistance in figuring it out. Presumably, the Lady provided that assistance.

Enoch's dream now turns to the Watchers and their posterity:

88.2. And one of them [*the four men from heaven*] drew a sword, and gave it to those elephants and camels and asses: then they began to smite each other, and the whole earth quaked because of them.

88.3. And as I was beholding in the vision, lo, one of those four who had come forth stoned (them) from heaven, and gathered and took all the great stars whose privy members were like those of horses, and bound them all hand and foot, and cast them in an abyss of the earth.

According to the passages above, the hybrid children of the Watchers were all killed by the four heavenly servants. The Watchers themselves were bound hand and foot and imprisoned in the abyss of the Earth. It is worth noting that all of the Watchers were described as male, having privy parts like horses. However, the first star that fell was not described as having male privy parts. I interpret this to mean the first star that fell was female, while the others were male. Time will tell.

Enoch's prophetic dream now turns to the next White Bull, signifying the keeper of the covenant.

89.1. And one of those four went to that white bull and instructed him in a secret, without his being terrified: he was born a bull and became a man, and built for himself a great vessel and dwelt thereon; and three bulls dwelt with him in that vessel and they were covered in.

The White Bull here is clearly Noah. Enoch saw that Noah would be born different from other men, which we confirmed in the first chapter of this book. Noah was so different that his father, Lamech, was convinced he was the offspring of a Watcher. However, Enoch assured him that Noah was his true son. The passage above also speaks of Noah's ark, which we learned was built in a collaborative process with the Lord.

89.2. And again I raised mine eyes towards heaven and saw a lofty roof, with seven water torrents thereon, and those torrents flowed with much water into an enclosure.

89.3. And I saw again, and behold fountains were opened on the surface of that great enclosure, and that water began to swell and rise upon the surface, and I saw that enclosure till all its surface was covered with water.

89.4. And the water, the darkness, and mist increased upon it; and as I looked at the height of that water, that water had risen above the height of that enclosure, and was streaming over that enclosure, and it stood upon the earth.

89.5. And all the cattle of that enclosure were gathered together until I saw how they sank and were swallowed up and perished in that water.

89.6. But that vessel floated on the water, while all the oxen and elephants and camels and asses sank to the bottom with all the animals, so that I could no longer see them, and they were not able to escape, (but) perished and sank into the depths.

89.7. And again I saw in the vision till those water torrents were removed from that high roof, and the chasms of the earth were levelled up and other abysses were opened.

89.8. Then the water began to run down into these, till the earth became visible; but that vessel settled on the earth, and the darkness retired and light appeared.

The passages above are consistent with the account told in the Book of Luminaries. In that account, the shortening of the days is described as the result of water soaking deep within the Earth's mantle. This portion of the vision ends with Noah stepping out of the ark.

89.9. But that white bull which had become a man came out of that vessel, and the three bulls with him, and one of those three was white like that bull, and one of them was red as blood, and one black: and that white bull departed from them.

Noah's three sons, Shem, Ham, and Japheth, are each described as being different colors: white, red, and black. We can deduce that Shem was the white bull because Abraham descended from Shem. Ham was likely the black ox because his posterity was cursed regarding the priesthood due to his marriage to a Canaanite woman, Egyptus. Lastly, Japheth was likely the red ox because his descendants founded the Persian, Greek, and Roman empires, which resulted in much bloodshed.

Chapter 20 – Epic Vision - Part II – The House of Israel

In the previous chapter, we began reviewing Enoch's epic vision, which encompassed everything that would befall the children of Adam from the beginning to the end. The prior chapter started with Adam and Eve and ended with the flood. This chapter picks up at the beginning of the post-diluvian world. Things become very interesting very quickly. Consider the following:

> **89.10.** And they [*Noah's posterity*] began to bring forth beasts of the field and birds, so that there arose different genera: lions, tigers, wolves, dogs, hyenas, wild boars, foxes, squirrels, swine, falcons, vultures, kites, eagles, and ravens; and among them was born a white bull.

The passage above speaks of the incredible diversity that arose in the post-diluvian world. Prior to this, there were oxen, elephants, camels, and burros. This diversity was due to the stars coming to Earth and intermarrying with the daughters of Eve. However, despite there being many stars, there was less diversity before the flood than what the above passage describes. What could have happened to introduce fourteen new lines in the human family?

According to the Book of Jubilees, the sons of the Watchers did return to Earth in the days of Noah's grandchildren, but this appears to have happened to a more limited degree than in the prediluvian world. Furthermore, the Lord caused ninety percent of the Watchers to die, and the remainder were confined to the lands of Canaan. However, the people were all one and had been reintroduced to ancient scripts, which unlocked the wisdom of the ancient world. In an attempt to make a name for themselves, the people of Earth began to build great cities, including the mysterious Tower of Babel. For reasons not fully elaborated upon in extant records, the Lord confounded the languages of the people. This confounding resulted in the diversity of cultures and languages across the Earth.

According to the Book of Mormon, it was during this time that the Jaredites left for North America. Curiously, Josephus stated that they were not the only ones. Consider the following extracts from the writings of Josephus:

> After this [*the Tower of Bable*] they were dispersed abroad on account of their languages and went out by colonies everywhere and each colony took possession of the land which they light upon, and to which God led them… there

were some also who passed over the sea in ships. (Josephus book 1 chapter 5)

It should be noted that the Earth was divided in the days of Peleg, which compounded the isolation and development of cultures upon the Earth. Elder Pratt also mentioned that a portion of the Earth was removed at this time. We are never told why or who was upon it, but Elder Pratt believed that the fragment was inhabited when it was taken. If this was true, such an event would have altered the Earth's gravitational portals once more, re-encrypting them from further interaction with the Watchers and their sons. The next time the Bible speaks of the Watchers returning to live openly upon the Earth as they did anciently will be in our days!

Of particular note, after the Earth was divided and the Tower of Babel incident occurred, as noted in **89.10** above, another white bull was born. The whiteness of this bull points us back to the righteousness and covenants of the prediluvian patriarchs belonging to the lineage of Seth. Therefore, we can deduce that this white bull is none other than Abraham. Abraham was born approximately two hundred years after the Tower of Babel and three hundred and fifty years after the flood. Shem, Noah's son who was also described as being white, was still alive at the time of Abraham's birth.

Because Shem was described as a white bull, he most likely preserved the records of the prediluvian fathers. Due to Shem's prediluvian longevity, he lived to be six hundred years old and was alive for most of Abraham's one hundred and seventy-five-year lifespan. As such, Abraham likely obtained the prediluvian records from Shem either directly or indirectly. Regardless, from Abraham's own record, the writings of his fathers greatly impacted him and caused him to seek the same promised blessings they obtained. President Nelson referred to this practice as the gospel of Abraham. If only more of us lived such a gospel!

The passage below speaks of the conditions of society in Abraham's day.

> **89.11.** And they began to bite one another; but that white bull which was born amongst them begat a wild ass [*Ishamel*] and a white bull [*Isaac*] with it, and the wild asses multiplied.
>
> **89.12.** But that bull which was born from him [*Isaac*] begat a black wild boar [*Esau*] and a white sheep [*Jacob*]; and the former begat many boars, but that sheep begat twelve sheep.
>
> **89.13.** And when those twelve sheep had grown, they gave up one of them [*Joseph*] to the asses, and those asses again

gave up that sheep to the wolves [*Egyptians*], and that sheep grew up among the wolves.

89.14. And the Lord brought the eleven sheep to live with it [*Joseph*] and to pasture with it among the wolves: and they multiplied and became many flocks of sheep.

In the passages above, Enoch clearly witnessed the rise of the House of Israel, beginning with the birth of Isaac, and then with Jacob and his twelve sons. Note that after Isaac, the lineage changes from bulls to white sheep. This change signifies something new: the introduction of the House of Israel.

Enoch foresaw that Joseph would be sold into slavery in Egypt, but that in time, the other eleven sheep would join him there. The history of the House of Israel in Egypt is well known and is recounted in detail in the Book of Genesis. What is curious is the individuals that the Lord highlighted in Enoch's vision: Abraham, Isaac, Jacob, and Joseph. This was done to emphasize the birthright. Each of these men went to great lengths to obtain the blessings they received from the Lord. These covenants were more important to them than anything else the world could offer. The same could not be said of the other sons of Jacob, who struggled with their faith and obedience throughout their lives.

Yet, the Lord used the trials and troubles associated with Joseph to teach and correct the House of Israel. Ultimately, all of Jacob's sons came to Egypt and settled in the land of Goshen, where they prospered until a Pharaoh arose who did not know Joseph. Then things changed for the House of Israel. This is where the vision continues:

89.15. And the wolves began to fear them [*the House of Israel*], and they oppressed them until they destroyed their little ones, and they cast their young into a river of much water: but those sheep began to cry aloud on account of their little ones, and to complain unto their Lord.

89.16. And a sheep which had been saved from the wolves fled [*Moses*] and escaped to the wild asses; and I saw the sheep how they lamented and cried, and besought their Lord with all their might, till that Lord of the sheep descended at the voice of the sheep from a lofty abode, and came to them and pastured them.

89.17. And He called that sheep which had escaped the wolves, and spake with it concerning the wolves that it should admonish them not to touch the sheep.

89.18. And the sheep went to the wolves according to the word of the Lord, and another sheep met it and went with it, and the two went and entered together into the assembly of those wolves, and spake with them and admonished them not to touch the sheep from henceforth.

89.19. And thereupon I saw the wolves, and how they oppressed the sheep exceedingly with all their power; and the sheep cried aloud.

89.20. And the Lord came to the sheep and they began to smite those wolves: and the wolves began to make lamentation; but the sheep became quiet and forthwith ceased to cry out.

89.21. And I saw the sheep till they departed from amongst the wolves; but the eyes of the wolves were blinded, and those wolves departed in pursuit of the sheep with all their power.

89.22. And the Lord of the sheep went with them, as their leader, and all His sheep followed Him: and His face was dazzling and glorious and terrible to behold.

89.23. But the wolves began to pursue those sheep till they reached a sea of water.

89.24. And that sea was divided, and the water stood on this side and on that before their face, and their Lord led them and placed Himself between them and the wolves.

89.25. And as those wolves did not yet see the sheep, they proceeded into the midst of that sea, and the wolves followed the sheep, and [those wolves] ran after them into that sea.

89.26. And when they saw the Lord of the sheep, they turned to flee before His face, but that sea gathered itself together, and became as it had been created, and the water swelled and rose till it covered those wolves.

89.27. And I saw till all the wolves who pursued those sheep perished and were drowned.

The passages above clearly speak of Moses and the deliverance of the House of Israel after four hundred years in Egypt, much of that time as slaves. While these events are clear to us in hindsight, they would have been very mysterious to the House of Israel at the time. It is very challenging to understand prophecy in advance, but looking back, things become very clear. So it will be with the prophecies of our days. We look at them now and they are mysterious, yet when the events play out, everything will make perfect sense.

The Lord knew all of these things when Enoch was still a boy and showed him these events long before they happened. This passage explains how the House of Israel knew to look forward to a deliverer. Given that the House of Israel had these writings of Enoch from Abraham, they surely knew of this prophecy and that a deliverer would come, but how it would all play out, no one understood—not even Moses.

Something that really stood out to me in the prophecy above is found in 89.24. I am speaking specifically of the prophecy wherein the Lord stated that He would place Himself between the wolves of Egypt and the House of Israel. The Lord wanted us to know that He was there with their sheep, protecting them during all their trials. However, while the Lord did deliver them, He did not shelter them from the stinging blows of the Egyptians' whips. They bore the bitter burdens of their slavery. Yet, they did not deliver themselves; the Lord did.

Today, many devote great energy and resources to speaking of the evils of slavery. However, they do so without any acknowledgment of the great emancipators who freed them. God delivered the American slaves every bit as much as He did the House of Israel. Yet, both the Lord and America, the tool of their liberation, are vilified. This highlights how easy it is to be blinded by the subtle craft of demons and men. If we focus on evil and darkness, evil and darkness are all we will see. However, if we focus on the hand of God, we will see it throughout our lives. Upon which do you focus, God or Satan? The Savior has always positioned Himself between His people and their oppressors. He will fight against the wolves for us, but we must retain our focus on Him so that we can hear His voice and follow His commands. These are very important lessons for us to retain for the coming days.

The vison now moves beyond the Egyptian Exodus:

89.28. But the sheep escaped from that water and went forth into a wilderness, where there was no water and no grass; and they began to open their eyes and to see; and I saw the Lord of the sheep pasturing them and giving them water and grass, and that sheep [*Moses*] going and leading them.

89.29. And that sheep ascended to the summit of that lofty rock, and the Lord of the sheep sent it to them [*meaning the Lord brought Israel to the base of Mt Siani*].

89.30. And after that I saw the Lord of the sheep who stood before them, and His appearance was great and terrible and majestic, and all those sheep saw Him and were afraid before His face.

89.31. And they all feared and trembled because of Him, and they cried to that sheep with them [which was amongst them]: "We are not able to stand before our Lord or to behold Him."

Consider the monumental significance of this passage, highlighted by the Lord to Enoch eighteen centuries prior! The passage above recounts the moment when the Lord summoned Moses to gather the House of Israel at the base of Mt. Horeb, also known as Mt. Sinai, to speak with them directly. I have often written about this profound experience. It was during this encounter that the House of Israel chose to outsource their spiritual education to Moses, rather than being educated directly from the Lord. This was never the Lord's intention and marked a crucial deviation from the righteous peoples that came before them.

The descendants of Adam's son Seth rejoiced in the Lord and communicated with Him directly. So did the people of Enoch, who formed a city called Zion, where the Lord dwelled among them. The same was true for the people of Melchizedek. Yet, Israel did not follow this divine pattern. They wanted Moses to act on their behalf—see Deuteronomy 5:22-27. Moses did not desire to be their sole intermediary; he wished for every Israelite to be a prophet and speak the word of the Lord directly—see Numbers 11:29.

This tradition of outsourced spiritual education persists in Israel to this day. Many saints believe they can only be taught by a modern Moses and not directly. Yet, how many times have our modern Moses's urged us to hear the Lord ourselves! We are as blind today as Israel ever has been. This is why the Lord highlighted and preserved this prophecy for you to read today. You simply cannot afford to outsource your spiritual education any longer! You will not survive the coming days without constant and direct communication with the Lord. Anyone who tells you differently is a blind guide, from such turn away!

The Lord's revelation continues with Moses ascending the mountain to be taught by the Lord alone on Israel's behalf. Therefore, consider how the Lord describes what happens next.

> **89.32.** And that sheep which led them again ascended to the summit of that rock, but the sheep began to be blinded and to wander from the way which he had showed them, but that sheep wot not thereof [*Moses did not know Israel was apostatizing while he was being instructed by the Lord on their behalf*].

> **89.33.** And the Lord of the sheep was wrathful exceedingly against them, and that sheep discovered it, and went down from the summit of the rock, and came to the sheep, and found the greatest part of them blinded and fallen away.

> **89.34.** And when they saw it [*the Lord's wrath*] they feared and trembled at its presence, and desired to return to their folds [*the slavery of Egypt*].

> **89.35.** And that sheep took other sheep with it, and came to those sheep which had fallen away, and began to slay them; and the sheep feared its presence, and thus that sheep brought back those sheep that had fallen away, and they returned to their folds.

This passage discusses the moment when Israel constructed a golden calf, reminiscent of Hathor, the Egyptian Queen of Heaven. This act became known as the first provocation in the wilderness. The Lord commanded Moses and those who followed Him to slay those who worshiped the Queen of Heaven, establishing a troubling pattern for Israel. According to 1 Kings 11:5, 10-11, the division of the kingdom into two parts occurred because Solomon began to worship Ashtoreth (the Queen of Heaven) and Milcom (Ba'al/Molech).

The Northern Kingdom of Israel did not endure for long. The heading in 2 Kings 17 refers to the destruction of this kingdom and the exile of the Ten Tribes. Verses 15-18 of that chapter explain that their downfall was due to their worship of the two golden calves, which symbolized the hosts of heaven—specifically Ba'al and the Queen of

Heaven, Asherah. Shortly thereafter, Judah faced destruction at the hands of Babylon. In Jeremiah 7:17-20, the Lord states that the Southern Kingdom of Judah was destroyed for worshiping the Queen of Heaven.

As you reflect on these events, remember that Enoch compiled this record to bless those living in the last days. Thus, we can presume that Enoch's vision was also intended to prepare the Saints of today. The lessons from Israel's history are relevant for us now. Understanding these truths is crucial.

Today, some Saints are reintroducing the troubling practice of worshiping a Heavenly Mother—the Queen of Heaven. You may recall that the Lady told Chris Bledsoe that in 2026, the world would enter the age of the Divine Feminine, led by her. This ancient concept of the Queen of Heaven is poised to resurface globally, and the spiritual blindness of the Saints may lead them down the same paths as our ancient forefathers. We must awaken to the seriousness of our situation and worship God alone.

When in Scripture have we ever been instructed to pray to the Queen of Heaven? As I outlined in Volume II of this series, while we all have heavenly mothers, they never taught us to worship them. Instead, they directed us to worship the One who is mighty to save. Let us remain faithful to the teachings of our mothers and worship God the Father, and no one else!

Enoch's vision continues:

> **89.36.** And I saw in this vision till that sheep became a man and built a house for the Lord of the sheep, and placed all the sheep in that house.

> **89.37.** And I saw till this sheep which had met that sheep which led them fell asleep: and I saw till all the great sheep perished and little ones arose in their place, and they came to a pasture, and approached a stream of water.

> **89.38.** Then that sheep, their leader which had become a man, withdrew from them and fell asleep, and all the sheep sought it and cried over it with a great crying.

> **89.39.** And I saw till they left off crying for that sheep and crossed that stream of water, and there arose the two sheep as leaders in the place of those which had led them and fallen asleep.

89.40. And I saw till the sheep came to a goodly place, and a pleasant and glorious land, and I saw till those sheep were satisfied; and that house stood amongst them in the pleasant land.

In the passages above, Enoch saw Israel being led into the land of Canaan across the Jordan River by Joshua and Caleb. We must understand this in the context of Israel's forty years of wandering in the wilderness, a consequence of their lack of faith in God's ability to deliver them from the giants of Canaan. We should remember that God will also deliver us from the Watchers and their sons in our day; we must not doubt it. This deliverance will rival the Exodus from Egypt, which was mirrored when Israel crossed the Jordan and the waters were divided.

Furthermore, the Lord emphasized that Moses did not enter the Promised Land. While this vision does not highlight that the Lord took Moses unto Himself, as noted in Alma 45:19, it is important to recognize. This vision is presented from the perspective of the blind and obstinate sheep of Israel, who lacked the foresight to understand the workings of their God. God has His reasons. What were His reasons for taking Moses? I believe the answer can be found in the following passage:

> How long will these people reject Me? And how long will they not believe Me, with all the signs which I have performed among them? I will strike them with the pestilence and disinherit them, and **I will make of you a nation greater and mightier than they**. (Numbers 14:11-12)

When Moses heard the Lord say these thing, he begged Him that He would not destroy Israel, but give them another chance. This is how the Lord responded:

> And the Lord said, I have pardoned [*Israel*] according to thy word: **But as truly as I live, all the Earth shall be filled with the glory of the Lord.** (Numbers 14:20-21)

While the Lord agreed to pardon Israel again, He stated that the day would come when the Earth would be filled with His glory. I believe that He was referring to the day when Moses would return from the cosmos with the nation that the Lord had raised up from him. We have learned little of Moses since his translation, but I am sure the Lord has made good on His word. The Lord says what He means, and he does what He says. The Lord knew that Israel would abandon Him and go after the Queen of Heaven. He wanted a people that would be faithful, and the literal sons and daughters of Moses will surely fit the bill. I believe that we of the latter-days will be delighted and awed by the workings of the Father when He fills the Earth with His glory! I absolutely expect that when Israel is restored to us, it will be joined by a mighty nation that has descended from Moses. Thus we see that like many before Him, Moses obtained the covenant of Abraham for himself!

The vision now returns to the House of Israel's occupation of their promised lands.

> **89.41.** And sometimes their eyes were opened, and sometimes blinded, till another sheep arose and led them and brought them all back, and their eyes were opened.

> **89.42.** And the dogs and the foxes and the wild boars began to devour those sheep till the Lord of the sheep raised up a ram from their midst, which led them.

> **89.43.** And that ram began to butt on either side those dogs, foxes, and wild boars till he had destroyed them †all†.

The passages above recount the rise and fall of many generations over approximately four hundred and fifty years. During this time, Israel's spiritual blindness ebbed and flowed like ocean tides. They witnessed the intervention of the Mazzaroth, the star kings, on their behalf, which opened their eyes to the profound reality of the multiverse in the days of Deborah. Yet, despite this enlightenment, they ultimately slipped back into darkness.

Following their victory over Sisera and his nine hundred iron chariots, others rose to persecute Israel in Sisera's stead. This cycle of persecution continued until the days of Saul and David, when the Philistines, Amalekites, and Ammonites finally began to be driven back once and for all. However, Saul's jealousy of David led him to seek David's life. The prophecy addresses this struggle next:

> **89.44.** And that sheep whose eyes were opened [*Samuel the prophet*] saw that ram [*King Saul*], which was amongst the sheep, till it [*Saul*]†forsook its glory† and began to butt those sheep, and trampled upon them, and behaved itself unseemly.

> **89.45.** And the Lord of the sheep sent the lamb [*Samuel*] to another lamb [*David*] and raised it to being a ram and leader of the sheep instead of that ram [*Saul*] which had †forsaken its glory†.

89.46. And it went to it and spake to it alone, and raised it to being a ram, and made it the prince and leader of the sheep; but during all these things those dogs oppressed the sheep.

89.47. And the first ram pursued that second ram, and that second ram arose and fled before it; and I saw till those dogs pulled down the first ram.

89.48. And that second ram arose and led the [little] sheep.

89.49. And those sheep grew and multiplied; but all the dogs, and foxes, and wild boars feared and fled before it, and that ram butted and killed the wild beasts [*the remaining giants*], and those wild beasts had no longer any power among the sheep and robbed them no more of ought. And that ram begat many sheep and fell asleep; and a little sheep became ram in its stead, and became prince and leader of those sheep.

The epic story of the prophet Samuel, born of his mother Hannah's unwavering faith, was foretold long ago. The Lord used Samuel to identify, call, and anoint Saul as King of Israel. Saul began his reign with strength but soon became consumed by jealousy over David's meteoric rise to popularity. In a fit of covetous rage, Saul hunted David throughout the kingdom, seeking to kill him. Yet David, despite having the opportunity to take Saul's life, refused to raise his hand against the Lord's anointed.

Ultimately, Saul was killed in battle after consulting a necromancer to speak with the deceased prophet Samuel. With Saul's death, David ascended to the throne and united all of Israel by defeating their enemies.

David had many wives and fathered numerous children. Tragically, like Saul before him, David lost his way. In a moment of unbridled passion, he had an affair with his neighbor's wife and sought to cover his sins by orchestrating her husband's death. The child born from this union was Solomon, who inherited his father's throne. Solomon's crowning achievement is discussed next:

89.50. And that house became great and broad, and it was built for those sheep: (and) a tower lofty and great was built on the house for the Lord of the sheep, and that house was low, but the tower was elevated and lofty, and the Lord of the sheep stood on that tower and they offered a full table before Him.

The passage above discusses the temple of Solomon, built from the wealth accumulated by David. However, the days of Israel's righteousness were short-lived. Why? As we see in 1 Kings 11, Solomon began to worship Ashtoreth, the Queen of Heaven. Consequently, ten tribes of Israel were torn from Solomon's kingdom and given to his servant, Jeroboam. Jeroboam established the Northern Kingdom of Israel, while Solomon's son Rehoboam became king over the significantly diminished Kingdom of Judah.

According to 2 Kings 17, the Northern Kingdom fully embraced the worship of the two calves (Baalim and Ashtoreth, the Queen of Heaven) and ultimately faced destruction at the hands of Assyria. However, before this destruction occurred, the Lord called prophets to reclaim His people. This sets the stage for the vision that follows.

> **89.51.** And again I saw those sheep that they again erred and went many ways, and forsook that their house, and the Lord of the sheep called some from amongst the sheep and sent them to the sheep, but the sheep began to slay them.

> **89.52.** And one of them was saved and was not slain, and it sped away and cried aloud over the sheep; and they sought to slay it, but the Lord of the sheep saved it from the sheep, and brought it up to me, and caused it to dwell there.

In the passage above, Enoch observed that the Lord was seeking to redeem His people, yet they were killing His servants, the prophets. During this time in Israel, there existed a prophetic guild known as the sons of the prophets. These were ordinary men and women who sought to be taught directly by the Lord rather than by Israel's blind guides. Jezebel, the queen of the Northern Kingdom of Israel, despised these saints because they exposed her apostasy. Consequently, she hunted them down and killed them.

Jezebel promoted the exclusive worship of Baal and Asherah. During this period, high places and groves containing Asherah poles were widespread throughout Israel. Archaeologists have uncovered thousands of Asherah figurines, testifying to Israel's surrender to the abominable practice of worshiping the Queen of Heaven. The sons of the prophets aimed to reclaim Israel from this diabolical worship of the Heavenly Mother, as she was often called. The most renowned prophet of this time was Elijah the Tishbite. The Lord bestowed upon Elijah a mighty mantle of priesthood power, granting him the ability to call down fire from heaven to destroy his enemies. Yet, despite these incredible displays of power, Jezebel refused to repent.

Interestingly, as part of this vision, Enoch saw that Elijah would be translated and brought up to reside with his people. This presents a curious contrast between Moses and Elijah, both of whom were translated. Enoch did not describe Moses as coming up to him and his people, but he did with Elijah. This distinction highlights that the Lord had other plans for Moses, who was taken up into heaven so that the Lord might create a mightier nation than exists anywhere else in Israel.

We understand why Moses was translated, but why Elijah? This is an important question. When Jesus Christ ascended the Mount of Transfiguration with Peter, James, and John, they encountered both Moses and Elijah. Each of these remarkable men has significant roles yet to fulfill. They both appeared to Joseph Smith and conferred upon him keys and priesthood power, one of which related to the gathering of the House of Israel.

As we reflect on these matters, we must remember Enoch's stated purpose in writing his record: to bless the saints living in the last days. We recognize that these are indeed the last days. Great trials are soon to come upon us here in America; just this morning, it was announced that Donald Trump won the 2024 election. If the prophecy of Ezra's Eagle is correct, he will never sit in the Oval Office as President again.

Enoch included this prophecy in his record because the people of the last days will be directly impacted by both Moses and Elijah, who will play prominent roles before the final curtain falls. They will do more than simply remind the children of the covenants of their fathers! Every year at Passover, the Jews set a place at their table for Elijah. We smile at this, knowing that Elijah has returned, having visited Joseph Smith in the Kirtland Temple. However, I believe the Jews are right to continue their practice of waiting for Elijah, and you will understand why by the end of this vision.

We now return to Enoch's incredible vision:

> **89.53.** And many other sheep He sent to those sheep to testify unto them and lament over them.

> **89.54**. And after that I saw that when they forsook the house of the Lord and His tower they fell away entirely, and their eyes were blinded; and I saw the Lord of the sheep how He wrought much slaughter amongst them in their herds until those sheep invited that slaughter and betrayed His place.

> **89.55.** And He gave them over into the hands of the lions and tigers, and wolves and hyenas, and into the hand of the foxes, and to all the wild beasts, and those wild beasts began to tear in pieces those sheep.

89.56. And I saw that He forsook that their house and their tower and gave them all into the hand of the lions, to tear and devour them, into the hand of all the wild beasts.

The passage above speaks of the period of time when despite the warning of many prophets, including the great Isaiah, both of the Kingdoms of Israel would be destroyed. This destruction came to the Northern Kingdom around 720 BC, and to the Kingdom of Judah between 605 BC and 585 BC. When the Jews were destroyed, so was the Temple of Solomon. Since this destruction, the Northern Kingdom has never been restored. The survivors were taken captive into Assyria and have since become the Lost Ten Tribes. Again, it is very important that we remember the reasons both these kingdoms were destroyed. Consider the following passages.

Regarding the destruction of the Northern Kingdom of Israel:

> Then the king of Assyria invaded the entire land, and for three years he besieged the city of Samaria. Finally, in the ninth year of King Hoshea's reign, Samaria fell, and the people of Israel were exiled to Assyria. They were settled in colonies in Halah, along the banks of the Habor River in Gozan, and in the cities of the Medes.

> This disaster came upon the people of Israel because they worshiped other gods. They sinned against the LORD their God, who had brought them safely out of Egypt and had rescued them from the power of Pharaoh, the king of Egypt. They had followed the practices of the pagan nations the LORD had driven from the land ahead of them, as well as the practices the kings of Israel had introduced.

> The people of Israel had also secretly done many things that were not pleasing to the LORD their God. They built pagan shrines for themselves in all their towns, from the smallest outpost to the largest walled city. They set up sacred pillars and **Asherah poles** at the top of every hill and under every green tree. They offered sacrifices on all the hilltops [*to the Queen of Heaven and Ba'al*], just like the nations the LORD had driven from the land ahead of them. So the people of Israel had done many evil things, arousing the LORD's anger. Yes, they worshiped idols, despite the LORD's specific and repeated warnings.

Again and again the LORD had sent his prophets and seers to warn both Israel and Judah: "Turn from all your evil ways. Obey my commands and decrees—the entire law that I commanded your ancestors to obey, and that I gave you through my servants the prophets." But the Israelites would not listen. They were as stubborn as their ancestors who had refused to believe in the LORD their God.

They rejected His decrees and the covenant He had made with their ancestors, and they despised all His warnings. They worshiped worthless idols, so they became worthless themselves. They followed the example of the nations around them, disobeying the LORD's command not to imitate them. They rejected all the commands of the LORD their God and **made two calves from metal** [*one of Ba'al, and one for Asherah*]. They set up an **Asherah pole** and **worshiped Baal** and all the forces of heaven. They even sacrificed their own sons and daughters in the fire. (2 Kings 17:5-17 – New Living Translation)

In the above passages, Asherah is mentioned either directly or indirectly three times as a key reason for the destruction of the Northern Kingdom of Israel. An Asherah pole was a tree shaped to symbolically represent Asherah, the Queen of Heaven—the mother of all living. The following image illustrates an example of an Asherah pole. In this depiction, as in many representations found in Israel, she is shown holding her breasts in a provocative manner.

Also noted is the creation of two molten calves, one representing Asherah and the other Baal. Both practices are directly tied to Canaanite worship and were embraced by King Solomon and many others. These practices were the reason for Israel's downfall!

Regarding the destruction of the Kingdom of Judah, it is important to illustrate that Judah was guilty of the same abominations as the Northern Kingdom. Consider the case of Manasseh—the king who killed Isaiah.

Manasseh was twelve years old when he became king, and he reigned in Jerusalem fifty-five years. He did what was evil in the LORD's sight, following the detestable practices of the pagan nations that the LORD had driven from the land ahead of the Israelites. He rebuilt the pagan shrines his father, Hezekiah, had broken down. He constructed altars for the images of Baal and set up Asherah poles. He also bowed before all the powers of the heavens and worshiped them.

He built pagan altars in the Temple of the LORD [*2 Kings 21:7 specifically states that this was an image of Asherah*],… He built these altars for all the powers of the heavens in both courtyards of the LORD's Temple. Manasseh also sacrificed his own sons in the fire in the valley of Ben-Hinnom…

So the LORD sent the commanders of the Assyrian armies, and they took Manasseh prisoner. They put a ring through his nose, bound him in bronze chains, and led him away to Babylon. But while in deep distress, Manasseh sought the LORD his God and sincerely humbled himself before the God of his ancestors. And when he prayed, the LORD listened to him and was moved by his request. So the LORD brought Manasseh back to Jerusalem and to his kingdom. Then Manasseh finally realized that the LORD alone is God! (2 Chr 33:1-5;11-13 – New Living Translation)

In the passages above, the Kingdom of Judah was heading in the same direction as the Northern Kingdom of Israel. The key difference was that Manasseh repented in sackcloth and ashes, was forgiven by the Lord, and returned to his throne. However, the Kingdom of Judah soon reverted to the worship of Asherah and Baal, like a dog returning to its vomit. Consider the Lord's words to Jeremiah regarding the sins of Judah and their imminent destruction at the hands of Babylon.

Pray no more for these people, Jeremiah. Do not weep or pray for them, and don't beg me to help them, for I will not listen to you. Don't you see what they are doing throughout the towns of Judah and in the streets of Jerusalem? No wonder I am so angry! Watch how the children gather wood and the fathers build sacrificial fires. See how the women knead dough and make cakes to offer to the Queen of Heaven [*Asherah*]. And they pour out liquid offerings to their other idol gods! Am I the one they are hurting? asks the LORD. Most of all, they hurt themselves, to their own shame. So this is what the Sovereign LORD says: I will pour out My terrible fury on this place. Its people, animals, trees, and crops will be consumed by the unquenchable fire of My anger." (Jer 7:16-20 – New Living Translation)

The destruction of both Israel and Judah stemmed from their worship of Asherah, the Queen of Heaven, and Ba'al. Israel crafted their own permissive version of the Lord, a god that allowed them to live after the manner of the flesh. The Father's responses to the ancient civilizations that embraced these practices are all we need to know about them. Yet, due to ignorance of such things, these abominable practices are experiencing a modern resurgence within the Church.

Enoch's writings contain significant warnings about these issues, highlighting their relevance for the saints of the last days. We will encounter these phenomena on a grand scale, which will lead many astray. Many unsuspecting saints have already begun the apostate practice of praying to "Heavenly Mother." This practice directly contradicts every teaching the Father's Hidden Son provided regarding prayer. It marks a clear deviation from the true path, echoing the apostate practices of ancient Israel, like a dog returning to its vomit.

If the Lady does make a global appearance around April 2026 to usher in the era of the Divine Feminine, what hope do the blind have of not being deceived? Already, this abominable resurgence of ancient apostate traditions signals that the old ways are returning. This is why the Lord commanded us to obtain a deeper understanding of countries, kingdoms, and the perplexity of nations. All the great kingdoms of the Earth fell for similar reasons—reasons we have begun to emulate on a grand scale. If we do not learn from the past, we will repeat it. Of this, there can be no doubt!

Chapter 21 – Epic Vision Part III – 70 Shepherds

In the prior chapter, we continued our analysis of Enoch's epic vision of all things that would befall the posterity of Adam from the beginning of time to the last generation. As part of that vision, the Lord highlighted specific scenes of Israel's fickleness that would be particularly relevant to our day. Specifically, the Lord emphasized Israel's outsourcing of their spiritual education to Moses and the catastrophes that followed as a result. We learned from the very beginning how Israel struggled to worship the true and living God for who He truly is. Instead, because they did not choose to know Him directly, they worshiped their own apostate versions of Him, along with a self-proclaimed mother goddess.

These practices turned the ancient world upside down. Indeed, every nation that indulged in such practices has been completely destroyed. Those with eyes to see can observe that the world is being flipped upside down once more. Only those with ears to hear the whispered truths of the Holy Spirit will be able to navigate Lucifer's maze of deception unscathed. The Lord has left us many warnings that such things are coming, yet many are too blind to see. As a result, they depend on someone else to warn them that they are about to go over the same cliff that every lemming-like nation of the past has gone over. Yet, even if they are warned by their neighbor, few will heed the warning. Why? Because they have outsourced their spiritual education to Moses, and not to their neighbor. However, while they listen to Moses, they do not heed his council, therefore, they are truly blind. All is not well in Zion!

We now return to Enoch's epic vision of all things, and the horrific consequences of Israel's blindness in antiquity.

> **89.57.** And I began to cry aloud with all my power, and to appeal to the Lord of the sheep, and to represent to Him in regard to the sheep that they were devoured by all the wild beasts.

> **89.58.** But [*the Lord of sheep*] remained unmoved, though He saw it, and rejoiced that they were devoured and swallowed and robbed, and left them to be devoured in the hand of all the beasts.

> **89.59.** And He called seventy shepherds, and cast those sheep to them that they might pasture them, and He spake to the shepherds and their companions: "Let each individual of

you pasture the sheep henceforward, and everything that I shall command you that do ye.

89.60. And I will deliver them over unto you duly numbered, and tell you which of them are to be destroyed--and them destroy ye." And He gave over unto them those sheep.

The number seventy is a reoccurring number in scripture. The Watchers were bound for seventy generations. Judah was in Babylonian captivity for seventy years. Now Enoch foresaw that Israel would be given over to seventy consecutive shepherds, many of which would not have Israel's best interests at heart. Who were these seventy shepherds? I believe these to be seventy consecutive leaders that would be given power over the Lord's flock.

The question becomes, why seventy? In order to answer this question we must look into Israel's ancient history, starting with the day the Lord delivered them into the hands of the first of these seventy shepherds. This started when Assyria attacked and over threw the Northern Kingdom of Israel. Using this as the starting point a remarkable list of seventy consecutive leaders appears. Consider the following consecutive list of seventy consecutive Shepards shown to Enoch by the Lord in vision:

Order	Name	Period	Kingdom	Note
1	Tiglath-Pileser III	745-727 BC	Assyrian	Began the conquest and deportation of Northern Israel
2	Sargon II	722-705 BC	Assyrian	Usurped his brother's throne. Venerated by the Nazis. Destroyed the Northern Kingdom of Israel and relocated all surviving Israelites
3	Sennacherib	705-681 BC	Assyrian	Tried to conquer Judah, but his entire army was defeated by divine intervention.
4	Esarhaddon	681-669 BC	Assyrian	Allowed some Israelites to return home, they became the Samaritans.
5	Nebuchadnezzar II	605-562 BC	Babylon	Destroyed the Kingdom of Judah and brought them into captivity. Destroyed the Temple of Solomon.
6	Merodach	562-560 BC	Babylon	Known for releasing Jehoiachin - King of Judah from prison after 37 years of captivity. Was murdered by his brother-in-law.
7	Nergal Sharezer	560-556 BC	Babylon	Killed Merodach and usurped his throne.
8	Labasi Marduk	556 BC	Babylon	Killed in a coup by Nabonidus and his son Belshazzar
9	Nabonidus	556-539 BC	Babylon	Sought to restore the ancient religions of the past through the world's first archaeological digs.

10	Belshazzar	539 BC	Babylon	Co-regent of Babylon with his father- a prophecy of their demise was written on the wall by the finger of the Lord - "You have been weighed, measured, and found wanting". The King of Persia conquered Babylon that same night without the shedding of blood.
11	Cyrus the Great	539-530 BC	Persia	Respected by the kingdom's he conquered. He liberated the Jews, and funded the rebuilding of the temple in Jerusalem. Established the Achaemenid or Persian empire.
12	Cambyses II	530-522 BC	Persia	Son of Cyrus the Great, conquered Egypt, was murdered by his own while returning home from his Egyptian conquest. Had a favorable disposition towards the Jews like his father.
13	Darius the Great	522-486 BC	Persia	Attempted to conquer Greece but was defeated at the famous battle of Marathon. He provided financial aid to the Jews in the construction of the temple.
14	Xerxes I, aka Ahasuerus	486-465 BC	Persia	Husband to Queen Ester, allowed the Jews to protect themselves from Haman's attempt to destroy them. Xerxes I was also Famous for invading Greece and fighting King Leonidas of Sparta. Xerxes was ultimately forced to withdraw from Greece.
15	Artaxerxes I	465-425 BC	Persia	Funded the rebuilding of Jerusalem's walls, contemporary of Ezra, Ester, and Nehemiah.
16	Xerxes II	425-424 BC	Persia	Reign only lasted 45 days. He was murdered.
17	Darius II	423-404 BC	Persia	Continued the tradition of religious tolerance towards the Jewish nation, permitting them to worship as they pleased.
18	Artaxerxes II	404-359 BC	Persia	Continued the tradition of religious tolerance towards the Jewish nation, permitting them to worship as they pleased.
19	Artaxerxes III	359-338 BC	Persia	Implemented a heavy tax upon the Jew's sacrifices in their temple - 50 drachmas for each lamb sacrificed. One drachma was equal to a day's wage!
20	Artaxerxes IV	338-336 BC	Persia	He was murdered upon the throne by Darius III
21	Darius III	336-330 BC	Persia	Did not lift the tax burden from the Jews, was the last king of Persia
22	Alexander the Great	330-312 BC	Macedonian Empire	Revered by the Jews for ending their tax burden, and honoring their religious freedoms. Died young, leaving the kingdom to his four generals.

23	Seleucus I Nicator	312-281 BC	Seleucid Empire	Alexander's general that ruled over Judea. He granted the Jews citizenship in the kingdom, which resulted in Jewish integration into Hellenistic society.
24	Antiochus I Soter	281-261 BC	Seleucid Empire	Courted the favor of the Jewish leadership by exempting the council of elders, priests and scribes from taxation.
25	Antiochus II Theos	261.246 BC	Seleucid Empire	Expanded Jewish freedoms by exempting Jews from taxation for three years, and donated funds to the temple.
26	Seleucus II Callinicus	246-225 BC	Seleucid Empire	His reign was marked by growing conflicts between his kingdom and other Hellenistic states. Maintained respected for the Jewish people.
27	Seleucus III Ceraunus	225-223 BC	Seleucid Empire	Reign marked with continued conflict with other rival Hellenistic states, but upheld respect for the Jewish people.
28	Antiochus III the Great	223-187 BC	Seleucid Empire	Ptolemaic empire in Egypt joined forces with Rome in his day, both of which were antagonists to his kingdom.
29	Antiochus IV Epiphanes	187-163 BC	Seleucid Empire	Attempted to force the Jews to convert to Hellenism through torture and fear. Was disposed by the Maccabean revolt.
30	Judah Maccabee revolt	167-140 BC	Jewish war for independence	The Maccabees were a family of Jewish priests who organized the people to fight for independence from the Greeks (Seleucid empire).
31	Simon Thassi Maccabeaus	140-134 BC	High priest	Negotiated with Demetrius II for Jewish self-governance
32	John Hyrcanus	134.104 BC	High priest	Ruler of the semi-autonomous Jewish state.
33	Aristobuls I	103-76 BC	Hasmonean	First High Priest of Israel to proclaim himself King.
34	Alexander Jannaeus	76-67 BC	Hasmonean	Semi-autonomous state of Israel
35	Salome Alexandra	67-66 BC	Hasmonean	Semi-autonomous state of Israel
36	Hyrcanus II	66-63 BC	Hasmonean	Semi-autonomous state of Israel
37	Aristobulus II	63-40 BC	Hasmonean	Semi-autonomous state of Israel
38	Antigonus II Mattathias	40-37 BC	Hasmonean	Semi-autonomous state of Israel
39	Herod the Great	37 BC-4 AD	Vassal King of Rome	Rebuilt the temple and expanded the temple mount. Killed many infants in an attempt to keep the Messiah from coming.
40	Herod Agrippa	4 BC -44 AD	Last vassal king of Rome	Killed John the Baptist and gave Christ over to Pilot to be judged.

41	Coponius	6-9 AD	Rome	Rome introduced concurrent Roman Prefects during the rule of Herod Agrippa. Coponius was the first Roman Prefect and was sent to crush a Galilean zealot revolt regarding Roman taxation. Jewish casualties were not reported by Josephus.
42	Marcus Ambivulus	9-12 AD	Rome	Maintained peace with Herod Agrippa without major conflict.
43	Annius Rufus	12-15 AD	Rome	Maintained peace with Herod Agrippa without major conflict.
44	Valerius Gratus	15-26 AD	Rome	Appointed four different high priests including Joseph Caiaphas. His appointments were political in nature, and were a source of consternation amongst the Jews.
45	Pontius Pilatus	26-36 AD	Rome	Roman Prefect during Christ's day who attempted to liberate Jesus, but was forced to crucify Him by the demand of Caiaphas, and the Jewish religious leaders.
46	Marcellus	36-37 AD	Rome	Prefect of Rome
47	Marullus	37-41 AD	Rome	Prefect of Rome
48	Marcus Julius Agrippa	41-44 AD	Rome	Prefect of Rome
49	Cuspius Fadus	44-46 AD	Rome	Roman Procurator
50	Tiberius Julius Alexander	46-48 AD	Rome	Roman Procurator
51	Ventidius Cumanus	48-52 AD	Rome	Roman Procurator
52	Marcus Antonius Felix	52-60 AD	Rome	Roman Procurator
53	Porcius Festus	60-62 AD	Rome	Roman Procurator
54	Lucceius Albinus	62-64 AD	Rome	Roman Procurator
55	Gessius Florus	64-66 AD	Rome	Roman Procurator
56	Marcus Antonius Julianus	66-70 AD	Rome	Roman Procurator
57	Sextus Vettulenus Cerialis	70-71 AD	Rome	Over a million Jews killed. Temple and Jerusalem destroyed. One hundred thousand Jews sold into slavery.
58	Sextus Lucilius Bassus	71-72 AD	Rome	Roman Legate
59	Lucius Flavius Bassus	72-81 AD	Rome	Roman Legate
60	Marcus Salvidienus	80-85 AD	Rome	Roman Legate
61	Gnaeus Longinus	85-89 AD	Rome	Roman Legate
62	Sextus Campanus	93-97 AD	Rome	Roman Legate
63	Tiberius Herodes	99-102 AD	Rome	Roman Legate
64	Gaius Bassus	102-104 AD	Rome	Roman Legate

65	Quintus Pompeius Falco	105-107 AD	Rome	Roman Legate
66	Tiberianus	114-117 AD	Rome	Roman Legate
67	Lusius Quietus	117-120 AD	Rome	Roman Legate
68	Quintus Antiquus	120-125 AD	Rome	Roman Prefect
69	Quintus Tineius Rufus	125-c. 132 AD	Rome	Roman Legate
70	General Julius Severus	132-135 AD	Rome	Roman General that destroyed all remaining Jewish settlements in the Holy Land as part of the Bar Kokhba revolt, leaving no surviving Israelites in Palestine.

This incredible list of consecutive leaders in Judea began with the Assyrian conquest of the Northern Kingdom of Israel and ended with the crushing defeat of the Jews in the last of the Roman wars, the Bar Kokhba revolt. After the Bar Kokhba revolt, all remaining Jews in Judea were either slaughtered or sold into captivity. This ended the Jews' 1,500-year occupation of the lands of Canaan, over half of which were presided over by these seventy shepherds.

Millions died at the hands of these shepherds. They came from Assyria, then Babylon, then Persia, and then Greece and the Seleucid dynasty. The Jews revolted against the Greeks in the famous Maccabean revolt. Yet, the Hasmonean dynasty was ultimately crushed by the Romans. The Romans represented the final stewards of the Jewish-occupied Holy Land. The Romans and the Jews would engage in three catastrophic wars. The first of these began in 66 AD and culminated with the destruction of both Jerusalem and the incredible siege of Masada in 73 AD. It is estimated that around 1.4 million Jews were killed in this war, with a hundred thousand survivors sold into slavery. The last of these wars, the Bar Kokhba revolt, resulted in the destruction of all remaining Jewish towns and villages, with approximately six hundred thousand Jews killed and all survivors sold into slavery. This last revolt left the Holy Land desolate and empty.

All this happened because of the blindness of the Lord's flock. Can we look back at this terrible period in the history of the House of Israel without asking ourselves if the same blindness exists among the Lord's people today? Have we learned any lessons from our forefathers? We probably think that we have, for it is easy to see the flaws in others but nearly impossible to see ourselves as we really are. The Lord did not include this account to highlight the fickleness of our fathers but so that we do not repeat their folly in the last days.

As the narrative returns, we will reference the above list again. We now return to Enoch's epoch vision of these seventy shepherds.

89.61. And He called another and spake unto him: "Observe and mark everything that the shepherds will do to those sheep; for they will destroy more of them than I have commanded them.

89.62. And every excess and the destruction which will be wrought through the shepherds, record how many they destroy according to my command, and how many according to their own caprice: record against every individual shepherd all the destruction he effects.

89.63. And read out before me by number how many they destroy, and how many they deliver over for destruction, that I may have this as a testimony against them, and know every deed of the shepherds, that I may comprehend and see what they do, whether or not they abide by my command which I have commanded them.

89.64. But they shall not know it, and thou shalt not declare it to them, nor admonish them, but only record against each individual all the destruction which the shepherds effect each in his time and lay it all before Me."

89.65. And I saw till those shepherds pastured in their season, and they began to slay and to destroy more than they were bidden, and they delivered those sheep into the hand of the lions.

89.66. And the lions and tigers eat and devoured the greater part of those sheep, and the wild boars eat along with them; and they burnt that tower and demolished that house.

89.67. And I became exceedingly sorrowful over that tower because that house of the sheep was demolished, and afterwards I was unable to see if those sheep entered that house.

89.68. And the shepherds and their associates delivered over those sheep to all the wild beasts, to devour them, and each one of them received in his time a definite number: it was written by the other in a book how many each one of them destroyed of them.

89.69. And each one slew and destroyed many more than was prescribed; and I began to weep and lament on account of those sheep.

89.70. And thus in the vision I saw that one who wrote, how he wrote down every one that was destroyed by those shepherds, day by day, and carried up and laid down and showed actually the whole book to the Lord of the sheep-- (even) everything that they had done, and all that each one of them had made away with, and all that they had given over to destruction.

89.71. And the book was read before the Lord of the sheep, and He took the book from His hand and read it and sealed it and laid it down.

89.72. And forthwith I saw how the shepherds pastured for twelve hours, and behold three of those sheep turned back and came and entered and began to build up all that had fallen down of that house; but the wild boars tried to hinder them, but they were not able.

89.73. And they began again to build as before, and they reared up that tower, and it was named the high tower; and they began again to place a table before the tower, but all the bread on it was polluted and not pure.

In the passages above, we learn of three of the sheep who returned to Jerusalem in the days of Cyrus, the eleventh shepherd in the list above, to rebuild the temple. These three sheep correlate with Esther, who was responsible for preserving the sheep, as well as Ezra and Nehemiah, who brought Esther's survivors back to Israel to rebuild the Temple. Ezra was a prolific prophet who restored all of the ancient scriptures that had been lost during the Babylonian siege of Jerusalem.

It was at this time that the prophecy of Ezra's Eagle was written, of which I have so often spoken. Despite rebuilding the temple during this time, the Jews remained blind. While Ezra restored the scriptures, the Jews went beyond the mark, editing and censoring them in their restored infancy. In so doing, they believed that they were protecting their people from worshiping Ba'al and Asherah, as their fathers before the Babylonian captivity had done. However, in erasing polytheism, they blinded the Israelites to the Father's Hidden Son.

Without Christ, no matter how ardent one's worship of God is, it falls short. Jesus Christ is the way to the Father. Without Christ, all is vain. As such, among the Jews, the blind were leading the blind right to the edge of the cliff. This is where the narrative picks up.

> **89.74.** And as touching all this the eyes of those sheep were blinded so that they saw not, and (the eyes of) their shepherds likewise; and they delivered them in large numbers to their shepherds for destruction, and they trampled the sheep with their feet and devoured them.

> **89.75.** And the Lord of the sheep remained unmoved till all the sheep were dispersed over the field and mingled with them, and they did not save them out of the hand of the beasts.

> **89.76.** And this one who wrote the book [*meaning Ezra who restored their scriptures*] carried it up, and showed it and read it before the Lord of the sheep, and implored Him on their account, and besought Him on their account as he showed Him all the doings of the shepherds, and gave testimony before Him against all the shepherds. And he took the actual book and laid it down beside Him and departed.

The passage above states that Ezra was taken up to the presence of the Lord of Sheep. This means that Ezra was translated, just as three others from this account were: Enoch, Moses, and Elijah. The Book of Enoch is not the only text that suggests that Ezra was translated. The book of Second Esdras, which also contains the prophecy of Ezra's Eagle, speaks of this as well. Consider the following:

> For thou shalt be taken away from all, and from henceforth
> thou shalt remain with my Son, and with such as be like thee,
> until the times be ended. (2 Esdras 14:9)

In the passage above, the Lord tells Ezra that he will be taken up into the heavens to dwell with those that are like him, until the times be ended. By this we are to understand that Ezra was translated and lives with other translated beings, such as Enoch, Melchizedek, Moses, and Elijah. Furthermore, like with Elijah, it seems to me that the Lord told Ezra that he would remain in the heavens, UNTIL THE TIMES BE ENDED.

I believe this indicates that, like Elijah, Ezra will return before the end and have a major role to play in the events of the latter days. Therefore, as the Jews continue to look for Elijah to return, they should pull up another empty chair for Ezra as well.

Ezra understood that he would be translated. As a result, he petitioned the Lord that he might leave something behind to bless his fellow man until his return. Consider Ezra's request:

> If I have found grace before thee, send the Holy Ghost into me, and I shall write all that hath been done in the world since the beginning, which were written in Thy law, that men may find the path, and that they which will live in the latter-days may live. (2 Esdras 14:22)

Similar to Enoch, Ezra's desire was to leave a message regarding the true history of the world. He understood that his history would bless those who would be called to spend mortality in the last days. Ezra knew that there would be those living in times of trial who would have his words, and that they would greatly benefit from them. Thus, the prominence of Ezra's writings among my own. It was Ezra's hope that, while many were blind, some in the last days would have eyes to see, and that his writings would be an integral part of that process. This has certainly come to pass in my own life, and I hope you can say the same. I will revisit this topic later, as there is more to be said.

The vision continues:

> **90.1.** And I saw till that in this manner thirty-five shepherds undertook the pasturing (of the sheep), and they severally completed their periods as did the first; and others received them into their hands, to pasture them for their period, each shepherd in his own period.

> **90.2.** And after that I saw in my vision all the birds of heaven coming, the eagles, the vultures, the kites, the ravens; but the eagles led all the birds; and they began to devour those sheep, and to pick out their eyes and to devour their flesh.

> **90.3.** And the sheep cried out because their flesh was being devoured by the birds, and as for me I looked and lamented in my sleep over that shepherd who pastured the sheep.

> **90.4.** And I saw until those sheep were devoured by the dogs and eagles and kites, and they left neither flesh nor skin nor

sinew remaining on them till only their bones stood there: and their bones too fell to the earth and the sheep became few.

According to Enoch, the events mentioned above all occurred during the time frame of the first thirty-five shepherds. During this period, the Lord's sheep would have been sorely tried and tortured, having their flesh consumed from their bodies in the most horrific ways. The first thirty-five shepherds bring us squarely into the Hasmonean dynasty, which was born from the Maccabean revolts. There can be little doubt about the tortures Enoch witnessed.

According to the first and second books of Maccabees, Antiochus Epiphanes, the last of the Seleucid kings, sought to force the conversion of the Jews to the religions of the Greeks. He did so in the most brutal ways, including mutilating children in front of their parents in attempts to force renouncements of their faith. People were skinned alive, roasted in frying pans, boiled alive in cauldrons, and children were thrown from high walls before their mothers' eyes, among other atrocities.

It was during these days that Mattathias Maccabee, a priest, and his sons began a formal rebellion. The Greeks commanded Mattathias to perform their hedonistic sacrifices, but he refused and fled to the mountains with his family, friends, and neighbors. They began resisting the Greeks, and the opposition grew until the yoke of Antiochus Epiphanes was broken, leading to the Greeks retreating from their lands. After this long line of foreign shepherds, the Jews were once again led by their own, but this time of independence did not last.

The vision continues marching through time:

> **90.5.** And I saw until that twenty-three had undertaken the pasturing and completed in their several periods fifty-eight times.

> **90.6.** But behold lambs were borne by those white sheep, and they began to open their eyes and to see, and to cry to the sheep.

> **90.7.** Yea, they cried to them, but they did not hearken to what they said to them, but were exceedingly deaf, and their eyes were very exceedingly blinded.

90.8. And I saw in the vision how the ravens flew upon those lambs and took one of those lambs, and dashed the sheep in pieces and devoured them.

90.9. And I saw till horns grew upon those lambs [*the white sheep grew in power and authority – think the birth of John the Baptist, and Jesus*], and the ravens cast down their horns [*the threat of Messiah caused many to be killed, the children of Bethlehem, and the beheading of John*]; and I saw till there sprouted a great horn of one of those sheep, and their eyes were opened [*the Lamb of God opened the eyes of many of the Jews*].

90.10. And it [*the great ram - Christ*] †looked at† them and their eyes opened, and it cried to the sheep, and the rams saw it and all ran to it.

90.11. And notwithstanding all this those eagles and vultures and ravens and kites still kept tearing the sheep and swooping down upon them and devouring them: still the sheep remained silent, but the rams lamented and cried out.

90.12. And those ravens fought and battled with it and sought to lay low its horn, but they had no power over it.

90.13. And I saw till the †shepherds and† eagles and those vultures and kites came, and †they cried to the ravens† that they should break the horn of that ram, and they battled and fought with it, and it battled with them and cried that its help might come.

The passages above speak of events that transpired during the reign of the next twenty-five shepherds, up until the 58th shepherd. This corresponds with the destruction of Jerusalem around 70 AD. Enoch saw that before Jerusalem was destroyed, during the time of the Maccabees and the destruction of Jerusalem, white sheep would return to Israel. As we have seen, white sheep are associated with the covenant. The most notable event during this period is the rise of a great Ram that opened the eyes of many of the people of Israel. This is none other than the Lamb of God, who atoned for the sins of the world.

Despite the fact that the Lamb of God was slain, His influence and authority only grew. There was nothing that the Romans or the Jews could do to suppress it. The more they tried, the more Christ's influence spread. As such, they had no power over it. Yet, this did not stop them from trying, and try they did. The Christians were hunted and persecuted, driven from Jerusalem, and forced to leave the lands of their fathers. When the Romans came to destroy Jerusalem, around the time of the 58th shepherd, the Christians were already gone. Thus, they survived the destruction of Jerusalem unscathed.

However, the blind Jews did not; they were obliterated. More than a million Jews were killed in and around Jerusalem at this time, with a hundred thousand survivors carried off captive to Rome, where they were sold as slaves. Yet, Jews remained in Judea, having regrouped in Galilee and the surrounding areas. They continued there until the days of the 70th and final shepherd of the series—General Julius Severus. General Julius Severus crushed what is known as the Bar Kokhba revolt, resulting in the destruction of all remaining Jewish settlements. Most were killed, and any surviving Jews were sold into slavery. Therefore, at the end of the 70th shepherd's reign, Israel was left bereft of Israelites.

This is the last time that this vision mentions these seventy shepherds. Therefore, the cries of the blind sheep for help represent the voice of Israel scattered among the nations of the Earth. They cried out that the Lord might remember them and restore them to the lands of their fathers. Yet, from the rise of the Great Ram until this day, those who accepted the Father's Hidden Son have been mocked, persecuted, and belittled by the wolves and vultures of the Earth. During this same period, the Jews became a hiss and a byword among all the nations of the Earth—why? Because of their exceedingly great blindness. Can you see a recurring theme? Oh, that this blindness were limited to the Jews, but it most certainly is not. It is as present among the Saints of God as it was among the Jews at the first coming of the Son of Man. Let us pray that the Lord opens our eyes so that we may see things as they really are!

Chapter 22 – Unto the Last Generation Part IV

In the prior chapter, we reviewed Enoch's prophecy of seventy shepherds. The Lord entrusted these seventy men with His flock—the House of Israel. These seventy shepherds were similar to the twenty feathers of Ezra's Eagle, except that instead of counting down to the cleansing of America, Enoch's vision counted down to the complete scattering of the Israelites from their ancestral homelands. Both of these visions demonstrate the magnificence of the Lord's foresight. He sees the end from the beginning with pristine clarity.

Now that we have come to the point in Enoch's dream where the lands of Abraham's inheritance have been left desolate, the dream takes a massive jump forward in time. We will discuss precisely how much time after we analyze the following passage:

> **90.14.** And I saw till that man, who wrote down the names of the shepherds and [*was*]carried up into the presence of the Lord of the sheep [*who*] came and helped it [*the prophet Ezra*] and showed it everything: he had come down for the help of that ram [*this ram is the latter-day antichrist who will attack Israel in the last days*].

This verse begins with the phrase, "I saw till," which denotes the passage of time. Therefore, Enoch is stating that he has jumped forward in time from the final scattering of Israel, which took place at the time of the seventieth shepherd in 135 AD, to a future date when Ezra would return to aid Israel against the antichrist. We will see that this ram is the antichrist in a future passage; for now, just know that is what the ram represents. This is simply stunning!

While Enoch is the one who originally had this dream, he was not the man to record the names of the shepherds. The man who recorded the shepherds' names was undoubtedly Ezra. Ezra restored the Jews' scriptures to them, along with other invaluable prophecies regarding the last days. Remember, the Jews' scriptures had been destroyed by Nebuchadnezzar, the 5th shepherd in the series, when he conquered the Jews and destroyed the temple of Solomon.

For context, it will be very helpful to review the fourteenth chapter of 2 Esdras, wherein we learn some incredible things regarding Ezra. I believe you will find it a fascinating read.

And it came to pass upon the third day, I sat under an oak, and, behold, there came a voice out of a bush over against me, and said, Esdras, Esdras. And I said, Here am I, Lord And I stood up upon my feet. Then said He unto me, In the bush I did manifestly reveal Myself unto Moses, and talked with him, when my people served in Egypt: and I sent him and led My people out of Egypt, and brought him up to the mount of where I held him by Me a long season, and told him many wondrous things, and shewed him the secrets of the times, and the end; and commanded him, saying, these words shalt thou declare, and these shalt thou hide.

And now I say unto thee, that thou lay up in thy heart the signs that I have shewed, and the dreams that thou hast seen, and the interpretations which thou hast heard: For thou shalt be taken away from all, and from henceforth thou shalt remain with my Son [*referring to the fact that Ezra would be translated*], and with such as be like thee, until the times be ended [*Ezra would remain with other translated beings until the last days – when he would return*]. For the world hath lost his youth, and the times begin to wax old. For the world is divided into twelve parts, and the ten parts of it are gone already, and half of a tenth part [*this refers to the 12 tribes of Israel, the Lord took the ten tribes away unto Himself*]: .

Now therefore set thine house in order, and reprove thy people, comfort such of them as be in trouble, and now renounce corruption, let go from thee mortal thoughts, cast away the burdens of man, put off now the weak nature [*the natural man*], and set aside the thoughts that are most heavy unto thee, and haste thee to flee from these times. For yet greater evils than those which thou hast seen happen shall be done hereafter. For look how much the world shall be weaker through age [*the world will become more blind to the reality of things with time*], so much the more shall evils increase upon them that dwell therein.

For the time is fled far away, and leasing is hard at hand: for now hasteth the vision to come, which thou hast seen. Then answered I before thee, and said, Behold, Lord, I will go, as thou hast commanded me, and reprove the people which are present: but they that shall be born afterward, who shall admonish them? Thus the world is set in darkness, and they that dwell therein are without light. For thy law is burnt, therefore no man knoweth the things that are done of Thee, or the work that shall begin. But if I have found grace before thee, send the Holy Ghost into me, and I shall write all that hath been done in the world since the beginning, which were written in thy law, that men may find Thy path, and that they which will live in the latter days may live.

And He answered me, saying, Go thy way, gather the people together, and say unto them, that they seek thee not for forty days. But look thou prepare thee many box trees, and take with thee Sarea, Dabria, Selemia, Ecanus, and Asiel, these five which are ready to write swiftly; and come hither, and I shall light a candle of understanding in thine heart, which shall not be put out, till the things be performed which thou shalt begin to write. And when thou hast done, some things shalt thou publish, and some things shalt thou shew secretly to the wise: tomorrow this hour shalt thou begin to write.

Then went I forth, as He commanded, and gathered all the people together, and said, Hear these words, O Israel. Our fathers at the beginning were strangers in Egypt, from whence they were delivered: and received the law of life, which they kept not, which ye also have transgressed after them. Then was the land, even the land of Sion, parted among you by lot: but your fathers, and ye yourselves, have done unrighteousness, and have not kept the ways which the Highest commanded you. And forasmuch as He is a righteous judge, He took from you in time the thing that He had given you. And now are ye here, and your brethren among you. Therefore if so be that ye will subdue your own understanding, and reform your hearts, ye shall be kept alive and after death ye shall obtain mercy.

For after death shall the judgment come, when we shall live again: and then shall the names of the righteous be manifest, and the works of the ungodly shall be declared. Let no man therefore come unto me now, nor seek after me these forty days. So I took the five men, as He commanded me, and we went into the field, and remained there.

And the next day, behold, a voice called me, saying, Esdras, open thy mouth, and drink that I give thee to drink. Then opened I my mouth, and, behold, He reached me a full cup, which was full as it were with water, but the colour of it was like fire. And I took it, and drank: and when I had drunk of it, my heart uttered understanding, and wisdom grew in my breast, for my spirit strengthened my memory: and my mouth was opened, and shut no more.

The Highest gave understanding unto the five men, and they wrote the wonderful visions of the night that were told, which they knew not: and they sat forty days, and they wrote in the day, and at night they ate bread. As for me. I spake in the day, and I held not my tongue by night. In forty days they wrote two hundred and four books. And it came to pass, when the forty days were filled, that the Highest spake, saying, The first that thou hast written publish openly, that the worthy and unworthy may read it:

But keep the seventy last, that thou mayest deliver them only to such as be wise among the people: for in them is the spring of understanding, the fountain of wisdom, and the stream of knowledge. And I did so. (2 Esdras 14)

In the passages above, the Lord tells Ezra that he will be translated and dwell with other translated beings until the last days. Before Ezra was translated, he petitioned the Lord on behalf of the remaining Jews, asking to restore their lost scriptures. The Lord conceded to Ezra's request and restored their scriptures through him by miraculous means. Many of the revelations given to Ezra were kept hidden from the body of the Jews and were known only to the wise. The names of the seventy shepherds of Israel were surely among these hidden records. According to Josephus, Alexander the Great was greeted by the High Priest, Shimon HaTzaddik, and welcomed with respect, for they had been expecting him. It is certainly possible that some of these priests had access to Ezra's private prophecies.

Also included in the narrative above is the fact that the Lord tracked world history by His dealings with the House of Israel. The Lord specifically stated that time had begun to wax old now that the ten and a half tribes were removed, leaving only the Jews and a scattering of Levites in the Kingdom of Judah. Based on the prophecies of this book, it is clear that the Lord fully understood that Judah would also be scattered to the four winds. When that happened, Israel's lands would be left bereft of the children of the covenant for many generations.

The restoration of Israel would happen in the reverse order of their destruction. As the Northern Kingdom was the first to be destroyed in 720 BC, it would be the last to be restored in the last days. Yet, their restoration would be the most incredible of all the houses of Jacob. The Jews were the second to be destroyed, having been completely removed from their homelands by 135 AD. Joseph was the last to be destroyed when the Nephite nation was destroyed, with any surviving members hunted down and killed until Moroni hid his father's record in the Hill Cumorah around 420 AD. As such, the Lord moved to restore Joseph in America first, and then He restored Judah to Israel in 1948. We now await the restoration of the Lost Ten Tribes of Israel.

Returning to Ezra's role in the events of the last days, Ezra lived during the reign of the 15th shepherd. According to Enoch's vision, both Elijah and Ezra were translated. Curiously, the Jews actively look forward to the day when Elijah will return to them. At Passover, Jewish families around the world leave an empty seat at their table for Elijah. As Latter-day Saints, we sometimes smile at this practice because we believe that Elijah has already returned. After all, D&C 110 speaks of how these incredible men gave Joseph Smith certain priesthood keys, which included keys pertaining to the oath and covenant of the priesthood, the sealing power, and keys for the gathering of Israel. However, this does not mean that Elijah, or Moses, who appeared with him, are done with us. To the contrary, I believe they will have major roles to play in the events of the last days.

Both Elijah and Moses appeared atop the Mount of Transfiguration, yet to this day we do not know why. Neither of these men held keys that the Lord did not already possess. Therefore, the Lord did not need them atop the mount for their keys. There was a different reason for their coming. The Lord stated that we do not have a full account of what happened atop the Mount of Transfiguration—see D&C 63:20-21. I believe that the primary purpose of their visitation was to coordinate with John, Peter, and James regarding the events of the last days. According to D&C 7, the Lord placed the keys for His Second Coming with John, another translated being. The reason we do not have a full account of this meeting is that it pertains to pending events meant to try the faith of the Lord's people.

With this background in mind, we return to the discussion of **90.14** in the Book of Enoch. According to Enoch, Ezra will also return to assist the Jews in the last days when a powerful ram confronts them.

> **90.15** And I saw till the Lord of the sheep came unto them
> in wrath, and all who saw Him fled, and they all fell †into
> His shadow† from before His face

90.16. All the eagles and vultures and ravens and kites were gathered together, and there came with them all the sheep of the field, yea, they all came together, and helped each other to break that horn of the ram.

The passages above commence once more with the phrase, "I saw till," signifying a pivotal period between the Lord's sending of Ezra to safeguard the Jews and the glorious Second Coming of Christ. This interim period is addressed in Revelation 13 as a span of three and a half years, during which two prophets shall arrive to protect Israel from the Antichrist and the Beast. Ezra will be one of these two prophets. But who will be the other one?

In this vision, Enoch spoke of two translated beings: Ezra and Elijah. If Ezra is indeed one of these latter-day prophets, it stands to reason that Elijah will be the other one. Together, these two stalwart men will command the elements and wield them against the encroaching forces of darkness with great skill and effect. These two men will be the bane of the antichrist's existence. Without these two prophets, Israel would find itself at the mercy of the antichrist and the beast.

In addition, the passages above referenced four distinct kinds of birds that will descend upon Israel in the last days. The Lord's sheep will accompany these birds, as such the birds and sheep are clearly affiliated. Curiously, while the sheep themselves have no inherent recourse against the antichrist and the beast, these birds do. Through the intervention of these four types of birds, the ram's power will be significantly diminished. Therefore, the symbolism of these four birds is crucial if we are to understand Enoch's vision. As such, we must consider these four birds more carefully.

Let us begin with the obvious: birds are fundamentally different from sheep. Sheep are grounded in the Earth, while birds soar in the heavens. Thus, while these birds are affiliated with the House of Israel, they will possess a familiarity with the heavens that the Lord's sheep simply do not have.

Next, let us consider the four types of birds mentioned: eagles, vultures, ravens, and kites. These four groups represent various species of birds. Notably, eagles and kites (hawks) are both birds of prey, while vultures and ravens are scavengers. The symbolism here suggests that eagles and kites will share a connection that the vultures and ravens do not, and vice versa. This distinction will become clearer as we work to identify the populations these four groups represent.

Throughout these volumes, particularly in Volume I of this series, I have written about the purifiers of the Hopi prophecy. These purifiers comprise distinct populations, the largest of which is described as descending from the heavens, to cover the Earth like ants. These will begin to purge America from the West, first bowing down to the children of Ephraim in the shadow of the everlasting hills. As such, this first group can only be the mighty Remnant of Jacob. Therefore, the eagles depict the Remnant of Jacob. Recall that in Revelation 12, the main body of the House of Israel was granted the wings of an eagle. Ezekiel also associated the head of an eagle with a host descending to Earth upon flying wheels (see Ezekiel 1 & 10).

I believe that the second of these initial three groups, the vultures, is represented by the crypto-terrestrial remnant of Joseph. This hidden body of Joseph is comprised of the repentant Germans who fled Nazi Germany during World War II. According to the Hopi prophecy, this group joined another crypto-terrestrial faction hidden beneath the Arctic ice (the ravens). I postulate that this is the same group referenced by the Lord in D&C 49:8—the righteous people we know not of. Given that both of these last two groups are crypto-terrestrials, they birds of a feather, like vultures and ravens. According to the Hopi prophecy, these two joint groups will initiate the purification of America, beginning on its East Coast.

This leaves us with the last group: the kites or hawks. As previously mentioned, kites, like eagles, are birds of prey. Birds of prey are hunters. Therefore, I contend that first and last groups represent off-world factions of the House of Israel. The first of these is the mighty Remnant of Jacob. The last group represents the nation of Moses. Therefore, I believe that the Eagles and the Kites shall be the long-prophesied hunters sent forth to gather Israel from the four corners of the Earth, from right under the Stout Horn's nose.

While all four of these groups will play a role in shattering the Stout Horn in the last days, the honor of vanquishing the Antichrist and the Beast shall be reserved for the Lord Himself. According to Revelation 19:20, the Lord will cast these two into Hell while they are yet alive. This fate is reserved for them because they have impersonated Him and led many of His blind sheep to slaughter. Thus, He shall unleash His vengeance upon them.

The Book of Enoch continues:

> **90.17.** And I saw that man, who wrote the book [*Ezra*] according to the command of the Lord, till he opened that book concerning the destruction which those twelve last shepherds had wrought [*referring to the last twelve roman leaders who removed the Jews from Israel*], and showed that they [*the antichrist and the Beast – the horns of the ram*] had destroyed much more than their predecessors, before the Lord of the sheep

90.18 And I saw till the Lord of the sheep came unto them [*the antichrist and the Beast*] and took in His hand the staff of His wrath, and smote the earth, and the earth clave asunder, and all the beasts and all the birds of the heaven fell from among those sheep, and were swallowed up in the earth and it covered them

90.19. And I saw till a great sword was given to the sheep, and the sheep proceeded against all the beasts of the field to slay them, and all the beasts and the birds of the heaven fled before their face.

The passages above speak of the great day when the Father's Hidden Son will descend from the heavens and divide the Mount of Olives in two, to the shock and horror of the beasts and other predators of Israel. On that day, the Lord of Hosts will execute vengeance and fury upon the wicked inhabitants of the Earth, a judgment unlike anything they have ever heard. In a single day, the wicked will be purged, and the Kingdom of God will be ushered in. The beasts and birds mentioned are all adversaries of the Lord. However, the sheep, eagles, vultures, ravens, and kites are exempt from His destruction, for they know Him, and He knows them.

The vision continues:

90.20. And I saw till a throne was erected in the pleasant land, and the Lord of the sheep sat Himself thereon, and the other [*meaning Ezra – now raised from the dead after lying in the streets of Jerusalem for three and a half days*] took the sealed books and opened those books before the Lord of the sheep.

90.21. And the Lord called those men the seven first white ones, [*Adam, Seth, Enos, Cainan, Mahalaleel, Jared, and Enoch*] and commanded that they should bring before Him, beginning with the first star which led the way, all the stars whose privy members were like those of horses, and they brought them all before Him [*the Lady is the first star that led the Watchers to Earth*].

90.22. And He said to that man who wrote before Him [*Enoch - the holy scribe who recorded the dream*], being one of those seven white ones, and said unto him: "Take those seventy shepherds to whom I delivered the sheep, and who taking them on their own authority slew more than I commanded them."

90.23. And behold they were all bound, I saw, and they all stood before Him.

90.24. And the judgement was held first over the stars [*the Watchers – both ancient and modern*], and they were judged and found guilty, and went to the place of condemnation, and they were cast into an abyss, full of fire and flaming, and full of pillars of fire.

90.25. And those seventy shepherds [*the wicked among the seventy*] were judged and found guilty, and they were cast into that fiery abyss.

90.26. And I saw at that time how a like abyss was opened in the midst of the earth, full of fire, and they brought those blinded sheep, and they were all judged and found guilty and cast into this fiery abyss, and they burned; now this abyss was to the right of that house.

90.27. And I saw those sheep burning †and their bones burning†.

The passages above clearly speak of the judgement that all who have lived upon the Earth must face. Sooner, or latter, all will account for their actions in mortality, whether they originated upon this planet, or came here from afar as the Watchers did. There is one cosmic law which governs all things. To this cosmic law, all must give an account. According to the prophecy of Enoch, the Watchers - both ancient and modern, will be judged according to their actions. Those that served the Father of Lies will receive the wages of their labors. Those among the seventy shepherds that thrashed and destroyed the Lord's chosen people beyond the Lord's command, will receive their recompense, as will the spiritual deaf and blind.

Many who have rejected God will suffer for their own sins in the fiery ranges at the edge of all things. Yet, all these will ultimately find redemption, except for those few sons of perdition who prefer darkness to light. Those few will reign forever in outer darkness with Lucifer and his minions. Yet Lucifer's end is not yet, but by and by, after the millennium. During the millennium, the Earth will rest, it is regarding this rest that Enoch's vision now turns.

90.28. And I stood up to see till they folded up that old house; and carried off all the pillars, and all the beams and ornaments of the house were at the same time folded up with it, and they carried it off and laid it in a place in the south of the land.

90.29. And I saw till the Lord of the sheep brought a new house greater and loftier than that first, and set it up in the place of the first which had been folded up: all its pillars were new, and its ornaments were new and larger than those of the first, the old one which He had taken away, and all the sheep were within it.

90.30. And I saw all the sheep which had been left, and all the beasts on the earth, and all the birds of the heaven, falling down and doing homage to those sheep and making petition to and obeying them in everything.

The passages above speak of the day when the modern Jewish people will finally set aside the Law of Moses and turn toward the New Covenant, forged in the blood of the Lamb of God. On that day, the old ordinances of the ancient temple will be replaced by the ordinances and covenants of the new. As it is written, in those days the Jews will open the gates of Jerusalem so that the righteous nation, which keeps the truth, may enter in—see Isaiah 26:2. There can be no doubt that this righteous nation is the newly purged and liberated nation of Joseph.

In that day, the Jews will follow in the footsteps of their restored brethren from the Northern Kingdom of Israel, humbling themselves before the children of Ephraim to receive their crowning ordinances in the Lord's holy sanctuary. This holy sanctuary will descend from the heavens, just as the New Jerusalem will—see Ether 13:3. This is the heritage of the servants of the Lord, the greater blessing that rests upon the head of Ephraim and his fellows. In that coming day, the surviving members of the Church of Jesus Christ of Latter-day Saints will finally be recognized for who they are—the birthright sons and daughters of Israel.

Now, Enoch's vision fast-forwards to the end of all things, when the work of this cycle of the Father's great plan of salvation has been completed. It is the last and great day when even those who rejected God, and as a result suffered for their own sins, will come forth to inherit their degrees of glory. The sight of this nearly overwhelms Enoch, reflecting the goodness and mercy of God toward those who betrayed Him. Consider the following:

90.31. And thereafter those three [*Michael, Raphel, and Gabriel*] who were clothed in white and had seized me by my hand, and the hand of that ram [*Christ*] also seizing hold of me, they took me up and set me down in the midst of those sheep before the judgement took place†.

90.32. And those sheep were all white, and their wool was abundant and clean.

90.33. And all that had been destroyed and dispersed, and all the beasts of the field, and all the birds of the heaven, assembled in that house, and the Lord of the sheep rejoiced with great joy because they were all good and had returned to His house.

The passages above are truly remarkable. They challenge traditional Christianity by presenting a different perspective on redemption. Rather than remaining in fiery damnation for eternity, the blind sheep that were lost and devoured—along with the beasts and birds that consumed them—are ultimately redeemed. This implies that they receive resurrected bodies through the power of Christ's resurrection, thereby becoming begotten sons and daughters of God according to the degrees of glory for which they are qualified. The most faithful among them will be clothed with the glory of the Son, others with the glory of the moon, and the least with the glory of the stars, wherein one star differs from another in glory.

The vision continues:

90.34. And I saw till they laid down that sword, which had been given to the sheep, and they brought it back into the house, and it was sealed before the presence of the Lord, and all the sheep were invited into that house, but it held them not.

90.35. And the eyes of them all were opened, and they saw the good, and there was not one among them that did not see.

90.36. And I saw that that house was large and broad and very full.

The passage above concludes the current iteration of the Father's plan of salvation. The sword of His vengeance is now sealed away. All the sons and daughters of heaven are redeemed, and at last, they see things as they truly are. This process has been a long time in coming—approximately two and a half billion years, according to McConkie's reckoning. However, the great wheel of heaven continues to turn, and when one cycle ends, another begins. Thus unfolds Enoch's vision of the future.

> **90.37.** And I saw that a white bull was born, with large horns and all the beasts of the field and all the birds of the air feared Him [*revered Him*] and made petition to Him all the time.

Given that the White Bull described above is born in heaven, we are speaking of the birth of a spirit. The presence of large horns symbolizes this being's tremendous spiritual strength and authority. We are discussing the emergence of the newest member of the Godhead, now that the Father has ascended to the northern slope of the Mount of the Congregation. With the Father's ascension, the Son takes His place on the Father's throne, the Holy Spirit now   becomes the Son, and the Great White Bull is created with awe-inspiring power and authority to fill the vacant position.

God once told Abraham that He was more intelligent than all the spirits of heaven. I believe the same can be said for all members of the Godhead. Thus, the reason the hosts of heaven are in awe of the newly born White Bull is that the same applies to Him. According to the seventy-sixth section of the Doctrine and Covenants, those of the Celestial Kingdom are ministered to by the Father, those of the Terrestrial Kingdom by the Son, and those of the Telestial world by the Holy Spirit. Given that the inhabitants of the Telestial Kingdom will dwell in the fiery mountain ranges at the edge of all things, the newly born White Bull will be ten thousand years old by the time they inherit their kingdoms of glory. They will all be in awe of the White Bull, who will resemble the Upper Case Gods in every respect, save that He will not yet possess a body of flesh and bone. It will be a very long time before He does.

Enoch's vision continues:

> **90.38.** And I saw till all their generations [*the children of the next iteration of the gods*] were transformed, and they all became white bulls; and the first among them [*meaning the current Holy Ghost*] became a Lamb [*meaning the Lamb of God*], and that Lamb became a great animal and had great black horns on its head; and the Lord of the sheep rejoiced over it and over all the oxen.

In Enoch's vision, he perceives the next generation of heaven. In other words, he beholds our future heavenly posterity growing to spiritual maturity, wherein they

322

themselves become great white bulls and heifers. When that joyous day arrives, they will be presented with the option of becoming like us. By and large, they will rejoice in this opportunity. While some may choose to pass, most will not. Instead, they will shout for joy at the prospect of participating in the Father's Plan of Salvation. As such, they will need a Savior.

Enoch foresaw that the first among them would become the Lamb of God. The Holy Ghost will be the foremost among them, for He, like the Great White Bull previously discussed, will have had His beginnings in the prior iteration of the Father's Plan. He will have witnessed the entire unfolding of events, observing Christ fulfill the will of His Father. Now, He is willing to do the same Himself, that our children might be redeemed as well. For this reason, the Lord of Spirits rejoices over Him, and we too rejoice, for He will pay the price for our children's redemption. Our children will rejoice in Him, for without Him, they have no hope of becoming like us.

Enoch now concludes his description of his epic vision:

> **90.39.** And I slept in their midst [*in the midst of the gods*]: and I awoke [*the eyes of his understanding were opened*] and saw everything.

> **90.40.** This is the vision which I saw while I slept, and I awoke and blessed the Lord of righteousness and gave Him glory.

> **90.41.** Then I wept with a great weeping and my tears stayed not till I could no longer endure it: when I saw, they flowed on account of what I had seen; for everything shall come and be fulfilled, and all the deeds of men in their order were shown to me.

> **90.42.** On that night I remembered the first dream, and because of it I wept and was troubled--because I had seen that vision.'

When Enoch awoke from his vision, he wept with both joy and sorrow. He understood that he had slept among the gods, recognizing that his vision revealed the true order of heaven. Overjoyed, he realized he could never have received such an incredible blessing had not the Father opened his eyes. Yet, he also wept bitterly at the profound blindness and hardheartedness of the children of men. Enoch lamented particularly for the House of Israel, for they possessed immense potential, but their blindness caused them to fall short of the prize they had once shouted for joy about in the premortal realms.

Spiritual blindness prevents individuals from attaining the full measure of their respective creations. Enoch understood this, and now you do as well. The question is, what will you do with this knowledge? Will you follow the path of the blind sheep of Israel, or will you recognize your Master's voice and follow Him? May the God of heaven open the eyes of our understanding as He did with Enoch, that we might have both the vision to see and the wisdom to act, enabling us to continue primordial joyous acclamations when the Father's Hidden Son finally arrives!

Chapter 23 – The Ten Week Prophecy

The previous chapter concluded with an analysis of a vision that Enoch had when he was still a young man regarding the history of the world. That vision fulfilled D&C 107:57, wherein the Lord stated that the Book of Enoch would speak of all things that would befall the posterity of Adam unto the latest generation. Indeed, the vision spanned from the days of Adam all the way through to the next iteration of the Father's plan of salvation. It is an absolutely stunning vision and a testament to the Book of Enoch's veracity.

The current chapter continues along the same prophetic vein as the last. However, unlike the previous epic vision, this is not a dream or vision but rather an outright prophecy that Enoch gave to his posterity right before he and his people were taken up into the heavens. The prophecy begins as counsel but then moves into a sweeping prophecy regarding the history of the Earth. In the subsequent section, Enoch divides the history of the world into ten-week segments and discusses what will transpire during each respective time period. Enoch believed that this prophecy would be of particular benefit to those living in the last days. As such, get ready to have your socks blown off!

The first part of Enoch's prophecy begins as follows:

> **91.1.** The book written by Enoch--Enoch indeed wrote this complete doctrine of wisdom, which is praised of all men and a judge of all the earth for all my children who shall dwell on the earth. And for the future generations who shall observe uprightness and peace.

> **91.2.** Let not your spirit be troubled on account of the times; For the Holy and Great One has appointed days for all things.

> **91.3.** And the Righteous One shall arise from sleep, Shall arise and walk in the paths of righteousness, And all His path and conversation shall be in eternal goodness and grace.

> **91.4.** He will be gracious to the righteous and give him eternal uprightness, And He will give him power so that he shall be endowed with goodness and righteousness. And he shall walk in eternal light.

91.5. And sin shall perish in darkness for ever, and shall no more be seen from that day for evermore.

Enoch's prophecy began with a scribal introduction comprising the first verse. We do not know who made this note, but it is clear that they recognized this prophecy was meant for the generation that would transition into the millennial reign of Jesus Christ—us! Immediately following the scribal insert, Enoch commenced his prophecy by discussing the life and ministry of Jesus Christ and how He will put an end to all unrighteousness. Enoch emphasized Christ's victory over death and sin as a reason for the righteous not to fear, for there is a time for all things. There is a time for war and struggle, and a time for peace and prosperity. These cycles are brought about by the agency of man.

The prophecy continues:

92.1. 'And now, my son Methuselah, call to me all thy brothers And gather together to me all the sons of thy mother; for the word calls me, And the spirit is poured out upon me, that I may show you everything That shall befall you forever.'

92.2 And there upon Methuselah went and summoned to him all his brothers and assembled his relatives.

92.3 And he spake unto all the children of righteousness and said: 'Hear, ye sons of Enoch, all the words of your father, And hearken aright to the voice of my mouth; For I exhort you and say unto you, beloved: Love uprightness and walk therein.

92.4. And draw not nigh to uprightness with a double heart, and associate not with those of a double heart, But walk in righteousness, my sons. And it shall guide you on good paths, and righteousness shall be your companion.

One of the very first things that Enoch counseled his posterity to do was to be genuine. Enoch did not want his children to have merely the appearance of righteousness but the substance of it. Christ despised hypocrites who were content with appearing righteous, describing such individuals as whited sepulchers—clean and orderly on the outside but filled with filth and decay within. This is what Enoch referred to as having a double heart.

To be human is to be a hypocrite, as we all act contrary to the light within us. However, true disciples of Christ rely on His grace to overcome their weaknesses and shortcomings. We receive Christ's grace as we strive to surrender our will to the Father. Enoch and his people did just this. They did not start out as a Zion-like society, but they learned to be of one heart and one mind through submission and obedience to God. We must learn to do the same. This is an individual process, not a collective one.

Enoch's counsel continues:

> **92.5.** For I know that violence must increase on the earth, and a great chastisement be executed on the earth, and all unrighteousness come to an end: Yea, it shall be cut off from its roots, and its whole structure be destroyed.

Enoch foresaw that the days were soon coming when the sins of the pre-diluvian world would be cleansed from the Earth through the great flood. According to Enoch, the precursor to this destruction was increased violence. We should expect this to be true in our day as well, highlighting the importance of standing in holy places. We are already witnessing an increase in violence in cities across the world. This is the result of Satan stirring up the hearts of men into frenzies of hate and rage.

Charity, the pure love of Christ, is the antidote to Satan's rage. Therefore, those who aspire to be true disciples of Christ should seek charity above all else, for God is love. However, the flood demonstrates that while God loves the children of heaven, He does not tolerate the willful indulgence of sin.

Enoch's vision quickly moves to the other side of the flood.

> **92.6.** And unrighteousness shall again be consummated on the earth, and all the deeds of unrighteousness and of violence and transgression shall prevail in a twofold degree.

> **92.7.** And when sin and unrighteousness and blasphemy and violence in all kinds of deeds increase, and apostasy and transgression and uncleanness increase, great chastisement shall come from heaven upon all these, and the holy Lord will come forth with wrath and chastisement to execute judgement on earth.

> **92.8.** In those days violence shall be cut off from its roots, and the roots of unrighteousness together with deceit, and they shall be destroyed from under heaven.

92.9. And all the idols of the heathen shall be abandoned, and the temples burned with fire, and they shall remove them from the whole earth, and they shall be cast into the judgement of fire, and shall perish in wrath and in grievous judgement for ever.

92.10. And the righteous shall arise from their sleep, and wisdom shall arise and be given unto them.

92.11. And after that the roots of unrighteousness shall be cut off, and the sinners shall be destroyed by the sword . . . shall be cut off from the blasphemers in every place, and those who plan violence and those who commit blasphemy shall perish by the sword.

92.18. And now I tell you, my sons, and show you the paths of righteousness and the paths of violence. Yea, I will show them to you again that ye may know what will come to pass.

92.19. And now, hearken unto me, my sons, and walk in the paths of righteousness, And walk not in the paths of violence; for all who walk in the paths of unrighteousness shall perish for ever.'

Enoch foresaw that after the Earth was destroyed in the great flood, the days would come when it would become twice as wicked as it was in antiquity. When that day arrives, Enoch stated that the wicked would destroy the wicked. As those days begin to draw near, Enoch urged his posterity to choose the path of righteousness rather than the path of violence. Many good people today have stocked up on guns and ammunition to protect themselves and their families when the day of violence arrives. We would be wise to heed Enoch's counsel in this regard.

What did Jesus Christ teach His people to do when confronted with violence? He taught them to turn the other cheek and not to return railing for railing. Have you considered why there are so many war chapters in the Book of Mormon? How did the Nephites treat the Lamanites during times of war? How often did the Nephites defeat the Lamanites only to allow them to return to their homes with a covenant of peace, rather than exacting revenge upon them?

If you study these accounts, you will find that the more righteous Nephites lamented the fact that they had to kill the Lamanites. They were horrified that they were the means by which so many of their brethren were sent unprepared to meet their Maker. Indeed, many of the Nephites prayed with all the energy of their souls that the Lamanites could be recovered and restored to the truth at some future time. This is the path of righteousness. In contrast, consider the depravity that existed among the Nephites when they embraced the path of violence near the end of their civilization. They delighted in horrific acts of violence. Men always find ways to justify the atrocities they commit.

John the Revelator saw our day and issued a warning similar to Enoch's: those who live by the sword will die by the sword. Violence begets violence. Disciples of Christ should do everything in their power to avoid bloodshed. The Anti-Nephi-Lehies preferred to be killed rather than defend themselves. Yet the time came when they armed their children. What was the tipping point? The cause of liberty. Their posterity became the two thousand stripling warriors, and because of their faith, none of them were killed. Therefore, let us be as careful and deliberate about taking up the sword as they were.

Up to this point, all of Enoch's words have served as a precursor to his prophecy. He wanted us to understand what he is about to say from the perspective of this preface. Enoch stated that he intended to reveal all things that would befall his posterity upon this Earth forever. By this, Enoch means that the prophecy he is about to reveal will guide his posterity through the end of the Earth's temporal history and into the eternities beyond, just as he did with his prior dream.

What is the temporal history of the Earth? The Book of Revelation and the Doctrine and Covenants teach that the temporal existence of the world can be divided into eight time periods. The first seven of these time periods are one thousand years each (see D&C 77:6-7). Regarding the eighth or final period of the Earth's temporal existence, John the Revelator described it as being "a little season" (see Revelation 20:3).

I believe that Satan will use this little season to move throughout the cosmos, amassing all the hosts of heaven in his last great rebellion. In my opinion, this last little season will last approximately three hundred years. I will explain my basis for this line of thinking as the narrative continues. For now, let us simply observe that John the Revelator placed this small "eighth period" at the end of his timeline.

I believe that Enoch did the opposite of John in his timeline, placing the abbreviated length of time at the beginning of his timetable and concluding his vision in even periods of time. This will become clear as we return to my analysis of Enoch's writings. Consider the following:

> **93.1.** And after that Enoch both †gave† and began to recount from the books. And Enoch said: 'Concerning the children of righteousness and concerning the elect of the world, and

concerning the plant of uprightness, I will speak these things,
Yea, I Enoch will declare (them) unto you, my sons:

It is very important to note that Enoch mentions three separate groups of people in the verse above: 1) the children of righteousness, 2) the elect of the world, and 3) the plant of uprightness. It will become clear later in this vision that the third group, the plant of uprightness, refers to the House of Israel. Therefore, the first two groups—the children of righteousness and the elect of the world—are distinct from the House of Israel.

The first group, the children of righteousness, is defined by Enoch in **92:3** as Enoch's children, or more generally, the translated citizens of his holy city. The elect of the world, as the title suggests, refers to a separate group of righteous people on Earth apart from the House of Israel. This group was hinted at in the remarkable Hopi prophecy, which was also touched upon in Enoch's prior vision. The Doctrine and Covenants also speaks of this group:

> Wherefore, I will that all men shall repent, for all are under sin, except those which I have reserved unto Myself, **holy men that ye know not of**. (D&C 49:8)

I believe that this group is the body of people Enoch refers to as the "Elect of this World." The important takeaway here is that we know almost nothing about two out of the three groups. Therefore, when Enoch begins to prophesy about historical events that are unknown to us, we must recognize that he is speaking in relation to one of these two other groups of righteous people. This makes Enoch's prophecy all the more exciting.

Consider the following:

> **93.2** According to that which appeared to me in the heavenly vision, and which I have known through the word of the holy angels, and have learnt from the heavenly tablets.'

> **93.3**. And Enoch began to recount from the books and said: 'I was born the seventh in the first week, while judgement and righteousness still endured.

> **93.4**. And after me there shall arise in the second week great wickedness…

You will recall that I stated Enoch would open his vision with an asymmetric time period. He quantified this period as the time between Adam and the time after him, referring to the period following the translation of his city. There was still righteousness

330

on the Earth prior to his people's departure, but afterwards, which marks the start of the second week, only wickedness remained.

Enoch was translated nine hundred and eighty-seven years after the Fall. To avoid a false sense of precision, let's state that the second week began around 3000 BC. Earlier in the chapter, I mentioned that I believed the little season referred to by John was 300 years, leading to a total temporal existence of the Earth of approximately 8,300 years. Given that Enoch's first period occupied the first 1,000 years of the Earth's history, this leaves 6,300 years for the remaining nine weeks of his prophecy. Each of the nine remaining weeks corresponds to a 700-year week, comprised of seven days of approximately 100 years each.

The timing of the little season is calculated as the difference between the normal weekly time increment of the first week (700 years) and the number of years until Enoch's translation (1,000). Thus, the little season should be approximately 300 years. According to this calculation, the temporal history of the Earth will conclude around the year 3300 AD.

With these assumptions in place, we return to Enoch's remarkable prophetic timeline.

> **93.4.** And after me [*after his people were translated*] there shall arise in the second week great wickedness, and deceit shall have sprung up; and in it there shall be the first end. And in it a man shall be saved; and after it is ended unrighteousness shall grow up, and a law shall be made for the sinners.

According to Enoch, the great flood occurs during the second week. Based on the Biblical timeline, the great flood took place around the year 2348 BC. Given my earlier assumptions, 2348 BC corresponds with the seventh day of the second week. Enoch's wording makes it clear that he delivered this prophecy before Noah was born, as Noah was born on the first day of the second week.

Now, we move to Enoch's prophecy of the third week:

> **93.5.** And after that in the third week at its close a man shall be elected as the plant of righteous judgement, and his posterity shall become the plant of righteousness for evermore.

This clearly speaks of the rise of the House of Israel. As noted in this volume, Jacob obtained the promised blessings of his grandfather Abraham, and the Lord changed his name to Israel. This occurred around 1750 BC, or on the sixth day of the third week. So far, Enoch's timing mirrors the Biblical timeline perfectly. Therefore, we can assume that my initial assumptions about week one were correct.

The vision continues:

> **93.6**. And after that in the fourth week, at its close, Visions of the holy and righteous shall be seen, and a law for all generations and an enclosure shall be made for them.

Based on my calculations, the fourth week corresponds to the period from 1600 BC to 900 BC. Moses received the Ten Commandments atop Mount Sinai on the second day of this week, around 1500 BC. On the last day of this week, King Solomon built his famous temple, which housed the Ark of the Covenant. So far, Enoch's prophecy continues to align perfectly.

The vision continues:

> **93.7**. And after that in the fifth week, at its close, the house of glory and dominion shall be built forever.

Enoch prophesied that during the fifth week, which corresponds to 900 BC to 200 BC, the house of glory would be built forever. This description does not correspond with any known earthly structure. However, this was a very eventful week for the House of Israel. On the second day of this week, the Northern Kingdom of Israel was destroyed, and the Lost Ten Tribes were given the wings of a great eagle and left the Earth. On the fourth day of this week, Lehi departed for America, the Temple of Solomon was destroyed, and the Jews were taken captive into Babylon. Therefore, the reference to the house of glory and dominion must pertain to a structure built among the Lost Ten Tribes during this period.

Curiously, on the fourth day of this week, Ezekiel had an incredible vision of a heavenly temple that existed somewhere at that time. Ezekiel describes this holy structure in the fortieth chapter of his writings. Consider the chapter heading:

> A heavenly messenger shows Ezekiel in vision a city where the temple is located—Ezekiel is shown the form and size of the temple and its courts.

You will have noticed that the heavenly messenger showed Ezekiel "a city where the temple is located." This sacred structure must be the house of glory and dominion that

Enoch testified was built during this fourth week. In Enoch's prior vision, he saw the following regarding this holy house:

> **90.29**. And I saw till the Lord of the sheep brought a new house greater and loftier than that first [*the temple of Solomon*], and set it up in the place of the first which had been folded up: all its pillars were new, and its ornaments were new and larger than those of the first, the old one which He had taken away, and all the sheep were within it.

The passage above speaks of the day when the Lord will bring a new temple to Jerusalem and will set it in the location formerly occupied by the Temple of Solomon. I believe that this structure will be the house of glory and dominion of which Enoch spoke. Ether prophesied in the Book of Mormon that the holy sanctuary of the Lord will descend from the heavens at the same time that the New Jerusalem does (Ether 13:3). Verse **90:29** above states that this temple will be newer and larger than the Temple of Solomon, which will be true, for this temple was built in the fifth week, while the Temple of Solomon was built in the fourth week.

It is my belief that this temple, which we are told will stand forever, is now in existence among the Remnant of Jacob and will return in a miraculous fashion that will be among the greatest miracles the world has ever seen. I believe that this sacred structure is the same temple that Ezekiel saw in vision, as noted above. Many consider the Second Coming to be far away because this temple has not been built. They are mistaken; it has been built, it just has not descended from the heavens yet. According to prophecy, the Dome of the Rock will be folded up and taken elsewhere, and this temple will reside in its place. This structure will literally be out of this world. Its presence will nourish the thirsty lands of Israel with living water and even heal the Dead Sea.

The vision continues:

> **93.8.** And after that in the sixth week all who live in it shall be blinded, and the hearts of all of them shall godlessly forsake wisdom. And in it a man shall ascend; and at its close the house of dominion shall be burnt with fire, and the whole race of the chosen root shall be dispersed.

According to Enoch's timetable, the sixth week corresponds to 200 BC to 500 AD. The Man that Enoch saw ascend during this week was Jesus Christ. During this week, He introduced the new covenant, fulfilled the Law of Moses, and atoned for the sins of the world through the shedding of His own blood. On the third day, He arose from the dead and administered to His people once more. At the end of forty days, Christ ascended into the heavens. Before His ascension, He called twelve apostles in Jerusalem and twelve disciples in America, sending them to proclaim His gospel throughout the world.

However, enemies crept in unawares and infiltrated the Church. These wolves in sheep's clothing usurped its governance and corrupted the pure doctrines that had once been taught. By the end of this week, the truth had been utterly corrupted and could not be found on the surface of the Earth. By this time, the Jews had been destroyed and scattered, Rome had fallen, the nation of Joseph in America was extinct, and the temple of Herod was gone. By 500 AD, every man, woman, and child on the surface of the Earth was completely blind.

It is important to note that each of the last three verses has spoken of three separate temples, each called by a different name. In verse **93:6**, the Temple of Solomon was referred to simply as the Enclosure. In verse **93:7**, a mysterious temple known as the House of Glory and Dominion was mentioned, which we were told would stand forever. This temple is currently not on Earth. In verse **93:8**, the temple of Herod was called the House of Dominion and was described as being destroyed. These are all important details that should be observed and remembered.

We now move onward to Enoch's vision of the seventh week. This is when things start to get really interesting. Consider the following:

> **93.9.** And after that in the seventh week shall an apostate generation arise, and many shall be its deeds, and all its deeds shall be apostate.

The seventh week covers the period from 500 AD to 1200 AD. During this time, the great apostasy spread across the four corners of the Earth. The Nephite nation, the last holdout of righteousness, never witnessed the seventh week. Moroni, the last Nephite prophet, buried his record on the seventh day of the sixth week. Therefore, throughout the entire seventh week, apostasy reigned supreme among all known peoples on the surface of the Earth.

However, this is where things become very interesting, as the last two days of this week overlap with John the Revelator's sixth seal, which refers to the period between 1000 AD and 2000 AD. Consider closely, then, the things that Enoch stated happened at the close of this seventh week:

> **93.10.** And at its close shall be elected the elect righteous of the eternal plant of righteousness, to receive sevenfold instruction concerning all His creation.

93.11. For who is there of all the children of men that is able to hear the voice of the Holy One without being troubled? And who can think His thoughts? And who is there that can behold all the works of heaven?

93.12. And how should there be one who could behold the heaven, and who is there that could understand the things of heaven and see a soul or a spirit and could tell thereof, or ascend and see all their ends and think them or do like them?

93.13. And who is there of all men that could know what is the breadth and the length of the earth, and to whom has been shown the measure of all of them?

93.14. Or is there any one who could discern the length of the heaven and how great is its height, and upon what it is founded, and how great is the number of the stars, and where all the luminaries rest?

Enoch stated that some amazing things would occur at the close of the seventh week, which ended in 1200 AD. As I have noted, the sixth seal opened in 1000 AD, creating a two-hundred-year overlap between these two time periods. According to Enoch, during this time, the elect righteous among the plant of righteousness were chosen. What are we to understand by this? You will remember that at the beginning of this chapter, Enoch mentioned three groups: 1) the Children of Righteousness, 2) the Elect of the World, and 3) the Plant of Righteousness. Notably, in discussing what transpired during this time period, Enoch seems to combine all three groups into one. He referred to this group as the Righteous Elect from the Eternal Plant of Righteousness. By this, I believe we are to understand that this group will possess full knowledge of the history of the Earth, and not just the Earth, but the complexities of the multiverse and its varied inhabitants.

This elite group would receive seven-fold instruction, which symbolizes complete understanding. In other words, those selected among this elite group will have an astounding fullness of knowledge regarding the Father's workings among the creations of the multiverse. Examples indicate that these individuals would be able to see a spirit in the cosmos and categorize it. They would know by sight whether it is a spirit after the order of the Lady, who opted out of the Father's plan of redemption, a child of heaven in their first estate, a spirit awaiting the resurrection of the dead, or a spirit that rebelled against the Father and is bound to the Earth as a result.

Additionally, we are told that these individuals would know the length and breadth of the multiverse itself, a staggering accomplishment. Perhaps most impressive of all is that those chosen to be counted among this group are all members of the Eternal Plant of Righteousness, meaning they are all members of the House of Israel. Furthermore, it is clear from Enoch's explanation that the election of this group did not take place on Earth but elsewhere in the cosmos. What are we to understand from all of this?

Given the overlap of Enoch's seventh week and John's sixth seal, if we are to comprehend what is being taught, we must examine these two accounts together. As we do so, the reader should be aware that John wrote his description of these events as a translated being. Thus, besides the Book of Enoch—largely written by Enoch after his translation—John's is the only other record written by a translated being of which I am aware. Ezra wrote his prophecies prior to being translated. Therefore, we ought to acknowledge the wonderful significance of these two remarkable men and their incredible literary contributions. Their writings are a gift from God to those with eyes to see.

Now, consider John's writings regarding the opening of the sixth seal as it pertains to Enoch's prophecy of the same period:

> And I beheld when he had opened the sixth seal, and, lo, there was a great earthquake; and the sun became black as sackcloth of hair, and the moon became as blood; and the stars of heaven fell unto the earth, even as a fig tree casteth her untimely figs, when she is shaken of a mighty wind.
>
> And the heaven departed as a scroll when it is rolled together; and every mountain and island were moved out of their places. And the kings of the earth, and the great men, and the rich men, and the chief captains, and the mighty men, and every bondman, and every free man, hid themselves in the dens and in the rocks of the mountains; and said to the mountains and rocks, fall on us, and hide us from the face of him that sitteth on the Throne, and from the wrath of the Lamb: for the great day of His wrath is come; and who shall be able to stand?
>
> And after these things I saw four angels standing on the four corners of the earth, holding the four winds of the earth, that the wind should not blow on the earth, nor on the sea, nor on any tree.

> And I saw another angel ascending from the east, having the seal of the living God: and he cried with a loud voice to the four angels, to whom it was given to hurt the earth and the sea, Saying, Hurt not the Earth, neither the sea, nor the trees, till we have sealed the servants of our God in their foreheads.
>
> And I heard the number of them which were sealed: *and there were* sealed an hundred *and* forty *and* four thousand of all the tribes of the children of Israel… (Rev 6:12-17; 7:1-4)

According to the writings of John, when the sixth seal opened, the Earth was shaken terribly, causing the inhabitants to fear that the end of the world had come. After this great and terrible event, an angel ascended from the East and commanded four destroying angels to stay their hands until the servants of God had been sealed in their foreheads. We learn that these servants are the one hundred and forty-four thousand called from all the tribes of Israel. There can be no question that the event involving the election of the righteous from the Eternal Plant of Righteousness and the election of the one hundred and forty-four thousand is one and the same. Therefore, we must believe that this event took place sometime between 1000 AD and 1200 AD, based on the overlap of Enoch and John's timelines.

Elsewhere in John's writings, we learn that these one hundred and forty-four thousand will all be virgin men who joined the first fruits of the resurrection. As such, they lived and died before 1200 AD. They suffered much affliction in the name of Christ but remained valiant in their extremities. These are the individuals whom Enoch stated would receive a seven-fold understanding of God's workings among the multiverse. They will know the length and breadth of the multiverse, for they have surely been traveling it for the last thousand years in the service of the Father. Who can tell of the wondrous works that these have done and are still doing in the service of the Father?

Regarding this group, we learn that they were anointed and sealed unto their ministry by none other than John the Revelator himself, for according to D&C 77:9 & 14, John is the angel who ascended from the East. Therefore, the one hundred and forty-four thousand have already been called, and they are known to Enoch and his people, as well as to the portions of the House of Israel that have been taken to the ends of heaven. They are even now doing the will of the Father throughout the multiverse. The days are soon coming when they will arrive upon this Earth to gather the righteous from the four corners of the globe into Asenath's City of Refuge. This wondrous city will descend from the heavens as a bride adorned for her husband. These are marvelous mysteries that few have come to understand, for few have sought to comprehend them.

We now turn to Enoch's vision of the eighth week, which falls entirely within John's sixth seal, approximately from 1200 AD to 1900 AD. Consider the following:

> **93.15.** And after that there shall be another, the eighth week, that of righteousness, And a sword shall be given to it that a righteous judgement may be executed on the oppressors, and sinners shall be delivered into the hands of the righteous. And at its close they shall acquire houses through their righteousness, And a house shall be built for the Great King in glory for evermore, and all mankind shall look to the path of uprightness.

According to the prophecy above, during the eighth week, righteousness would be restored to the Earth, and another temple would be built for the Great King. This temple would hold the keys to the covenant path, so that all mankind who wish to obtain that covenant must do so by entering into that house. That holy temple can be none other than the Salt Lake City, Utah temple, built during the seventh day of the eighth week. Enoch's passage above is mirrored by Isaiah. Consider the following:

> And it shall come to pass in the last days, that the mountain of the Lord's house shall be established in the top of the mountains, and shall be exalted above the hills; and all nations shall flow unto it. And many people shall go and say, Come ye, and let us go up to the mountain of the Lord, to the house of the God of Jacob; and He will teach us of His ways, and we will walk in His paths: for out of Zion shall go forth the law, and the word of the Lord from Jerusalem. (Isaiah 2:2-3)

The beautiful symmetry between the prophecies of God is breathtaking. How many times has the Book of Enoch proven itself through its prophecies? Given the precise timing of this event, there can be no doubt that the Book of Enoch is referring to the Salt Lake Temple, which was dedicated in 1893, seven years before the conclusion of Enoch's eighth week. This temple has become one of the most significant symbols of the restoration. This prophecy should also remove any doubt regarding the continuity of the Church and of Brigham Young, under whose stewardship the Salt Lake Temple was built.

Yet, the restoration did not come without great sacrifice. Blessed be all those who have borne the shame of the world in order to walk the covenant path that runs through this sacred house. Great shall be their reward.

Now, the vision moves into the ninth week, which overlaps with John's seventh seal, traditionally associated with the millennial reign of Jesus Christ upon the Earth. However, before the millennium arrives, the wicked will be purged from the face of the Earth. Therefore, consider this stark reality alongside Enoch's prophecy regarding this same period.

> **93.16** And after that, in the ninth week, the righteous judgement shall be revealed to the whole world, And all the works of the godless shall vanish from all the earth, and the world shall be written down for destruction.

Enoch's ninth week runs from 1900 AD to 2600 AD. By the end of the second day of this week, godlessness will have vanished from the Earth, leaving only the righteous, who will usher in the millennium. It is during this period that the Earth shall finally experience its Sabbath day of rest. However, before that rest comes, the Earth will be baptized with fire. We are currently in the second day of Enoch's ninth week, and the destruction of the wicked is drawing ever nearer with each passing day.

We are the very last laborers that the Lord will send into His vineyard before it is burned. As such, we will witness this destruction with our own eyes. We live in a glorious day where blindness is no longer mandatory. If we have eyes to see, we can see! May the Lord prompt us to open our eyes and the eyes of those around us so that we may perceive things as they truly are!

Now, we turn to the tenth and final week of Enoch's prophecy. Based on my understanding, this week covers 2600 AD to 3300 AD. It encompasses the last half of the millennium and the brief season during which Satan is unbound. Consider the following:

> **93.17.** And after this, in the tenth week in the seventh part [*the last day*], there shall be the great eternal judgement, in which He will execute vengeance amongst the angels [*the hosts of heaven*].

According to Enoch, in the last one hundred years of the tenth week, God the Father will unleash His final great eternal judgment. This judgment will not be executed upon the angels. By "angels," we refer to those who dwell within the heavens—i.e., the inhabitants of other worlds. After Lucifer is released from his prison for a brief season, he will roam freely throughout the cosmos. The Lady and her minions will have been preparing for generations to make way for the darkest, vilest entities the multiverse has ever seen. This third of the host of heaven will run roughshod over the belief systems of the cosmos and will turn the hearts of many against the House of Israel and Israel's God.

The host of heaven that will come in rebellion will not consist solely of humans but will include malevolent creatures of incredible variety. Over the course of several hundred years, Satan will succeed in flipping the cosmic narrative, and under his leadership, the heavens will gather to battle against the Earth and lay siege to the New Jerusalem. The innumerable opposing forces that will assemble against us in that day will be absolutely staggering. Their numbers and technology will give this formidable host an illusory confidence that they can achieve victory.

Yet, they shall not prevail. Isaiah prophesied as much. Consider the following:

> And **ALL THE HOST OF HEAVEN** shall be dissolved, and the heavens shall be rolled together as a scroll [*that is to say the hosts of heaven will gather to the earth*]: and ALL THEIR HOSTS SHALL FALL DOWN, as the leaf falleth off from the vine, and as a falling fig from the fig tree.
>
> For my sword shall be bathed in heaven [*meaning the Sword of the Father will be bathed in the blood of the opposing comic forces*]: behold, it [*the Lord's sword*] shall come down upon Idumea, and upon the people of my curse, to judgment.
>
> The sword of the Lord is filled with blood, it is made fat with fatness, and with the blood of lambs and goats, with the fat of the kidneys of rams: for the Lord hath a sacrifice in bozrah [*the sheepfold*], and a great slaughter in the land of Idumea.
>
> And the unicorns [*incredible creatures of myth and legend such as Leviathans and dragons*] shall come down [*from the heavens*] with them, and the bullocks with the bulls [*symbols of the false gods of the ancient world*]; and THEIR land shall be soaked with blood, and THEIR dust made fat with fatness.
>
> For it is the day of the Lord's vengeance, and the year of recompences for the controversy of Zion [*the controversy of Zion is that the heavens will rebel and not want to be subject to the House of Israel*]. And the streams thereof [*meaning the streams of their worlds*] shall be turned into pitch, and the dust thereof into brimstone, and the land thereof shall become burning pitch. It shall not be quenched night nor day; the smoke thereof shall

go up for ever: from generation to generation it shall lie waste;
none shall pass through it for ever and ever. (Isaiah 34:4-10)

In the passages above, Isaiah speaks of a cosmic battle in which the God of the Multiverse utterly destroys the rebellious hosts of heaven, as well as the worlds upon which they dwell. Their worlds will be so completely destroyed that they will never again be inhabitable. Therefore, before the next cycle of salvation can begin, all things will need to be created anew—at the hands of the Savior of the next cycle.

For behold, there are many worlds that have passed away by
the word of my power (Moses 1:35)

There is no force in the multiverse more powerful than God the Father, and those who have been deceived into thinking otherwise will soon learn the error of their ways. However, the Lord does not delight in the shedding of blood or in sending the unrepentant hosts of heaven into eternal damnation. Therefore, as we have learned throughout these volumes, the Merciful God of the Multiverse has prepared a way for their deliverance. All those who chose to participate in the Father's plan of redemption will have another chance. Consider the following passages from earlier in Enoch's writings:

18.12. And beyond that abyss I saw a place which had no firmament of the heaven above, and no firmly founded earth beneath it: there was no water upon it, and no birds, but it was a waste and horrible place.
18.13. I saw there seven stars like great burning mountains, and to me, when I inquired regarding them,
18.14. The angel said: 'This place is the end of heaven and earth: this has become a prison for the stars and the host of heaven.
21.3. And there I saw seven stars of the heaven bound together in it, like great mountains and burning with fire.
21.4. Then I said: 'For what sin are they bound, and on what account have they been cast in hither?'
21.5. Then said Uriel, one of the holy angels, who was with me, and was chief over them, and said: 'Enoch, why dost thou ask, and why art thou eager for the truth?
21.6. These are of the number of the stars [of heaven], which have transgressed the commandment of the Lord, and are bound here till ten thousand years, the time entailed by their sins, are consummated.'

The hosts of heaven that rebel against the Father in this last great battle will, due to their rebellion, pay the price for their own sins. Enoch uses the term "seven stars bound together" to indicate the universality of this heavenly rebellion. Thus, we see that the Father's great plan of salvation began with a war in heaven, and it shall end with a war in heaven. The first war was fought and won because of our testimony in the sovereign Lord Jesus Christ. Those who will be victorious in the second battle will do so for the exact same reason. Thus, we see that history repeats itself. Those who are blind to this fact are destined for great sorrow. So it has always been, and so it will always be.

Enoch's ten-week vision now concludes with the following prophecy regarding those who overcome Lucifer and his cosmic deceptions:

> **93.18.** And the first heaven shall depart and pass away, and a new heaven shall appear, and all the powers of the heavens shall give sevenfold light.

> **93.19.** And after that there will be many weeks without number for ever, and all shall be in goodness and righteousness, and sin shall no more be mentioned for ever.

Those who have chosen the Father and His Son through both faith and deed will receive the light of heaven seven-fold. In other words, they will receive the fullness of the Father. As such, they will become joint heirs with Christ and receive all that the Father has. They will be magnified with an exceedingly great weight of glory. Consequently, power in the priesthood will flow unto them without compulsory means, through all generations of time and throughout all eternity. Such is the destiny of those who put their full trust in the Father's Hidden Son.

Chapter 24 - Woes and Warnings

In the previous chapter, we analyzed Enoch's ten-week vision. Of particular note was the building of the temple that will be established in Jerusalem in the last days and the calling and administration of the one hundred and forty-four thousand. We also discussed the epic conclusion of this iteration of the Father's plan of salvation, which will end as it began—with a war in heaven. At the conclusion of that war, the cycle will be over, and we will all realize how quickly it passed, as if it were a dream. Yet the actions and choices we made in mortality will have everlasting repercussions that will echo throughout eternity.

Therefore, how important it is to make these truths known to the inhabitants of the multiverse! We must strive to pierce the veil of our unbelief while still in the throes of our second estate and live the kinds of lives we were so resolute in living during the preexistence. The fact is, while these concepts may seem crazy and far-fetched to some, none of this is new. These truths are inextricably woven throughout the fabric of reality. All things bear witness to their truthfulness, if we only have eyes to see.

The days will come when the wicked will lament their own stiff-neckedness and blindness. Yet, it is only because of the veil and our ability to truly act on faith that progress of this nature is possible. The risks of mortality are every bit as real as the rewards it offers. The Father's plan has been devised to exalt us to the utmost degree that we are willing to accept from His hand.

Enoch now concludes his record by urging us to eschew wickedness and cleave unto righteousness. Consider the wisdom in his words of warning and counsel:

> **94.1**. And now I say unto you, my sons, love righteousness and walk therein; for the paths of righteousness are worthy of acceptation, but the paths of unrighteousness shall suddenly be destroyed and vanish.

94.2. And to certain men of a generation shall the paths of violence and of death be revealed, and they shall hold themselves afar from them, and shall not follow them.

94.3. And now I say unto you the righteous: Walk not in the paths of wickedness, nor in the paths of death, and draw not nigh to them, lest ye be destroyed.

94.4. But seek and choose for yourselves righteousness and an elect life, and walk in the paths of peace, and ye shall live and prosper.

94.5. And hold fast my words in the thoughts of your hearts, and suffer them not to be effaced from your hearts; for I know that sinners will tempt men to evilly-entreat wisdom, so that no place may be found for her, and no manner of temptation may diminish.

In the passages above, Enoch urges the righteous among his posterity to separate themselves from wickedness. Satan's pleasures are illusions that consume those who indulge in them, leaving them hollow and empty. Conversely, the righteous, who gain the strength to resist the temptations of the adversary, become beings of legendary substance and power. Enoch's primary purpose in writing this portion of his book is to help his posterity discern between these two paths and the inevitable destination of each. To this end, he now focuses on the behaviors and practices of the wicked, so that if these traits are found in our lives, we might repent of them while it is yet called day, avoiding the pains and sorrows that such choices will inevitably bring upon our own heads when the night falls.

94.6. Woe to those who build unrighteousness and oppression and lay deceit as a foundation; for they shall be suddenly overthrown, and they shall have no peace.

This is a warning to those who, wittingly or unwittingly, are building and sustaining Satan's kingdom. All who engage in such activities did not start out along this path but were led to it by personal choices and conditioning. We are all born innocent and pliable. Yet today, there is an absolute infrastructure in place to corrupt the innocent at ever earlier ages. Filth and sin are paraded before the young and innocent in ways that none of us would have ever imagined possible when we were young.

Such a hellish program of indoctrination requires willing participants to uphold and promote it. Without such supporters, the narratives of Satan would collapse. Therefore, the Kingdom of the Devil is a house of cards, sustained by those who once knew full well that the Emperor was naked and still know it deep within their souls. To such individuals, Enoch is speaking, calling them to repentance before it is everlastingly too late!

> **94.7.** Woe to those who build their houses with sin; for from all their foundations shall they be overthrown, and by the sword shall they fall. [And those who acquire gold and silver in judgement suddenly shall perish.]

The problem with houses made of cards is that they will ultimately collapse. Every major kingdom in this world has crumbled under the weight of its own sins. Lucifer knows this, yet he still has the audacity to tempt us into willingly giving up our eternal inheritances for the fleeting glory of the world. Where is the glory of Assyria now? Where is the pomp of Babylon? Where is the power of Egypt or the might of Rome? All these kingdoms, once the envy of the world, are now nothing more than crumbling artifacts in musty museums that many do not bother to visit, even when admission is free.

As such, the world must awaken to the reality around us and not waste our lives pursuing damning ideologies and things of no worth. As the history of the world attests, Satan's kingdoms inevitably perish—and suddenly. So it has ever been, and so it will always be.

> **94.8.** Woe to you, ye rich, for ye have trusted in your riches, and from your riches shall ye depart, because ye have not remembered the Most High in the days of your riches.

> **94.9.** Ye have committed blasphemy and unrighteousness, and have become ready for the day of slaughter, and the day of darkness and the day of the great judgement.

> **94.10.** Thus I speak and declare unto you: he who hath created you will overthrow you, and for your fall there shall be no compassion, and your Creator will rejoice at your destruction.

> **94.11.** And your righteous ones in those days shall be a reproach to the sinners and the godless.

The world is suffering under a great delusion. We have largely created an alternate reality in which the Great God of the Multiverse will accept us in our sins because He is a God of love. Yet the fact remains that God is a God of purity, and nothing impure can dwell in His presence. The alternate reality on which our society is now constructed is as unsustainable today as it has been in past kingdoms. With wanton blindness, modern societies flaunt ancient sins as exciting and liberating lifestyles. Yet, there is nothing new under the sun.

The ancient world was filled with men and women who burned with desire for one another, they engaged in unseeming behaviors, and proclaimed it love. Where are such civilizations today? Where will they be tomorrow? All such things are vanity and will be purged from the Earth. Interestingly, Enoch stated that the Father will delight in the purging of such societies. What did Enoch mean by this? Does the Father delight in destroying the children of heaven? Of course not. If He did, He would not allow civilizations to persist for so long before destroying them. He waits until they are fully ripened in iniquity to give every last person the opportunity to repent. If they repent, even in the eleventh hour, He receives them with more joy than a hundred just men.

Therefore, it is not that the Lord delights in destroying the wicked; rather, He delights in righteousness. For righteousness to flourish, the wicked who burden His vineyard must be purged so that the righteous may flourish and grow. Thus, it is what comes after the burning of the vineyard that brings joy to the Father, not the destruction that precedes it. If the Lord delighted in destruction, He would not provide so many warnings and prophecies about the future. Yet His children become past feeling and turn away from Him. Enoch has provided this entire chapter filled with woes and warnings in the hope that some might read them and turn back. Sadly, many of the saints themselves are not seeking knowledge. Instead, they wait to be led by the hand and told exactly what they must do in all things. We wonder at the blindness of those who prescribe the exact number of steps to walk but overlook the weightier matters of the law. What could be more important than being taught by the Lord Himself so that we may become like Him?

Enoch now expresses his desire to be unburdened by the heaviness of our sins and his sadness at our choices.

> **95.1.** Oh that mine eyes were [a cloud of] waters that I might weep over you, and pour down my tears as a cloud †of† waters: that so I might rest from my trouble of heart!

> **95.2.** †Who has permitted you to practice reproaches and wickedness? And so judgement shall overtake you, sinners†

In other words, Enoch longs to cry out all his tears over us in one great storm and be done with sorrow. Yet that is not how human emotions work. He cannot simply turn off his sorrow for the wickedness of mankind; sorrow is his constant companion. Jesus Christ was a man of sorrows, acquainted with grief. He mourned continuously for the blindness of the House of Israel. Sadly, that blindness persists today, just as it has throughout history.

Enoch witnessed the Father weeping over the wickedness on this Earth and wondered how such a great being could feel so much sorrow for a world so small and insignificant compared to the vastness of the multiverse. Yet He does. Why? Because His Son taught us to love one another, not to judge each other, and to seek charity above all things. We do not comply. Instead, we post hateful comments in the anonymity of online communities, fostering division and anger. We highlight the faults of others and condemn them openly. We are as blind as any generation that has ever walked the Earth—doubly so, for we have the truth among us but refuse to see it for what it is.

Yet, there are true disciples of Jesus Christ among us. They stand out from the crowd. Despite the darkness of the world, they are filled with light, love, and hope. These are the ones who will inherit the Earth when the vineyard is purged. Let us pray that the light from such individuals spreads, and that we ourselves can be filled with this light.

> **95.3.** Fear not the sinners, ye righteous; For again will the Lord deliver them into your hands, that ye may execute judgement upon them according to your desires.

From the passage above, we understand that the Lord will not always allow the righteous to be oppressed by the wicked. The day will come when He will turn the tables. How will He do this? He will send our righteous brothers and sisters to aid us, over whom the wicked will have no power. This righteous group will execute judgment upon the wicked of the Earth and purge the vineyard for our sake. In essence, they will do to the wicked of our day what the Israelites did to the Canaanites in times of old. That is to say, they will make a full end of the unrepentant Gentiles in America, and no weapon formed by man will stop them.

Enoch's vision continues.

> **95.4.** Woe to you who fulminate anathemas which cannot be reversed: healing shall therefore be far from you because of your sins.

To fulminate anathemas is to issue unrighteous judgment in anger, rather than in wisdom and understanding. It is not for us to judge our fellow man when we ourselves are stained with sin. Joseph Smith taught that the closer we come to God, the more inclined we are to look past the sins of others, seeking their salvation rather than their condemnation. Let us focus on and magnify the good in others. The world has more than enough people highlighting people's faults; we need not pick up stones and join these hypocritical masses. Such actions are not becoming of disciples of the Living Christ!

> **95.5.** Woe to you who requite your neighbor with evil; for ye shall be requited according to your works.

True disciples of Christ do not return railing for railing. They do not inflict anger and pain; instead, they absorb it and radiate light in its place. They are able to do this because they rely on the redemptive power of Christ, whose yoke is light. They see things as they truly are, and thus, they do not wallow in the darkness they absorb. Instead, they utilize the atoning power of Christ to obliterate it, ensuring that such darkness finds an end within them rather than continuing its destructive path like a hurricane over a hot and turbulent sea.

> **95.6.** Woe to you, lying witnesses, and to those who weigh out injustice, for suddenly shall ye perish.

> **95.7.** Woe to you, sinners, for ye persecute the righteous; for ye shall be delivered up and persecuted because of injustice, and heavy shall its yoke be upon you.

We live in a time with a two-tiered legal system. The wicked are held above the law, while others are crushed beneath its weight. This injustice will come to a sudden end. Those who have taken refuge in the corruption of this system will find that they have no refuge at all when their world burns around them. In contrast, those who have been condemned under such tyrannical systems will find mercy in the Hidden Son and will inherit the Earth.

> **96.1.** Be hopeful, ye righteous; for suddenly shall the sinners perish before you, and ye shall have lordship over them according to your desires.

> **96.2.** And in the day of the tribulation of the sinners, your children shall mount and rise as eagles, and higher than the vultures will be your nest, and ye shall ascend and enter the crevices of the earth, and the clefts of the rock forever as coneys before the unrighteous, and the sirens shall sigh because of you-and weep.]

96.3. Wherefore fear not, ye that have suffered; for healing shall be your portion, and a bright light shall enlighten you, and the voice of rest ye shall hear from heaven.

Despite the darkness that is soon to befall the Earth and the trials unlike any we have faced before, these challenges will last only for a small moment. Yes, we will witness things that we cannot comprehend, which may cause our hearts to falter with fear, as the world has no framework for such events. Yet, the human soul is resilient. The terror of those days will eventually normalize, and deliverance will come.

When that deliverance arrives, the righteous will rise above the vultures like glorious eagles. We will inherit the greatest civilization ever witnessed among the mortal worlds of men. Then we will experience joy and happiness beyond our current comprehension, and all fear and sorrow will be cast away. Therefore, let us retain hope in the growing darkness; great things lie in store for the righteous! The same cannot be said for the wicked.

96.4. Woe unto you, ye sinners, for your riches make you appear like the righteous, but your hearts convict you of being sinners, and this fact shall be a testimony against you for a memorial of (your) evil deeds.

96.5. Woe to you who devour the finest of the wheat, and drink wine in large bowls, and tread under foot the lowly with your might.

96.6. Woe to you who drink water from every fountain, for suddenly shall ye be consumed and wither away, because ye have forsaken the fountain of life.

96.7. Woe to you who work unrighteousness and deceit and blasphemy: It shall be a memorial against you for evil.

96.8. Woe to you, ye mighty, who with might oppress the righteous; for the day of your destruction is coming. In those days many and good days shall come to the righteous--in the day of your judgement.

Through the twisted lies and deceptions of Satan, many have wholly given themselves over to the Whore of Babylon in pursuit of gain in this life. Yet this life is fleeting. We spend less than two handfuls of decades on this Earth, and then the illusion of Satan's treasures will be ripped away. Why would we trade eternity for such insanity as this passing dream? After this comes a life that never ends; why exchange the riches of the next life for the baubles and trinkets of this one?

There is but one thing that matters: doing the will of the Father. Those who follow the Father's will find futures filled with light and joy. In contrast, those who place their faith in Satan's lies will reap the whirlwind for thousands of years. The change they could have achieved in mortality will be forged in burning flames hereafter.

> **97.1.** Believe, ye righteous, that the sinners will become a shame and perish in the day of unrighteousness.

There are many times in mortality when it seems that the sinful are living their best lives while the righteous mourn out their days. Yet, Enoch would have us see beyond this transitory illusion and believe in the coming day when the Lord raises us as His jewels. On that day, all mankind will be able to discern between those who served the Lord and those who did not.

Have faith and develop eyes to see beyond Satan's masterful illusions, for that is what they truly are. If the wicked are so happy, why must they constantly seek stimulation—be it through sex, drugs, or the praise of man? Without this constant distraction, they are forced to confront the emptiness of their own souls, and they tremble before the void.

Do not be deceived by Lucifer's light; it is, in reality, a terrible and consuming darkness.

> **97.2.** Be it known unto you ye sinners that the Most High is mindful of your destruction, and the angels of heaven rejoice over your destruction.

> **97.3.** What will ye do, ye sinners, and whither will ye flee on that day of judgement, when ye hear the voice of the prayer of the righteous?

> **97.4.** Yea, ye shall fare like unto them, against whom this word shall be a testimony: "Ye have been companions of sinners."

> **97.5.** And in those days the prayer of the righteous shall reach unto the Lord, and for you the days of your judgement shall come.

97.6. And all the words of your unrighteousness shall be read out before the Great Holy One, and your faces shall be covered with shame, and He will reject every work which is grounded on unrighteousness.

97.7. Woe to you, ye sinners, who live on the mid ocean and on the dry land, whose remembrance is evil against you.

97.8. Woe to you who acquire silver and gold in unrighteousness and say: "We have become rich with riches and have possessions; and have acquired everything we have desired.

97.9. And now let us do what we purposed: For we have gathered silver, and many are the husbandmen in our houses." And our granaries are (brim) full as with water,

97.10 Yea and like water your lies shall flow away; For your riches shall not abide But speedily ascend from you; For ye have acquired it all in unrighteousness, And ye shall be given over to a great curse.

98.1. And now I swear unto you, to the wise and to the foolish, for ye shall have manifold experiences on the earth.

98.2. For ye men shall put on more adornments than a woman, and coloured garments more than a virgin: In royalty and in grandeur and in power, and in silver and in gold and in purple, and in splendor and in food they shall be poured out as water.

98.3. Therefore, they shall be wanting in doctrine and wisdom, and they shall perish thereby together with their possessions; and with all their glory and their splendor, and in shame and in slaughter and in great destitution, their spirits shall be cast into the furnace of fire.

98.4. I have sworn unto you, ye sinners, as a mountain has not become a slave, and a hill does not become the handmaid of a woman, even so sin has not been sent upon the earth, but man of himself has created it, and under a great curse shall they fall who commit it.

98.5. And barrenness has not been given to the woman, but on account of the deeds of her own hands she dies without children.

98.6. I have sworn unto you, ye sinners, by the Holy Great One, that all your evil deeds are revealed in the heavens, and that none of your deeds of oppression are covered and hidden.

In the verses above, Enoch states plainly that those who willfully rebel against the commandments of God by seeking to do their own will and placing their own lusts and desires above all else shall perish. Specifically, Enoch has sworn that the wicked will die without children. This is not because they are barren or sterile, but due to their actions in mortality. Being a father or mother is one of the greatest blessings there is. The unbreakable family bond in the heavens is not the result of a biological process in mortality; it is the product of God's power made manifest through the covenants and ordinances of His holy temples.

Without the sealing power of God, the formal familial relationships that exist on Earth will fade away as nothing more than a pleasant dream. The relationships between us and our heavenly parents are absolute and cannot be broken by any power on Earth. However, any familial relationship on Earth must be forged deliberately and in righteousness by one with the authority to do so. When the scriptures speak of the wicked being cut off both root and branch, they speak the truth. While the relationship between the wicked and their heavenly parents can never be severed, their earthly relationships can and will be.

Yet, among the righteous, families will continue both on Earth and in heaven. If we are not worthy of our children, they will be sealed to others in our family lines who are worthy of them. Furthermore, Enoch stated that none of the sins of the righteous shall be covered. The Hebrew word for atonement literally means "to cover." Therefore, those who willfully rebel against God will not be covered by the atonement of His Son; rather, they will atone for their own sins. This will be the largest category of people, for broad is the road and easy is the way to rebellion against the Lord. Yet, in the end, the wicked do not rebel against God but against their own self-interests. They can never become what God could have made of them had they placed themselves in His hands, like clay on the potter's wheel.

Enoch's council and warnings continue:

98.7. And do not think in your spirit nor say in your heart that ye do not know and that ye do not see that every sin is every day recorded in heaven in the presence of the Most High.

98.8. From henceforth ye know that all your oppression wherewith ye oppress is written down every day till the day of your judgement.

98.9. Woe to you, ye fools, for through your folly shall ye perish: and ye transgress against the wise, and so good shall not be your portion.

98.10. And now, know ye that ye are prepared for the day of destruction: wherefore do not hope to live, ye sinners, but ye shall depart and die; for ye know no ransom; for ye are prepared for the day of the great judgement, for the day of tribulation and great shame for your spirits.

98.11. Woe to you, ye obstinate of heart, who work wickedness and eat blood: Whence have ye good things to eat and to drink and to be filled? From all the good things which the Lord the Most High has placed in abundance on the earth; therefore, ye shall have no peace.

Christ once atoned for the sins of all creation, His perfect life serving as a ransom for sin. The path to redemption for all creation is as simple as it was for the Israelites to look upon the brass serpent that Moses, the high priest of Israel, hung upon a pole. Yet, due to their stiff-neckedness and rebellion, many will refuse the ransom made for their sins and will instead atone for their own, in a process that will last longer than the temporal history of this Earth. The fruit of that suffering will be glorious, but far less so than any degree of glory they could have freely obtained from God had they chosen Him to be their Father from the beginning rather than the end. For in the end, every knee shall bend, and every tongue shall confess that Jesus is Lord of all creation.

Enoch continues:

98.12. Woe to you who love the deeds of unrighteousness: wherefore do ye hope for good unto yourselves? know that ye shall be delivered into the hands of the righteous [*the Remnant of Jacob*], and they shall cut off your necks and slay you, and have no mercy upon you.

98.13. Woe to you who rejoice in the tribulation of the righteous; for no grave shall be dug for you.

98.14. Woe to you who set at nought the words of the righteous; for ye shall have no hope of life.

98.15. Woe to you who write down lying and godless words; for they write down their lies that men may hear them and act godlessly towards (their) neighbor.

98.16. Therefore they shall have no peace but die a sudden death.

99.1. Woe to you who work godlessness, and glory in lying and extol them: Ye shall perish, and no happy life shall be yours.

Wickedness can produce a transitory illusion of happiness, but the wicked find no true satisfaction in their sins. Like the cursed pirates of the Black Pearl, they can never satiate their desires; it forever burns and consumes them. Like heroin addicts, they are drawn to that which destroys and torments them above all else. The wicked cannot take pleasure in yesterday's sins but are trapped in a hellish loop, trying to fill a bottomless pit that will become their future habitation.

Why, then, will they die, seeing that a ransom has been paid and a way of escape provided? Is it not because the chains they have bound themselves with have become too strong? In their desperate misery, they look to God and curse His name, infuriated that they cannot always indulge in their sins. Yet it is not God who has bound them; it is their chosen father, the Father of Lies, who has ensnared them and delivered them into a hell of their own making.

Given the truth of these matters, should not the wicked rebel against the Father of Lies, who leads them to destruction, rather than against the Almighty God, who can, if they choose, deliver them from bondage? Yet, as the life of Alma the Younger shows, such deliverance does not come without a fight, for Lucifer will not relinquish his own easily. Thus, we see the awful state of the wicked, caught in the swift currents of their sins, pulling them ever downward in a relentless current from which no one can escape by their own power.

99.2. Woe to them who pervert the words of uprightness, and transgress the eternal law, and transform themselves into what they were not: They shall be trodden under foot upon the earth.

Satan has deceived many into becoming evangelists of his false gospel. Through the false premises of political correctness and demonic morality, they set themselves up as something they are not. Millions of youth have become willing disciples of these satanic clergy, embracing doctrines that defy the spirit and essence of God. While such doctrines cannot produce salvation, they do foster hate, rage, and blindness. In their blind and hate-filled state, they mindlessly advocate for the right to slaughter innocence, discarding all propriety and accountability, and promoting behaviors that will accelerate their own demise.

Thus, we see that while they proclaim themselves to be "woke", their souls are asleep. In this state of sullen stupor, they have allowed Satan to drag them into darkness, far enough that they are beyond the Spirit's light. Consequently, the only testimony they will receive is that of earthquakes and thunderous sounds loud enough to collapse the world around them. Only then, when their world is crumbling, as with every "woke" society before them, will they finally recognize the gravity of their situation. However, it will already be everlastingly too late.

Enoch's council and warnings continue:

> **99.3.** In those days make ready, ye righteous, to raise your prayers as a memorial, And place them as a testimony before the angels, that they may place the sin of the sinners for a memorial before the Most High.

> **99.4.** In those days the nations shall be stirred up, and the families of the nations shall arise on the day of destruction.

> **99.5.** And in those days the destitute shall go forth and carry off their children, and they shall abandon them, so that their children shall perish through them: Yea, they shall abandon their children that are still sucklings, and not return to them And shall have no pity on their beloved ones.

> **99.6.** And again I swear to you, ye sinners, that sin is prepared for a day of unceasing bloodshed.

Enoch gives us a sign that indicates when the great and dreadful day of the Lord is at hand. The sign he provides is that the love of mothers will run cold. In that day, women will abandon their children in pursuit of their own fulfillment. This does not refer to young women giving their children up for adoption, that is a kindness which ensures that a child is placed in a loving home. Rather, Enoch speaks of days when young children are simply abandoned in their homes while their mothers leave them to fend for themselves. He describes young mothers leaving their babies in the woods or in bathroom stalls, or selling their children for drugs or money.

Women are the best that humanity has to offer; however, when the love of mothers begins to run cold and they show no pity for their own children, society becomes ripe for destruction. Unfortunately, headlines about mothers abandoning their children are increasingly commonplace today.

Yet, there are many who, rather than abandoning their children, have chosen to indoctrinate them in the ways of sin. The sexualization of children by their parents and teachers has become commonplace in many places around the world. These parents have not abandoned their children; but it would have been better if they had. Instead, they poison their minds.

According to Enoch, the Lord will not have mercy on those who offend His little ones. As He has said, it would be better for them to have a millstone tied around their necks and be cast into the sea than to offend one of these. Is raising a child on bile and filth not an offense? The righteous know how to give their children good gifts, while the blind and wicked give them serpents and stones. This perverse generation is ripening in iniquity, and its fullness is not far off.

These atrocities are signs that we are getting close. Therefore, we ought to engage in fervent prayer that the Lord will open the eyes of the blind and turn the hearts of the fathers back to the best interests of their children, lest the whole world be smitten with a curse at the Lord's coming. Let us pray that the Lord will strengthen His little ones so that they might remarkably survive the wickedness of their parents and find His Beloved Son in spite of them.

> **99.7.** And they who worship stones, and grave images of gold and silver and wood and clay, and those who worship impure spirits and demons, and all kinds of idols not according to knowledge, shall get no manner of help from them.

> **99.8.** And they shall become godless by reason of the folly of their hearts, and their eyes shall be blinded through the fear of their hearts and through visions in their dreams.

99.9. Through these they shall become godless and fearful; For they shall have wrought all their work in a lie, and shall have worshiped a stone: therefore in an instant shall they perish.

In ancient days, societies literally worshiped idols made of stone, metal, wood, and clay. Such objects were demonic counterfeits of the true and living God. Satan does not care what you worship, as long as you do not worship the Almighty in wisdom and truth. He has crafted alternate versions of God and has always taken delight in how easily the world can be led to worship false deities. Today, we have many more options for our devotion. Yet, there is but one true and living God, and the righteous, like all wise men before them, still seek Him.

99.10. But in those days blessed are all they who accept the words of wisdom, and understand them, and observe the paths of the Most High, and walk in the path of His righteousness, and become not godless with the godless; For they shall be saved.

Enoch prophesied that in the last days, there would be those who both understand his words of wisdom and walk in the Lord's covenant path. He foretold that those who do so would be saved. They are saved because they have eyes to see, and thus are not deceived like the godless all around them. Despite the blindness and hard-heartedness of their generation, these individuals will have felt the promptings of the Holy Ghost and acted upon them. There is no other way they could have come to read and understand Enoch's words in modern times.

Enoch now speaks in contrast to those that understand truth:

99.11. Woe to you who spread evil to your neighbors; For you shall be slain in Sheol.

99.12. Woe to you who make deceitful and false measures, and (to them) who cause bitterness on the earth; for they shall thereby be utterly consumed.

99.13. Woe to you who build your houses through the grievous toil of others, and all their building materials are the bricks and stones of sin; I tell you ye shall have no peace.

99.14. Woe to them who reject the measure and eternal heritage of their fathers and whose souls follow after idols; for they shall have no rest.

The passages above discuss the exchange of wisdom for foolishness—publishing demonic doctrines instead of the Father's gospel of peace. The days are coming when all will receive the wages of their masters. In that day, all who have rejected the measure and eternal heritage of their fathers will weep, mourn, and gnash their teeth for their own blindness and wanton foolishness. The truth is known: the gospel of Abraham is real, and it is up to us to seek the promises and blessings of the fathers as he did. If we do so, we are worthy to be called the children of Abraham, for we have acted as he did. However, if we do not perform the works of Abraham, how can we be his children?

99.15. Woe to them who work unrighteousness and help oppression, and slay their neighbors until the day of the great judgement.

99.16. For He shall cast down your glory, and bring affliction on your hearts, and shall arouse His fierce indignation, and destroy you all with the sword; and all the holy and righteous shall remember your sins.

The days are coming—though thankfully not yet—when neighbor will rise against neighbor, father against son, and mother against daughter. However, before that day arrives, the righteous will be driven from their homes. In that time, the righteous may feel abandoned and forgotten by the Lord. Yet, this separation must occur for wickedness to reach its fullness. When that day comes, we must trust that the Father is able to guide us through the most fertile parts of the wilderness. Though we will suffer, our sufferings will bring us closer to Him.

While, our sufferings will be both real and intense, they will be of limited duration. The holy race will begin to walk among us to help and protect us. Enoch has told us as much, and he is not alone in that witness; both ancient and modern prophets have said the same. Therefore, we can rest assured that if we endure these trials well, God will magnify us in our extremities and turn the bitter into sweet. Such will surely be the case.

Enoch now describes the depravity that will exist in societies that have cast out the righteous from among them:

100.1. And in those days in one place the fathers together with their sons shall be smitten and brothers one with another shall fall in death till the streams flow with their blood.

100.2. For a man shall not withhold his hand from slaying his sons and his sons' sons, and the sinner shall not withhold his hand from his honored brother: From dawn till sunset they shall slay one another.

100.3. And the horse shall walk up to the breast in the blood of sinners, and the chariot shall be submerged to its height.

The passages above speak of the last days when the Son of Man will harvest the Earth, as spoken of in the Book of Revelation. There can be little doubt that Enoch saw the same end times event that John spoke of in the following manner:

> And the winepress was trodden without the city, and blood came out of the winepress, even unto the horse bridles, by the space of a thousand and six hundred furlongs. (Rev 14:20)

Both Enoch and John saw that in the last days, the blood of the wicked would run deep. John even provided a measurement equivalent to 125,000 square miles, which would be submerged in blood up to the bridle of a horse. As a result, at the end of this destruction, the wicked will be nowhere to be found; only the righteous will remain on that day. Ezra offers one of the most haunting descriptions of the apocalyptic destruction that I have encountered, which speaks of this same time. Consider the following:

> Behold, victuals shall be so good and cheap upon earth, that they shall think themselves to be in good case, and even then shall evils grow upon earth, sword, famine, and great confusion. For many of them that dwell upon earth shall perish of famine; and the other, that escape the hunger, shall the sword destroy.

> And the dead shall be cast out as dung, and there shall be no man to comfort them: for the earth shall be wasted, and the cities shall be cast down. There shall be no man left to till the earth, and to sow it

> The trees shall give fruit, and who shall gather them? The grapes shall ripen, and who shall tread them? for all places shall be desolate of men: So that one man shall desire to see another, and to hear his voice.

For of a city there shall be ten left, and two of the field, which shall hide themselves in the thick groves, and in the clefts of the rocks. As in an orchard of Olives upon every tree there are left three or four olives; or as when a vineyard is gathered, there are left some clusters of them that diligently seek through the vineyard: even so in those days there shall be three or four left by them that search their houses with the sword.

And the earth shall be laid waste, and the fields thereof shall wax old, and her ways and all her paths shall grow full of thorns, because no man shall travel therethrough.

The virgins shall mourn, having no bridegrooms; the women shall mourn, having no husbands; their daughters shall mourn, having no helpers. In the wars shall their bridegrooms be destroyed, and their husbands shall perish of famine.

Hear now these things and understand them, ye servants of the Lord. Behold, the word of the Lord, receive it: believe not the gods of whom the Lord spake. (2 Esdras 16:21-36)

Curiously, Ezra's warning begins by stating that the price of food in the last days will decrease significantly. Price is a function of supply and demand. If the supply of food remains constant while the population decreases precipitously, the price of food will fall. While the passages above suggest a massive decrease in global population due to famine and war, it seems that the famine is self-inflicted. It will be caused by a complete collapse of the global supply chain rather than by a collapse in food production.

Farmers in Idaho will continue to grow enough potatoes to feed the entire country, yet the means of distribution will collapse. As a result, food will be available in great abundance locally but will be non-existent in large population centers. Ironically, the hungrier the population becomes, the more dangerous it will be to supply them. Therefore, the danger created by the starving populace ensures the continuation and escalation of the famine. Why would a trucker risk his life to deliver food into a city? He will not, and thus, within days, the complex global supply chain will come to a complete halt.

Food that once traveled thousands of miles to feed a city of millions will be cut off. Within hours, grocery shelves will be bare, gas stations will be empty, and population centers will become prisons. All of these destructions will befall our societies because we will have abandoned the God of our fathers in favor of the gods and philosophies of the ancient world. Yet these gods will have no power to save us. Those who follow these strange gods will be forsaken by them. These same events are also spoken of by Isaiah in the following manner:

> I, even I, am the Lord; and beside Me there is no Savior. I have declared, and have saved, and I have shewed, **when there was no strange god among you**: therefore ye are My witnesses, saith the Lord, that I am God.
>
> Yea, before the day was I am He; and there is none that can deliver out of My hand: I will work, and who shall let it? Thus saith the Lord, your redeemer, the Holy One of Israel; For your sake I have sent to Babylon, and have brought down all their nobles, and the Chaldeans, whose cry is in the ships.
>
> I am the Lord, your Holy One, the creator of Israel, your King. Thus saith the Lord, which maketh a way in the sea, and a path in the mighty waters; which bringeth forth the chariot and horse, the army and the power; they shall lie down together, they shall not rise: they are extinct, they are quenched as tow.
>
> Remember ye not the former things, neither consider the things of old. Behold, I will do a new thing; now it shall spring forth; shall ye not know it? (Isaiah 43:11-19)

The things that are about to transpire upon the Earth will be astounding. While the supply chains of men will collapse overnight, God is not dependent on humanity to do His work. He can solve problems in miraculous ways never considered by men, such as dividing the sea. Salvation will come quickly in that day. By miraculous means, the wicked will be trodden down, and only the righteous will remain.

Those who have placed their trust in strange gods, such as the Lady, the Beast, and the Antichrist, will be consumed, for they that come shall burn them (JSH 1:37). Jesus Christ alone is our Savior; there is none other. If we know Him, we will not be deceived by those false gods that come in His name with their tricks and deceptions. Let us look to Him and hold fast to our faith in the face of the strange gods that will soon overcome the faithless people of this generation.

Amid all the chaos that will soon be unleashed upon this world, it is vital to remember that the Lord will not forsake us, even though it may feel as though He has. You may recall from a prior vision of Enoch's that he saw angels sent to provide lifelines to the righteous in the last days. At that time, the holy race will begin to dwell among us. This is now reconfirmed anew by Enoch once more. Consider the following:

> **100.4** In those days the angels shall descend into the secret places and gather together into one place all those who brought down sin [*meaning that highlighted and rejected the sins of the world*] and the Most High will arise on that day of judgement to execute great judgement amongst sinners.

> **100.5.** And over all the righteous and holy He will appoint guardians from amongst the holy angels to guard them as the apple of an eye, until He makes an end of all wickedness and all sin, and though the righteous sleep a long sleep, they have nought to fear.

> **100.6.** And then the children of the earth shall see the wise in security, and shall understand all the words of this book, and recognize that their riches shall not be able to save them in the overthrow of their sins.

When it comes to sin in the last days, we have two choices: to bring it down or to be brought down by it. According to Enoch, those who overcome sin will be gathered by angels into a single location. This location can be none other than the New Jerusalem on the North American continent. Sinners—those who embrace sin rather than resist it—will be purged. This last great purge of the Earth will come by way of fire, "for they that come will burn them" (JSH 1:37).

In that day, the world will be shocked by how the righteous have been made secure and how the wicked are helplessly exposed. Prior to the day of the sinners, the righteous appeared weak. The wicked expelled them from their houses and drove them like dumb animals. Yet now, it is the wicked who flee in vain for their lives, while the righteous are made fast and immovable. There will be no doubt about who was right and who was wrong in those days. According to Enoch, it is only at this stage that the wicked will understand the words of his book. Until this point, they will have been completely blind to the truth.

As I consider these things, I find it hard to fault the blind. The scriptures speak of things that are simply too fantastic to be believed at face value. Those who come to believe in them arrive at that conclusion through the promptings of the Holy Ghost, and in no other way. This is by design. As such, rather than condemning the unbelieving, I marvel at those capable of believing such things.

Enoch continues to speak to us of the latter days, hoping that his admonitions will find fertile ground and inspire us to change while there is still time to do so.

100.7. Woe to you, Sinners, on the day of strong anguish, Ye who afflict the righteous and burn them with fire: Ye shall be requited according to your works.

100.8. Woe to you, ye obstinate of heart, who watch in order to devise wickedness: Therefore shall fear come upon you and there shall be none to help you.

100.9. Woe to you, ye sinners, on account of the words of your mouth, and on account of the deeds of your hands which your godlessness has wrought, in blazing flames burning worse than fire shall ye burn.

100.10 And now, know ye that from the angels He will inquire as to your deeds in heaven, from the sun and from the moon and from the stars in reference to your sins because upon the Earth ye execute judgement on the righteous.

100.11. And He will summon to testify against you every cloud and mist and dew and rain; for they shall all be withheld because of you from descending upon you, and they shall be mindful of your sins.

100.12. And now give presents to the rain that it be not withheld from descending upon you, nor yet the dew, when it has received gold and silver from you that it may descend.

100.13. When the hoar-frost and snow with their chilliness, and all the snow-storms with all their plagues fall upon you, in those days ye shall not be able to stand before them.

Enoch concludes this portion of his writings by telling the wicked that the day of judgment is most assuredly coming for them. Prior to this day, the wicked used their wealth and influence to spare themselves from the consequences of their sins. They were able to pay off judges and witnesses. However, this will not always be true. Can you pay off the elements of the Earth to withhold their testimonies against you? Justice is coming for the wicked, and the only recourse is sincere repentance.

Unlike the Book of Mormon, Enoch's words were preserved and brought forth through mundane means. As such, many within the Church may not consider them. This is truly a shame, for they were meant to bless the righteous who would be called to endure the trials and hardships of the last days.

If we read and believe these words, we should act upon them by putting our lives in order and preparing ourselves speedily for the coming day. The greatest preparations we can make have little to do with guns and food, and everything to do with repentance and faith in Jesus Christ. Through repentance and faith in Jesus Christ, even the most vile of sinners may become saints and joint heirs with Him. This is the reason we have these words: that we might resolve to overcome our sins rather than be overcome by them.

Chapter 25 – The Promised Books

In the prior chapter, Enoch emphatically warned the world of the fearful vengeance that will soon befall it. Ironically, we have all waited eons for our opportunity to come to Earth and prove ourselves. Now that we are here, due to the skill of the adversary, we have become spiritually blind to one degree or another. The struggle is to pierce this blindness and choose light over darkness. We all make that choice every day. Some have been able to overcome the darkness, while others continue to claw their way toward it. In the end, it is a matter of choice, for whether we acknowledge it or not, every single one of us will eventually stand before the Throne of God and recognize that we knew the emperor was naked all along.

Therefore, we are all engaged in the greatest struggle of our existence: the struggle between what we know to be true and the desires of the natural man. The fight is real and unrelenting. The current does not stop for us to rest; its pull is constant. Yet, the Lord will never allow us to drown as long as we look to Him for strength. His power is inexhaustible. Just as a chick must hatch from its egg of its own accord, we need this struggle to reach our full potential. However, not all have the strength to overcome on their own. They need our help to persuade them that their lives are worth fighting for. This is the sole purpose of Enoch's writings: to help us have hope and to endure to the end, despite the complexities of nations and demons.

Enoch's writings are now drawing to a close; only fifty-five verses remain to be discussed in the remaining pages of this book. However, while we are nearing the end of Enoch's writings, we are about to explore some of his most profound prophecies. These prophecies are meant for all, but only those with eyes to see and hearts to feel will truly receive them. Consider how Enoch begins his closing remarks:

> **101.1.** Observe the heaven, ye children of heaven, and every work of the Most High, and fear ye Him and work no evil in His presence.

In the passage above, Enoch refers to the inhabitants of the Earth as the children of heaven. This is consistent with his teachings throughout these volumes. We came to this Earth trailing clouds of glory, with every intent of following in the footsteps of our heavenly parents. None of us ever intended to lose our way or to be overcome by sin. Indeed, we cast the great deceiver out of the heavenly realms by the power of our testimonies in Jesus Christ. As the children of heaven upon this Earth, this is who we are. Our inheritance should be of the Lord, not of demons.

Therefore, Enoch reminds us to look heavenward and remember who we are. We are the grandchildren of the Most High God, created in His image. His power and influence flow within us, warning us of the sin and folly all around. Our very existence is a testament to His raw power and might. His power is made manifest in the eternal bodies of our beautiful and perfected heavenly parents—His direct offspring. All eternity hears His voice and obeys His commands. The only reason the Great Dragon has any power at all on Earth is that the Great God of Heaven wills it so. Why? So that we might be able to choose for ourselves according to our instincts and desires. God will not compel us to return to His side.

Enoch continues by addressing the power and will of God.

> **101.2.** If He closes the windows of heaven, and withholds the rain and the dew from descending on the earth on your account, what will ye do then?

> **101.3.** And if He sends His anger upon you because of your deeds, ye cannot petition Him; for ye spake proud and insolent words against His righteousness: therefore ye shall have no peace.

> **101.4.** And see ye not the sailors of the ships, how their ships are tossed to and fro by the waves, and are shaken by the winds, and are in sore trouble?

> **101.5.** And therefore do they fear because all their goodly possessions go upon the sea with them, and they have evil forebodings of heart that the sea will swallow them and they will perish therein.

> **101.6.** Are not the entire sea and all its waters, and all its movements, the work of the Most High, and has He not set limits to its doings, and confined it throughout by the sand?

> **101.7.** And at His reproof it is afraid and dries up, and all its fish die and all that is in it; But ye sinners that are on the earth fear Him not.

Enoch likens the sojourn of the children of heaven upon the Earth to sailors traveling upon a treacherous sea. The sea has always been a symbol of mystery and wonder. Humanity cannot know its depths, for they are too great for us to penetrate. Many have set sail upon mortality with a veil of forgetfulness that is as impenetrable as the depths of the sea. Enoch would have us remember that, although sailors fear losing their cargo and their lives to the sea, for the children of heaven, such worries are illusory.

Just as God is the maker of heaven and Earth, He is also the maker of the sea and all that is within it. Those things lost in the depths of the sea are not lost to the Lord. He holds all things in His Almighty Hand. Everything in life and beyond the grave is before Him, just as all eternity is before Him. If this is true, why should we fear, even if we are cast into the depths of the sea? There is no place in heaven or on Earth where we are beyond His power or reach. If we have faith and trust in Him, all will be well; nothing can be lost to the sea that He cannot restore.

Enoch continues with this analogy:

> **101.8.** Has He not made the heaven and the earth, and all that is therein? Who has given understanding and wisdom to everything that moves on the earth and in the sea.

> **101.9.** Do not the sailors of the ships fear the sea? Yet sinners fear not the Most High.

> **102.1.** In those days when He hath brought a grievous fire upon you, Whither will ye flee, and where will ye find deliverance? And when He launches forth His Word against you Will you not be affrighted and fear?

The sea demands respect, and experienced sailors readily grant it, fully aware of their vulnerability to the elements. Enoch teaches us to revere the Lord as sailors revere the sea, for we are just as much in the Lord's hands as a ship is in the ocean. Whether we are tossed among mountainous waves or transported to the farthest reaches of heaven, we are never beyond God's reach.

Those who remember God at all times and in all places lead lives that are markedly different from those who do not. Those who forget God quickly fall prey to the deceptions and shortsightedness inherent in human nature. The spiritually blind navigate the cosmic sea like pirates, believing their secret deeds go unnoticed. They fail to realize that the very elements will bear witness against them.

Enoch now broadens his warning to the entire multiverse:

102.2. And all the luminaries shall be affrighted with great fear, and all the earth shall be affrighted and tremble and be alarmed.

102.3. And all the †angels shall execute their commands† And shall seek to hide themselves from the presence of the Great Glory, and the children of earth shall tremble and quake; and ye sinners shall be cursed forever, and ye shall have no peace.

These passages describe the last great war in heaven, when the inhabitants of the stars, in their foolish arrogance, seek to overthrow God's chosen people—the House of Israel. On that day, the cosmic forces of evil will unleash the most advanced technology in the mortal multiverse against the Lord's chosen. The numbers of opposing forces will be beyond measure; by all calculations, they should prevail. Yet they will not, for God is the most powerful force in the multiverse. At His command, their worlds will cease to exist, dissolved in a grievous fire.

While the host of heaven will heed Satan's council, they will ultimately fail. The elements are not as feckless as God's other creations; they will not rise up against Him. Although there may be technology capable of shaking the heavens, nothing can threaten the might and power of God the Father or His Almighty Son. Therefore, in this final day, Satan and his minions will flee in fear before Him, their plans in ruins. As a consequence of their rebellion, they will be cast into outer darkness forever, beyond the burning mountain ranges at the end of all things.

Enoch now speaks to the righteous and to those who have turned to righteousness while waiting in the spiritual confines of Sheol (the spirit world). Consider his words:

102.4. Fear ye not, ye souls of the righteous, and be hopeful ye that have died in righteousness.

102.5. And grieve not if your soul into Sheol has descended in grief, and that in your life your body fared not according to your goodness, but wait for the day of the judgement of sinners and for the day of cursing and chastisement.

102.6. And yet when ye die the sinners speak over you: "As we die, so die the righteous, and what benefit do they reap for their deeds?

102.7. Behold, even as we, so do they die in grief and darkness, and what have they more than we? From henceforth we are equal.

102.8. And what will they receive and what will they see forever? Behold, they too have died, and henceforth forever shall they see no light."

In this mortal life, it often appears that the wicked prosper while many of the Lord's most humble and devout followers endure their days in sorrow. Indeed, the members of the Whore of Babylon are often described as living life indulgently. They justify their actions by claiming to live fully on their own terms, believing that the grave alone makes all men equal. However, this premise is fundamentally flawed.

In death, both the righteous and the wicked enter Sheol, the waiting place for the dead. Yet, Sheol is a continuum, much like the eternities themselves, with paradise and hell at its extremes. Most will likely find themselves somewhere in between. If this were not the case, faith would not be necessary to accept the gospel in the Spirit World, but we know it is. Even in death, the blind will preach to the blind.

However, the day will come when the scales will fall from the eyes of all men. On that day, every inhabitant of the multiverse—whether created in the image of God or otherwise—will clearly distinguish between those who serve God and those who do not. The difference will be as striking as that between the light of the sun and the stars.

102.9. I tell you, ye sinners, ye are content to eat and drink, and rob and sin, and strip men naked, and acquire wealth and see good days.

102.10. Have ye seen the righteous how their end turns out, that no manner of violence is found in them till their death?

102.11. "Nevertheless they perished and became as though they had not been, and their spirits descended into Sheol in tribulation."

103.1. Now, therefore, I swear to you, the righteous, by the glory of the Great and Honored and the Mighty One in dominion, and by His greatness I swear to you:

103.2. I know a mystery and have read the heavenly tablets, and have seen the holy books, and have found written therein and inscribed regarding them:

103.3. That all goodness and joy and glory are prepared for them, and written down for the spirits of those who have died in righteousness, and that manifold good shall be given to you in recompense for your labors, and that your lot is abundantly beyond the lot of the living.

103.4. And the spirits of you who have died in righteousness shall live and rejoice, and their spirits shall not perish, nor their memorial from before the face of the Great One unto all the generations of the world: wherefore no longer fear their contumely [*vilification*].

Enoch swore by the God of the Multiverse that the righteous have no need to fear. While some may endure terrible acts of violence, such suffering is but for a moment. The trials of the righteous are bound to mortality, which passes like a fleeting dream. Thus, all sorrow and hardship on this Earth are transitory, destined to fade as if they had never occurred.

In the name of the Almighty, Enoch declared that all negative effects of mortality will ultimately come to an end. Indeed, even the weakest among the saints will one day be transformed into beings of glory and strength beyond reckoning. Conversely, the fleeting pleasures of the wicked will also vanish, just like the pomp of Babylon. What remains for them is the horror and regret of a squandered mortal existence. For such individuals, death is merely the beginning of their sorrows.

103.5. Woe to you, ye sinners, when ye have died, if ye die in the wealth of your sins, and those who are like you say regarding you: 'Blessed are the sinners: they have seen all their days.

103.6. And how they have died in prosperity and in wealth, and have not seen tribulation or murder in their life; and they have died in honor, and judgement has not been executed on them during their life."

103.7. Know ye, that their souls will be made to descend into Sheol and they shall be wretched in their great tribulation.

103.8. And into darkness and chains and a burning flame where there is grievous judgement shall your spirits enter; and the great judgement shall be for all the generations of the world. Woe to you, for ye shall have no peace.

For those who have squandered their mortal experiences, there will be weeping, wailing, and gnashing of teeth. Yet, the Lord is merciful. This pain and suffering are not intended as punishment, but rather as agents of transformative change. The days will come when these transformations will be complete. When that day arrives, they will be gathered as jewels, shining like the stars above.

103.9. Say not in regard to the righteous and good who are in life: "In our troubled days we have toiled laboriously and experienced every trouble, and met with much evil and been consumed, and have become few and our spirit small.

103.10. And we have been destroyed and have not found any to help us even with a word: We have been tortured [and destroyed], and not hoped to see life from day to day.

103.11. We hoped to be the head and have become the tail: We have toiled laboriously and had no satisfaction in our toil; and we have become the food of the sinners and the unrighteous, and they have laid their yoke heavily upon us.

103.12. They have had dominion over us that hated us †and smote us; and to those that hated us† we have bowed our necks but they pitied us not.

103.13. We desired to get away from them that we might escape and be at rest, but found no place whereunto we should flee and be safe from them.

103.14. And are complained to the rulers in our tribulation, and cried out against those who devoured us, but they did not attend to our cries and would not hearken to our voice.

103.15. And they helped those who robbed us and devoured us and those who made us few; and they concealed their oppression, and they did not remove from us the yoke of those that devoured us and dispersed us and murdered us, and they concealed their murder, and remembered not that they had lifted up their hands against us.

104.1. I swear unto you, that in heaven the angels remember you for good before the glory of the Great One: and your names are written before the glory of the Great One.

104.2. Be hopeful; for aforetime ye were put to shame through ill and affliction; but now ye shall shine as the lights of heaven, ye shall shine and ye shall be seen, and the portals of heaven shall be opened to you.

104.3. And in your cry, cry for judgement, and it shall appear to you; for all your tribulation shall be visited on the rulers, and on all who helped those who plundered you.

104.4. Be hopeful, and cast not away your hopes for ye shall have great joy as the angels of heaven.

Enoch's counsel is for all the innocent who will be persecuted throughout every age of the Earth, but it is particularly meant for those who will live in the last days. He stated as much in **1.1** of his writings. In these final days, the righteous will be driven, persecuted, and overcome. Many will give their lives for their testimonies in Jesus Christ, and their suffering in His name will become a badge of honor they will wear for eternity.

Yet, despite the coming trials, as surely as there is a God in heaven, a bright and glorious dawn is approaching. Our kingdoms are not of this world; let the wicked have their power, gold, fame, and honor. They may glory in it, but it will not last—it will wilt like a cut flower. The reward of the righteous, however, will be everlasting, spanning from all eternity to all eternity. When the kingdom of the Gentiles comes to an end, the eternal kingdom of the saints will be ushered in.

To those who will inherit the Earth, the portals of heaven will be opened. They alone will be able to traverse the entirety of the multiverse unimpeded, while all others will face varying degrees of eternal damnation. The righteous will experience joy beyond reckoning, while the wicked will weep, wail, and gnash their teeth. In that last and great day, when the God of the Multiverse raises up His jewels, those who subjugated, oppressed, and abused them will be as dross and ash beneath their feet.

All things will be open to the righteous, while all things will be shut before the wicked. The righteous will know true and everlasting freedom, while the wicked will know only damnation, confined to the haunts of lesser souls. Therefore, hold fast to your hope in that great and coming day, and let that hope carry you through the dark horrors of the falling night. The Father's Hidden Son is coming!

Enoch continues speaking to the downtrodden and oppressed:

> **104.5.** What shall ye be obliged to do? Ye shall not have to hide on the day of the great judgement and ye shall not be found as sinners, and the eternal judgement shall be far from you for all the generations of the world.

> **104.6.** And now fear not, ye righteous, when ye see the sinners growing strong and prospering in their ways: be not companions with them, but keep afar from their violence; for ye shall become companions of the hosts of heaven.

Those who bear the evils, shame, and scorn of sinners will soon be counted worthy to rise as companions and peers of the gods, the hosts of heaven. Such alone receive a full and exceedingly great weight of glory. For God is just in all things, and as He has promised, so He will deliver. While the wicked will be cut off, both root and branch, the righteous will increase and multiply. Their posterity will fill the worlds of the multiverse, and they will rejoice in their descendants forevermore.

Unto the rising generation of gods, the experiences of sorrow, darkness, and oppression that they received throughout the fallen worlds of this multiverse will become treasures unto them. Such experiences could be obtained in no other way, and will work for their good in the coming days. Such experiences will empower their future children in ways that would not be have been possible in any other way.

Therefore, cast not away your confidence. Have hope that the end will justify the means, and that all things will eventually work together for your good. The harrowing experiences of today will bring unfathomable blessings to your posterity - throughout all generations of time and throughout all eternity. As such, do not allow yourself to become embittered by this life's bitter cup. Though you may wish to have it pass from your hands, it shall work for your good, just as it did for the Son of Man.

The Lord will give us beauty for our ashes, hope and joy for our despair. On the other hand, our enemies would rather have millstones chained to their necks and be cast into the crushing depths of the sea, than to be confronted with the consequences of their own spiritual blindness and debauchery. It is unto such that Enoch now speaks:

104.7. And, although ye sinners say: "All our sins shall not be searched out and be written down," nevertheless they shall write down all your sins every day.

104.8. And now I show unto you that light and darkness, day and night, see all your sins.

104.9. Be not godless in your hearts, and lie not and alter not the words of uprightness, nor charge with lying the words of the Holy Great One, nor take account of your idols; for all your lying and all your godlessness issue not in righteousness but in great sin.

104.10. And now I know this mystery, that sinners will alter and pervert the words of righteousness in many ways, and will speak wicked words, and lie, and practice great deceits, and write books concerning their words.

Enoch saw deep into the future, and understood that in the last days the wicked would understand dark sayings. They would have amongst them books of darkness, books of sorceries, and magic. Yet, these books contain the worthless mysteries of the Watchers. While such things will seem great and mighty in contrast to the mundane world we have been led to believe in, they will be sorry and mournful substitutes for the inheritance that God has in store for those that love Him. As such, resist the allure of such things.

However, the wicked will not be the only ones in the last days to obtain the hidden knowledge of the ancient world. I nearly fell out of my chair when I read Enoch's next prophecy concerning his own record. Consider the following:

104.11. But when they [*the men of the last days*] write down truthfully all my words in their languages, and do not change or minish ought from my words but write them all down truthfully--all that I first testified concerning them.

104.12. Then, I know another mystery, that books will be given to the righteous and the wise to become a cause of joy and uprightness and much wisdom.

Incredibly, Enoch foresaw that his writings would be lost to the world for a time, but in the last days, people would work diligently to create faithful translations of his words. The first of these translations was made by Richard Laurence in 1821, sparking a flurry of additional translations into other languages, as discussed in Volume I of this series.

Furthermore, Enoch foresaw that after this, other books would be given to the righteous, and these additional books would supplement and enhance his own. A similar prophecy is included in the Pearl of Great Price. Consider the following:

> And the day shall come that the earth shall rest, but before that day the heavens shall be darkened, and a veil of darkness shall cover the earth; and the heavens shall shake, and also the earth; and great tribulations shall be among the children of men, but my people will I preserve; and righteousness will I send down out of heaven; and truth will I send forth out of the earth, to bear testimony of mine Only Begotten; His resurrection from the dead; yea, and also the resurrection of all men; and righteousness and truth will I cause to sweep the earth as with a flood, to gather out mine elect from the four quarters of the earth, unto a place which I shall prepare, an Holy City, that my people may gird up their loins, and be looking forth for the time of my coming; for there shall be my tabernacle, and it shall be called Zion, a New Jerusalem. (Moses 7:61-62)

The Father promised Enoch that He would bring forth truth from the Earth in the last days, a truth that would sweep across the entire globe. This does not imply that all inhabitants of the Earth would recognize and embrace the truths found in these supplemental books; rather, they are referenced because they are essential for understanding Enoch's writings. Indeed, I believe it would be nearly impossible for the world to grasp the true meaning of Enoch's writings without the insights provided by the writings of the Restoration.

Consider what Enoch states next:

> **104.13.** And to them [*the righteous*] shall the books be given, and they shall believe in them and rejoice over them, and then shall all the righteous who have learnt therefrom all the paths of uprightness be recompensed.'

Enoch specifically states that a subset of the righteous would hold together the books of the Restoration and the Book of Enoch itself. Those who do will not only believe in these texts but also rejoice in them. Enoch prophesied that this subset of the Saints would be rewarded with knowledge and guided on the true path they should follow. I believe Enoch is directly referring to the readers of this book. While I understand this may seem audacious, who else could it apply to? What other group on the planet accepts both the scriptures of the Restoration and the Book of Enoch? I know of none. This makes it an exceedingly hopeful prophecy, as it suggests that Enoch is speaking about you specifically. Enoch continues by elaborating on what this recompense will entail, and it is truly incredible! Consider the following:

> **105.1.** In those days the Lord bade them [*meaning those that understand Enoch's writings in conjunction with the scriptures of the restoration*] to summon and testify to the children of Earth concerning their wisdom: Show it unto them; for ye are their guides, and a recompense over the whole earth.

In this passage, the Lord commands those He has instructed in these matters to teach them to the entire world. The days are approaching when the blind will be desperate to make sense of the changing world around them. Due to the hidden nature of these truths, most will have no idea where to turn for understanding. Without such knowledge, even the very elect are at tremendous risk of being deceived.

The coming days will be the most perilous in history, as events will unfold not gradually, as in the past, but at breakneck speed. When the secret combinations spring their trap, it will begin. Soon, the Antichrist will uproot them and destroy the Whore of Babylon. In doing so, he will overwhelm the princes of the covenant and simultaneously overcome the saints of God. Without their shepherds to guide them, the Lord's sheep will be left to rely solely on their ability to listen to their Master's voice.

The sobering reality that most of the Father's sheep have little awareness of these impending events is a terrifying indication of the world's general ability to act upon the promptings of the Spirit. Without their official shepherds, many will be at great risk. This is why the Lord has made these truths known to all who seek to be taught. This is the meaning of the following passage:

> And such as do wickedly against the covenant shall [*the antichrist*] corrupt by flatteries: but the people that do know their God shall be strong, and do *exploits*. And they that understand among the people shall instruct many: yet [*the people of the world*] shall fall by the sword, and by flame, by captivity, and by spoil, *many* days. Now when they shall fall, they shall be holpen with a little help: but many shall cleave to them with flatteries.

> And *some* of them of understanding shall fall, to try them, and to purge, and to make *them* white, *even* to the time of the end: because *it is* yet for a time appointed. And they that be

376

wise shall shine as the brightness of the firmament; and they
that turn many to righteousness as the stars for ever and ever.
But thou, O Daniel, shut up the words, and seal the book,
even to the time of the end: many shall run to and fro, and
knowledge shall be increased. (Dan 11:32-35; 12:3-4)

Daniel speaks of the events that are now at our doors. Those who understand Enoch's words in conjunction with the books of the Restoration will be called to teach the world—not in an official capacity, but as a labor of love. These people of understanding will teach the Father's sheep, and they will hear them. The testimonies of the righteous will help many retain their faith in the Son of Man, whereas they might otherwise have been deceived.

The true meaning of Daniel's vision was sealed until the last days, when knowledge would be increased upon the Earth. What would cause knowledge to increase? The coming forth of the Book of Enoch and the other books of the Restoration. Who are these people of understanding upon whom the Lord will depend to minister to His flocks in the last and great day? These are those who ascended Mount Sinai when all the other sheep fled to the far valley as the mountain began to shake and tremble. They accepted the Father's invitation, while others were content to outsource their understanding.

I have ascended Mount Horeb. I have taken the Father at His word, and He has fulfilled His promises. While I have not seen the burning bush, I have felt it in my heart and could no more deny these experiences than I could stop breathing. The instruction of the Lord has become like fire in my bones. Though the world at large has been unwilling to do what I have done, many others have. These too have had their eyes opened by the Lord. I do not believe you would be reading this book now had you not embarked upon a similar journey. Surely, you must know that it is not happenstance that your eyes have been opened. The time is soon coming, and is not far off, when you will be called to witness for the Lord in the face of the greatest deceptions the world has ever known.

As you consider these things in your heart, reflect on the promises of the Father and His Hidden Son to all those who find and teach these truths to the lost sheep of Israel:

> **105.2.** For I and My son will be united with them forever in
> the paths of uprightness in their lives; and ye shall have
> peace: rejoice, ye children of uprightness. Amen!

In this passage, God the Father speaks specifically to those who have received Enoch's words along with the other books of the Restoration and have based their lives upon them. To such individuals, God promises that they will enter His presence and never go out again. Why? Because, despite all the temptations and lies the adversary places in their path, these are the ones who truly know the Father and the Son. Flesh and blood did not reveal this knowledge to them, but the Spirit of the Almighty Father. They have paid the price to obtain true knowledge—not the worthless mysteries of the world, but the true nature of the Father's Hidden Son. Dear reader, let me be perfectly clear: the Father is speaking about you!

The world will not receive these truths; they are too much for them. Even the mere hint of such things is overwhelming for most. Truly, these are hard sayings, which can only be understood by those seeking to comprehend them in the light in which they were given. From the beginning of the Earth, it has always been so. This is my seventh book, and I expect that it will not be long after its publication before the chaos foretold within its pages begins to unfold at an ever-increasing pace. Know that this chaos arises from the wickedness of mankind and is a direct result of belief in the twisted, demonic doctrines of the father of Lies. He is a master deceiver. Hold fast to what you know to be true.

Nephi, who saw these things as clearly as day, was forbidden to write about them. Yet he also knew that the Lord would instruct the righteous, and as a result, the righteous need not fear the coming day. I do not doubt Nephi's words, and I understand why the Lord hid these truths from the world. The Lord will test the faith of His people, and the Earth's greatest trial will unfold in the coming days. Those who listen to God's counsel will come to know everything that Nephi knew, for God is no respecter of persons. We may not be transported to some glorious high mountain peak by the power of the Spirit, nor do we need to be, for the still, small workings of the Spirit produce the same result.

The righteous who have sought the Father's Hidden Son have become the salt of the Earth. You are the salt of the Earth. As such, you must prepare to share the wisdom that the Lord has imparted to you with others. The writings of Enoch can only be fully understood in conjunction with the restored gospel of Jesus Christ. Therefore, no other people on Earth can understand Enoch's writings like the Saints of God. It is a travesty that so few have made a study of them. However, it takes very little salt to savor the world. Therefore, dear reader, it now falls to you to take these truths to the world.

The time is not yet, but it will soon be upon us. You will know with absolute certainty when it arrives—just as the wise men of old knew. For in that day, men and women will be running to and fro, frantically seeking to hear the word of God and reconcile their faith with the collapsing Newtonian world around them. Of all the things you have known in your life, the arrival of this great and terrible day will be the clearest.

God has given you a box for the strange work He is about to perform. You must now give others the same box. In the coming days, the Lord will magnify your gifts, open your mouth, and you will be able to speak with great power and authority. For God will pour out upon His Saints and upon the covenant people tremendous power from on high. With this power, you will perform great exploits. Through such incredible power, the hungry will be fed, the naked will be clothed, the wicked will be scattered, the dead will rise, the lame will walk, the sick will be healed, the elements will be rearranged, and places and peoples will descend from the heavens. While you will witness the most terrible events the world has ever seen, you will also witness the most incredible miracles God has ever performed.

As such, do not fear these days. God has not called you forth and given you this knowledge for you to fear the coming day, but so that you might receive it in the strength of His Hidden Son. When evil is poured out upon the Earth without measure, the Father will be with us in amazing ways. The veil will be thin, and we will receive divine aid. God the Father will go before us and behind us; He will be on our right side and on our left. Through His astonishing power, the vast majority of the righteous will be preserved, while 100% of the wicked will be swept from the face of the Earth. This is the heritage and destiny of the servants of the Lord, and the greater blessing that shall be poured out upon Ephraim and his fellows.

Chapter 26 - Launchpads

In the previous chapter, Enoch prophesied of the restoration of his writings in the last days. He also foretold that his writings would be accompanied by other books, which would reveal the mysteries of God to those who seek them. Enoch stated that the righteous would rejoice at the receipt of such things. Enoch then said that such would be called upon to testify of these things to the world. Knowledge of these things will make the difference between abandoning faith in the Son of God, and enduring to the end. The Father concluded by promising that His faithful servants would have a place by His side forever.

In this chapter, Enoch shares his final words to the righteous that will live through the Great and Terrible Day of the Lord. His words hold profound significance for those who will be called to share them with the world in the days to come. You should consider them in this light:

> **108.1.** Another book which Enoch wrote for his son Methuselah and for those who will come after him, and keep the law in the last days.

> **108.2.** Ye who have done good shall wait for those days till an end is made of those who work evil; and an end of the might of the transgressors.

> **108.3.** And wait ye indeed till sin has passed away, for their names shall be blotted out of the book of life and out of the holy books, and their seed shall be destroyed forever, and their spirits shall be slain, and they shall cry and make lamentation in a place that is a chaotic wilderness, and in the fire shall they burn; for there is no earth there.

In the passages above, Enoch speaks of the sons of perdition, who will be eternally cut off from the glory of God. They will be cast into outer darkness, beyond the burning mountain ranges at the edge of the created multiverse. There, they will exist in a hellish void of empty space, as the faithful elements will not be confined to a kingdom devoid of glory. Of all creation, only the sons of perdition will never know redemption.

As Enoch contemplates outer darkness and the fate of the unfortunate souls destined for it, he perceives something else. Consider the following:

108.4. And I saw there something like an invisible cloud; for by reason of its depth I could not look over, and I saw a flame of fire blazing brightly, and things like shining mountains circling and sweeping to and fro.

108.5. And I asked one of the holy angels who was with me and said unto him: 'What is this shining thing? for it is not a heaven but only the flame of a blazing fire, and the voice of weeping and crying and lamentation and strong pain.'

108.6. And he said unto me: 'This place which thou seest-- here are cast the spirits of sinners and blasphemers, and of those who work wickedness, and of those who pervert everything that the Lord hath spoken through the mouth of the prophets--even the things that shall be.

It seems that Enoch's perspective has shifted. Whereas he once viewed outer darkness up close, he now observes it from a greater distance. From afar, he sees cloud-like masses swirling and burning with chaotic fire. At first, he believes he is witnessing solid objects, like asteroids. However, upon closer inspection, to his horror, he discerns that these are not solid; rather, they are swarming hives of the spirits of the damned themselves. Just as gravitational forces consolidate matter, these wicked souls have congregated into hateful swarms of anger and rage. There is no solid matter upon which they can rest.

On Earth, Satan once reveled in the greatness and glory of its kingdoms. He offered these kingdoms to those who would follow him, along with power and wealth. In reality, he had nothing to offer, for none of it was his. Now, he and his kind have been cast out from the organized multiverse itself, into the great void beyond. There, they are alone, with naught but the souls of the damned for company—swirling storm clouds of negative energy. It is a mournful fate and a terrible, depressing sight to behold.

Enoch's vision now shifts to the kingdoms of glory. It is important to note that these outcomes depend entirely on the agency of the children of heaven:

108.7. For some of them [*prophecies regarding the fates of the children of heaven*] are written and inscribed above in the heaven, in order that the angels may read them and know that which shall befall the sinners, and the spirits of the humble, and of those who have afflicted their bodies, and been recompensed by God; and of those who have been put to shame by wicked men:

108.8. Who love God and loved neither gold nor silver nor any of the good things which are in the world, but gave over their bodies to torture.

108.9. Who, since they came into being, longed not after earthly food, but regarded everything as a passing breath, and lived accordingly, and the Lord tried them much, and their spirits were found pure so that they should bless His name.

108.10. And all the blessings destined for them I have recounted in the books. And he hath assigned them their recompense, because they have been found to be such as loved heaven more than their life in the world, and though they were trodden under foot of wicked men, and experienced abuse and reviling from them and were put to shame, yet they blessed Me.

The Father caused descriptions of the various kingdoms to be recorded and displayed in heaven so that they might be considered by all. The contrasts among the kingdoms are evident in the attitudes of their occupants. Those who place the kingdom of heaven first and foremost obtain the greatest inheritance the heavens have to offer, while those who care for nothing but themselves are quarantined to quarters of the multiverse where they can do no harm but to themselves. Enoch's writings are filled with such descriptions.

From Enoch's writings, we know that there will be those whose countenances shine like lightning, brighter than the sun. Others will reflect the sun's light, like the moon. Still others will be lights unto themselves, having atoned for their own sins. These will shine like the stars, one star differing from another in glory. Yet all of these will reside in kingdoms of glory, and they will all bless the Lord and seek to honor and serve Him. Only those in the chaotic void of outer darkness will be worse off than if they had never chosen to participate in the Father's plan of salvation to begin with.

Enoch highlights that those who attain the highest heights of the Celestial Kingdom are those who sought it during their mortal probation, in spite of the veil. Such individuals esteem the things of God above all the transitory treasures that Satan's prison planet has to offer. It should not be lost on the reader that in the passages above, Enoch writes in the first person on behalf of God the Father. Therefore, when God speaks of those who will be persecuted in the last days because they bless Him, Enoch is letting us know that God is personally aware of everything transpiring on this Earth. Nothing escapes His notice. He will remember all those who blessed Him, as Job did, despite their temporary trials and tribulations. Therefore, let us be faithful as Job was faithful, and the Father will magnify us as He magnified Job.

Indeed, the magnification of the righteous is what the Father speaks of next. Consider what He says:

> **108.11.** And now I will summon the spirits of the good who belong to the generation of light, and I will transform those who were born in darkness, who in the flesh were not recompensed with such honor as their faithfulness deserved.

> **108.12.** And I will bring forth in shining light those who have loved My holy name, and I will seat each on the throne of his honor.

> **108.13.** And they shall be resplendent for times without number; for righteousness is the judgement of God; for to the faithful He will give faithfulness in the habitation of upright paths.

In the passages above, the Father clearly states through the words of Enoch that He will reward the righteous with eternal thrones of honor. By this, we understand that the glory of the fathers shall become our own. The righteous become joint heirs in salvation with the Father's Hidden Son, who now sits on His Father's throne while the Father ascends to the Mount of the Congregation. In this brief vision, we see the stark contrast between those who love the Lord and the swarming masses in outer darkness who hate Him. The incomprehensible joy of the magnified righteous stands in sharp contrast to the hellish void of outer darkness, where the glory of God is completely absent.

In this last and great day, all the inhabitants of the multiverse will know, see, and comprehend each other for who they truly are. Nothing will be hidden—so states the Father in the concluding two passages of Enoch's writings:

> **108.14.** And they shall see those who were, born in darkness led into darkness, while the righteous shall be resplendent.

> **108.15.** And the sinners shall cry aloud and see them resplendent, and they indeed will go where days and seasons are prescribed for them.'

The final passages included in this book's analysis of Enoch's writings pertain to the agency of man. We are in control of our destiny; we can choose the Lord or choose darkness. Satan, the great deceiver, has tried to blur the lines between light and dark, between sin and sanctification. Yet, the distinction between the path of darkness and that of glory is as clear as ever. One path leads to light and salvation, while the other leads to darkness and despair. Do not be deceived by Satan and his omnipresent counterfeits. Such things are only difficult to discern if you rely on the logic and reason of men. If you depend on the light and wisdom of God, the way of life and salvation is as clear as it has ever been.

This brings us to the conclusion of this three-part series on Enoch's writings. The understanding I have shared in this book is only possible because of the restored light and knowledge of the gospel of Jesus Christ. There is so much more to Christ's teachings than meets the eye. Those of you who have joined me on this journey have done so because you receive Enoch's testimony with gladness and joy. His words resonate with you because the Spirit has moved upon you as it has upon all those with eyes to see and hearts to feel.

Thus, we see that the gospel of Jesus Christ is far more than words on a page. I liken the gospel of Jesus Christ to a launchpad. Baptism into the kingdom is not the end, but the beginning. Baptism opens the gate to a path, and the path leads to a launchpad. Many who enter by the gate walk the path to their respective launchpad sites and find themselves perplexed. In their confusion, many saints suppose that the launchpad is their intended destination. As a result, these saints rejoice in the launchpad itself. They clean and scrub their launchpads, paint and decorate them with potted plants and hanging lights, and host BBQs and parties, celebrating that they have entered by the gate. Sadly, this is the extent of their utilization of their respective launchpads.

However, while most are decorating their launchpads with the latest rugs and designer patio furniture, others engage with their launchpads as the Lord intended. Like Nephi of old, these individuals begin working with the Lord to construct ships in a collaborative process. These ships are not built after the manner of men, but after the manner of the Lord. For them, the gospel is more than glad tidings; it is the most powerful propellant in the multiverse. They use the gospel's fuel and the launchpads they have received to propel themselves into the cosmos on epic voyages of discovery and becoming that most have never contemplated. It is the attitudes of these individuals that separate the inhabitants of the various kingdoms of glory.

> O then despise not, and wonder not, but hearken unto the words of the Lord, and ask the Father in the name of Jesus for what things soever ye shall stand in need. Doubt not, but be believing, and begin as in times of old, and come unto the Lord with all your heart, and work out your own salvation with fear and trembling before him. (Mormon 9:27)

The End

(OR IS IT THE BEGINNING – YOU CHOOSE!)

APPENDIX ONE – THE BOOK OF THE LUMINARIES

72.1. The book of the courses of the luminaries of the heaven, the relations of each, according to their classes, their dominion and their seasons, according to their names and places of origin, and according to their months, which Uriel, the holy angel, who was with me, who is their guide, showed me; and he showed me all their laws exactly as they are, and how it is with regard to all the years of the world and unto eternity, till the new creation is accomplished which dureth till eternity.

72.2. And this is the first law of the luminaries: the luminary the Sun has its rising in the eastern portals of the heaven, and its setting in the western portals of the heaven.

72.3. And I saw six portals in which the sun rises, and six portals in which the sun sets and the moon rises and sets in these portals, and the leaders of the stars and those whom they lead: six in the east and six in the west, and all following each other in accurately corresponding order: also many windows to the right and left of these portals.

72.4. And first there goes forth the great luminary, named the Sun, and his circumference is like the circumference of the heaven, and he is quite filled with illuminating and heating fire.

72.5. The chariot on which he ascends, the wind drives, and the sun goes down from the heaven and returns through the north in order to reach the east, and is so guided that he comes to the appropriate (lit. 'that') portal and shines in the face of the heaven.

72.6. In this way he rises in the first month in the great portal, which is the fourth [those six portals in the cast].

72.7. And in that fourth portal from which the sun rises in the first month are twelve window-openings, from which proceed a flame when they are opened in their season.

72.8. When the sun rises in the heaven, he comes forth through that fourth portal thirty mornings in succession, and sets accurately in the fourth portal in the west of the heaven.

72.9. And during this period the day becomes daily longer and the night nightly shorter to the thirtieth morning.

72.10. On that day the day is longer than the night by a ninth part, and the day amounts exactly to ten parts and the night to eight parts.

72.11. And the sun rises from that fourth portal, and sets in the fourth and returns to the fifth portal of the east thirty mornings, and rises from it and sets in the fifth portal.

72.12. And then the day becomes longer by †two† parts and amounts to eleven parts, and the night becomes shorter and amounts to seven parts.

72.13. And it returns to the east and enters into the sixth portal, and rises and sets in the sixth portal one-and-thirty mornings on account of its sign.

72.14. On that day the day becomes longer than the night, and the day becomes double the night, and the day becomes twelve parts, and the night is shortened and becomes six parts.

72.15. And the sun mounts up to make the day shorter and the night longer, and the sun returns to the east and enters into the sixth portal, and rises from it and sets thirty mornings.

72.16. And when thirty mornings are accomplished, the day decreases by exactly one part, and becomes eleven parts, and the night seven.

72.17. And the sun goes forth from that sixth portal in the west, and goes to the east and rises in the fifth portal for thirty mornings, and sets in the west again in the fifth western portal.

72.18. On that day the day decreases by †two† parts, and amounts to ten parts and the night to eight parts.

72.19. And the sun goes forth from that fifth portal and sets in the fifth portal of the west, and rises in the fourth portal for one-and-thirty mornings on account of its sign, and sets in the west.

72.20. On that day the day is equalized with the night, [and becomes of equal length], and the night amounts to nine parts and the day to nine parts.

72.21. And the sun rises from that portal and sets in the west, and returns to the east and rises thirty mornings in the third portal and sets in the west in the third portal.

72.22. And on that day the night becomes longer than the day, and night becomes longer than night, and day shorter than day till the thirtieth morning, and the night amounts exactly to ten parts and the day to eight parts.

72.23. And the sun rises from that third portal and sets in the third portal in the west and returns to the east, and for thirty mornings rises in the second portal in the east, and in like manner sets in the second portal in the west of the heaven.

72.24. And on that day the night amounts to eleven parts and the day to seven parts.

72.25. And the sun rises on that day from that second portal and sets in the west in the second portal, and returns to the east into the first portal for one-and-thirty mornings, and sets in the first portal in the west of the heaven.

72.26. And on that day the night becomes longer and amounts to the double of the day: and the night amounts exactly to twelve parts and the day to six.

72.27. And the sun has (therewith) traversed the divisions of his orbit and turns again on those divisions of his orbit, and enters that portal thirty mornings and sets also in the west opposite to it.

72.28. And on that night has the night decreased in length by a †ninth† part, and the night has become eleven parts and the day seven parts.

72.29. And the sun has returned and entered into the second portal in the east, and returns on those his divisions of his orbit for thirty mornings, rising and setting.

72.30. And on that day the night decreases in length, and the night amounts to ten parts and the day to eight.

72.31. And on that day the sun rises from that portal, and sets in the west, and returns to the east, and rises in the third portal for one-and-thirty mornings, and sets in the west of the heaven.

72.32. On that day the night decreases and amounts to nine parts, and the day to nine parts, and the night is equal to the day and the year is exactly as to its days three hundred and sixty-four.

72.33. And the length of the day and of the night, and the shortness of the day and of the night arise--through the course of the sun these distinctions are made (lit. 'they are separated').

72.34. So it comes that its course becomes daily longer, and its course nightly shorter.

72.35. And this is the law and the course of the sun, and his return as often as he returns sixty times and rises, *i.e.* the great luminary which is named the sun, for ever and ever.

72.36. And that which (thus) rises is the great luminary, and is so named according to its appearance, according as the Lord commanded.

72.37. As he rises, so he sets and decreases not, and rests not, but runs day and night, and his light is sevenfold brighter than that of the moon; but as regards size they are both equal.

73.1. And after this law I saw another law dealing with the smaller luminary, which is named the Moon.

73.2. And her circumference is like the circumference of the heaven, and her chariot in which she rides is driven by the wind, and light is given to her in (definite) measure.

73.3. And her rising and setting change every month: and her days are like the days of the sun, and when her light is uniform (*i.e.* full) it amounts to the seventh part of the light of the sun.

73.4. And thus she rises. And her first phase in the east comes forth on the thirtieth morning: and on that day she becomes visible, and constitutes for you the first phase of the moon on the thirtieth day together with the sun in the portal where the sun rises.

73.5. And the one half of her goes forth by a seventh part, and her whole circumference is empty, without light, with the exception of one-seventh part of it, (and) the fourteenth part of her light.

73.6. And when she receives one-seventh part of the half of her light, her light amounts to one-seventh part and the half thereof.

73.7. And she sets with the sun, and when the sun rises the moon rises with him and receives the half of one part of light, and in that night in the beginning of her morning [in the commencement of the lunar day] the moon sets with the sun, and is invisible that night with the fourteen parts and the half of one of them.

73.8. And she rises on that day with exactly a seventh part, and comes forth and recedes from the rising of the sun, and in her remaining days she becomes bright in the (remaining) thirteen parts.

74.1. And I saw another course, a law for her, (and) how according to that law she performs her monthly revolution.

74.2. And all these Uriel, the holy angel who is the leader of them all, showed to me, and their positions, and I wrote down their positions as he showed them to me, and I wrote down their months as they were, and the appearance of their lights till fifteen days were accomplished.

74.3. In single seventh parts she accomplishes all her light in the east, and in single seventh parts accomplishes all her darkness in the west.

74.4. And in certain months she alters her settings, and in certain months she pursues her own peculiar course.

74.5. In two months the moon sets with the sun: in those two middle portals the third and the fourth.

74.6. She goes forth for seven days, and turns about and returns again through the portal where the sun rises, and accomplishes all her light: and she recedes from the sun, and in eight days enters the sixth portal from which the sun goes forth.

74.7. And when the sun goes forth from the fourth portal she goes forth seven days, until she goes forth from the fifth and turns back again in seven days into the fourth portal and accomplishes all her light: and she recedes and enters into the first portal in eight days.

74.8. And she returns again in seven days into the fourth portal from which the sun goes forth.

74.9. Thus I saw their position--how the moons rose and the sun set in those days.

74.10. And if five years are added together the sun has an overplus of thirty days, and all the days which accrue to it for one of those five years, when they are full, amount to 364 days.

74.11. And the overplus of the sun and of the stars amounts to six days: in 5 years 6 days every year come to 30 days:

and the moon falls behind the sun and stars to the number of 30 days.

74.12. And **the sun** and the stars bring in all the years exactly, so that they do not advance or delay their position by a single day unto eternity; but **complete** the years with perfect justice in 364 days.

74.13. In 3 years there are 1092 days, and in 5 years 1820 days, so that in 8 years there are 2912 days.

74.14. For the moon alone the days amount in 3 years to 1062 days, and in 5 years she falls 50 days behind: [*i.e.* to the sum (of 1770) there is to be added (1000 and) 62 days.]

74.15. And in 5 years there are 1770 days, so that for the moon the days in 8 years amount to 2832 days.

74.16. [For in 8 years she falls behind to the amount of 80 days], all the days she falls behind in 8 years are 80.

74.17. And the year is accurately completed in conformity with their world-stations and the stations of the sun, which rise from the portals through which it (the sun) rises and sets 30 days.

75.1. And the leaders of the heads of the thousands, who are placed over the whole creation and over all the stars, have also to do with the four intercalary days, being inseparable from their office, according to the reckoning of the year, and these render service on the four days which are not reckoned in the reckoning of the year.

75.2. And owing to them men go wrong therein, for those luminaries truly render service on the world-stations, one in the first portal, one in the third portal of the heaven, one in the fourth portal, and one in the sixth portal, and the exactness of the year is accomplished through its separate three hundred and sixty-four stations.

75.3. For the signs and the times and the years and the days the angel Uriel showed to me, whom the Lord of glory hath set for ever over all the luminaries of the heaven, in the heaven and in the world, that they should rule on the face of the heaven and be seen on the earth, and be leaders for the day and the night, *i.e.* the sun, moon, and stars, and all the ministering creatures which make their revolution in all the chariots of the heaven.

75.4. In like manner twelve doors Uriel showed me, open in the circumference of the sun's chariot in the heaven, through which the rays of the sun break forth: and from them is warmth diffused over the earth, when they are opened at their appointed seasons.

75.5. [And for the winds and the spirit of the dew† when they are opened, standing open in the heavens at the ends.]

75.6. As for the twelve portals in the heaven, at the ends of the earth, out of which go forth the sun, moon, and stars, and all the works of heaven in the east and in the west.

75.7. There are many windows open to the left and right of them, and one window at its (appointed) season produces warmth, corresponding (as these do) to those doors from which the stars come forth according as He has commanded them, and wherein they set corresponding to their number.

75.8. And I saw chariots in the heaven, running in the world, above those portals in which revolve the stars that never set.

75.9. And one is larger than all the rest, and it is that that makes its course through the entire world.

76.1 And at the ends of the earth I saw twelve portals open to all the **quarters** of heaven, from which the winds go forth and blow over the earth.

76.2. Three of them are open on the face (*i.e.* the east) of the heavens, and three in the west, and three on the right (*i.e.* the south) of the heaven, and three on the left (*i.e.* the north).

76.3. And the three first are those of the east, and three are of †the north, and three [after those on the left] of the south†, and three of the west.

76.4. Through four of these come winds of blessing and prosperity, and from those eight come hurtful winds: when they are sent, they bring destruction on all the earth and on the water upon it, and on all who dwell thereon, and on everything which is in the water and on the land.

76.5. And the first wind from those portals, called the east wind, comes forth through the first portal which is in the east, inclining towards the south: from it come forth desolation, drought, heat, and destruction.

76.6. And through the second portal in the middle comes what is fitting, and from it there come rain and fruitfulness and prosperity and dew; and through the third portal which lies toward the north come cold and drought.

76.7. And after these come forth the south winds through three portals: through the first portal of them inclining to the east comes forth a hot wind.

76.8. And through the middle portal next to it there come forth fragrant smells, and dew and rain, and prosperity and health.

76.9. And through the third portal lying to the west come forth dew and rain, locusts and desolation.

76.10. And after these the north winds: from the seventh portal in the east come dew and rain, locusts and desolation.

76.11. And from the middle portal come in a direct direction health and rain and dew and prosperity; and through the third portal in the west come cloud and hoar-frost, and snow and rain, and dew and locusts.

76.12. And after these [four] are the west winds: through the first portal adjoining the north come forth dew and hoar-frost, and cold and snow and frost.

76.13 And from the middle portal come forth dew and rain, and prosperity and blessing; and through the last portal which adjoins the south come forth drought and desolation, and burning and destruction.

76.14. And the twelve portals of the four **quarters** of the heaven are therewith completed, and all their laws and all their plagues and all their benefactions have I shown to thee, my son Methuselah.

77.1. And the first **quarter** is called the east, because it is the first: and the second, the south, because the Most High **will descend** there, yea, there in quite a special sense will He who is blessed for ever **descend**.

77.2. And the west **quarter** is named the diminished, because there all the luminaries of the heaven wane and go down.

77.3. And the fourth **quarter**, named the north, is divided into three parts: the first of them is for the dwelling of men: and the second contains seas of water, and the abysses and forests and rivers, and darkness and clouds; and the third part contains the garden of righteousness.

77.4. I saw seven high mountains, higher than all the mountains which are on the earth: and thence comes forth hoar-frost, and days, seasons, and years pass away.

77.5. I saw seven rivers on the earth larger than all the rivers: one of them coming from the west pours its waters into the Great Sea.

77.6. And these two come from the north to the sea and pour their waters into the Erythraean Sea in the east.

77.7. And the remaining four come forth on the side of the north to their own sea, ⟨two of them⟩ to the Erythraean Sea, and two into the Great Sea and discharge themselves there [and some say: into the desert].

77.8. Seven great islands I saw in the sea and in the mainland: two in the mainland and five in the Great Sea.

78.1. And the names of the sun are the following: the first Orjârês, and the second Tômâs.

78.2. And the moon has four names: the first name is Asônjâ, the second Eblâ, the third Benâsê, and the fourth Erâe.

78.3. These are the two great luminaries: their circumference is like the circumference of the heaven, and the size of the circumference of both is alike.

78.4. In the circumference of the sun there are seven portions of light which are added to it more than to the moon, and in definite measures it is s transferred till the seventh portion of the sun is exhausted.

78.5. And they set and enter the portals of the west, and make their revolution by the north, and come forth through the eastern portals on the face of the heaven.

78.6. And when the moon rises one-fourteenth part appears in the heaven: [the light becomes full in her]: on the fourteenth day she accomplishes her light.

78.7. And fifteen parts of light are transferred to her till the fifteenth day (when) her light is accomplished, according to the sign of the year, and she becomes fifteen parts, and the moon grows by (the addition of) fourteenth parts.

78.8. And in her waning (the moon) decreases on the first day to fourteen parts of her light, on the second to thirteen parts of light, on the third to twelve, on the fourth to eleven, on the fifth to ten, on the sixth to nine, on the seventh to eight, on the eighth to seven, on the ninth to six, on the tenth to five, on the eleventh to four, on the twelfth to three, on the thirteenth to two, on the fourteenth to the half of a seventh, and all her remaining light disappears wholly on the fifteenth.

78.9. And in certain months the month has twenty-nine days and once twenty-eight.

78.10. And Uriel showed me another law: when light is transferred to the moon, and on which side it is transferred to her by the sun.

78.11. During all the period during which the moon is growing in her light, she is transferring it to herself when opposite to the sun during fourteen days [her light is accomplished in the heaven], and when she is illumined throughout, her light is accomplished full in the heaven.

78.12. And on the first day she is called the new moon, for on that day the light rises upon her.

78.13. She becomes full moon exactly on the day when the sun sets in the west, and from the east she rises at night, and the moon shines the whole night through till the sun rises over against her and the moon is seen over against the sun.

78.14. On the side whence the light of the moon comes forth, there again she wanes till all the light vanishes and all the days of the month are at an end, and her circumference is empty, void of light.

78.15. And three months she makes of thirty days, and at her time she makes three months of twenty-nine days each, in which she accomplishes her waning in the first period of time, and in the first portal for one hundred and seventy-seven days.

78.16. And in the time of her going out she appears for three months (of) thirty days each, and for three months she appears (of) twenty-nine each.

78.17. At night she appears like a man for twenty days each time, and by day she appears like the heaven, and there is nothing else in her save her light.

79.1. And now, my son, I have shown thee everything, and the law of all the stars of the heaven is completed.

79.2. And he showed me all the laws of these for every day, and for every season of bearing rule, and for every year, and for its going forth, and for the order prescribed to it every month and every week:

79.3. And the waning of the moon which takes place in the sixth portal: for in this sixth portal her light is accomplished, and after that there is the beginning of the waning:

79.4. ⟨And the waning⟩ which takes place in the first portal in its season, till one hundred and seventy-seven days are accomplished: reckoned according to weeks, twenty-five (weeks) and two days.

79.5. She falls behind the sun and the order of the stars exactly five days in the course of one period, and when this place which thou seest has been traversed. **79.6.** Such is the picture and sketch of every luminary which Uriel the archangel, who is their leader, showed unto me.

80.1. And in those days the angel Uriel answered and said to me: 'Behold, I have shown thee everything, Enoch, and I have revealed everything to thee that thou shouldst see this sun and this moon, and the leaders of the stars of the heaven and all those who turn them, their tasks and times and departures.

80.2. And in the days of the sinners the years shall be shortened, And their seed shall be tardy on their lands and fields, and all things on the earth shall alter, And shall not appear in their time: And the rain shall be kept back And the heaven shall withhold (it).

80.3. And in those times the fruits of the earth shall be backward, And shall not grow in their time, And the fruits of the trees shall be withheld in their time.

80.4. And the moon shall alter her order, And not appear at her time.

80.5. [And in those days the **sun** shall be seen and he shall journey in the **evening** †on the extremity of the great chariot† in the west] And shall shine more brightly than accords with the order of light.

80.6. And many chiefs of the stars shall transgress the order (prescribed). And these shall alter their orbits and tasks, and not appear at the seasons prescribed to them.

80.7. And the whole order of the stars shall be concealed from the sinners, And the thoughts of those on the earth shall err concerning them, [And they shall be altered from all their ways], Yea, they shall err and take them to be gods.

80.8. And evil shall be multiplied upon them, And punishment shall come upon them So as to destroy all.'

81.1. And he said unto me: 'Observe, Enoch, these heavenly tablets, And read what is written thereon, And mark every individual fact.'

81.2 And I observed the heavenly tablets, and read everything which was written (thereon) and understood everything, and read the book of all the deeds of mankind, and of all the children of flesh that shall be upon the earth to the remotest generations.

81.3. And forthwith I blessed the great Lord the King of glory for ever, in that He has made all the works of the world, And I extolled the Lord because of His patience, And blessed Him because of the children of men.

81.4. And after that I said: 'Blessed is the man who dies in righteousness and goodness, concerning whom there is no book of unrighteousness written, And against whom no day of judgement shall be found.'

81.5. And those seven holy ones brought me and placed me on the earth before the door of my house, and said to me: 'Declare everything to thy son Methuselah, and show to all thy children that no flesh is righteous in the sight of the Lord, for He is their Creator.

81.6. One year we will leave thee with thy son, till thou givest thy (last) commands, that thou mayest teach thy children and record (it) for them, and testify to all thy children; and in the second year they shall take thee from their midst.

81.7. Let thy heart be strong, for the good shall announce righteousness to the good; the righteous with the righteous shall rejoice, and shall offer congratulation to one another.

81.8. But the sinners shall die with the sinners, and the apostate go down with the apostate.

81.9. And those who practice righteousness shall die on account of the deeds of men, and be taken away on account of the doings of the godless.'

81.10. And in those days they ceased to speak to me, and I came to my people, blessing the Lord of the world.

82.1. And now, my son Methuselah, all these things I am recounting to thee and writing down for thee, and I have revealed to thee everything, and given thee books concerning all these: so preserve, my son Methuselah, the books from thy father's hand, and (see) that thou deliver them to the generations of the world.

82.2. I have given Wisdom to thee and to thy children, [And thy children that shall be to thee], That they may give it to their children for generations, This wisdom (namely) that passeth their thought.

82.3. And those who understand it shall not sleep, But shall listen with the ear that they may learn this wisdom, And it shall please those that eat thereof better than good food.

82.4. Blessed are all the righteous, blessed are all those who walk in the way of righteousness and sin not as the sinners, in the reckoning of all their days in which the sun traverses the heaven, entering into and departing from the portals for thirty days with the heads of thousands of the order of the stars, together with the four which are intercalated which divide the four portions of the year, which lead them and enter with them four days.

82.5. Owing to them men shall be at fault and not reckon them in the whole reckoning of the year: yea, men shall be at fault, and not recognize them accurately.

82.6. For they belong to the reckoning of the year and are truly recorded (thereon) for ever, one in the first portal and one in the third, and one in the fourth and one in the sixth, and the year is completed in three hundred and sixty-four days.

82.7. And the account thereof is accurate and the recorded reckoning thereof exact; for the luminaries, and months and festivals, and years and days, has Uriel shown and revealed to me, to whom the Lord of the whole creation of the world hath subjected the host of heaven.

82.8. And he has power over night and day in the heaven to cause the light to give light to men--sun, moon, and stars, and all the powers of the heaven which revolve in their circular chariots.

82.9. And these are the orders of the stars, which set in their places, and in their seasons and festivals and months.

82.10. And these are the names of those who lead them, who watch that they enter at their times, in their orders, in their seasons, in their months, in their periods of dominion, and in their positions.

82.11. Their four leaders who divide the four parts of the year enter first; and after them the twelve leaders of the orders who divide the months; and for the three hundred and sixty (days) there are heads over thousands who divide the days; and for the four intercalary days there are the leaders which sunder the four parts of the year.

82.12. And these heads over thousands are intercalated between leader and leader, each behind a station, but their leaders make the division. And these are the names of the leaders who divide the four parts of the year which are ordained: Mîlkî'êl, Hel'emmêlêk, and Mêl'êjal, and Nârêl.

82.13. And the names of those who lead them: Adnâr'êl, and Îjâsûsa'êl, and 'Elômê'êl--these three follow the leaders of the orders, and there is one that follows the three leaders of the orders which follow those leaders of stations that divide the four parts of the year.

82.14 [Not used]

82.15. In the beginning of the year Melkejâl rises first and rules, who is named †Tam'âinî† and sun, and all the days of his dominion whilst he bears rule are ninety-one days.

82.16. And these are the signs of the days which are to be seen on earth in the days of his dominion: sweat, and heat, and calms; and all the trees bear fruit, and leaves are produced on all the trees, and the harvest of wheat, and the rose-flowers, and all the flowers which come forth in the field, but the trees of the winter season become withered.

82.17. And these are the names of the leaders which are under them: Berka'êl, Zêlebs'êl, and another who is added a head of a thousand, called Hîlûjâsĕph: and the days of the dominion of this (leader) are at an end.

82.18. The next leader after him is Hêl'emmêlêk, whom one names the shining sun, and all the days of his light are ninety-one days.

82.19. And these are the signs of (his) days on the earth: glowing heat and dryness, and the trees ripen their fruits and produce all their fruits ripe and ready, and the sheep pair and become pregnant, and all the fruits of the earth are gathered in, and everything that is in the fields, and the winepress: these things take place in the days of his dominion.

82.20. These are the names, and the orders, and the leaders of those heads of thousands: Gîdâ'îjal, Kê'êl, and Hê'êl, and the name of the head of a thousand which is added to them, Asfâ'êl': and the days of his dominion are at an end.

Made in the USA
Columbia, SC
28 January 2025

52388660R00220